The Human Person and the Church

CHRISTIAN TEXTS IN PERSPECTIVE

The Orbis series *Christian Texts in Perspective* provides readers with a selection of foundational texts upon which the Christian tradition has been built, as well as texts that move the tradition in new directions. The texts and their introductions, along with biographical sketches and a timeline, will aid students and other readers in understanding central Christian doctrines in the context of both church and general western history.

The series — edited by William Madges and Gillian T. W. Ahlgren of Xavier University, Cincinnati — focuses on specific doctrines and traces their development from the origins of the church to the present. Each volume introduces major periods with a substantive interpretative essay, and the editors' selections aim to widen the canon by including texts by significant female authors. The timeline places in context events in Christian history, theological authors, and major political, social, intellectual, and cultural achievements in western civilization from the first to the twentieth century.

In addition to the present volume, the series includes the following:

- *God and the World,* edited by William Madges (published simultaneously with this volume)

- *Spirituality,* edited by Gillian T. W. Ahlgren (forthcoming)

- *Christ and Salvation,* edited by William Madges (forthcoming)

- *Sacraments of the Christian Life,* edited by Gillian T. W. Ahlgren and William Madges (forthcoming)

The Human Person and the Church

Christian Texts in Perspective

Gillian T. W. Ahlgren

ORBIS BOOKS

Maryknoll, New York 10545

The Catholic Foreign Mission Society of America (Maryknoll) recruits and trains people for overseas missionary service. Through Orbis Books, Maryknoll aims to foster the international dialogue that is essential to mission. The books published, however, reflect the opinions of their authors and are not meant to represent the official position of the society. To obtain more information about Maryknoll or Orbis Books, please visit our website at http://www.maryknoll.org.

Library of Congress Cataloging-in-Publication Data

Ahlgren, Gillian T. W., 1964-
     The human person and the church / Gillian T.W. Ahlgren.
        p.   cm. – (Christian texts in perspective)
     Includes bibliographical references.
     ISBN 1-57075-213-3 (pbk.)
     1. Man (Christian theology) 2. Church.   I. Title. II. Series.
BT701.2.A35   1999
233–dc21   98-48315

Contents

Preface ix

Acknowledgments xii

Part One

THE DOCTRINE OF THE HUMAN PERSON

1. The Early Period 3

   INTRODUCTION   3

   TEXTS   9

      Irenaeus of Lyons, *Against Heresies*   9

      Origen, "Commentary on the Song of Songs"   12

      Augustine of Hippo, *On the Trinity*   15

      Augustine of Hippo, *The Spirit and the Letter*   17

2. The Medieval and Reformation Period 19

   INTRODUCTION   19

   TEXTS   27

      Bernard of Clairvaux, "Sermon 80 on the Song of Songs"   27

      Bernard of Clairvaux, *On Grace and Free Choice*   29

      Bonaventure, *The Soul's Journey into God*   30

      Thomas Aquinas, *Summa theologiae*   31

      Catherine of Siena, *The Dialogue*   33

      Julian of Norwich, *Showings*   36

      Martin Luther, "Sermon on Two Kinds of Righteousness"   38

      John Calvin, *Institutes of the Christian Religion*   40

      Teresa of Avila, *The Interior Castle*   41

3. **The Modern Period** 44

    Introduction   44

    Texts   50

        Friedrich Schleiermacher, *The Christian Faith*   50

        Reinhold Niebuhr, *The Nature and Destiny of Man*   54

        Karl Rahner, *Foundations of Christian Faith*   57

        Vatican II, *Gaudium et Spes*   59

        Rita Nakashima Brock, *Journeys by Heart*   64

        Marjorie Hewitt Suchocki, *The Fall to Violence*   68

Part Two

THE DOCTRINE OF THE CHURCH

4. **The Early Period** 75

    Introduction   75

    Texts   84

        Clement of Rome, *1 Clement*   84

        Ignatius of Antioch, *Letter to the Ephesians*   86

        Ignatius of Antioch, *Letter to the Magnesians*   87

        The *Didache*   88

        Irenaeus of Lyons, *Against Heresies*   89

        Cyprian of Carthage, "Unity of the Catholic Church"   90

        Augustine of Hippo, "On Baptism, against the Donatists"   92

5. **The Medieval and Reformation Period** 95

    Introduction   95

    Texts   105

        Bernard of Clairvaux, "Sermon 27 on the Song of Songs"   105

        Thomas Aquinas, "Exposition on the Apostles' Creed"   107

        Catherine of Siena, *The Dialogue*   109

        Martin Luther, "Sermons on the Catechism"   112

        John Calvin, *Institutes of the Christian Religion*   114

6. **The Modern Period** 118

INTRODUCTION 118

TEXTS 124

Friedrich Schleiermacher, *The Christian Faith* 124
Vatican II, *Lumen Gentium* 128
Vatican II, *Gaudium et Spes* 131
Hans Urs von Balthasar, *Church and World* 133
Karl Rahner, *Foundations of Christian Faith* 137
Leonardo Boff, *Church: Charism and Power* 142
Congregation for the Doctrine of the Faith,
    "Notification to Father Leonardo Boff" 147
John Macquarrie, *Principles of Christian Theology* 152
Rita Nakashima Brock, *Journeys by Heart* 160
Pedro Casaldáliga, "A New Way of Being Church" 161
Elisabeth Schüssler Fiorenza, *Discipleship of Equals* 163
Avery Dulles, *The Catholicity of the Church* 167
Edward Schillebeeckx, *Church: The Human Story of God* 172

Part Three
BIOGRAPHICAL AND TEXTUAL
INFORMATION

Augustine of Hippo 181
Bernard of Clairvaux 184
Leonardo Boff 185
Bonaventure 186
Rita Nakashima Brock 188
John Calvin 189
Pedro Casaldáliga 190
Catherine of Siena 191
Clement of Rome 193
Cyprian of Carthage 194
The Didache 195
Avery Dulles 196

Ignatius of Antioch   197
Irenaeus of Lyons   198
Julian of Norwich   199
Martin Luther   201
John Macquarrie   204
Reinhold Niebuhr   205
Origen   206
Karl Rahner   207
Edward Schillebeeckx   210
Friedrich Schleiermacher   212
Elisabeth Schüssler Fiorenza   215
Marjorie Hewitt Suchocki   216
Teresa of Avila   216
Thomas Aquinas   218
Vatican II   221
Hans Urs von Balthasar   224

For Further Reading 227

Part Four

TIMELINE

Chronological Relationships among Political and Social Events,
Intellectual and Cultural Developments, Christian History,
Major Christian Writers / 231

Preface

Christian Texts in Perspective is a series that offers readers an understanding of the development of central Christian doctrines within the context of western church history. This series not only provides the reader with important theological texts from all periods of church history. It also puts those texts within their historical contexts so that the new directions taken in the doctrine's development become intelligible and meaningful. Although there are other collections of primary sources on the market, the Christian Texts in Perspective series is designed to meet a need unmet by most of the other currently available collections.

First, each volume in the series focuses on a specific doctrine and traces its development from the origins of the church to the present. This volume, which is divided into two major parts, examines the doctrines of the human person and the church. Each part of *The Human Person and the Church* is further divided into three historical periods: early church (up to 600), medieval and Reformation church (600–1600), and modern church (1600 to present). Part One deals with the question, "What is the nature of the human person?" It traces the development of ideas about human nature, its potentiality, and its limitations in the three time periods. Part One concludes with a review of Christianity's evolving understanding of original sin, its effects on humanity, and the continuing hope for wholeness and redemption. Part Two deals with the question, "What is the church?" with attention to two major subquestions: "What is the church's role?" and "How should the church be organized to accomplish its roles?" Part Two examines the interplay between theological and sociohistorical approaches to theologians' understandings of the nature of the church and ends with a consideration of the role of the church in the world today.

Second, each volume in this series includes a wider range of theological authors than what can usually be found in standard "readers" in Christian thought or theology. That is, each volume includes not only the classic authors who have given definitive shape to the doctrine in question. Each volume also includes other authors who have challenged the received understanding of the doctrine or who have pointed its interpretation in new directions. Consequently, you will find in these volumes the writings of authors such as Hildegard of Bingen, James Cone, Dorothee Soelle, Leonardo Boff, and Elizabeth Johnson, as well as writings from Irenaeus of Lyons, Augustine, Aquinas, Luther, and Calvin. In the selection of authors, we have sought to give a fuller picture of the richness of theological reflection upon the church's doctrines by including significant female authors, often excluded from standard histories of doctrine. For example, the writings of authors such as Hadewijch of Brabant, Catherine of Siena, Julian of Norwich, and Teresa of Avila have been included. In addition, texts that might traditionally be regarded as more "spiritual" than "theological" have been included in the series when the texts offer a significant or illuminating perspective from which the doctrine in question can be understood.[1]

Third, the series offers more than a collection of texts. It offers appropriate tools for helping the reader to understand the texts in context and to identify the continuities or divergences among them. The principal tool that assists this process of understanding is the interpretative essay that precedes each set of texts from the three different periods of the church's history (early, medieval and Reformation, and modern periods). In this volume you will find three interpretative essays in each of the book's two main parts. These essays introduce the texts, describe the main lines of doctrinal development in each period, and situate the texts within their historical context. In addition to the essays, each volume in the series contains a biography and bibliography for each of the authors whose writings are included. These biographical and textual introductions are often more extensive than what can be found in other available readers in Christian theology.

Fourth, each volume in the series contains a detailed timeline, in which church events and theological authors are set into relation with the major political, social, intellectual, and cultural achievements in western civilization from the first to the twentieth century. By consulting the timeline, the reader can not only learn the dates of important events in the church and western civilization, but also see connections between the cultural temperament or social development of a period and the theological creativity of authors who lived during that period. Use of the timeline can help the reader avoid thinking of theological reflection upon Christian doctrines as disconnected from the sweep of other historical events.

This series was developed according to certain guidelines. Because we wanted to provide a broad portrait of theological thinking about central Christian doctrines, we did not write the series as a history of official dogmatic statements. Although they refer substantively to the official (that is, ecclesiastically approved) development of doctrine, the books in the series do not restrict themselves to official statements, but include other theological analyses of the doctrines in question. Our intent thereby is to help the reader not only to understand the foundations of the classic understanding of the doctrine, but also to appreciate the theological creativity and to assess the theological adequacy of the new directions that understanding of the doctrine has taken over time.

Moreover, the series does not purport to provide a complete picture of how specific doctrines developed in both the eastern and western traditions of the church. Such an undertaking would exceed the competence of the authors and stretch the length of these volumes beyond acceptable levels. In general, we have selected authors who stand within the western Christian tradition or whose thoughts have contributed in a significant way to doctrinal development in the

---

1. The authors of this series are in substantial agreement with Joan Nuth, who writes: "Present parameters for what designates legitimate theology need to be stretched to include the more experientially oriented mystical and devotional writings, many of which were produced by women. Careful investigation might reveal in such writings valuable doctrinal insights to add to our record of how the Christian faith has been experienced and understood in history, thereby enriching our own experience and understanding" (*Wisdom's Daughter: The Theology of Julian of Norwich* [New York: Crossroad, 1991], 1–2).

West. This choice does not mean to suggest that the eastern Christian tradition has no significant contributions to make toward understanding central Christian doctrines. Rather, the exclusion of the East was a pragmatic decision, not an evaluative judgment. In general, philosophers have also been excluded from the series. An occasional exception is made if the author's writing is judged to be sufficiently "theological" in character and sufficiently influential upon the thinking of theologians in the West. Of course, a case could be made to include authors, both theological and philosophical, who have been excluded from this series. Although our selection of texts will not please everyone, we believe that we have put together a judicious collection that includes both foundational texts and texts that move in new directions.

The texts and the interpretative essays are arranged in chronological order. If you wish to acquire a more comprehensive sense of the development of theological thinking upon a specific doctrine, you should begin at the beginning of the book and read the subsequent material in order. If you are primarily interested in understanding developments within a particular historical period, you should go directly to that portion of the book. Each historical period is indicated in the table of contents. Before reading the selections from each historical period, you are encouraged to read the biographical introduction for the respective authors. The biographical introductions, listed in alphabetical order, are located toward the end of the book. If you are already very familiar with the life and work of the author in question, you might choose to read the text without consulting the biographical introduction. The bibliography for each author, however, might still be useful. You will find these bibliographies at the end of each biographical introduction.

The translations we have included in the series represent solid English translations or, in some cases, the only English translations currently available. Unfortunately, most of these translations are not sensitive to issues of gender-inclusive language. Because of copyright and related laws, the authors of the Christian Texts in Perspective series have not been able to rectify this situation.

We have attempted to make the Christian Texts in Perspective series useful to a range of readers, from the adult nonspecialist to graduate theology and seminary students. Whatever your situation or need, we hope that you will find this book an aid in understanding the development of Christian thinking about the doctrines of the human person and the church from the first century to the beginning of the third millennium.

Acknowledgments

The production of this book was a complicated process. Initially begun as a response to student complaints about reserve readings, this project took on ever-deepening dimensions in conversations with my Xavier colleague Bill Madges. As we combined our curricular concerns with aspects of our scholarly work, we began to conceptualize a resource that would serve as a broad review of the Christian tradition. For the intense and jovial conversations, interpretive discussions on finer points, and personal support he has given me throughout this project, I express heartfelt thanks.

I would like to thank Edmund Cueva for his review of sections of the timeline. Elena Procario-Foley deserves special thanks for her comments on the "Human Person" portion of the manuscript. Darleen Frickman directed much of her energies into the timeline with its multitude of additions, corrections, and formatting problems. Thanks as well are due to the chair of my department, Brennan Hill, and the Dean of the College of Arts and Sciences, Max Keck, for their support. Bill Burrows, managing editor at Orbis, has been a warm and patient colleague.

Part One

THE DOCTRINE OF
THE HUMAN PERSON

– 1 –

The Early Period

INTRODUCTION

The discipline of theological anthropology attempts to address a number of questions about human nature, God's intent and purpose for creation, the damage done to human potential in the fall of humanity, and the process of restoration in God through Christ. Generally speaking, Christian theologians must juggle a number of assumptions as they work out a theory of human nature. First, they must affirm the goodness of God and God's creation. In keeping with the first account of creation, they recognize that humanity was created in God's image and likeness. Second, as described in the account of the Fall (Genesis 3), they must affirm that humanity fell short of the Creator's expectations. Conceptualized primarily as the sin of disobedience, theologians often describe a wrongly ordered operation of the human will which leads to the perpetuation of sin in the world. Third, they struggle with the human experience of goodness, compassion, and love as well as violence, hatred, and oppression. They observe both the individual and communal aspects of goodness and evil, accounting for them in various ways, but, generally speaking, conclude that goodness occurs through the operation of grace in the human person and evil as a result of various aspects of the human condition, but most commonly the perversity of the human will. Finally, Christian theologians attach their understandings of human nature to the saving work of Jesus Christ, establishing a circular movement of creation out of God, fall, and restoration to God in Christ. Within Christianity, then, no understanding of human nature can be seen as operating independently of Christ.

The earliest theologians who developed theories and systems to account for these difficult questions relied upon three primary resources: scripture, contemporary philosophical reflections, and their own human experience. As the centuries passed, theologians also built upon a growing tradition of Christian theological writings. The thought of Augustine, in particular, took on special importance in questions of theological anthropology.

The messages of Christian scripture with respect to human nature are numerous and diverse. For the purposes of introducing the thinkers contained in this volume, the central paradox contained in Genesis is sufficient to develop the questions theologians attempted to answer. The first account of creation (Gen. 1:1–2:4a) affirms the goodness of God and creation. The text states explicitly that humanity is made "in our image, after our likeness."[1] In this account God

---

1. Genesis 1:26. See also 1:27.

blesses humanity, urging us to multiply and granting us dominion over creation. Humanity's creation out of nothing during the last day of creation suggests here that humanity is the pinnacle of God's creative activity. The second account of creation (Gen. 2:4b–25) and the account of the Fall which follows introduce another theological perspective. In this account Adam is formed out of clay and Eve from the rib of Adam. The act of creation is a more collaborative process: Adam names the wild animals and birds as God forms them out of the ground. God places Adam in Eden and orders him not to eat from the tree of knowledge of good and evil. Eve is created from Adam, and the two eat of the fruit, resulting in banishment from Eden and mortality.[2] Reconciling the two perspectives is difficult, as the texts taken together raise a host of theological questions: If humanity is created good by an all-powerful God, why does God allow for alienation between God and humanity? Is the human will so strong as to overcome or undo the goodness of God's creative activity? How free is the human will if, in a context where it was easiest to be good, it chose to disobey God's will? Will humans, now that they are banished from the environment of God's presence, not inevitably sin? Is obedience to divine order the primary aim of the human person, and does this make obedience the primary religious virtue? What lessons about the nature and actions of God are we to draw from this story?

Early Christian answers to such questions were informed by various traditions. Specifically, Paul devoted considerable attention to anthropological issues, articulating several concepts which would give rise to reflection over the course of Christian history. Paul first considered the account of the Fall, recognizing in Christ the second Adam. Unlike the first Adam, i.e., all of humanity, Christ is not a slave to sin but lives in a freedom which humanity enjoyed in paradise but has not experienced since. In the thought of Paul, then, there is a pronounced sense of sin as a power which dominates individuals. The power of sin keeps us in an ontological state in which we are unable to do the good we actually will to do (see Rom. 7:14–25). But, through Christ, we are also enabled by spiritual gifts, and made into the body of Christ, in which distinctions among people are no longer significant (see 1 Corinthians 12). In Christ, because of Christ, all are made just; the grace of God completely overcomes the offense of sin (see Rom. 5:15–19). Paul speaks clearly, then, of the restoration of humanity to the image of God. Finally, Paul distinguishes between the inner and outer person, both of whom are transformed in Christ allowing for the full appearance of the "new" person in Christ. This new person lives in a psychosomatic unity which enables good works, righteousness, and ethical action.

The philosophical traditions of the first centuries of Christianity also provided theologians with a framework for understanding human nature. Consistent with an interpretation of the first account of creation, Christian Platonism identified the divine image in humanity as its capacity for attaining the knowledge of God. Thus, the soul retains a memory of God's presence not entirely obliterated by the Fall, and that memory impels it into a search for union with God, a union

---

2. See esp. Genesis 3:19: "By the sweat of your face shall you get bread to eat, until you return to the ground, from which you were taken; for you are dirt, and to dirt you shall return."

of knowledge and love. This desire for union with God is the seed of humanity's salvation; it is fed by the renewed knowledge of God brought to humanity in Jesus Christ. Christ, both as the template of perfected humanity and as the model of godly life, centers humanity in its desire for God. The model of Platonic thought offered Christianity the introduction of eros as a motivating principle: humanity's innate desire for union with God propels humanity ever forward, even though humans must still struggle to overcome or change those habits, behaviors, or limitations which keep them from God. Obedience to divine precepts is supplemented — or even replaced — by the pursuit of intimacy with God.

Additionally, the platonic model affirmed a conceptualization of the God of wisdom, a cosmic intelligence in which human beings could participate. The task of humanity is to grow in enlightenment. The platonic framework was highly adaptable to scripture, as it both affirmed the wisdom tradition of the Old Testament and allowed for a more developed christology, such as the one found in the Gospel of John. As reflected in John 1:1–4, the wisdom of God (or Logos [Word]) was present and active in the creation of the world and became flesh in Christ. Christ therefore imparts divine knowledge within which humans can grow and develop, preparing themselves for union with God. As Christian theologians adopted this platonic framework, a view of human nature emerged which preserved both the goodness of creation and the separation between God and humanity, with the promise of restoration in God through Christ the Word.

The thought of Irenaeus of Lyons (d. ca. 200), one of the earliest Christian thinkers to address the major questions of theological anthropology, provided a model for explaining the inherent separation between God and humanity without diminishing the goodness of human nature as God's creation. Human beings, because they were created, are by definition imperfect. Only uncreated things are perfect. Thus, the separation between God and humanity existed at the moment of creation and was not attributable solely to the Fall. Further, this separation was foreknown by a loving Creator who recognized humanity as good but immature. Through our separation from God we actually learn of the goodness of God, grow to desire God more, and are eventually restored to God's perfection in Christ. Arguing against the gnostics, Irenaeus wanted to affirm that the fallen condition of humanity was not contrary to God's plan. God is patient as humans learn from the consequences of disobedience the goodness of obeying and honoring God. Irenaeus holds out the promise of God's plan, not thwarted by human disobedience in the Fall: "To create belongs to God's goodness; to be created belongs to human nature. If therefore, you commit to him the submission and trust in him which are yours, then you hold onto his artistry and will be God's perfect work."[3]

The soul's yearning for wisdom, satiable only in God, actually underscores God's omnipotence, for humans are inevitably attracted to God — indeed, driven back toward God. In the thought of Origen, for example, humanity's loving affection for God provides both the proof that humanity is created from Christ and God, who share in the same loving affection, and the possibility of being

---

3. Irenaeus of Lyons, *Against Heresies;* see below.

brought back into full relationship with the trinity.[4] Origen's insistence upon the irresistibility of God does not move him toward a deterministic view of the soul or of salvation. Even though the soul's free will caused its falling away from God in the first place, its continued capacity to choose allows it to choose to return to God. Thus, while Origen affirms the power of God to draw us back into God, he also recognizes humanity's ability to assent to and work for that return.

Regarding the extent of the damage done to humanity in the Fall, there is a wide range of opinion and even disagreement. Reflection on the Fall is directly related to questions of christology and God. To affirm that creation is good and created by a good and loving God makes it difficult to account for human suffering. Evil and the suffering it produces cannot be imputed to God but must be attributed to a shortcoming in humanity. The story of the Fall is subject to many interpretations.[5] Most early commentators focused on humanity's first sin, characterizing it as disobedience or pride, and, although some saw in the Fall the introduction of sexual passion as a further expression of sin, others struggled to redeem marital sexuality for its procreative purposes.[6]

It is in the thought of Augustine where we observe an extraordinary tension between the two major themes of obedience and eros. Through Adam and Eve humanity lived in a state of joy and union with God, but that union was predicated upon humanity wanting what God commanded. In the moment that human desire contradicted a divine edict, an ontological rupture occurred in which Adam and Eve lost the grace of innocence and moved into a state in which the human will lost its primary orientation to God. In many passages from his *Confessions* Augustine captures and expresses the natural desire of humanity for God, perhaps most notably when he writes: "Our hearts are restless until they find their rest in You." But over the course of his life, particularly after debates with Pelagius, Augustine came to understand that insatiable desire as part of the redeemed soul, not the created soul. Thus the spirit of Christ which allows for the grace of God to operate in the soul is what ultimately moves a person toward God. Metaphorically, as Augustine expresses it, the fire of desire for God must be lit and enkindled by the Holy Spirit; only God's love can beget true love for God.[7] But the human will must be overcome by grace in order for this to occur; thus the individual learns an obedience which paradoxically allows it far greater liberty. As one commentator puts it, "Grace for Augustine was delight in the good, a new form of liberty that required an internal modification of the human will."[8]

In order to explain the inability of human beings to do good without the driving impulse of grace, Augustine distinguished between sin as a series of actions or behaviors and sin as an ontological state. Born into original sin, a state in-

---

4. In this sense, for Origen, loving affection can be understood to comprise the "same substance" of God and Christ (see selection below). Understanding God's nature as loving affection in which humans participate is critical in the theological systems of both Julian of Norwich and Rita Nakashima Brock.

5. For a range of interpretations see Elaine Pagels, *Adam, Eve, and the Serpent* (New York: Vintage Books, 1988).

6. See, for example, commentaries by Tatian, Clement of Alexandria, and Irenaeus.

7. See text below from *The Spirit and the Letter*: "And that it may be loved, the love of God is shed abroad in our hearts, not by the free choice whose spring is in ourselves, but through the Holy Spirit which is given us."

8. Roger Haight, *The Experience and Language of Grace* (New York: Paulist Press, 1979), 36.

herited from Adam and Eve in their fallen nature, humans act sinfully because sinfulness is embedded in their very being. In Christ, however, the effects of this state on human behavior are lessened. For Augustine, original sin is characterized by the human will which seeks satisfaction in sensuality and other selfish pursuits. Such an orientation, by definition, does not enhance the individual's spiritual growth. While Augustine appreciates the soul's natural desire to love and be connected with others (eros), he understood this desire, without being informed by the movements of the Holy Spirit and tamed by obedience to the will of God, to be a tragic shortcoming, leading people into inappropriate and ultimately damaging forms of behavior. Thus individuals need grace continually to orient their lives toward God; the necessity of grace justifies the primary role of the church as mediator of the sacraments.

Although the Council of Ephesus in 431 condemned Pelagianism, Augustine did not have the last word on all aspects of theological anthropology. In his arguments with the Pelagians, Augustine formulated a definition of predestination based on God's foreknowledge of future events. Such foreknowledge necessitated that the events could not be changed as they were already known. This formula prioritized prescience over God's power to change. His position on predestination was interpreted at the Synod of Orange in 529 to preclude the predestination of damnation. The synod issued a restatement of Augustine's theological views on humanity, sin, and grace, equating them with official church doctrine and making many of Augustine's teachings on human nature normative throughout the medieval period.

Theological positions on human nature vary in degrees and emphases: Does the theologian develop the idea that the image and likeness of God imprinted in the soul is never completely effaced? Does the theologian devote energy to the idea that humans are characterized by sinful behavior? Is the human experience characterized by a frustrated or thwarted yearning for God? How much joy in God can the human person experience in this life? The set of questions a theologian chooses to answer is as important as the answers he or she develops, since the questions precondition the range of the theologian's thought. Yet, after the thought of Augustine, theological anthropology in the West was preconditioned by the questions, vocabulary, and interpretive framework Augustine had introduced.

There was, however, a differing orthodox view on the nature of humanity, particularly in light of the predestinarian perspectives Augustine had expressed. A major spokesperson, who asserted the importance of human ascetical activity in the pursuit of God, was the monk John Cassian (ca. 360–433). Highly influenced by Egyptian monasticism and the thought of Evagrius Ponticus and Origen, he spent time in Rome and finally settled in Gaul around 415. There he founded two monasteries at Marseilles and wrote the *Conferences* and the *Institutes* to bring the Egyptian monastic tradition to Europe. For Cassian, the monastic ideal is to achieve a state of continuous prayer which propels us into union with God, a union predicated on the same love that binds the persons of the trinity.[9] This

---

9. See commentary in Bernard McGinn, *The Foundations of Mysticism* (New York: Crossroad, 1991), 218–27, esp. 222–23.

kind of union is predicated upon grace, but human effort clearly plays a part and might even attract grace.

Another important voice, emerging around 500, presented a theological system which belied the ontological separation between God and humanity that Augustine's anti-Pelagian views had introduced. From Syria came a series of treatises which gave substance and structure to the spiritual traditions surrounding union with God, traditions which the author identified as "mystical theology." He is known as "Pseudo-Dionysius" because he took the name of Dionysius the Areopagite, although he was not the convert to Christianity mentioned in Acts 17:34. The obscure Pseudo-Dionysius was highly influential within the mystical tradition of the West, beginning with the thought of John the Scot and continuing throughout the medieval period in figures such as Bonaventure and the author of the *Cloud of Unknowing*.

Thoroughly imbued with Neoplatonism, Pseudo-Dionysius's orientation to metaphysics drives his commentary, and certain Christian theological categories receive more attention than others. Theological anthropology is not one of Pseudo-Dionysius's central concerns; however, his affirmation of the goodness and beauty of creation could certainly be said to extend to humanity. Creation proceeds out of God and eventually returns to its source. Pseudo-Dionysius, following Proclus, attributes the "yearning" for union both to God and humanity; indeed, because God is good, God brings all things into perfection, returning them into Godself. Thus Pseudo-Dionysius describes a circle of love which forms the universe, from the outpouring of God's love that resulted in creation to the eventual restoration of creation into God. The implicit anthropology behind such a system directly contradicts many of Augustine's views. Interestingly, both see eros as a primary motivating force; however, for Augustine, the erotic urge between God and humanity is fundamentally different. Eros is not by its nature good; it becomes perverted within humanity because of humanity's disordered will. For Pseudo-Dionysius one force drives the entire cosmos, and it is the force of divine goodness.

These differing views are not, ultimately, reconcilable, and they continue in the medieval period but do not share the same priority within theological circles. While Augustine's views on predestination are soft-pedaled throughout the medieval period, his emphasis on the separation of God and humanity in the Fall dominate much of medieval anthropological discussion. Pseudo-Dionysius's views are extremely important in the mystical tradition and are taken up again in most metaphysical discussions. Thomas Aquinas, for example, makes much use of his treatises in his discussions of the nature of God and the discipline of theology.

Pseudo-Dionysius's expression of mysticism represented a contemplative ideal which was possible to achieve only within a specific monastic context. In the sixth century, many such monastic options were developing; indeed, between 400 and 700, there were thirty different monastic rules circulating in the West.[10] For the medieval period, however, the most important monastic rule was that of Benedict of Nursia (ca. 480–ca. 547), which would become normative for monasticism in

---

10. See Bernard McGinn, *The Growth of Mysticism* (New York: Crossroad, 1994), 27.

the ninth century. Benedict was an aristocrat educated in Rome, who withdrew from public life for a time as a hermit, but eventually established a monastery at Monte Cassino. Benedict's rule emphasized the importance of stability in establishing a spiritual life. The monk entered a permanent community with a fixed daily routine consisting of work and prayer. The religious ideals which permeate Benedict's rule reflect an Augustinian view of human nature in that they associate spiritual progress with disciplining the human will. For Benedict the ascetic ideal was best expressed through the cultivation of the virtues of humility and obedience; the mortification of the will was more important than the mortification of the body. Benedict's perspectives on the ascetical contributions of the human person and the need for a supportive monastic context for spiritual growth were brought into the mainstream life of the church with the person of Gregory the Great (ca. 540–604), bishop of Rome from 590 until his death. As his papacy represents many of the characteristics of the medieval period, we will consider his influence in the next section.

TEXTS

Irenaeus of Lyons (ca. 130–202)

Against Heresies (ca. 180)*

Someone might say, "Why is this? Was God unable to make humanity perfect from the start?" He should realize that because God was not born and always remains the same, he can do anything, as far as depends on himself. The things he made had to be lesser than himself, however, precisely because they were to be made and have a beginning. What was only recently created could not be uncreated; such things fall short of perfection by the very fact of not being uncreated. Because they come later, they are immature; as such they are inexperienced and not trained to perfect understanding. A mother, for example, can provide perfect food for a child, but at that point he cannot digest food which is suitable for someone older. Similarly, God himself certainly could have provided humanity with perfection from the beginning. Humanity, however, was immature and unable to lay hold of it. When our Lord came in the last age to gather all things in himself, therefore, he did not come in the way he was able, but in the way we were able to see him. He could have come to us in his indescribable glory; we, however, could not have borne the greatness of his glory. For this reason, the one who was the perfect bread of the Father offered himself to us as milk for children: he came in human form. His purpose was to feed us at the breast of his flesh, by nursing us to make us accustomed to eat and drink the Word of God, so that we would be able to hold in ourselves the one who is the bread of immortality, the Spirit of the Father.

---

*Reprinted from *Theological Anthropology,* trans. and ed. J. Patout Burns (Philadelphia, 1981), 23–28, by permission of Fortress Press.

Thus Paul says to the Corinthians, "I gave you milk to drink, not solid food, because you could not yet receive solid food" [1 Cor. 3:2]. He means: I taught you about the coming of the Lord in a human way; because of your weakness, the Spirit of the Father has not yet rested upon you. "For when envy, strife, and factions exist among you," he says, "are you not being carnal and walking in human ways?" [1 Cor. 3:3]. This means that they did not yet have the Spirit of the Father because of their imperfection and the inconstancy of their conduct. Still, the Apostle could have given them solid food. Anyone upon whom the apostles imposed hands received the Holy Spirit, who is the food of life. They could not hold him, however, because their capacity for dealing with God was still weak and undeveloped. Similarly, God could have given humanity perfection in the beginning. Humanity, however, had just been made; it could not receive it, or hold it once received, or preserve it once held. The Word of God, then, did not take on humanity's immaturity for his own sake, since he was perfect; rather, because of humanity's immaturity was he made susceptible of being grasped by humans. The inadequacy and impossibility were not on God's part but on the part of humanity, since it was not uncreated but had just been made.

God's power, wisdom, and goodness are all demonstrated at once: power and goodness in his freely creating and establishing things which do not yet exist; wisdom in his making things which follow in order, which go together, which are well arranged. Through his immense goodness, some of them develop, continue for a long time, and reach the glory of the uncreated. God generously bestows on them what is good. Though as created, they are not uncreated; still since they continue for long ages, they will take on the strength of the uncreated. God will give them everlasting endurance.

God therefore has dominion over all things since he alone is uncreated, is before all things, and is the cause of the existence of all things. All else remains subjected to God. Submission to God is incorruption, and continuance in incorruption is the glory of the uncreated. Through this system, such arrangement, and this kind of governance, humanity was created according to the image and established in the likeness of the uncreated God. The Father decided and commanded; the Son molded and shaped; the Spirit nourished and developed. Humanity slowly progresses, approaches perfection, and draws near to the uncreated, God. It was therefore appropriate for humanity first to be made; having been made, to grow; having grown, to be strengthened; having become stronger, to multiply; having multiplied, to recover from illness; having recovered, to be glorified; and once glorified, to see its Lord. God is the one who is going to be seen; the vision of God produces incorruptibility; incorruptibility makes a person approach God.

People who do not wait for the period of growth, who attribute the weakness of their nature to God, are completely unreasonable. They understand neither God nor themselves; they are ungrateful and never satisfied. At the outset they refuse to be what they were made: human beings who are subject to passions. They override the law of human nature; they already want to be like God the Creator before they even become human beings. They want to do away with all the differences between the uncreated God and created humans. Thus they are more unreasonable than the dumb animals. The beasts do not blame God for not making them human; rather, by the fact of its creation each gives thanks for being made. We, however, complain that instead of being made gods from the beginning, we are first human and then divine. Yet God followed the simplicity of his goodness in doing this. To prevent anyone from considering him jealous or lacking in generosity, he says, "I said that you are gods, all children of the Most High." To us, however, who could not stand to bear the might of divinity, he said, "You, however, will die like human beings" [Ps. 82:6, 7]. He speaks here of two things: of the generosity of his gift, then of our weakness and our having dominion over ourselves. In his generosity he freely gave what was good and made human beings like himself in their having control over themselves. In his foresight he knew human weakness and what would result from it. In his love and power he will surpass the substance of our created nature. It was appropriate that the nature first appear and only later that the mortal be surpassed and absorbed by immortality, the corruptible by incorruptibility; that by acquiring the knowledge of good and evil, human beings should be made according to the image and likeness of God.

Human beings acquired the knowledge of good and evil. Good is to obey God, to believe in him, to keep his command; this means life for human beings. On the other hand, not to obey God is evil; this is death for human beings. God has exercised patience, and human beings have come to know both the good of obedience and the evil of disobedience. Thus by experiencing them both the mind's eye would choose the better things with discernment and never become sluggish or negligent of God's command. By learning through experience the evil of not obeying God, which would deprive them of life, human beings would never try it. Rather, knowing the good of obeying God, which preserves their life, they would diligently maintain it. Human beings have this twofold power of perception which gives the knowledge of good and evil so that they might choose the better things intelligently. How can someone be intelligent about good when he does not know what is contrary to it? Certain understanding of the issue to be decided is more solid than a conjecture based on guessing. The tongue experiences sweet and sour by tasting; the eye distinguishes black from white by seeing; the ear perceives the difference between sounds by hearing. In this same way, by experiencing good and evil, the mind comes to understand good and is strengthened to preserve it by obeying God. First by repentance it rejects disobedience because it is bitter and evil. By grasping the nature of what is opposed to the sweet and good, it will never again try to taste disobedience to God. If a person avoids the twofold power of perception and the knowledge of both of these, therefore, he implicitly destroys his humanity.

How will one who has not yet become human be God? How can one just created be perfect? How can one who has not obeyed his Maker in a mortal nature be immortal? You should first follow the order of human existence and only then share in God's glory. You do not make God; God makes you. If you are God's artifact, then wait for the hand of the Master which makes everything at the proper time, at the time proper for you who are being created. Offer him a soft and malleable heart; then keep the shape in which the Master molds you. Retain your moisture, so that you do not harden and lose the imprint of his fingers. By preserving your structure you will rise to perfection. God's artistry will conceal what is clay in you. His hand fashioned a foundation in you; he will cover you inside and out with pure gold and silver. He will so adorn you that the King himself will desire your beauty [Ps. 45:11]. If, however, you immediately harden yourself and reject his artistry, if you rebel against God and are ungrateful because he made you human, then you have lost not only his artistry but life itself at the same time. To create belongs to God's goodness; to be created belongs to human nature. If, therefore, you commit to him the submission and trust in him which are yours, then you hold onto his artistry and will be God's perfect work.

Origen (ca. 185–254)

"Commentary on the Song of Songs" (ca. 233)*

At the beginning of Moses' words, where he describes the creation of the world, we find reference to two men that were created, the first made after the image and likeness of God (cf. Gen 1:26) and the second formed from the dust of the ground (cf. Gen. 2:7). Paul the Apostle well knew this and possessed a clear understanding of these matters. In his letters he wrote more openly and clearly that every person is two different men. This is what he said, "Though our outer man is wasting away, our inner man is being renewed every day" (2 Cor. 4:16) and further, "For I delight in the law of God in my inner man" (Rom. 7:22)....He mentions that one of them, that is, the inner man, is renewed every day; but he asserts that the other, the outer man, in the saints and in people like Paul, is wasting away and growing weak. (p. 220)

•

Therefore, this material man, who is also called the outer man, has food and drink related to his nature, specifically corporeal and earthly. And in a similar way, the spiritual man, who is called the inner man, also has his own food, that living bread which came down from heaven (cf. John 6:33, 41). And his drink is from that water which Jesus promised when He said, "Whoever drinks of the water that I shall give him will never thirst" (John 4:14). And so through everything a similarity of designations is applied according to each of the men; but the special properties of what each of them is are distinguished from one another and kept separate. Corruptible things are granted to the corruptible man, but incorruptible things are set forth for the incorruptible man. Because of this it happens that certain of the simpler Christians, since they do not know how to distinguish and to keep separate what in the divine Scriptures must be allotted to the inner man and what to the outer man, misled by the similarities in the designations, have turned themselves to certain foolish stories and vain fic-

---

*Reprinted from Origen, *An Exhortation to Martyrdom, Prayer, and Selected Works*, trans. Rowan A. Greer (New York, 1979), 220, 222–23, 225–27, by permission of Paulist Press.

tions, so that even after the resurrection they believe that corporeal foods must be used and drink taken not only from that true Vine which lives forever, but also from vines and fruits of wood (cf. John 15:1). But we shall turn our attention to them another time.

Now, therefore, as we have noted in our earlier observations, there is one person according to the inner man without children and "barren," but another abounding in "children." In this regard we have noticed the verse "The barren has borne seven, and she who has many children is deprived of strength" (1 Sam. 2:5). And as it is said among the blessings, "No one among you shall be without children and barren" (cf. Exod. 23:26). Thus, if these conclusions are sound, just as there is said to be a fleshly love, which the poets also call Love, according to which the person who loves sows in the flesh, so also there is a spiritual love according to which the inner man when he loves sows in the Spirit (cf. Gal. 6:8). And to speak more plainly, if there is someone who still bears the image of the earthly according to the outer man, he is led by an earthly desire and love. But the person who bears the image of the heavenly according to the inner man is led by a heavenly desire and love (cf. 1 Cor. 15:49). Indeed, the soul is led by a heavenly love and desire when once the beauty and glory of the Word of God has been perceived, he falls in love with His splendor and by this receives from Him some dart and wound of love. For this Word is the image and brightness of the invisible God, the First Born of all creation, in whom all things were created, in heaven and on earth, visible and invisible (cf. Col. 1:15f.; Heb. 1:3). Therefore, if anyone has been able to hold in the breadth of his mind and to consider the glory and splendor of all things created in Him, he will be struck by their very beauty and transfixed by the magnificence of their brilliance or, as the prophet says, "by the chosen arrow" (Isa. 49:2). And he will receive from Him the saving wound and will burn with the blessed fire of His love. (pp. 222–23)

•

Quite obviously, as well, in the book we have in hand the term love has been changed into the designation "loving affection" in the passage where it says, "I adjure you, O daughters of Jerusalem, if you find my beloved, that you tell Him I am wounded with loving affection" (Song of Songs 5:8). This certainly stands for what might be said, "I have been struck by the dart of His love." Thus, there is no difference in the divine Scriptures whether "love" is used or "loving affection" or "affectionate love," save insofar as the term "loving affection" is given a higher place, because God Himself is also called "loving Affection." For example, John says, "Beloved, let us affectionately love one another, for loving affection is from God, and he who affectionately loves is born of God and knows God. He who does not affectionately love does not know God; for God is loving Affection" (1 John 4:7–8). And although there may be another opportunity to say something about the verses we have used as an example from John's letter, nonetheless it does not seem foolish to touch briefly upon some other points made by his letter. He says, "Let us affectionately love one another, for loving affection is from God" and a little further on, "God is loving Affection." Here he shows both that God is Himself loving Affection and that loving Affection is from God. Who, then, is "from God" save He who said, "I came from God and have come into this world" (cf. John 16:28)? But if God the Father is loving Affection and the Son is loving Affection, and if "loving affection" and "loving affection" are one and the same and differ in no respect, it follows that the Father and the Son are one and the same and differ in no respect.

Moreover, Christ is quite suitably called loving Affection, just as He is called Wisdom and power and righteousness and Word and truth (cf. 1 Cor. 1:24, 30; John 1:1, 14:6). And so Scripture says that "if loving affection remains in us, God remains in us" (cf. 1 John 4:12). And "God," that is, the Father and the Son, "come to him" who is perfected in loving affection according to the word of our Lord and Savior, who says, "I and my Father will come to him and make our home with him" (cf. 1 John 4:18, John 14:23).

Therefore, we must know that this loving affection, which is God and takes its existence in Him, affectionately loves nothing earthly, nothing material, nothing corruptible. For it is against its nature to love anything corruptible affectionately, since it is itself the source of incorruption. And it alone has immortality, if indeed God is loving Affection, who alone has immortality and dwells in unapproachable light (1 John 4:8; 1 Tim. 6:16). And what else is immortality but the eternal life that God promises He will give to those who believe in Him the only true God and in Jesus Christ, His Son, whom He has sent (cf. John 17:3)? Furthermore, then, first of all and before all else this is said to be worthy of God's love and good pleasure, that a person should "affectionately love the Lord his God with all his heart and with all his soul and with all his strength" (cf. Luke 10:27). And because God is loving Affection, He demands something like Himself from us, so that through that loving affection which is in Christ Jesus we may be brought into fellowship with God, who is loving Affection, as by a relationship made kindred by the term loving affection.

Thus it is that he who was already united with Him said, "Who shall separate us from the loving affection of God which is in Christ Jesus our Lord?" (cf. Rom. 8:35, 39). And this loving affection makes everyone a neighbor. It was because of this that the Savior confounded a man who thought that a righteous soul should not observe the rights of friendship toward a soul fallen among wicked deeds. And for this reason He told in a secret way the parable that says that a certain man fell among robbers while he was going down from Jerusalem to Jericho. And He finds fault with the priest and the Levite, who saw him half dead and passed by. But he cherishes the Samaritan, who had compassion. And he asserted in His answer that he was the neighbor of the man who had raised the question, and He told him, "Go and do likewise" (Luke 10:29ff.). Indeed, by nature we are all neighbors of one another; but by deeds of loving affection that person becomes a neighbor who can do good to the one who has no power. That is why our Savior was also made our neighbor, and He did not pass us by when we were lying half dead from the wounds inflicted by the robbers. Therefore, we must know that loving affection for God always strives toward God from whom it took its origin, and it has regard for the neighbor with whom it shows participation, since he was similarly created in incorruption. (pp. 225–27)

Augustine of Hippo (354–430)

On the Trinity (404–20)*

It is written: "So long as we are in the body, we are sojourners away from the Lord; for we walk by faith, not by sight." Accordingly, so long as the just lives by faith, though his life be that of the inward man, he can only strive for the truth and make his way towards the eternal by means of the faith which is temporal: not yet can there be in the holding and contemplation and love of this temporal faith a trinity fit to be called the image of God. Else that which must be established in the eternal would seem to be established in things temporal. When the mind of a man sees its own faith, believing what it does not see, it is not looking upon what is everlasting. What it sees will not always be so, will assuredly not be so, when at the end of the sojourning in which we are absent from the Lord and must walk by faith, shall come the turn of sight in which we shall see face to face. We see not so now; but because we believe, we shall be found worthy to see, and shall rejoice that faith has brought us home to sight. Instead of the faith by which the unseen is believed, will come the sight by which things formerly believed are seen. It may be then that we shall remember this mortal life that will be past, and recall our former belief of what we did not see; but that faith will be set down among things past and gone, not present and ever abiding. It will be found, therefore, that the trinity which now appears in the remembering, beholding, and loving of the faith now present and abiding, is then a thing not permanent but past and gone. We must conclude that if that trinity is indeed the image of God, this image itself must be counted as belonging not to that which always is, but to that which passes away. But if the soul's nature is immortal, so that after its original creation it can never cease to be, God forbid that the soul's most precious possession should not endure with its own immortality; and what can be more precious in its created nature than its making in the image of its Creator? Not therefore in the holding, contemplation, and love of faith, which may not be forever, but in what shall always be, we must find the image of God worthy of that name. (pp. 100–101)

•

Hence we developed an account of the mental trinity, in which memory supplied the source from which the thinker's view receives its form, the conformation itself being a kind of image imprinted by the memory, and the agency by which the two are conjoined being love or will. Thus when the mind regards itself in the act of thought, it understands and takes knowledge of itself: we may say that it begets this self-understanding and self-knowledge. For an object that is incorporeal is seen when it is understood, and is known by the act of understanding. But this begetting by the mind of self-knowledge, when it regards itself as understood in thought, does not imply that it was previously unknown to itself. It was

---

*Reprinted from Augustine, *Later Works*, trans. John Burnaby (Philadelphia, 1955), 100–101, 105–6, 108–9, 113–14, by permission of Westminster/John Knox Press.

so known, in the way that things held in the memory are known, though not thought upon: as we say that a man knows letters, even when he is thinking not of letters but of other things. And to these two, the begetter and the begotten, we have to add the love which joins them together, and is simply the will, pursuing or embracing an object of enjoyment. Accordingly, for the indication of our mental trinity we found these three names appropriate: memory, understanding, and will. (pp. 105–6)

•

Now we have reached the point in our discussion at which we have undertaken to consider that highest element in the human mind whereby it knows or can know God, with a view to our finding therein the image of God. Although the human mind is not of that nature which belongs to God, yet the image of that nature which transcends every other in excellence is to be sought and found in the element which in our own nature is the most excellent. But first we have to consider the mind in itself, before it has participation in God, and discover his image there. We have said that it still remains the image of God, although an image faded and defaced by the loss of that participation. It is in virtue of the fact that it has a capacity for God and the ability to participate in God, that it is his image; only because it is his image can so high a destiny be conceived for it. Here then is the mind, remembering itself, understanding itself, loving itself. Perceiving this, we perceive a trinity — a trinity still less than God, but already an image of God. In this trinity, the memory has not imported from outside what it should retain, nor has the understanding discovered in the outer world the object for its beholding, like the body's eye. The will has not in this case made an outward union of these two, as of the material form and its derivative in the sight of the beholder. An image of the external object seen, taken up as it were and stored in the memory, has not been discovered by thought directed towards it, and thence form been given to the recollecting attention, while the two are united by the further activity of will. This was the system displayed in those trinities which we found to exist in material processes, or to pass somehow into our inward experience from the external body through the bodily sense. (pp. 108–9)

•

Now this trinity of the mind is God's image, not because the mind remembers, understands, and loves itself; but because it has the power also to remember, understand, and love its Maker. And it is in so doing that it attains wisdom. If it does not so, the memory, understanding, and love of itself is no more than an act of folly. Let the mind then remember its God, in whose image it was made, let it understand him and love him. In a word, let it worship the uncreated God who created it with the capacity for himself, and in whom it is able to be made partaker. For this cause it is written: "Behold, the worship of God is wisdom." Wisdom will be the mind's not by its own illumination, but by partaking in that supreme Light; and only when it enters eternity will it reign in bliss. But to say that a man may possess such wisdom is not to deny that it is the property of God. God's is the only true wisdom: were it human, it would be vain. Yet when we call it the wisdom of God, we do not mean the wisdom wherewith God is wise: he is not wise by partaking in himself, as is the mind by partaking in God. It is rather as we speak of the righteousness of God, not only in the sense of that whereby God is righteous, but of that which he gives to man when he "justifies the ungodly": to which the apostle refers when he speaks of those who "being ignorant of God's righteousness, and willing to establish their own righteousness, were not subject to the righteousness of God." In the same way we might speak of some who being ignorant of the wisdom of God, and willing to establish their own, were not subject to the wisdom of God.

There is an uncreated Being who has made all other beings great and small, unquestionably surpassing all that he has made, and so surpassing also the reasonable and spiritual being of which we have been speaking, namely the mind of man, made in the image of its Creator. And the Being surpassing all others is God. He is, indeed "Not far from each one of us," as the apostle says, adding, "for in him we live and move, and have our being." If this were spoken in a material sense, it could be understood of our material world: for in it too, so far as our body is concerned, we live and move and are. We must take the text, then, as spoken of the mind which is made in his image, and of a manner of being more excellent, not visible, but spiritual. What is there indeed that is not "in him," of whom Holy Scripture says: "for from him and through him and in him are all things"? If in him are all things, in whom, save in him in whom they are, can the living live or the moving move? Yet all men are not with him after the manner of the saying "I am always with thee." Nor is he with all after the manner of our own saying, "the Lord be with you." It is man's great misery, not to be with him, without whom man cannot be. Certainly, man is never without him, in whom he is; yet if a man does not remember him, does not understand him, nor love him, he is not with him. But complete oblivion makes it impossible even to be reminded of what we have forgotten. (pp. 113–14)

Augustine of Hippo, *The Spirit and the Letter* (412/3)*

Our own assertion, on the contrary, is this: that the human will is divinely assisted to do the right in such manner that, besides man's creation with the endowment of freedom to choose, and besides the teaching by which he is instructed how he ought to live, he receives the Holy Spirit, whereby there arises in his soul the delight in and the love of God, the supreme and changeless Good. This gift is his here and now, while he walks by faith, not yet by sight; that having this as earnest of God's free bounty, he may be fired in heart to cleave to his Creator, kindled in mind to come within the shining of the true light; and thus receive from the source of his being the only real well-being. Free choice alone, if the way of truth is hidden, avails for nothing but sin; and when the right action and the true aim has begun to appear clearly, there is still no doing, no devotion, no good life, unless it be also delighted in and loved. And that it may be loved, the love of God

---

*Reprinted from *Augustine: Later Works,* trans. John Burnaby (Philadelphia, 1955), 197–99, by permission of Westminster/John Knox Press.

is shed abroad in our hearts, not by the free choice whose spring is in ourselves, but through the Holy Spirit which is given us.[1]

The truth is that the teaching which gives us the commandment of self-control and uprightness of life, remains, without the presence of the life-giving Spirit, a letter that killeth. That text — "The letter killeth, but the Spirit giveth life"[2] — is naturally taken to mean that we are not to understand the figurative sayings of Scripture in their literal sense, which may be irrational, but to look for their deeper significance, and find nourishment for the inward man in a spiritual understanding of them; inasmuch as "to be carnally minded is death, but to be spiritually minded is life and peace."[3] I wish to show, if I can, the apostle's words: "the letter killeth, but the Spirit giveth life," do not refer primarily to figurative modes of speech — although that sense may fit them — but rather to the law's express forbidding of what is evil. That being demonstrated, it will be the more evident that the good life is a divine gift; not only because God has given man the power of free choice, without which moral life were impossible; not only because he has given the commandment to teach us how to live; but because through the Holy Spirit he sheds abroad charity in the hearts of those whom he foreknew that he might predestinate, predestinated that he might call, called that he might justify, and justified that he might glorify. If I can make this clear, I think you will see that the proposed objection falls to the ground: I mean the argument that nothing is to be called possible in the absence of an instance but works of God, like my case of the camel's passing through the needle's eye, and all else that with us is impossible but not with God; and that human righteousness cannot be included in this class, as belonging not to God's work but man's: so that there can be no reason for disbelieving in any example of its perfection, if that perfection is possible in this life. This argument, I say, must clearly fall to the ground, once we are assured that human righteousness itself, though not arising independently of man's will, is yet to be ascribed to the operation of God. We cannot deny the possibility of its perfection in this life, just because all things are possible for God — both what he does by his own will alone, and what he has ordained to be accomplished by himself with the cooperation of the wills of his creatures. Anything in either kind that he does not do will be without example in fact, but will have the reason of its possibility in God's power and the reason of its non-occurrence in God's wisdom. Such reason may be hidden from a man; but he must not forget his humanity, and attribute unwisdom to God because the wisdom of God exceeds his grasp.

---

1. See Romans 5:5.
2. 2 Corinthians 3:6.
3. Romans 8:6.

– 2 –

The Medieval and Reformation Period

INTRODUCTION

Theological anthropology received considerable attention during the medieval and Reformation periods, generating debates at least as intense as Augustine's with Pelagius. Although many of Augustine's positions proved normative after the Synod of Orange (529), by no means can Augustine be said to have had the last word. Perhaps the best way to characterize Augustine's influence on the medieval and Reformation period is to say that he remained a constant "conversation partner." Most theologians consciously addressed theological problems Augustine had originally raised, although certainly not all came to the same conclusions he did. Still, it proved impossible to make significant theological statements about human nature without reference to Augustine's thought.

The early medieval period (600–800) was characterized by the renewed growth and expansion of Christianity throughout Europe after a long period of political instability. This expansion was accomplished primarily by Benedictine monks who became the major representatives of the Christian tradition into the reign of Charlemagne. The monastic tradition continued to develop the notion of original sin as pride, but affirmed that through ascetic discipline Christians could grow in humility and self-knowledge, which would allow them to approach the image and likeness of God in their own interiors. The stability emphasized in the Rule of Saint Benedict, which was the definitive monastic rule by the time of the Carolingian period (ca. 800), established on a religious level precisely what the early medieval period lacked on the political level. The life of Gregory the Great (ca. 540–604), a Benedictine who promoted political and religious stability throughout his life, reflects what Christianity could offer a beleaguered Europe. Gregory was born into an aristocratic Roman family. He observed destruction by both the Ostrogoths and the Lombards after 568. At first a civil servant, Gregory retired to establish monasteries with his inheritance. In 579 he was pressed into papal service as ambassador to the imperial court in Constantinople. A natural diplomat, Gregory became pope upon the death of his predecessor, Pelagius II, in 590. As pope, his agenda included managing the papal estates, developing relief for the poor in Rome, and extending Christianity throughout Europe through the foundation of Benedictine monasteries. Benedictinism became normative for Christianity with important implications for the medieval period, most notably the establishment of the monastery as a place of learning and culture as well as of prayer and contemplation.

In terms of Gregory's position on human nature, his contribution, through the

Christian mystical tradition, was to develop its understanding that a vision of God through contemplation was possible in this lifetime. Critical in the movement toward God was the reading of scripture. This emphasis is both consistent with his Benedictine focus and also uniquely developed in a way which emphasized "the personal relation of the reader to the Bible."[1] At the same time, Gregory retained a pessimism about the fallen world, particularly as manifested in the disharmony between body and spirit. The equilibrium we seek is not attained on earth, but we must nonetheless strive toward integration throughout our lifetimes.

For the next several centuries Benedictine monasticism maintained the integrity of the Christian tradition through the copying of manuscripts and meditation on Christian scripture. Many of the key figures during this period have been called "compilers" or "transmitters," because they were the points of contact between the early and medieval periods. As redactors of earlier texts they played a less creative role than either their predecessors or their successors. Writers like Isidore of Seville (ca. 570–636), Ildefonsus of Toledo (ca. 610–67), and the venerable Bede (673–735) shaped the tradition by establishing a canon of authoritative texts for the medieval period.

A revival of learning known as the Carolingian Renaissance allowed for more theological questions based upon the discussion and interpretation of these "compiled" texts. The tensions over human nature, grace, and predestination in the thought of Augustine generated continued controversy over the primacy of grace or free will in the ninth century. Distinctive positions were developed by Gottschalk of Orbais and Hincmar of Reims, with Florus of Lyons. Gottschalk asserted that humans could not use their free will to do any good, but only evil. Florus asserted that the human will was not so corrupt as that, yet after the Fall humanity had lost its ability to cling to God freely. Hincmar clarified that human free will had been dealt a great blow in the Fall but had been equally restored by the grace of Christ. Hincmar's position emerged at the Council of Quiercy in 853, but his rejection of a doctrine of double predestination, in which God foreknows both salvation and damnation, was reversed at a synod in Valence in 855 and at another synod in Langres in 859.

The rejection of double predestination was not the primary focus of John the Scot, or John Scotus Erigena (ca. 810–77), who was more concerned with applying the resources of the neoplatonic tradition to Christianity, but it was a clear corollary of his thought. Born in Ireland, this thinker moved forward the neoplatonic mystical tradition earlier developed by Pseudo-Dionysius and offered another anthropological alternative in the wake of controversies over how to interpret Augustine. An intellectual associated with the court of Charles the Bald, John the Scot intervened in controversies over Augustine's doctrine of predestination and translated the works of Pseudo-Dionysius. His *Periphyseon,* or *On the Division of Nature,* is a systematic theology sketching out the essential organization of nature as a process of emanation from and return to God. Within this system the Fall is more a fall into ignorance of our relationship with God than an ontological separation. Indeed, the restoration humans experience in Christ is

---

1. Bernard McGinn, *The Growth of Mysticism* (New York: Crossroad, 1994), 41.

predicated upon the common humanity we share with Christ.[2] Whether or not we know Christ, because we are humans we resemble Christ and are joined to him through our common form.

It took many centuries to produce further theological reflection of significance on christology, human nature, and the process of salvation. With the important figure of Anselm of Canterbury (ca. 1033–1109), however, we see how the Augustinian synthesis combined with an emerging reliance on Aristotelian thought to produce new perspectives for the twelfth century. An anthropological view becomes apparent in Anselm, even though his primary focus in *Why God Became Human* is on Christ and salvation. Anselm is considered an important bridge figure who ushers theology into a new phase. His incorporation of parts of the newly translated Aristotelian corpus reflects an important turn in twelfth-century theological method (thus he is called a "protoscholastic"), and his balance between contemplative prayer and theological speculation models a personal commitment to intellectual faith and spiritual depth to which many in the twelfth century aspired.

Anselm was born in northern Italy and became a monk in Normandy at Bec. He served as abbot there for fifteen years until he was named archbishop of Canterbury in 1093. The author of many works, he is probably best known for his two treatises on God, the *Monologion* and the *Proslogion,* as well as his work on redemption (*Why God Became Human*). In this third treatise Anselm devotes his attention to proving by reason alone why restoration to God, part of the divine plan, was impossible without the entrance of Christ into human history. Anselm's distinction between what God can do and what it is fitting for God to do maintained Augustine's ontological separation between God and humanity, a gap which necessitated redemption through Christ. Indeed, for Anselm, humanity is characterized by its obligation both not to sin and also to make satisfaction for sin, or to make amends for the loss of God's honor through sin. Yet because of the stain of original sin humanity was unable to do either. Anselm characterizes humanity as essentially trapped in the circumstances of original sin, trapped by its inability to do what it ought and, by implication, stricken with guilt because it continually dishonors God through sin.

The theologian Peter Abelard (ca. 1079–1142) critiqued the thought of Anselm, introducing the "moral influence" theory, in which it was Christ's moral example, not his ability to make satisfaction for sin, that was critical in the redemption of humanity. While Abelard, like Anselm, focuses more on redemption than on anthropology, the implications for an understanding of human nature are clear. If Christ saved us by providing us with the example of behavior pleasing to God and by taking on suffering out of love, humanity must have the ability to follow Christ's example. The extent to which grace was necessary for the moral life and the idea that redemption has an objective as well as a subjective value were the points of contention raised by Bernard of Clairvaux (1090–1153) in his response to Abelard.

The thought of Abelard signals a significant paradigm shift which occurred

---

2. Our return to God is also mediated by the sacraments and our growth in virtue.

over the course of the century. Both within monastic circles and lay groups (such as the Waldensians and Beguines) many Christian writers described a more human, suffering Christ than had previously been appreciated. Christ's victory over death and the majesty of God became less significant, devotionally and theologically, than Christ's willingness to take on human suffering. The *imitatio Christi* which characterized the medieval period, beginning in the twelfth century, was not primarily priestly but involved a greater sense of poverty, ascetical practice, and charitable work. Signs of this new orientation are found in hagiographical literature, mystical treatises, the later proliferation of writings on the life of Christ, and, of course, in the theological questions raised by Christian writers.[3]

New reflection on the humanity of Christ is apparent in the thought of Bernard of Clairvaux, an influential abbot of the Cistercian order (a reformed branch of the Benedictines). A prolific writer, one of Bernard's significant contributions was his sermon cycle on the Song of Songs, in which he reflects upon the nuptial relationship as a metaphor for humanity's collective and individual relationship with Christ. The intimacy of the relationship underscores the potential for deep union with Christ (Bernard's mysticism is often called "christocentric") and belies a radical ontological separation between God and humanity, although, when explicitly addressing this question, Bernard affirms that, of necessity, mystical union in this life is fleeting. Additionally, Bernard develops a variety of positions on human nature in his direct reflections on Genesis 1:26. In various texts Bernard argues that the soul retains the image of God, at least in part, even after the Fall. Similarly the likeness is lost, entirely or in part, through sin. Bernard of Clairvaux, according to Bernard McGinn's summary, outlines several ways of interpreting humanity's progression from its formation in God, to its deformation through sin, and to its reformation or restoration of similarity to God through Jesus Christ.[4] Although Bernard is keenly aware of the power of humanity's fallen nature, which weighs down the soul in corruption, he also affirms the possibility of conversion in God as a lifelong process toward self-knowledge and rightly ordered love. His poignant reflections on this theme produced some of the most important mystical literature in the Christian tradition.

With the advent of Scholasticism in the medieval universities, the method, sources, and context for theological inquiry changed, and reflection on the nature of humanity changed. The synthesis of Aristotelian thought into the Christian theological tradition, a task taken up most notably by Thomas Aquinas (ca. 1224–74), allowed for refining the details of how grace operated in the human person, enabling both the salvation and the sanctification of the Christian. For Thomas, grace is a necessity for humanity "to do or will any good whatsoever."[5]

---

3. For a review of the hagiographical tradition see Donald Weinstein and Rudolph M. Bell, *Saints and Society: The Two Worlds of Western Christendom, 1000–1700* (Chicago: University of Chicago Press, 1982). For a review of the representation of the humanity of Christ in the mystical tradition and especially of the influence of women see Caroline Walker Bynum, *Holy Feast, Holy Fast: The Religious Significance of Food to Medieval Women* (Berkeley: University of California Press, 1987), and idem, " '…and women his humanity': Female Imagery in the Religious Writing of the Later Middle Ages," in *Fragmentation and Redemption: Essays on Gender and the Human Body in Medieval Religion* (New York: Zone Books, 1991), 151–80.

4. See McGinn, *Growth of Mysticism*, 171–73, esp. 172.

5. See *Summa theologiae*, I-II, q. 109, art. 2; see below.

Echoing Augustine, Aquinas understood that this grace is necessary both in humanity's pre-fallen and fallen nature. It is also necessary for salvation as well as for meritorious (sanctifying) activities. Thomas distinguishes between grace as an infused habit and as a motivator impelling the soul toward individual acts of goodness. This distinction between state and activity is both a recognition of Aristotelian categories and a development of an Augustinian position on original sin as a way of being, preceding any sinful activity.

Aquinas's explanation of how grace operates in the soul suggests that grace becomes a true part of the soul without being part of the soul's essence. Here Aquinas develops an Aristotelian distinction between substance and accident: grace is accidentally part of the soul, not intrinsic to its substance. Grace enters the human person as the expression of God's love, and then the person cooperates with it as both a way of being, or a habit, and as a way of acting. Thus, with the continued help of grace, the infused habit of grace is developed in each human person as that person becomes more and more a Christian person, abiding by Christian precepts and growing in Christian charity. Yet Aquinas also develops the other major strand of Augustinian anthropology, the indwelling of the trinity in the human soul, the manifestation of God's image in creation. In his *Summa theologiae* Aquinas refers to Augustine's *On the Trinity* when he declares "we recognize in ourselves the image of God, that is, of the supreme Trinity."[6]

Within theological circles at the universities, other later medieval theologians parted ways with Aquinas's system in the movement known as nominalism. In this movement concern for the omnipotence of God led to a rejection of too-formalized a system for God's operations in the world. While some theologians could agree with Aquinas that God tended to operate the way Aquinas had described, they wanted to allow God the ability to circumvent whatever observations about God's activity human beings could make. One of the early theologians to criticize Aquinas's system was John Duns Scotus (ca. 1265–1308), who developed a clearer sense of God's will as completely independent of human activity. Scotus drove a further separation between God and humanity, suggesting that God, by definition, was not bound to a specific way of operating or of loving humanity. Further, God's desire to redeem an individual person was more important than anything that person had done, and, indeed, more important than any salvation system that God had established.

Another Franciscan, William of Ockham (ca. 1285–1347), pushed the ideas of Scotus even further when he asserted that whatever God produced through secondary causes God could also produce directly without the use of those secondary causes. Ockham's most basic theological principle was a distinction between God's absolute and ordained powers. God's absolute power rests in God's ability to do anything; it is infinite with unlimited possibilities. God's ordained power is the way that God exercises power according to the way God has chosen to do things. Thus God can do anything God wants, even though we as humans have come to expect God to act in particular ways. Ockham's insistence upon God's freedom reinforced a corresponding powerlessness or finitude in humanity and in-

---

6. Augustine, *The City of God*, book 11, chapter 26.

troduced a certain anxiety about how God might will to respond to the individual soul. Because nothing could really characterize God, nothing could characterize the relationship between God and humanity at large and God's relationship with individual Christians striving to know God.

Several representatives of the medieval mystical tradition described humanity's relationship with God in such a way as to reassure Christians of the primacy of God's infinite love. For example, Catherine of Siena (1347–80), a Dominican tertiary who was certainly familiar with the teachings of Thomas Aquinas, develops a different emphasis while not directly contradicting Thomas's sense of the necessity of grace even in humanity before the Fall. Rather than stressing the rupture between God and humanity caused by the Fall, in her *Dialogue* Catherine emphasizes the process of restoration in Christ by developing the metaphor of humanity as a sick infant restored to health by a wet nurse. This restorative process is so powerful that the soul can withstand any temptation to sin and is under obligation to strive toward goodness and the service of God. Heavily influenced by a theology of atonement, Catherine writes that the tools of the soul in the process of restoration are hunger and longing for God and willingness to suffer on behalf of human sin.

In texts developed by the English anchorite known to us as Julian of Norwich (ca. 1342–1423), there is no focus on the fallen state of humanity (its deformation), but rather much theological attention is given to the process of reformation, which, for Julian, affirms the soul's formation in God. Indeed, Julian states plainly that humanity is made for union with God: "Our natural will is to have God, and God's good will is to have us, and we can never stop willing or loving until we possess God in the fullness of joy."[7] And humanity is caught up in the process of longing for God, just as God longs for humanity: "It is God's will that we seek on until we see him, for it is through this that he will show himself to us, of his special grace, when it is his will." Searching and longing is both appropriate to the soul's nature and "right" ontologically: "The soul's constant search pleases God greatly. For it cannot do more than seek, suffer, and trust."[8] Trusting in God's love is critical in the human journey toward God, as humanity can be hindered in its ability to love itself, God, and others without that trust.

The key to understanding Julian's contributions to theological anthropology is to recognize that her approach takes most seriously the definition of God as love. This is an ontological definition, and a systematic theology develops around it. Love is God's way of being, a state leading to creative activity. Through God's loving creation, humanity is endowed with the gifts of loving, suffering, and joy. These gifts are never taken away from the soul, and through them the soul partakes and exists in God's substance (love). Because the human will loves out of its very nature as God's creation, the human will is not completely overcome by original sin, as Julian asserts: The human will consists of two parts, one which assents to sin and one which "never assents to sin and never will."[9]

---

7. Julian of Norwich, *Showings* (New York: Paulist Press, 1978), 186.
8. Ibid., 195.
9. Ibid., 241–42.

The context of nominalism certainly helps to understand the thought of Julian of Norwich. Philosophically, Julian rejects the idea that God's will is radically free and inscrutable. Julian's God is indeed bound, not by theological systems, but by an ordained way of behaving consistent with God's being in love. Thus a pastoral orientation characterizes her theological method, and she understands her task to be the demonstration that God's being is love, and that all creative activity (divine and human) is rooted in the ontological state of loving. Suffering and bliss, which characterize the human experience, also characterize the life of Christ and God; these activities are rooted in the condition of loving. The human capacity to love, instilled in humanity by the loving Creator, is not effaced in the Fall; indeed, in her retelling of the Fall story, Julian suggests that the Fall is a result not of the perversity of the human will but of an accident occasioned by the force of humanity's desire to love and serve God. Once failen, it is difficult for humanity to perceive the love of God as strongly as it could in its pre-fallen state, but as it learns to live in love, humanity also realizes how united it is to God in God's loving nature.

The breadth of thought in the fourteenth and fifteenth centuries about human nature should make us cautious about overgeneralizing; however, we must also account for the explosion of ideas about theological anthropology which occurs in the sixteenth century. The diversity of thought certainly makes it safe to say, as Heiko Oberman argues, that two centuries of dialogue and debate on issues of justification precede the escalated disagreements of the sixteenth century, and that both Catholics and Protestants drew from a common theological heritage.[10] Further, we should observe that medieval appreciation of the humanity of Christ led to profound development in reflection on human nature. For the most part, medieval theologians dwelled less on the rupture between God and humanity established in the Fall and more on the inborn image of God and its continued restoration in Christ.

The thought of Martin Luther (1483–1546) contains both old and new themes in theological anthropology. Luther both affirms and updates Augustine's sense of original sin and insists that faith alone saves us. For Luther original sin is a personal disorientation which ruptures one's relationship to God. Because of original sin, humans seek themselves before God. Original sin is a powerful force, so powerful that, in debates with his contemporary Erasmus, Luther maintained that free will exists only in theory. Redemption from sin comes through the power of grace, yet the power of sin remains in humanity even though the human being can be understood to be saved or justified. Retaining a rigid sense of humanity's separation from God, Luther allowed that grace could enable a person to overcome the power of sin, but only through a radical experience of faith which frees the human will from its servitude to the devil.

---

10. See Heiko Oberman, *Forerunners of the Reformation: The Shape of Late Medieval Thought Illustrated by Key Documents* (Philadelphia: Fortress Press, 1981), 38. In making the case for these "forerunners," Oberman proposes the following: "(1) the concept of Forerunner proves to be anything but alien to the period concerned, (2) the Forerunner is *not* a product of Protestant apologetics, (3) the rejection of the Forerunner is the outcome of an ahistorical disjunction of medieval and Reformation thought" (ibid.).

While he agreed with Luther on the doctrine of justification by faith alone, the thought of the reformer John Calvin (1509–64) advanced Augustinian thought on human nature in different ways. In his massive work, the *Institutes*, revised many times throughout his life, Calvin affirms the image of God in humanity, suggesting that this reality is apparent to all, even non-Christians. Further, God's image, imprinted in the human mind, "can never be effaced" (see text below). However, Calvin reiterated Augustine's sense of the depravity and disorientation of the human will after the Fall and the tendency to seek fulfillment in the intellect, outside the presence of God. He also extended Augustine's sense of double predestination referring to the elect, not the entire church, as the true body of Christ.

In light of the challenges to the hierarchical church and the sacramental system posed by the Protestant reformers, a Roman Catholic perspective (probably best understood as a range of perspectives) on human nature emerged over the course of the sixteenth century. Catholic positions may be grouped in two primary ways: first, the official church teaching coming out of the Council of Trent and, second, the positions enunciated by mystical theologians who carried the medieval mystical tradition into the sixteenth century and beyond. The Council of Trent was held in several phases from 1545 to 1563. During the first phase (1545–47) the council issued a decree on original sin and another on justification. One of the major concerns in these decrees was to reaffirm the role of human cooperation in salvation and sanctification, and a restatement of Aquinas's position that indwelling grace both saved and stimulated individuals to perform meritorious acts served this purpose well.

Within the context of controversy over the extent to which union with God is possible, Teresa of Avila (d. 1582) asserted what became the definitive Catholic position throughout the Counter-Reformation and Baroque periods. Teresa's thought, rooted heavily in that of Augustine and Catherine of Siena, and informed by thinkers as diverse as Jerome, Gregory the Great, Angela of Foligno, and her own contemporaries Francisco de Osuna, Bernardino de Laredo, Pedro de Alcantara, and John of the Cross, served to solidify and promote much of the medieval mystical tradition, preserving and updating it for the next several centuries. From Augustine, Teresa takes the idea of the presence of the trinity in the soul, but for Teresa this image is completely recoverable as the soul moves through the seven mansions of its interior. Indeed, an intellectual vision of the trinity welcomes the soul's entrance into the deepest center of itself. Teresa was also moved by Augustine's sense of yearning for God's presence, and found the *Confessions* an intimate portrait of spiritual growth. Probably no less flamboyant than Augustine, Teresa's own spiritual journey was anchored in a deliberately contemplative setting, the Discalced Carmelite convents she founded throughout Spain; thus her accounts of her spiritual journey convey a sense of regularity and rhythm punctuated by moments of grace, but moving steadily forward toward a spiritual profundity often absent in Augustine's theological texts. No stranger to rhetoric herself, Teresa's polemical words are reserved primarily for Roman Catholics of the *letrado* school, who viewed the mystical life with suspicion.

Apparently informed by sixteenth-century debates over grace, Teresa reshapes the medieval mystical tradition by injecting a reverence for the majesty of God and peppering her analysis of the mystical way with references to her own lowliness. Referring to her own journey toward God, Teresa is careful to attribute all spiritual progress to God's grace. Yet the ascetical discipline inherent in such spiritual progress — reflected in obedience, the pursuit of prayer, and, in one of Teresa's characteristic phrases, "a very determined determination" to progress — underscores our active human participation in the spiritual life.

Substantial debate among Teresa's peers, including a lengthy inquisitional review of her writings, preceded the readmittance of the mystical tradition into Catholic orthodoxy. However, the transition to seventeenth-century Catholic spirituality and anthropology was characterized by an affirmation of the possibility of union with God and the quest for concrete experiences of the holy.

In some senses, the necessity of God's grace or love as it is developed in the passages considered in this reader reveals a question of perspective; the core of a theologian's beliefs about human nature are suggested in how the author develops the reality of God's love as a way of being. For example, Aquinas and Luther devote a considerable amount of time to articulating how grace works and how dependent humanity is on grace. This tends to accentuate the difference or separation between God and humanity. Julian of Norwich (and Catherine of Siena, to a lesser extent) spends more time developing the idea of God's love as an ontological reality, which reinforces the bond between Creator and creation, who engage in creative and redemptive activity together out of love. God's love, for Julian, is part of our substance, and for that reason she can affirm, "Our soul is united to him who is unchangeable goodness. And between God and our soul there is neither wrath nor forgiveness in his sight. For our soul is so wholly united to God, through his own goodness, that between God and our soul nothing can interpose."[11] The prioritization of the attributes of God and the resultant doctrine of human nature which emerges may differ, but these authors share a common set of assumptions about God which were about to be challenged by the intellectual and cultural developments of the modern period.

TEXTS

Bernard of Clairvaux (1090–1153)

"Sermon 80 on the Song of Songs" (ca. 1148)*

But someone says to me, "Why do you take these two together? What have the Word and the soul in common?" Much, on all counts. In the first place, there is a natural kinship, in that the one is the Image of God, and the other is made in that image. Next, their resemblance argues some affinity. For the soul is made not

---

11. Julian of Norwich, *Showings,* 259.

*Reprinted from Bernard of Clairvaux, *On the Song of Songs IV,* trans. Irene Edmonds (Kalamazoo, Mich., 1980), 146–49, by permission of Cistercian Publications.

only in the image of God but in his likeness. In what does this likeness consist? you ask. Take first the Image. The word is truth, it is wisdom and righteousness. These constitute the Image. The image of what? Of righteousness, wisdom, and truth. For the image, the Word, is righteousness from righteousness, wisdom from wisdom, truth from truth, as he is light and God from God. The soul is none of these things, since it is not the image. Yet it is capable of them and yearns for them; that perhaps is why it is said to be made in the image. It is a lofty creature, in its capacity for greatness, and in its longing we see a token of its uprightness. We read that God made man upright and great; his capacity proves that, as we have said. For what is made in the image should conform to the image, and not merely share the empty name of image — as the image [of God] himself is not merely called by the empty name of image. You know that it is said of him who is the image of God that although he was in the form of God, he did not think it robbery to be equal with God. You see that his uprightness is indicated because he is in the form of God, and his greatness in his equality with God, so that in the comparison of uprightness with uprightness and greatness with greatness, it appears on two accounts that what is made in the image agrees with the image, just as the image also corresponds in both respects to that of which it is the image. For he is the one of whom you have heard holy David sing in his Psalm "Great is the Lord, and great is his power"; and again "The Lord our God is upright, and in him there is no unrighteousness." He is the image of this upright and great God; therefore the soul which is in his image is like him.

But I ask: Is there no difference between the image of God and the soul which is made in its image, since we attribute greatness and uprightness to it, too? Indeed there is. For the soul receives according to its capacity, but the image receives in equal measure with God. Is there no more to say? You must mark this as well: the soul is endowed with both by God who created him and made him great, but the image of God receives them by God's begetting. And who can deny that this is a much greater dignity. Although man received his gifts from God's hands, the image received them from God's being, that is from his very substance. For the image of God is of the same substance as God, and everything which he seems to share with his image is part of the substance of both, and not accident.... But if, as I argued before, the soul is great in proportion to its capacity for the eternal, and upright in proportion to its desire for heavenly things, then the soul which does not desire or have a taste for heavenly things, but clings to earthly things, is clearly not upright but bent, but it does not for all this cease to be great, and it always retains its capacity for eternity. For even if it never attains to it, it never ceases to be capable of doing so, and so the Scripture is fulfilled. Truly man "passes as an image," yet only in part, so that the superiority of the Word may be seen in its completeness. For how can the Word fail to be great and upright, since it possesses these qualities as part of its nature? Man possesses these gifts in part also because if he were completely deprived of them there would be no hope of salvation, for if he ceased to be great he would lose his capacity, and, as I have said, the soul's greatness is measured by its capacity. What hope of salvation could there be for one who had no capacity for receiving it?

And so by the greatness which it retains even when it has lost its uprightness, "man passes as an image," but he limps, as it were, on one foot, and has become an estranged son. Of someone like this, it can, I think, be said: "the estranged sons have lied to me, they have become weak, and have limped away from the path." They are well called "estranged sons," for they are sons inasmuch as they keep their greatness, and estranged because they have lost their uprightness. If they had completely lost the image, the psalmist would not have said "they have fallen away" or some such thing. But now "man passes as an image" because of his greatness; but as far as his uprightness is concerned, he limps, he is troubled, and he is torn away from the image.

Bernard of Clairvaux, *On Grace and Free Choice* (ca. 1128), 6:18*

Created, then, to a certain extent, as our own in freedom of will, we become God's as it were by good will. Moreover he makes the will good, who made it free; and makes it good to this end, that we may be a kind of first fruits of his creatures; because it would have been better for us never to have existed than that we should remain always our own. For those who wished to belong to themselves, became indeed like gods, knowing good and evil; but then they were not merely their own, but the devil's. Hence, free will makes us our own; bad will, the devil's; and good will, God's. This is the meaning of the words: "The Lord knows those who are his." For to those who are not his he says: "Amen I say to you, I do not know you." As long, therefore, as by bad will we belong to the devil, we are, in a certain sense, no longer God's; just as, when by good will we pass over to God, we cease to belong to the devil. "No one," in fact, "can serve two masters." Furthermore, whether we belong to God or to the devil, this does not prevent us from being also our own. For on either side freedom of choice continues to operate, and so the ground of merit remains, inasmuch as, when we are bad we are rightly punished, since we have become so of our own free choice, or when we are good we are glorified, since we could not have become so without a similar decision of our will. It is our own will that enslaves us to the devil, not his power; whereas, God's grace subjects us to God, not our own will. Our will, created good (as must be granted) by the good God, shall nevertheless be perfect only when perfectly subjected to its Creator. This does not mean that we ascribe to it its own perfection, and to God, only its creation; since to be perfect is far more than to be made. The attributing to God of what is less than excellent, and to ourselves of what is more, surely stands condemned in the very statement. Finally, the Apostle, feeling what he really was by nature and what he hoped to be by grace, said: "I can will what is right, but I cannot do it." He realized that to will was possible to him as a result of free choice, but that for this will to be perfect he stood in need of grace. For, if to will what is evil is a defect of the willing faculty, then undoubtedly to will what is good marks a growth in this same faculty. To measure up to every good thing that we will, however, is its perfection.

In order, then, that our willing, derived from our free choice may be perfect,

---

*Reprinted from Bernard of Clairvaux, *On Grace and Free Choice*, trans. Daniel O'Donovan (Kalamazoo, Mich., 1988), 73–74, by permission of Cistercian Publications.

we need the twofold gift of grace: namely, true wisdom, which means the turning of the will to good, and full power, which means its confirmation in good.

Bonaventure (ca. 1221–74)

The Soul's Journey into God (1259)*

The two previous stages, by leading us into God through his vestiges, through which he shines forth in all creatures, have led us to the point of reentering ourselves, that is, into our mind, where the divine image shines forth. Here is that, now in the third stage, we enter into our very selves, and, as it were, leaving the outer court, we should strive to see God through a mirror in the sanctuary, that is, in the forward area of the tabernacle. Here the light of truth, as from a candelabrum, glows upon the face of our mind, in which the image of the most blessed Trinity shines in splendor. Enter into yourself, then, and see that your soul loves itself most fervently; that it could not love itself unless it knew itself, not know itself unless it remembered itself, because our intellects grasp only what is present in our memory. From this you can observe, not with the bodily eye, but with the eye of reason, that your soul has a threefold power. Consider, therefore, the operations and relationships of these three powers, and you will be able to see God through yourself as through an image, which is to see through a mirror in an obscure manner.

The function of memory is to retain and represent not only present, corporeal and temporal things but also successive, simple, and eternal things. For the memory retains the past by remembrance, the present by reception and the future by foresight. It retains also simple things, such as the principles of continuous and discrete quantities like the point, the instant, and the unit. Without these it is impossible to remember or to think of things which originate from them. The memory also retains the principles and axioms of the sciences, as everlasting truths held everlastingly. For while using reason, one can never so completely forget these principles that he would fail to approve and assent to them once they are heard, not as if he perceives them anew, but rather as if he recognizes them as innate and familiar. This is clearly shown when we propose to someone the following: "On any matter, one must either affirm or deny," or "Every whole is greater than its part," or any other axiom which cannot be contradicted "by our inner reason."

In its first activity, therefore — the actual retention of all temporal things, past, present, and future — the memory is an image of eternity, whose indivisible presence extends to all times. From its second activity, it is evident that memory is informed not only from outside by sensible images, but also from above by receiving and holding within itself simple forms which cannot enter through the doors of the senses by means of sensible images. From the third activity, we hold that the memory has an unchangeable light present to itself in which it remembers

---

*Reprinted from Bonaventure, *The Soul's Journey into God,* trans. Ewert Cousins (New York, 1979), 79–81, by permission of Paulist Press.

immutable truths. And so from the activities of the memory, we see that the soul itself is an image of God and a likeness to present to itself and having God so present that the soul actually grasps him and potentially "is capable of possessing him and to being a partaker in him."[1]

Thomas Aquinas (1225–74)

Summa theologiae (1256–73), I-II, q. 77, art. 2; q. 109, art. 2; q. 109, art. 9*

Question 77: What Belongs to the Powers of the Soul in General

Second Article: Whether There Are Several Powers of the Soul?

Of necessity we must place several powers in the soul. To make this evident, we observe that, as the Philosopher says, the lowest order of things cannot acquire perfect goodness, but they acquire a certain imperfect goodness, by few movements. Those which belong to a higher order acquire perfect goodness by many movements. Those yet higher acquire perfect goodness by few movements, and the highest perfection is found in those things which acquire perfect goodness without any movement whatever. Thus he is least of all disposed to health, who can only acquire imperfect health by means of a few remedies. Better disposed is he who can acquire perfect health by means of many remedies, and better still, he who can by few remedies; but best of all is he who has perfect health without any remedies. We conclude, therefore, that things which are below man acquire a certain limited goodness, and so have a few determinate operations and powers. But man can acquire universal and perfect goodness, because he can acquire beatitude. Yet he is in the lowest degree, according to his nature, of those to whom beatitude is possible; and therefore the human soul requires many and various operations and powers. But to angels smaller variety of powers is sufficient. In God, however, there is no power or action beyond His own Essence.

There is yet another reason why the human soul abounds in a variety of power: it is on the confines of spiritual and corporeal creatures, and therefore the powers of both meet together in the soul.

Question 109: Necessity of Grace

Second Article: Whether Man Can Will or Do Any Good without Grace?

Man's nature may be looked at in two ways: first, in its integrity, as it was in our first parent before sin; secondly, as it is corrupted in us after the sin of our first parent. Now in both states human nature needs the help of God as First Mover, to do or will any good whatsoever, as was stated above. But in the state of

---

1. A reference to Augustine, *On the Trinity,* book 19, chapter 8, no. 11.

*Reprinted from *Introduction to Saint Thomas Aquinas,* ed. Anton C. Pegis (New York: Modern Library, 1948), 315–16, 655–56, 669–70, by permission of the estate of Anton Pegis.

integrity of nature, as regards the sufficiency of operative power, man by his natural endowments could will and do the good proportioned to his nature, which is the good of acquired virtue; but he could not do the good that exceeded his nature, which is the good of infused virtue. But in the state of corrupted nature, man falls short even of what he can do by his own nature, so that he is unable to fulfill all of it by his own natural powers. Yet because human nature is not altogether corrupted by sin, namely, so as to be shorn of every good of nature, even in the state of corrupted nature it can, by virtue of its natural endowments, perform some particular good, such as to build dwellings, plant vineyards, and the like; yet it cannot do all the good natural to it, so as to fall short in nothing. In the same way, a sick man can of himself make some movements, yet he cannot be perfectly moved with the movement of one in health, unless by the help of medicine he be cured.

Hence in the state of the integrity of nature, man needs a gratuitous strength superadded to natural strength for one reason, viz., in order to do and will supernatural good; but in the state of corrupted nature he needs it for two reasons, viz., in order to be healed and, furthermore, in order to carry out works of supernatural virtue, which are meritorious. Beyond this, in both states man needs the divine help that he may be moved to act well.

Article 9: Whether One Who Has Already Obtained Grace Can, of Himself and without Further Help of Grace, Do Good and Avoid Sin?

. . . [I]n order to live righteously a man needs a twofold help of God — first, a habitual gift whereby corrupted human nature is healed, and after being healed is lifted up so as to work deeds meritorious of eternal life, which exceed the capability of nature. Secondly, man needs the help of grace in order to be moved by God to act.

Now with regard to the first kind of help, man does not need a further help of grace, that is, a further infused habit. Yet he needs the help of grace in another way, i.e., in order to be moved by God to act righteously; and this for two reasons: first, for the general reason that no created thing can put forth any act, unless by virtue of the divine motion; secondly, for this special reason — the condition of the state of human nature. For, although healed by grace as to the mind, yet it remains corrupted and poisoned in the flesh, whereby it serves the law of sin. In the intellect, too, there remains the darkness of ignorance, whereby, as is written, We know not what we should pray for as we ought; since, because of the various turns of circumstances, and because we do not know ourselves perfectly, we cannot fully know what is for our good, according to Wisdom 9:14: For the thoughts of mortal men are fearful and our counsels uncertain. Hence we must be guided and guarded by God, Who knows and can do all things. For this reason also it is becoming in those who have been born again as sons of God to say: Lead us not into temptation, and Thy Will be done on earth as it is in heaven, and whatever else is contained in the Lord's Prayer pertaining to this.

The gift of habitual grace is not therefore given to us that we may no longer need the divine help; for every creature needs to be preserved in the good received from Him. Hence, if after having received grace man still needs the divine help, it cannot be concluded that grace is given to no purpose, or that it is imperfect, since man will need the divine help even in the state of glory, when grace shall be fully perfected. But here grace is to some extent imperfect, inasmuch as it does not completely heal man, as was stated above.

Catherine of Siena (1347–80)

The Dialogue (ca. 1378)*

God let himself be forced by her tears and chained by her holy desire. And turning to her with a glance at once full of mercy and of sadness God said:

Dearest daughter, because your tears are joined to my charity and are shed for love of me, your weeping has power over me and the pain in your desire binds me like a chain. But look how my bride has disfigured her face! She is leprous with impurity and selfishness. Her breasts are swollen because of the pride and avarice of those who feed there: the universal body of Christianity and the mystic body of holy Church. I am speaking of my ministers who feed at her breasts. They ought not only to feed themselves, but hold to those breasts the whole body of Christianity as well as whoever would rise from the darkness of unbelief and be bound into the body of my Church.

Do you see how ignorantly and blindly they serve out the marvelous milk and blood of this bride — how thanklessly and with what filthy hands? And do you see with what presumption and lack of reverence it is received? And so the precious life-giving blood of my only-begotten Son, which dispelled death and darkness, confounded falsehood, and brought the gift of light and truth, all too often, because of their sinfulness, brings them death instead.

For those who are receptive this blood bestowed and accomplished all that they need to be saved and made perfect. But since its gift of life and grace is in proportion to the soul's readiness and desire, it deals death to the wicked. So it gives death rather than life to those who receive it unworthily, in the darkness of deadly sin. The fault for this is not in the blood. Nor does it lie in the ministers. The latter may be just as evil or worse, but their sin cannot spoil or contaminate the blood or lessen its grace and power, nor can it harm those they serve. They are, however, bringing on themselves the evil of sin, which will certainly be punished unless they set themselves right through true contrition and contempt for sin.

Those who receive the blood unworthily then, I repeat, are harmed not through any fault in the blood nor because of any fault on the ministers' part, but because of their own evil disposition and their own sin. For they have defiled their minds and bodies with such wretched filth, and have been so cruel to themselves and to their neighbors. They have cruelly deprived themselves of grace, willfully trampling underfoot the fruit of the blood, since it was by virtue of the blood that

---

*Reprinted from Catherine of Siena, *The Dialogue*, trans. Suzanne Noffke (New York, 1980), 50–55, by permission of Paulist Press.

they were freed in holy baptism from the taint of original sin, which they had contracted when they were conceived by their father and mother.

This is why I gave the Word, my only-begotten Son. The clay of humankind was spoiled by the sin of the first man, Adam, and so all of you, as vessels made from that clay, were spoiled and unfit to hold eternal life. So to undo the corruption and death of humankind and to bring you back to the grace you had lost through sin, I, exaltedness, united myself with the baseness of your humanity. For my divine justice demanded suffering in atonement for sin. But I cannot suffer. And you, being only human, cannot make adequate atonement. Even if you did atone for some particular thing, you still could make atonement only for yourself and not for others. But for this sin you could not make full atonement either for yourself or for others since it was committed against me, and I am infinite Goodness.

Yet I really wanted to restore you, incapable as you were of making atonement for yourself. And because you were so utterly handicapped, I sent the Word, my Son; I clothed him with the same nature as yours — the spoiled clay of Adam — so that he could suffer in that same nature which had sinned, and by suffering in his body even to the extent of the shameful death of the cross he would placate my anger.

And so I satisfied both my justice and my divine mercy. For my mercy wanted to atone for your sin and make you fit to receive the good for which I had created you. Humanity, when united with divinity, was able to make atonement for the whole human race — not simply through suffering in its finite nature, that is, in the clay of Adam, but by virtue of the eternal divinity, the infinite divine nature. In the union of those two natures I received and accepted the sacrifice of my only-begotten Son's blood, steeped and kneaded with his divinity into the one bread, which the heat of my divine love held nailed to the cross. Thus was human nature enabled to atone for its sin only by virtue of the divine nature.

So the pus was drained out of Adam's sin, leaving only its scar, that is, the inclination to sin and every sort of physical weakness — like the scar that remains after a wound has healed. Now Adam's sin oozed with a deadly pus, but you were too weakened to drain it yourself. But when the great doctor came (my only-begotten Son) he tended that wound, drinking himself the bitter medicine you could not swallow.[1] And he did as the wet nurse who herself drinks the medicine the baby needs, because she is big and strong and the baby is too weak to stand the bitterness. My son was your wet nurse, and he joined the bigness and strength of his divinity with your nature to drink the bitter medicine of his painful death on the cross so that he might heal and give life to you who were babies weakened by sin.

Only the scar remains of that original sin as you contract it from your father and mother when you are conceived by them. And even this scar is lifted from the soul — though not completely — in holy baptism, for baptism has power to communicate the life of grace in virtue of this glorious and precious blood. As soon as the soul has received holy baptism, original sin is taken from her and grace is

---

1. Cf. Augustine, *Homilies on 1 John,* "Sermon 9:4," in *Augustine: Later Works,* ed. John Burnaby (Philadelphia: Westminster Press, 1955), 332–33.

poured in. The inclination to sin, which is the trace that remains from original sin, is a weakness as I have said, but the soul can keep it in check if she will.

Then the soul is as a vessel ready to receive grace and to make it grow within her as much as she chooses to fit herself, through affection and desire, to love and serve me. Or she can fit herself for evil instead, even though she has received grace in holy baptism. And when she is old enough to discern the one from the other, in her freedom she can choose good or evil as it pleases her.

But such is the freedom of your humanity, and so strong have you been made by the power of this glorious blood, that neither the devil nor any other creature can force you to the least sin unless you want it. You were freed from slavery so that you might be in control of your own powers and reach the end you were created for. How wretched you would be, then, to wallow in the mud like an animal, ignoring the great gift I had given you! A miserable creature full of such foolishness could not receive more.

I want you to understand this, my daughter: I created humankind anew in the blood of my only-begotten Son and reestablished them in grace, but they have so scorned the graces I gave them and still give them! They go from bad to worse, from sin to sin, constantly repaying me with insults. And they not only fail to recognize my graces for what they are, but sometimes even think I am abusing them — I who want nothing but their sanctification! I tell you it will go harder for them in view of the grace they have received, and they will be deserving of greater punishment. They will be more severely punished now that they have been redeemed by my Son's blood than they would have been before that redemption, before the scar of Adam's sin was removed.

It is only reasonable that those who receive more should give more in return, and the greater the gift, the greater the bond of indebtedness. How greatly were they indebted to me, then, since I had given them their very existence, creating them in my image and likeness! They owed me glory, but they stole it from me and took it to themselves instead. They violated the obedience I had laid on them and so became my enemies. But with humility I destroyed their pride: I stooped to take on their humanity, rescued them from their slavery to the devil, and made them free. And more than this — can you see? — through this union of the divine nature with the human, God was made human and humanity was made God.

What indebtedness — to have received the treasure of the blood by which they are created anew in grace! So you see how much more they owe me after their redemption than before. For now they are bound by the example of the incarnate Word, my only-begotten Son, to give me glory and praise. And then they will pay their debt of love for me and for their neighbors, as well as true and solid virtue as I described for you earlier.

Because they owe me so much love, if they refuse it their sin is all the greater, and my divine justice punishes them so much more severely in eternal damnation. False Christians fare much worse there than do pagans. The fire of divine justice torments them the more, burning without consuming; and in their torment they feel themselves being eaten by the worm of conscience, which eats away without eating up — for the damned for all their torment cannot cease to exist. By their sin they can lose the life of grace, but not their very being.

So sin is punished far more severely after people have been redeemed by the blood than before. For they have received more, but they seem to ignore it and to take no notice of their evil deeds. Though I once reconciled them to myself through the blood of my Son, they have become my enemies.

But I have one remedy to calm my wrath: my servants who care enough to press me with their tears and bind me with the chain of their desire. You see, you have bound me with that chain — and I myself gave you that chain because I wanted to be merciful to the world. I put into my servants a hunger and longing for my honor and the salvation of souls so that I might be forced by their tears to soften the fury of my divine justice.

Bring, then, your tears and your sweat, you and my other servants. Draw them from the fountain of my divine love and use them to wash the face of my bride. I promise you that thus her beauty will be restored. Not by the sword or by war or by violence will she regain her beauty, but through peace and through the constant and humble prayers and sweat and tears poured out by my servants with eager desire.

And so I will fulfill your desire by giving you much to suffer, and your patience will spread light into the darkness in all the world's evil. Do not be afraid: Though the world may persecute you, I am at your side and never will my providence fail you.

Julian of Norwich (1342–ca. 1423)

Showings (1373)*

Greatly ought we to rejoice that God dwells in our soul; and more greatly ought we to rejoice that our soul dwells in God. Our soul was created to be God's dwelling place, and the dwelling of our soul is God, who is uncreated. It is a great understanding to see and know inwardly that God, who is our Creator, dwells in our soul, and it is a far greater understanding to see and know inwardly that our soul, which is created, dwells in God in substance, of which substance, through God, we are what we are.

And I saw no difference between God and our substance, but, as it were, all God; and still my understanding accepted that our substance is in God, that is to say that God is God, and our substance is a creature in God. For the almighty truth of the Trinity is our Father, for he made us and keeps us in him. And the deep wisdom of the Trinity is our Mother, in whom we are enclosed. And the high goodness of the Trinity is our Lord, and in him we are enclosed and he in us. We are enclosed in the Father, and we are enclosed in the Son, and we are enclosed in the Holy Spirit. And the Father is enclosed in us, the Son is enclosed in us, and the Holy Spirit is enclosed in us, almighty, all wisdom and all goodness, one God, one Lord. And our faith is a power which comes from our natural substance into our sensual soul by the Holy Spirit, in which power all our powers come to

*Reprinted from Julian of Norwich, *Showings*, trans. Edmund Colledge and James Walsh (New York, 1978), 285–89, by permission of Paulist Press.

us, for without that no one can receive power, for it is nothing else than right understanding with true belief and certain trust in our being, that we are in God and he in us, which we do not see.

And this power with all the others which God has ordained for us, entering there, works great things in us; for Christ is mercifully working in us, and we are by grace according with him, through the gift and the power of the Holy Spirit. This working makes it so that we are Christ's children and live Christian lives.

... [D]espite all our feelings of woe or of well-being, God wants us to understand and to believe that we are more truly in heaven than on earth. Our faith comes from the natural love of our soul, and from the clear light of our reason, and from the steadfast memory which we have from God in our first creation. And when our soul is breathed into our body, at which time we are made sensual, at once mercy and grace begin to work, having care of us and protecting us with pity and love, in which operation the Holy Spirit forms in our faith the help that we shall return up above to our substance, into the power of Christ, increased and fulfilled through the Holy Spirit. So I understood that our sensuality is founded in nature, in mercy and in grace, and this foundation enables us to receive gifts which lead us to endless life. For I saw very surely that our substance is in God, and I also saw that God is in our sensuality, for in the same instant and place in which our soul is made sensual, in that same instant and place exists the city of God, ordained for him from without beginning. He comes into this city and will never depart from it, for God is never out of the soul, in which he will dwell blessedly without end.

And this was said in the sixteenth revelation, where it says: The place that Jesus takes in our soul he will never depart from. And all the gifts which God can give to the creature he has given to his Son Jesus for us, which gifts he, dwelling in us, has enclosed in him until the time that we are fully grown, our soul together with our body and our body together with our soul. Let either of them take help from the other, until we have grown to full stature as creative nature brings about; and then in the foundation of creative nature with the operation of mercy, the Holy Spirit by grace breathes into us gifts leading to endless life.

And so my understanding was led by God to see in him and to know, to understand and to recognize that our soul is a created trinity, like the uncreated blessed Trinity, known and loved from without beginning, and in the creation united to the Creator, as is said before. This sight was sweet and wonderful to contemplate, peaceful and restful, secure and delectable. And because of the glorious union which was thus made by God between the soul and the body, humankind had necessarily to be restored from a double death, which restoration could never be until the time when the second person in the Trinity had taken the lower part of human nature, whose highest part was united to him in its first creation. And these two parts were in Christ, the higher and the lower, which are only one soul. The higher part was always at peace with God in full joy and bliss. The lower part, which is sensuality, suffered for the salvation of humankind. ...

And so I saw most surely that it is quicker for us and easier to come to the knowledge of God than it is to know our own soul. For our soul is so deeply grounded in God and so endlessly treasured that we cannot come to knowledge of it until we first have knowledge of God, who is the Creator to whom it is united. But nevertheless I saw that we have, naturally from our fullness, to desire wisely and truly to know our own soul, through which we are taught to seek it where it is, and that is in God. And so by the leading through grace of the Holy Spirit we shall know them both in one; whether we are moved to know God or our soul, either motion is good and true. God is closer to us than our own soul, for he is the foundation on which our soul stands, and he is the mean which keeps the substance and the sensuality together, so that they will never separate. For our soul sits in God in true rest, and our soul stands in God in sure strength, and our soul is naturally rooted in God in endless love. And therefore if we want to have knowledge of our soul, and communion and discourse with it, we must seek in our Lord God in whom it is enclosed. . . .

That honorable city in which our Lord Jesus sits is our sensuality, in which he is enclosed; and our natural substance is enclosed in Jesus, with the blessed soul of Christ sitting in rest in the divinity. And I saw very certainly that we must necessarily be in longing and in penance until the time when we are led so deeply into God that we verily and truly know our own soul; and I saw certainly that our good Lord himself leads us into this high depth, in the same love with which he created us and in the same love with which he redeemed us, by mercy and grace, through the power of his blessed Passion.

And all this notwithstanding, we can never come to the full knowledge of God until we first clearly know our own soul. For until the time that it is in its full powers, we cannot be all holy; and that is when our sensuality by the power of Christ's Passion can be brought up into the substance, with all the profits of our tribulation which our Lord will make us obtain through mercy and grace.

Martin Luther (1483–1546)

"Sermon on Two Kinds of Righteousness" (1519)*

There are two kinds of Christian righteousness, just as man's sin is of two kinds.

The first is alien righteousness, that is the righteousness of another, instilled from without. This is the righteousness of Christ by which he justifies through faith, as it is written in 1 Cor. 1[:30]: "Whom God made our wisdom, our righteousness and sanctification and redemption." In John 11[:25–26], Christ himself states: "I am the resurrection and the life; he who believes in me . . . shall never die." Later he adds in John 14[:6], "I am the way, and the truth, and the life." This righteousness, then, is given to men in baptism and whenever they are truly repentant. . . .

Through faith in Christ, therefore, Christ's righteousness becomes our righteousness and all that he has becomes ours; rather, he himself becomes ours.

*From Luther Work's, ed. Harold J. Grimm, vol. 31 (Philadelphia: Muhlenburg Press, 1957), 297–306, as reprinted in Martin Luther: Selections from His Writings, ed. John Dillenberger (New York: Doubleday, 1961), 86–89.

Therefore the Apostle calls it "the righteousness of God" in Rom. 1[:17]: For in the gospel "the righteousness of God is revealed...; as it is written, 'The righteous shall live by his faith.'" Finally, in the same epistle, chapter 3[:28], such a faith is called "the righteousness of God": "We hold that a man is justified by faith." This is an infinite righteousness, and one that swallows up all sins in a moment, for it is impossible that sin should exist in Christ. On the contrary, he who trusts in Christ exists in Christ; he is one with Christ, having the same righteousness as he. It is therefore impossible that sin should remain in him. This righteousness is primary; it is the basis, the cause, the source of all our own actual righteousness. For this is the righteousness given in place of the original righteousness lost in Adam. It accomplishes the same as that original righteousness would have accomplished; rather, it accomplishes more....

Therefore this alien righteousness, instilled within us without our works by grace alone — while the Father, to be sure, inwardly draws us to Christ — is set opposite original sin, likewise alien, which we acquire without our works by birth alone. Christ daily drives out the old Adam more and more in accordance with the extent to which faith and knowledge of Christ grow. For alien righteousness is not instilled all at once, but it begins, makes progress, and is finally perfected at the end through death.

The second kind of righteousness is our proper righteousness, not because we alone work it, but because we work with that first and alien righteousness. This is that manner of life spent profitably in good works, in the first place, in slaying the flesh and crucifying the desires with respect to the self, of which we read in Gal. 5[:24]: "And those who belong to Christ Jesus have crucified the flesh with its passions and desires." In the second place, this righteousness consists in love to one's neighbor, and in the third place, in meekness and fear toward God. The Apostle is full of references to these, as is all the rest of Scripture. He briefly summarizes everything, however, in Titus 2[:12]: "In this world let us live soberly (pertaining to crucifying one's own flesh), justly (referring to one's neighbor), and devoutly (relating to God)."

This righteousness is the product of the righteousness of the first type, actually its fruit and consequence, for we read in Gal. 5[:22]: "But the fruit of the spirit [i.e., of a spiritual man, whose very existence depends on faith in Christ] is love, joy, peace, patience, kindness, goodness, faithfulness, gentleness, self-control." For because the works mentioned are works of men, it is obvious that in this passage a spiritual man is called "spirit." In John 3[:6] we read: "That which is born of the flesh is flesh, and that which is born of the Spirit is spirit." This righteousness goes on to complete the first for it ever strives to do away with the old Adam and to destroy the body of sin. Therefore it hates itself and loves its neighbor; it does not seek its own good, but that of another, and in this its whole way of living consists. For in that it hates itself and does not seek its own, it crucifies the flesh. Because it seeks the good of another, it works love. Thus in each sphere it does God's will, living soberly with self, justly with neighbor, devoutly toward God.

This righteousness follows the example of Christ in this respect [1 Pet. 2:21] and is transformed into his likeness [2 Cor. 3:18]. It is precisely this that Christ requires. Just as he himself did all things for us, not seeking his own good but ours only — and in this he was most obedient to God the Father — so he desires that we also should set the same example for our neighbors.

John Calvin (1509–64)

Institutes of the Christian Religion (1559)*

There is within the human mind, and indeed by natural instinct, an awareness of divinity. This we take to be beyond controversy. To prevent anyone from taking refuge in the pretense of ignorance, God himself has implanted in all men a certain understanding of his divine majesty. Ever renewing its memory, he repeatedly sheds fresh drops. Since, therefore, men one and all perceive that there is a God and that he is their Maker, they are condemned by their own testimony because they have failed to honor him and to consecrate their lives to his will. If ignorance of God is to be looked for anywhere, surely one is most likely to find an example of it among the more backward folk and those more remote from civilization. Yet there is, as the eminent pagan says, no nation so barbarous, no people so savage, that they have not a deep-seated conviction that there is a God. And they who in other aspects of life seem least to differ from brutes still continue to retain some seed of religion. So deeply does the common conception occupy the minds of all, so tenaciously does it inhere in the hearts of all! Therefore, since from the beginning of the world there has been no region, no city, in short, no household, that could do without religion, there lies in this a tacit confession of a sense of deity inscribed in the hearts of all.

Indeed, even idolatry is ample proof of this conception. We know how man does not willingly humble himself so as to place other creatures over himself. Since, then, he prefers to worship wood and stone rather than to be thought of as having no God, clearly this is a most vivid impression of a divine being. So impossible is it to blot this from man's mind that natural disposition would be more easily altered, as altered indeed it is when man voluntarily sinks from his natural haughtiness to the very depths in order to honor God! (pp. 326–27)

•

Men of sound judgment will always be sure that a sense of divinity which can never be effaced is engraved upon men's minds. Indeed, the perversity of the impious, who though they struggle furiously are unable to extricate themselves from the fear of God, is abundant testimony that this conviction, namely, that there is some God, is naturally inborn in all, and is fixed deep within, as it were in the very marrow. Although Diagoras and his like may jest at whatever has been believed in every age concerning religion, and Dionysius may mock the heavenly judgment, this is sardonic laughter, for the worm of conscience, sharper than any cauterizing iron, gnaws away within. I do not say, as Cicero did, that errors disappear with the lapse of time, and that religion grows and becomes better each day.

---

*Reprinted from *John Calvin: Selections from His Writings*, ed. John Dillenberger (Missoula, Mont., 1975), 326–27, 328–29, 336, by permission of Scholars Press.

For the world (something will have to be said of this a little later) tries as far as it is able to cast away all knowledge of God, and by every means to corrupt the worship of him. I only say that though the stupid hardness in their minds, which the impious eagerly conjure up to reject God, wastes away, yet the sense of divinity, which they greatly wished to have extinguished, thrives and presently burgeons. From this we conclude that it is not a doctrine that must first be learned in school, but one of which each of us is master from his mother's womb and which nature itself permits no one to forget, although many strive with every nerve to this end.

Besides, if all men are born and live to the end that they may know God, and yet if knowledge of God is unstable and fleeting unless it progresses to this degree, it is clear that all those who do not direct every thought and action in their lives to this goal degenerate from the law of their creation. This was not unknown to the philosophers. Plato meant nothing but this when he often taught that the highest good of the soul is likeness to God, where, when the soul has grasped the knowledge of God, it is wholly transformed into his likeness. In the same manner also Gryllus, in the writings of Plutarch, reasons very skillfully, affirming that, if once religion is absent from their life, men are in no wise superior to brute beasts, but are in many respects far more miserable. Subject, then, to so many forms of wickedness, they drag out their lives in ceaseless tumult and disquiet. Therefore, it is worship of God alone that renders men higher than the brutes, and through it alone they aspire to immortality. (pp. 328–29)

•

Here, however, the foul ungratefulness of men is disclosed. They have within themselves a workshop graced with God's unnumbered works and, at the same time, a storehouse overflowing with inestimable riches. They ought, then, to break forth into praises of him but are actually puffed up and swollen with all the more pride. They feel in many wonderful ways that God works in them; they are also taught, by the very use of these things, what a great variety of gifts they possess from his liberality. They are compelled to know — whether they will or not — that these are the signs of divinity; yet they conceal them within. Indeed, there is no need to go outside themselves, provided they do not, by claiming for themselves what has been given them from heaven, bury in the earth that which enlightens their minds to see God clearly. (p. 336)

Teresa of Avila (1515–82)

The Interior Castle (First Mansions) (1577)*

We should consider our soul to be a castle made entirely of a diamond or very clear crystal, in which there are many rooms, just as in heaven there are many mansions.[1] And, if we consider this carefully, sisters, the soul of the just is nothing

---

*Translated by Gillian T. W. Ahlgren for this volume.

1. See John 14:2.

less than a paradise where our Lord himself says he will take his pleasure.[2] So what do you think the room where a king so powerful, so wise, so pure, and so full of all good things takes his pleasure will be like? I myself cannot find anything with which to compare the great beauty of a soul and its great potential; and truly our understanding can hardly arrive at comprehending this, as keen as it might be, any more than we can understand God, in whose image and likeness he himself says he has created us.[3] So, if this is how things are, there is no reason to wear ourselves out trying to comprehend the beauty of this castle, because there is between it and God the same difference as between the Creator and the creature, and, since it is created, it is enough for his Majesty to say that it is made in his image for us to begin to understand the great dignity and beauty of the soul.

Is it not a great shame that through our own fault we do not ourselves understand or know who we are? Would it not show great ignorance, my daughters, for someone to be asked who he is and him not know nor even to know who his father and mother were nor his homeland? If this would be great stupidity, ours is much greater without comparison when we do not attempt to know what we are, but instead detain ourselves in these bodies and we understand only vaguely that we have souls, because we have heard it and because the faith tells us so. But the riches which this soul might possess or who is within it or its great value we rarely even consider, and thus we do not work at conserving its beauty very carefully. We spend all our energy in the outskirts of this castle, which are our bodies.

But let us consider that this castle has, as I have said, many mansions: some up high, some down below, some on the sides; and in the center and midpoint of all of these it has its most principal, which is where all the secret things between God and the soul occur....

Now, turning to our beautiful and delectable castle, we must see how to enter into it. Perhaps it seems that I say something silly here, because, if this castle is the soul, it is clear that one need not enter but rather simply be [the castle], just as it would seem crazy to tell someone to enter a room being already inside it. But you must understand that there are many ways of being: there are many souls who are in the outskirts of the castle, where its guards are, and they do not attempt to enter inside, nor do they know what is inside such a precious place, nor who is inside it, nor even what rooms it has. You will already have heard in some books on prayer that the soul should enter inside itself: this is exactly the same thing....

Before we go any further I want to tell you to consider what it will be to see this castle, so resplendent and beautiful, this oriental pearl, this tree of life which is planted in the same living waters of life which is God, when it falls into mortal sin. There is no darkness any darker, nor anything so obscure and black than this. Let it suffice to say that, even though the same sun that was giving such splendor and beauty to the soul is still within its center, it is as if it were no longer there for its participation, even though [the soul] is still capable of delighting in his Majesty as the crystal is to reflect inside it the splendor of the sun. But nothing helps it; and thus all of the good works it may do, being in this state of mortal sin, are

---

2. See Proverbs 8:31.
3. See Genesis 1:26.

of no merit in gaining glory, because they do not proceed from that foundation that is God, from whom our virtue is virtue, and apart from Him, it cannot be agreeable to his eyes. And, after all, the intent of someone who commits mortal sin is not to please God, but rather to please the devil, who is darkness itself, so the poor soul remains in that same darkness.

I know of a person[4] to whom our Lord wanted to show what a soul becomes when it sins mortally. That person says that it seems to her, that if they were to understand it, it would not be possible for anyone to sin, although they might have to make a great effort to avoid occasions of sin. And thus she desired that all should understand this, and so should you, daughters, pray earnestly to God for those who are in this state, since they are in darkness and so are their works. For just as all the streams of water emitted by a very clear fountain are themselves [clear], so is a soul which is in a state of grace and from it its works become pleasing in the eyes of God and humans, because they come from this fountain of life where the soul is like a tree planted within it, and this sustains it and waters it and allows it to give off good fruit. In the same way the soul which through its own fault removes itself from this fountain and plants itself in another with very black and malodorous water can only give rise to things of the same misery and filth.

Here it is significant that the fountain and that resplendent sun which is in the center of the soul does not lose its splendor and beauty, which it always has, and nothing can take away its beauty. But, if one puts a very dark cloth over the crystal which is in the sunlight, it's obvious that, even though the sun still gives off light in it, it will not make its same operation in the crystal. . . .

Now let us turn to our castle with many mansions. You should not understand these mansions to be one behind another like things in a row, but rather place your eyes in the center which is the room or palace where the king is, and consider a palmito plant, how in getting to the part you eat you must get through all the coverings which surround the delicious heart. It is the same here, all around this room there are many others and the same above; because the things pertaining to the soul must be considered with fullness and breadth and grandeur, and they will not puff the soul up, since it is capable of much more than we can ever realize, and in all parts of her this sun communicates with her in this palace.

---

4. I.e., Teresa herself.

– 3 –

The Modern Period

INTRODUCTION

The first half of the seventeenth century was characterized by intense conflict over how to control national and regional boundaries, conflict which, because it was rooted in cultural identities, was both political and religious in nature. The Edict of Nantes (1598) had provided for an uneasy peace between church and state, allowing for religious freedom. But in 1617 controversy over religious expression ignited once again when Ferdinand of Styria (1578–1637) began closing Protestant churches in Bohemia. The local conflict escalated into a series of full-fledged wars throughout Europe, known as the Thirty Years' War (1618–48). This war reveals the extent to which regional groups achieved social and political unity through adherence to particular religious confessions. By the time of the Peace of Westphalia (1648), the destruction of war had convinced many Europeans that a dogmatic approach to religion, which had fostered doctrinal conflict, would have to be replaced by a more universal and rational approach, in which the truth of a religious tradition could be assessed by human reason.

On the level of thought about the human person this approach tended to create a distinction between the life of the mind and the life of the heart, a dichotomy readily apparent in the ways that theology and religious experience grew apart over the course of the next two centuries, and symbolized by two movements, the Enlightenment and Pietism. The *Enlightenment* is a term used to describe intellectual advancements, primarily in the sciences and in philosophy, of the seventeenth and eighteenth centuries. Scientific advances and the movement toward empirical thought gave rise to significant questions about the nature and order of the universe. Scientists proposed explanations of phenomena and processes according to natural law, a law which was increasingly seen to operate independent of God. Additionally, as scientists proposed more scientific theories, confidence in the human ability to comprehend the universe increased. Increasingly, humans were understood to be primarily rational creatures, and human reason became separable from revealed, religious knowledge.

Enlightenment traditions cultivated the link between philosophy and politics more than the link between philosophy and theology. Still, theologians could not but be affected by the new reflections on the nature of rights, which resulted in so much political transformation. The American Declaration of Independence included language about the rights to "life, liberty, and the pursuit of happiness" and declared such rights to be "self-evident." Natural law and God's law converged in affirming human equality, with the intended result of political systems that support life and religious toleration. Religion's primary purpose, within Enlightenment thought, was the perpetuation of ethical norms and behaviors.

The popularization and extension of the mystical tradition into devout religious practices, so typical of the Baroque period, continued in the movement known as *Pietism,* in which a faithful and devout life was seen to be more important than technically correct doctrine. There was a new emphasis on the spiritual and ethical development of the individual person, an orientation which followed Kant's "turn to the subject." At the same time, however, as religiosity was understood as personal devotion, a greater dichotomy between faith and reason emerged.

Pietism relied on revelation for authority and thus downplayed the rational or intellectual content of a statement about God or human nature. In movements like those involving the Quakers, for example, the direct inspiration of the Holy Spirit took on primary importance. The Quakers, or Society of Friends, emerged from the Puritan movement in the 1650s in England. They were concerned about the authenticity of religion, and they claimed that an unmediated experience of God was the only thing that could keep religion genuine. Rather than observing the traditional prayers or religious ceremonies, their worship consisted of silence, interrupted only by the spontaneous witness of the Holy Spirit through one of the participants. The Quakers quickly spread throughout New England, where they experienced persecution. Both in their affirmation of humanity's direct experience of God and their adherence to strict moral guidelines, the Quakers affirmed both humanity's dependence upon God and humanity's ability to respond to grace.

Eighteenth-century American Catholicism was also characterized by pietism of the same quality as was true of the post-Tridentine period. >From the colonial period through the mid–nineteenth century, after a literal explosion in the development of religious orders, Catholicism was experienced primarily in the home where devotional activities centered. Thus women played an important role in the maintenance of Catholicism through their instruction of children. Catholic sacramental life was severely hampered by a shortage of priests; devotional practices such as the rosary and other forms of prayer were the hallmarks of Catholic religiosity, affirming an interior religiosity and a personal relationship with Christ and Mary.[1]

Beginning in the mid–eighteenth century Americans experienced a series of religious "awakenings" which continued throughout the nineteenth century. Although more associated with Protestantism than Catholicism, revivalism had a pervasive influence on American religiosity at large. Revivals, or attempts to revitalize individual commitment to religion through stimulating a peak experience (or "conversion") in a group setting, played a large role in "awakening" the religious consciousness of Americans. Revivalism originated as early as the 1620s among Scottish Presbyterians and was enacted within Puritan communi-

---

1. Jay P. Dolan reviews the growth of Catholic devotionalism of the nineteenth century in *The American Catholic Experience: A History from Colonial Times to the Present* (Notre Dame, Ind.: University of Notre Dame Press, 1992), 211–20. Using the work of Ann Taves, Dolan asserts that Catholic devotionalism combined with Catholic revivalism to produce a new style of religiosity in the mid–nineteenth century.

ties in the career of Jonathan Edwards (1703–58). In 1734, Edwards described how over three hundred men and women claimed to have experienced salvation and joined the church as a result of preaching, prayers, and Bible reading. For Edwards knowledge was derived from the senses; therefore Christianity must appeal to the emotions, will, and the intellect in order to effect true contrition and conversion.

The 1830s brought another wave of revivals known as the Second Great Awakening, which generated new religious traditions (including the Disciples of Christ, the Universalists, the Mormons, and the Shakers) as well as truly Americanized forms of older traditions. By putting the universal need for conversion in order to receive salvation before denominational and confessional concerns, the revivalist movement reinforced a common unity among Christians. Further, it fostered a perspective on human nature as totally dependent upon an experience of grace for rebirth. For Catholics, too, the revivalist movement allowed itinerant priests to administer the sacraments of baptism, confession, and the Eucharist efficiently, if irregularly. The recognition of sin and the desire for conversion fostered at revival meetings could receive an immediate response through the sacraments.

It was in Germany, in the person of Friedrich Schleiermacher (1768–1834), that many of the tendencies of both the Pietist movement and the Enlightenment came together. Taking seriously the critiques of religion leveled by Enlightenment thinkers, Schleiermacher made assertions about the universal condition of humanity, and attempted to move religiosity out of the particularity of personalism. And, in direct response to the increased valuation of rational processes, he affirmed the importance of nonrational operations in the human person. His ideas both synthesized the two movements and moved them into a new era of theological development.

Schleiermacher's thought, developed during the early part of the Romantic period, reflects the desire to affirm an aesthetical theology. Schleiermacher argues that consciousness is the lens through which humans can actually come to know God, Christ, the world, themselves, their own nature; only, in other words, through a radical entry into one's personal being could one enter cognitively into being itself. Thus it is impossible to engage in theological reflection without a deep knowledge of and affirmation of selfhood. In terms of theological anthropology, Schleiermacher used the theme of consciousness to explain the human perception and understanding of God as well as the human understanding of sin. Self-consciousness, mediated primarily through feeling and then stimulating knowing and doing, leads us to a world consciousness, a consciousness of God, and a consciousness of sin. This consciousness beyond selfhood is the key to religion and spiritual growth, a reflection of the potentiality of humanity. In *The Christian Faith,* Schleiermacher insisted that the reality of sin did not "annul" the original perfection of humanity, for, he argued, we could not be conscious of sin if we were not working out of a state of goodness which enabled our consciousness of how things could be better. Further, he stated that the first sin of Adam and Eve did not bring about an "alteration in human nature" or an ontological change of the type Augustine had posited and Luther had echoed. The entry of Christ into the world remained salvific, since it moved human consciousness back to the good, but in effect it was the completion of the initial creative act.[2] Further, Schleiermacher articulated a powerful ethical responsibility associated both with the growing consciousness of grace and our inability to blame sinful actions on our ontological state.

In the United States the eighteenth and nineteenth centuries saw many instances of theological reflection on human nature in light of the phenomenon of slavery. While there was little significant theological reflection justifying slavery, both church and public policy often supported its existence. For example, in 1667 the Virginian Assembly declared that baptism did not require that a slave be freed, a position subsequently endorsed by the Anglican Church. However, a range of more compelling theological positions was developed by other Christians who denounced slavery as a sin. The Quakers, for example, had a long history of opposing slavery on religious grounds. In 1685 Virginia law forbade slaves to attend Quaker meetings for fear of agitation. For many Quakers, slaveholding was cause for being banned from the church, a policy put into practice in Philadelphia when in 1758 the Quakers forbade members from buying or selling slaves. By the nineteenth century, debate over slavery had caused real divisions within religious communities. Within the Presbyterian tradition, for example, a single church policy proved impossible to develop. In 1837 the church split into the Old and New schools; doctrinal issues as well as the issue of slavery were factors in this division. Although some of the New congregations were abolitionist, they still admitted slaveholders into their congregations, and in 1841 John Rankin, a Presbyterian minister, established the Free Presbyterian Church. Disturbed when he received news that his brother had purchased slaves, Rankin wrote to him, calling slavery "a never failing fountain of the grossest immorality and one of the deepest sources of human misery" and informing him that the law of God forbade such an institution.[3] Rankin and his wife Jean often provided shelter, food, and safety to fugitive slaves.

During the same time period, suffragists, or supporters of equal rights for women — who also spoke out on the abolitionist platform — made other contributions to the understanding of human nature based on their reflections about the nature of womanhood. Although humanity had often been treated as universal, theologians from previous periods had often also carried with them certain assumptions about gender.[4] In the nineteenth century, with women like Angela and Sarah Grimke, Lucretia Mott, Antoinette Brown, and Mary Baker Eddy, these issues grew more explicit. In 1837, in a series of letters addressed to Mary S. Parker, president of the Boston Female Anti-Slavery Society, Sarah Grimke based her arguments for the equality of women and men in ministry and marriage on her scriptural exegesis. In her defense of women's equality in ministry, she wrote:

---

2. Friedrich Schleiermacher, *The Christian Faith* (Edinburgh: T. & T. Clark, 1976), 366–69.

3. John Rankin to Thomas Rankin, *The [Ripley] Castigator,* August 17, 1824.

4. The theology of gender is complex and deserves the attention of an additional volume. In this collection of essays I have attempted to represent a range of gendered perspectives on human nature without addressing explicitly the "nature" of manhood or womanhood. Concern over this question is not limited to the modern period, however. For an interesting collection of medieval reflections on womanhood, see Alcuin Blamires, ed., *Woman Defamed and Woman Defended: An Anthology of Medieval Texts* (Oxford: Clarendon Press, 1992).

"Surely there is nothing either astonishing or novel in the gifts of the Spirit being bestowed on woman: nothing astonishing, because there is no respect of persons with God; the soul of the woman in his sight is as the soul of the man, and both are alike capable of the Holy Spirit."[5] And, in a letter written on October 20, 1837, Grimke explicitly addressed the equal guilt of men and women in the Fall.

However, religion in the nineteenth century continued to promote the cult of domesticity, and, because Catholicism continued to be rooted in the spiritual environment of the home, many Catholic women promoted a domestic ideology. The increased forms of nineteenth-century devotionalism — for example, to the Sacred Heart and the Immaculate Conception — coupled with the growth of Catholic revivalism, tended to reinforce the reality and the concreteness of human sin. American Catholics distinguished themselves from their Protestant peers by the examinations of conscience their devotional practices encouraged. Combating sin meant immersion in the rituals of prayer and devotion; the cycle perpetuated itself and even gathered steam.

At the same time, waves of immigration from Europe were changing the demographics of American Catholicism. In 1830 there were an estimated 318,000 American Catholics; by 1920 that number had grown to nearly eighteen million. The influx of Catholic immigrants after the 1830s turned American Catholicism into primarily a working-class church. After the Civil War, with the growth of industrialization, Catholics were also invested in the questions of economic and social justice raised by the rise of big business. A spirit of religious reform known as the Social Gospel addressed such concerns, championing social reform as well as private conversion. This movement, while made up of Protestant leaders, affected Protestants and Catholics alike. Both at the level of the parish and within the growing networks of religious orders an intense drive toward charitable work developed, more typical of the conservative social tendencies of American Catholics. However, immersion in these corporal acts of mercy often led Catholics to a new orientation to the need for larger social reform. Further, the rise of the labor movement, to which many Catholics were committed, contributed to a growing Catholic voice for reform. Although at first controversial, Catholic association with the labor movement was endorsed with the appearance in 1891 of Leo XIII's papal encyclical *Rerum Novarum,* which offered a critique of capitalism and a new program of social reform. By the First World War, Jay Dolan concludes, "American Catholicism had acquired a social-gospel tradition."[6] For Protestants and Catholics alike, the Social Gospel movement encouraged a new perspective on sin; it had a clear social dimension which dehumanized creation. Further, the Social Gospel tradition indicated a new orientation in the understanding of human nature, a religious affirmation of human rights and the dignity of the human person. Advocacy of a living wage was a concrete sign that societies affirmed the innate worth of each person. In 1919 the American Bishops drafted a "Program of Social Reconstruction" which advocated minimum-wage legislation, a minimum working age, public housing, unemployment insurance,

---

5. Sarah M. Grimke, *Letters on the Equality of the Sexes and the Condition of Woman* (New York: Source Book Press, 1970), 103.

6. Dolan, *The American Catholic Experience,* 329.

regulation of public utility rates, and other measures. Public response to the document was limited during the relatively prosperous 1920s; however, the movement toward affirming human dignity took on renewed importance during the Depression era.

Although not an academically trained theologian, Dorothy Day (1897–1980), founder with Peter Maurin of the Catholic Worker Movement in the 1930s, was an eloquent advocate of the essential link between following Christ and recognizing the dignity of the human person. In the numerous articles she wrote for the *Catholic Worker* newspaper, Day spoke of the daily struggles workers faced: exploitation, hunger, anxiety, disease. For over thirty years, in a practical blend of christology and anthropology, Day presented her readers with the dilemmas of the modern world in their numerous concrete forms in such a way as to cause a crisis of conscience: if Christ was indeed incarnate in the poor how could Christians contribute to the unjust conditions of the poor?

Meanwhile, academic theology addressed questions of human nature within the context of a new form of theology known as process theology. Rooted in the philosophy of Alfred North Whitehead, process theologians reflected on the nature of God as a creative force in the world whose acts of creation were not limited to any time period but were continuous. God is thus bound up in the process of creation and in the enfolding story of creation. Without equating God and humanity, process theologians affirmed the powerful bond between them.

The thought of Reinhold Niebuhr (1892–1971) reflects the new orientations of process theology after the chastening effects of the Second World War. Humanity, he explains, is characterized by a desire to deny its finitude, primarily out of anxiety and the desire to control its circumstances; however, this is an inappropriate use of power and reflects the tendency to sin: "The ego which falsely makes itself the center of existence in its pride and will-to-power inevitably subordinates other life to its will and thus does injustice to other life." In other words, humans experience the intimacy between God and humanity in a way which confuses them and paradoxically causes anxiety: "Anxiety is the inevitable concomitant of the paradox of freedom and finiteness in which man is involved" (see text below.)

The reflections of Karl Rahner (1904–84) recognize the same inherent tension between finitude and infinity within humanity, suggesting that humanity must accept its ontological situation as inherently incomprehensible. Humanity, Rahner writes, "is not the unquestioning and unquestioned infinity of reality. He is the question which rises up before him, empty, but really and inescapably, and which can never be settled and never adequately answered by him" (see text below). Rahner agrees that humanity is not so free as to be able to assert its own power, and that assertions of power often result in abuse. Thus Rahner proposes that humanity can only understand its true nature by patiently enduring and accepting the knowledge that its own reality is not in its own hands (see text below).

Continuing reflection on the nature of sin in collectivities and the resultant damage to the image of God inherent in humanity led to other statements affirming human dignity and the role Christians must take in promoting and defending it. The document *Gaudium et Spes* from the Second Vatican Council, held in four periods from 1962 to 1965, recognizes the image of God in humanity and states categorically that this image does not derive from individuality. "For by his innermost nature man is a social being, and unless he relates himself to others he can neither live nor develop his potential" (see text below).

Contemporary feminists have moved process theology and liberation theology in important new directions, and this phenomenon has had a significant influence on contemporary theological anthropology. Modern theologians continue to assess the doctrine of original sin. While some are inclined to reject a notion of sin as an ontological state, arguing that sin is more learned than inherited, many affirm sin as a way of being leading to sinful actions. For both Rita Nakashima Brock and Marjorie Hewitt Suchocki, original sin is the denial of humanity's primary ontological reality: that all humans are interconnected. When that reality is denied — that is, when humans live in another reality which denies or ignores interrelatedness — sinful, violent, and abusive behaviors ensue. For Brock, original sin is brokenheartedness, a damaged way of being, from which we can be healed when we place ourselves within a context of relationships which enhance our wholeness and form a loving community. For Suchocki, original sin exists in the human urge toward violence, the destruction of well-being — one's own, that of others, and that of the earth.

The combination of process theology and feminism is leading to important new insights about the nature of sin, but more importantly such insights affirm the critical characteristic of human nature: its interconnectedness. However, these insights are hardly new. Interesting parallels can be found in a careful reading of Christian mystics, which suggests that the new directions in theological anthropology offer important contributions to the fundamental insights of the Christian tradition at large. In its own way each of the texts from this section reflects upon human nature as interdependent; indeed, our consciousness of God leads us to this primary insight. The challenge, as posed to us by so many prophets of this century, is to apply this insight in our interpersonal relationships, in our communities, and in our societies in such a way that the image of God in each of us flourishes.

TEXTS

Friedrich Schleiermacher (1768–1834)

The Christian Faith (1830–31)*

God-consciousness could not be excited by these world-impressions if they were of a nature discordant with it, or if man were not so constituted that these impressions reached, as it were, the region of his higher self-consciousness and the higher self-consciousness to each other which occasions the whole process of

---

*Reprinted from Friedrich Schleiermacher, *The Christian Faith*, trans. and ed. H. R. Mackintosh and J. S. Stewart (Edinburgh: T. & T. Clark; Philadelphia: Fortress Press, 1976), 236, 238–39, 244–46, 271–72, by permission of T. & T. Clark.

the excitation of the God-consciousness. Accordingly, these two conditions come to be considered each in itself. It could of course be said that man himself, with his constitution, is an integral part of the world, and that it is only in virtue of this constitution that he is precisely the part he is; and hence that the original perfection of man is already included in the original perfection of the world. This is quite correct; and in a purely scientific inquiry, where what was in question was a view of finite existence in itself, such a division would only be permissible insofar as other divisions were made, and the idea of the perfection of the world analyzed into the perfection of all its different parts, and their relations to one another. It is different in the dogmatic sphere, where the original object is not the objective consciousness at all but self-consciousness, especially insofar as in self-consciousness man contrasts himself with the world, and stands in the relationship of interaction to the rest of existence. (p. 236)

•

It has been taken for granted above that the God-consciousness may develop in every state of consciousness which has risen above animal confusion, so that in it there is expressed the contrast between the self and the "given," and the contrast between self-consciousness and objective consciousness, inasmuch as the two elements in the antithesis confront each other simultaneously. The same holds good also of the contrast between passive and active. But while in the sphere we are dealing with the God-consciousness, owing to the teleological character of Christian piety, can unite with the passive only as it is related to self-activity, the interposition of the passive nonetheless is necessary to mark out clearly the moments of self-activity, because clarity of consciousness only arises through a successive contrast of distinct moments. Passive states, however, can only arise through operative influences, and hence the original perfection of the world in relation to men consists primarily in this, that in it is temporally grounded the excitation of passive states which are to pass into active states (these we name *incentives*), or, in other words, that they sufficiently determine the receptivity of man to the awakening and shaping of his self-activity. If now we take man first of all purely on his inner side, as a self-active being in whom God-consciousness is possible — that is, as spirit; then, from this point of view, his bodily side, which is not the man himself, belongs originally to this material world into which the spirit enters. Only gradually does it become for the spirit instrument and means of expression — as later, mediately through it, all other things likewise become instrument and means of expression — but first of all and primarily it mediates the stimulating influences of the world upon the spirit. Thus the whole of this aspect of the original perfection of the world can be summarily expressed by saying that in it there is given for the spirit such an organism as the human body in living connection with all else — an organism which brings the spirit into contact with the rest of existence. (pp. 238–39)

•

If the God-consciousness in the form of the feeling of absolute dependence can only become actual in connection with a sensible determination of self-consciousness, the tendency towards God-consciousness would be altogether nugatory if the condition necessary for it in human life could not be evoked; and we should be no more able to think of it as actual than in the case of the beasts, because the confused state of man's consciousness would not exhibit the conditions under which alone that feeling could emerge. Religious experience, however, consists precisely in this, that we are aware of this tendency to God-consciousness as a living impulse; but such an impulse can only proceed for the true inner nature of the being which it goes to constitute. Hence, at least insofar as we are religious men, we reckon the whole range of these states with which the God-consciousness can unite as belonging to this true inner nature. And as it would be an absolute imperfection of human nature — that is to say, a complete absence of inner coherence — if the tendency were indeed present latently, but could not emerge, so it is an essential element in the perfection of human nature that those states which condition the appearance of the God-consciousness are able to fill the clear and waking life of man onwards from the time when the spiritual functions are developed. And as we consider it an imperfect state of religious life in the individual if many moments of clear sensibly-determined self-consciousness occur without the God-consciousness being combined with them, so we account it part of the original perfection of man that in our clear and waking life a continuous God-consciousness as such is possible; and on the contrary, we should have to regard it as an essential imperfection if the emergence of the feeling of absolute dependence, though not abrogating any feeling of partial dependence or freedom, were confined as such to separate and scattered moments.

The God-consciousness, moreover, combines not only with those sensible excitations of self-consciousness which express life-enhancements or life-hindrances immediately arising out of the impression of the world, but also with those which accompany the cognitive activities, and finally with those which are connected with every kind of outwardly directed action. Hence all these mental life-functions and the relative disposition of the organism belong together to the original perfection of man, though only insofar as the demand which we make for God-consciousness is conditioned by them, and in such a way that the first place always belongs to it. Thus, first of all, there is the physical basis of spiritual life, i.e., the fact that the spirit, become soul in the human body, acts also on the rest of the world in innumerable ways, and asserts its nature, just as the other living forces assert their nature relatively to it, so that life-feeling in general takes shape as the consciousness of interaction; from which it follows that to the original perfection of man this also belongs, that opposite life-moments, hindrances and furtherance, have one and the same bearing on the excitation of the God-consciousness. Next, there is the intellectual basis of spiritual life, i.e., the fact that the spirit by means of sense-impressions can obtain that knowledge of existence which is one element in its own nature, as also knowledge of what we ourselves by our activity can produce in and from existence, and can express this knowledge with actual consciousness in the most varied degrees of general and particular ideas, and that thereby it arrives at the accompanying consciousness of a natural order in connection with which the God-consciousness develops. Upon the agreement of these ideas and judgments with the being and relations of things depends all the influence of man on external nature which is more than simply instinctive, and also the connection between knowledge and practical life. But though the knowledge of God, in this sphere, is bound up pre-eminently and fundamentally with the idea of a natural order, the excitation of the God-consciousness is not at all imperiled though certain ideas should not agree with the actual being of the object presented; as indeed the comprehensive interconnection of all being would not be mirrored in our idea if we did not assume that so long as the whole of existence is not reflected in our thought every act of thought contains an element of error. (pp. 244–46)

•

Without running counter to our method we cannot at the outset give an objective elucidation of sin, but must revert to the personal self-consciousness which attests an inner state as sin — a procedure all the less open to objection because sin cannot emerge in the life of the Christian apart from such a consciousness. To lack this consciousness would simply be an additional sin, of which, as such, we could not fail subsequently to become conscious. If, then, it is our primary object to ascertain the characteristic element in the consciousness of sinfulness, we ought not, within the sphere of Christian piety, to look for it except in relationship to God-consciousness, and accordingly the only course open to us is to reckon everything as sin that has arrested the free development of the God-consciousness. Now, if in any particular moment under examination God has formed part of our self-consciousness, but this God-consciousness has not been able to permeate the other active elements therein, thus determining the moment, then sin and the consciousness of sin are simultaneous, and the sensuous self-consciousness by reason of its having been gratified is affected with pleasure, but the higher, owing to the importance of the God-consciousness, with pain. If, on the other hand, God has not formed part of the moment at all, that is to say, the occurrence of the moment excludes the God-consciousness, showing that the God-consciousness cannot make the moment its own, which also means that it cannot be supposed to accord and acquiesce in it, then the consciousness of sin follows on the sin itself. Supposing, however, that the God-consciousness has determined the moment, and that pleasure is present in the higher self-consciousness, still every attendant feeling of effort implies a consciousness of sin — in some degree, consequently, annulling that pleasure — since we thereby are made aware that if the sensuous elements which have been overcome had been reinforced from without, the God-consciousness would have been unable to determine the moment. In this sense, therefore — but only because there exists a living seed of sin ever ready to burst forth — there is such a thing as an abiding consciousness of sin, now preceding the sin itself as a warning presentiment, now accompanying it as an inward reproof, or following it as penitence. That no God-consciousness, however, should ever be directed at all upon a moment such as that described could only happen if in the person acting there were no relationship between the moment and the class of actions under discussion (in which case he would be in a state of innocence), or if the God-consciousness were no longer active within him (which would be the state of hardening). (pp. 271–72)

Reinhold Niebuhr (1892–1971)

The Nature and Destiny of Man, vol. 1: *Human Nature* (1941/1964)*

The Christian view of man is sharply distinguished from all alternative views by the manner in which it interprets and relates three aspects of human existence to each other: (1) It emphasizes the height of self-transcendence in man's spiritual stature in its doctrine of "image of God." (2) It insists on man's weakness, dependence, and finiteness, on his involvement in the necessities and contingencies of the natural world, without, however, regarding this finiteness as, of itself, a source of evil in man. In its purest form the Christian view of man regards man as a unity of God-likeness and creatureliness in which he remains a creature even in the highest spiritual dimensions of his existence and may reveal elements of the image of God even in the lowliest aspects of his natural life. (3) It affirms that the evil in man is a consequence of his inevitable though not necessary unwillingness to acknowledge his dependence, to accept his finiteness, and to admit his insecurity, an unwillingness which involves him in the vicious circle of accentuating the insecurity from which he seeks escape. (p. 150)

•

Without going into further historical analysis it will suffice to assert by way of summary that the Biblical conception of "image of God" has influenced Christian thought particularly since Augustine (when not under a too strong Platonic or Aristotelian influence), to interpret human nature in terms which include his rational faculties but which suggest something beyond them.... Man is self-determining not only in the sense that he transcends natural process in such a way as to be able to choose between various alternatives presented to him by the processes of nature but also in the sense that he transcends himself in such a way that he must choose his total end. In this task of self-determination he is confronted with endless potentialities and he can set no limit to what he ought to be, short of the character of ultimate reality. Yet this same man is a creature whose life is definitely limited by nature and he is unable to choose anything beyond the bounds set by the creation in which he stands.... In Christian faith the place of Christ as both the revelation of the character of God and of the essential nature of man (the "second Adam") does justice to the fact that man can find his true norm only in the character of God but is nevertheless a creature who cannot and must not aspire to be God. (pp. 161, 163–64)

•

Man is insecure and involved in natural contingency; he seeks to overcome his insecurity by a will-to-power which overreaches the limits of human creatureliness. Man is ignorant and involved in the limitations of a finite mind; but he pretends that he is not limited. He assumes that he can gradually transcend finite

---

*Reprinted from Reinhold Niebuhr, *The Nature and Destiny of Man,* vol. 1: *Human Nature* (New York: Charles Scribner's Sons, 1964), 150, 161, 163–64, 178–79, 270–72, by permission of Simon and Schuster.

limitations until his mind becomes identical with universal mind. All of his intellectual and cultural pursuits, therefore, become infected with the sin of pride. Man's pride and will-to-power disturb the harmony of creation. The Bible defines sin in both religious and moral terms. The religious dimension of sin is man's rebellion against God, his effort to usurp the place of God. The moral and social dimension of sin is injustice. The ego which falsely makes itself the center of existence in its pride and will-to-power inevitably subordinates other life to its will and thus does injustice to other life.

Sometimes man seeks to solve the problem of the contradiction of finiteness and freedom, not by seeking to hide his finiteness and comprehending the world into himself, but by seeking to hide his freedom and by losing himself in some aspect of the world's vitalities. In that case his sin may be defined as sensuality rather than pride. Sensuality is never the mere expression of natural impulse in man. It always betrays some aspect of his abortive effort to solve the problem of finiteness and freedom. Human passions are always characterized by unlimited and demonic potencies of which animal life is innocent.

In short, man, being both free and bound, both limited and limitless, is anxious. Anxiety is the inevitable concomitant of the paradox of freedom and finiteness in which man is involved. Anxiety is the internal precondition of sin. It is the inevitable spiritual state of man, standing in the paradoxical situation of freedom and finiteness. Anxiety is the internal description of the state of temptation. It must not be identified with sin because there is always the ideal possibility that faith would purge anxiety of the tendency toward sinful self-assertion. The ideal possibility is that faith in the ultimate security of God's love would overcome all immediate insecurities of nature and history. That is why Christian orthodoxy has consistently defined unbelief as the root of sin, or as the sin which precedes pride. It is significant that Jesus justifies his injunction, "Be not anxious" with the observation, "for your heavenly Father knoweth that ye have need of these things." The freedom from anxiety which he enjoins is a possibility only if perfect trust in divine security has been achieved. Whether such freedom from anxiety and such perfect trust are an actual possibility of historic existence must be considered later. For the present it is enough to observe that no life, even the most saintly, perfectly conforms to the injunction not to be anxious. (pp. 178–79)

•

It is important to distinguish between the essential nature of man and the virtue and perfection which would represent the normal expression of that nature. The essential nature of man contains two elements; and there are correspondingly two elements in the original perfection of man. To the essential nature of man belong, on the one hand, all his natural endowments, and determinations, his physical and social impulses, his sexual and racial differentiations, in short his character as a creature imbedded in the natural order. On the other hand, his essential nature also includes the freedom of his spirit, his transcendence over natural process, and finally his self-transcendence.

The virtue and perfection which corresponds to the first element of his nature is usually designated as the natural law. It is the law which defines the proper performance of his functions, the normal harmony of his impulses, and the normal social relation between himself and his fellows within the limitations of the natural order. Since every natural function of man is qualified by his freedom and since a "law" defining normality is necessary only because of his freedom, there is always an element of confusion in thus outlining a law of nature. It has nevertheless a tentative validity; for it distinguishes the obvious requirements of his nature as a creature in the natural order from the special requirements of his nature as free spirit.

The virtues which correspond to the second element in his nature, that is, to the freedom of the spirit, are analogous to the "theological virtues" of Catholic thought, namely faith, hope, and love. They must be analyzed at greater length presently. For the moment it is necessary to identify and validate them only provisionally as basic requirements of freedom. Faith in the providence of God is a necessity of freedom because, without it, the anxiety of freedom tempts man to seek a self-sufficiency and self-mastery incompatible with his dependence upon forces which he does not control. Hope is a particular form of that faith. It deals with the future as a realm where infinite possibilities are realized and which must be a realm of terror if it is not under the providence of God; for in that case it would stand under either a blind fate or pure caprice. The knowledge of God is thus not a supernatural grace which is a "further gift" beyond man's essential nature. It is the requirement of his nature as free spirit.

Love is both an independent requirement of this same freedom and a derivative of faith. Love is a requirement of freedom because the community to which man is impelled by his social nature is not possible to him merely upon the basis of his gregarious impulse. In his freedom and uniqueness each man stands outside of, and transcends, the cohesions of nature and the uniformities of mind which bind life to life. Since men are separated from one another by the uniqueness and individuality of each spirit, however closely they may be bound together by ties of nature, they cannot relate themselves to one another in terms which will do justice to both the bonds of nature and the freedom of their spirit if they are not related in terms of love. In love spirit meets spirit in the depth of the innermost essence of each. The cohesions of nature are qualified and transmuted by this relationship, for the other self ceases to be merely an object, serviceable to the self because of affinities of nature and reason. It is recognized as not merely object but as itself a subject, as a unique center of life and purpose. This "I" and "Thou" relationship is impossible without the presupposition of faith for two reasons: (1) Without freedom from anxiety man is so enmeshed in the vicious circle of egocentricity, so concerned about himself, that he cannot release himself for the adventure of love. (2) Without relation to God, the world of freedom in which spirit must meet spirit is so obscured that human beings constantly sink to the level of things in the human imagination. The injunction, "love thy neighbor as thyself," is therefore properly preceded both by the commandment, "love the Lord thy God," and by the injunction, "be not anxious."

These ultimate requirements of the Christian ethic are therefore not counsels of perfection or theological virtues of the sort which merely complete an otherwise incomplete natural goodness or virtue. Nor can they be subtracted from man without making his freedom a source of sinful infection. They are indeed counsels of perfection in the sense that sinful man lacks them and is incapable of achieving them. But they are basic and not supplementary requirements of his freedom. (pp. 270–72)

Karl Rahner (1904–84)

Foundations of Christian Faith (1976/1978)*

There is no need to explain in any great detail that a notion of person and subject is of fundamental importance for the possibility of Christian revelation and the self-understanding of Christianity. A personal relationship to God, a genuinely dialogical history of salvation between God and man, the acceptance of one's own, unique, eternal salvation, the notion of responsibility before God and his judgment, all of these assertions of Christianity, however they are to be explained more precisely, imply that man is what we want to say here: person and subject. The same thing is true when we speak of a verbal revelation in Christianity, when we say that God has spoken to man, has called him into his presence, that in prayer man can and should speak with God. All of these assertions are terribly obscure and difficult, but they make up the concrete reality of Christianity. And none of this would be intelligible unless we include in our understanding of Christianity explicitly or implicitly what we mean here by "person" and "subject." (p. 26)

•

Man experiences himself precisely as subject and person insofar as he becomes conscious of himself as the product of what is radically foreign to him. This element, namely, that man also *knows* about his radical origins in these causes, is not explained by these origins. When he analyzes and reconstructs himself, it is not yet explained by this process that he does this analysis and reconstruction *himself* and knows about it. Precisely in the fact that man experiences himself as something alien imposed upon himself and as produced; precisely insofar as he gives free rein to every conceivable possibility of analysis in the empirical anthropologies, analysis which reduces and dissolves man into what is not himself, and he does this even when this analysis in fact has not yet reached its conclusion; precisely in the fact that man gives his particular empirical anthropologies the right to explain him more and more, to reduce and dismantle him, and, as spirit's retort to all of this as it were, perhaps in the future even actually to reconstruct him, in all of this he experiences himself as subject and as person. But he can overlook this fact because he loses sight of it in its apparent opposite.

In the fact that man raises analytical questions about himself and opens himself to the unlimited horizons of such questioning, he has already transcended himself and every conceivable element of such an analysis or of an empirical reconstruction of himself. In doing this he is affirming himself as more than the sum of such

*Reprinted from Karl Rahner, *Foundations of Christian Faith: An Introduction to the Idea of Christianity*, trans. William V. Dych (New York: Seabury Press, 1978), 26, 29–30, 31–32, 42–43, by permission of the Crossroad Publishing Company.

analyzable components of his reality. Precisely this consciousness of himself, this confrontation with the totality of all his conditions, and this very being conditioned show him to be more than the sum of his factors. For a finite system of individual, distinguishable elements cannot have the kind of relationship to itself which man has to himself in the experience of his multiple conditioning and his reducibility. A finite system cannot confront itself in its totality. From its point of departure, which ultimately is imposed upon it, a finite system receives a relationship to a definite operation, although this might consist in maintaining the system itself, but it does not have a relationship to its own point of departure. It does not ask questions about itself. It is not a subject. The experience of radical questioning and man's ability to place himself in question are things which a finite system cannot accomplish. (pp. 29–30)

•

In spite of the finiteness of his system man is always present to himself in his entirety. He can place everything in question. In his openness to everything and anything, whatever can come to expression can be at least a question for him. In the fact that he affirms the possibility of a merely *finite* horizon of questioning, this possibility is already surpassed, and man shows himself to be a being with an *infinite* horizon. In the fact that he experiences his finiteness radically, he reaches beyond this finiteness and experiences himself as a transcendent being, as spirit. The infinite horizon of human questioning is experienced as a horizon which recedes further and further the more answers man can discover.

Man can try to evade the mysterious infinity which opens up before him in his questions. Out of fear of the mysterious he can take flight to the familiar and the everyday. But the infinity which he experiences himself exposed to also permeates his everyday activities. Basically he is always still on the way. Every goal that he can point to in knowledge and in action is always relativized, is always a provisional step. Every answer is always just the beginning of a new question. Man experiences himself as infinite possibility because in practice and in theory he necessarily places every sought-after result in question. He always situates it in a broader horizon which looms before him in its vastness. He is the spirit who experiences himself as spirit in that he does not experience himself as *pure* spirit. Man is not the unquestioning and unquestioned infinity of reality. He is the question which rises up before him, empty, but really and inescapably, and which can never be settled and never adequately answered by him. (pp. 31–32)

•

In spite of his free subjectivity, man experiences himself as being at the disposal of other things, a disposal over which he has no control. First of all, being constituted as transcendental subject, he is in the presence of being as mystery which constantly reveals itself and at the same time conceals itself. We mentioned earlier that his transcendentality cannot be understood as that of an absolute subject which experiences and possesses what opens before it as something subject to its own power. His transcendentality is rather a relationship which does not establish itself by its own power, but is experienced as something which was established by and is at the disposal of another, and which is grounded in the abyss of ineffable mystery.

Beyond that, man always experiences himself both in his activity in the world and also in his theoretical, objective reflection as one to whom a historical situation in a world of things and of persons has been given in advance, given without his having chosen it for himself, although it is in and through it that he discovers and is conscious of transcendence. Man is always conscious of his historical limitations, his historical origins, and the contingency of his origins. But this places him in the quite specific situation which characterizes man's nature: insofar as he experiences his historical conditioning, he is already beyond it in a certain sense, but nevertheless he cannot really leave it behind. Being situated in this way between the finite and the infinite is what constitutes man, and is shown by the fact that it is in his infinite transcendence and in his freedom that man experiences himself as dependent and historically conditioned.

Man never establishes his own freedom in some absolute sense, in the sense of a freedom which could make complete use of the material which is given to him in his freedom, or could cast it off in an absolute self-sufficiency. He never realizes completely his possibilities in the world and in history. Nor can he distance himself from them and withdraw into the pure essence of a pseudo-subjectivity or pseudo-interiority in such a way that he could honestly say that he had become independent of the world and the history that was given him. In an ultimate and inescapable way, man even as doer and maker is still receiving and being made. What he experiences in himself is always a synthesis: of possibilities presented to his freedom and his free disposition of self, of what is himself and what is the other, of acting and suffering, of knowing and doing, and these elements are synthesized in a unity which cannot be completely and objectively analyzed. Therefore insofar as reflection can never control or master or grasp the totality of the ground from out of which and towards which the subject is actualizing himself, man is the unknown not only in this or that area of his concrete reality, but he is the subject whose origin and end remain hidden from himself. He comes to the real truth about himself precisely by the fact that he patiently endures and accepts this knowledge that his own reality is not in his own hands. (pp. 42–43)

Vatican II (1962–65)

Gaudium et Spes, "The Role of the Church in the Modern World" (1965)*

The Dignity of the Human Person: Man as Made in God's Image

According to the almost unanimous opinion of believers and unbelievers alike, all things on earth should be related to man as their center and crown.

---

*From *The Documents of Vatican II*, ed. Walter M. Abbott (New York: Guild Press, 1966), 210–15, 240–41.

But what is man? About himself he has expressed, and continues to express, many divergent and even contradictory opinions. In these he often exalts himself as the absolute measure of all things or debases himself to the point of despair. The result is doubt and anxiety.

The Church understands these problems. Endowed with light from God, she can offer solutions to them so that man's true situation can be portrayed and his defects explained, while at the same time his dignity and destiny are justly acknowledged.

For sacred Scripture teaches that man was created "to the image of God," is capable of knowing and loving his Creator, and was appointed by Him a master of all earthly creatures that he might subdue them and use them to God's glory (Gen. 1:26; Wisd. 2:23). "What is man that thou art mindful of him or the son of man that thou visitest him? Thou hast made him a little less than the angels, thou hast crowned him with glory and honor: thou hast set him over the works of thy hands, thou hast subjected all things under his feet" (Ps. 8:5–6).

But God did not create man as a solitary. For from the beginning "male and female he created them" (Gen. 1:27). Their companionship produces the primary form of interpersonal communion. For by his innermost nature man is a social being, and unless he relates himself to others he can neither live nor develop his potential.

Therefore, as we read elsewhere in holy Scripture, God saw "all the things that he had made, and they were very good" (Gen. 1:31).

Sin

Although he was made by God in a state of holiness, from the very dawn of history man abused his liberty, at the urging of personified Evil. Man set himself against God and sought to find fulfillment apart from God. Although he knew God, he did not glorify Him as God, but his senseless mind was darkened and he served the creature rather than the Creator.

What divine revelation makes known to us agrees with experience. Examining his heart, man finds that he has inclinations toward evil, too, and is engulfed by manifold ills which cannot come from his good Creator. Often refusing to acknowledge God as his beginning, man has disrupted also his proper relationship with his own ultimate goal. At the same time he became out of harmony with himself, with others, and with all created things.

Therefore, man is split within himself. As a result, all of human life, whether individual or collective, shows itself to be a dramatic struggle between good and evil, between light and darkness. Indeed, man finds that by himself he is incapable of battling the assaults of evil successfully, so that everyone feels as though he is bound by chains.

But the Lord Himself came to free and strengthen man, renewing him inwardly and casting out that prince of this world (cf. John 12:31) who held him in the bondage of sin. For sin has diminished man, blocking his path to fulfillment.

The call to grandeur and the depths of misery are both a part of human experience. They find their ultimate and simultaneous explanation in the light of God's revelation.

The Make-Up of Man

Though made of body and soul, man is one. Through his bodily composition he gathers to himself the elements of the material world. Thus they reach their crown through him, and through him raise their voice in free praise of the Creator.

For this reason man is not allowed to despise his bodily life. Rather, he is obliged to regard his body as good and honorable since God has created it and will raise it up on the last day. Nevertheless, wounded by sin, man experiences rebellious stirrings in his body. But the very dignity of man postulates that man glorify God in his body and forbid it to serve the evil inclinations of his heart.

Now, man is not wrong when he regards himself as superior to bodily concerns, and as more than a speck of nature or a nameless constituent of the city of man. For by his interior qualities he outstrips the whole sum of mere things. He finds re-enforcement in this profound insight whenever he enters into his own heart. God, who probes the heart, awaits him there. There he discerns his proper destiny beneath the eyes of God. Thus, when man recognizes in himself a spiritual and immortal soul, he is not being mocked by a deceptive fantasy springing from mere physical or social influences. On the contrary he is getting to the depths of the very truth of the matter.

The Dignity of the Mind; Truth; Wisdom

Man judges rightly that by his intellect he surpasses the material universe, for he shares in the light of the divine mind. By relentlessly employing his talents through the ages, he has indeed made progress in the practical sciences, technology, and the liberal arts. In our times he has won superlative victories, especially in his probing of the material world and in subjecting it to himself.

Still he has always searched for more penetrating truths, and finds them. For his intelligence is not confined to observable data alone. It can with genuine certitude attain to reality itself as knowable, though in consequence of sin that certitude is partly obscured and weakened.

The intellectual nature of the human person is perfected by wisdom and needs to be. For wisdom gently attracts the mind of man to a quest and a love for what is true and good. Steeped in wisdom, man passes through visible realities to those which are unseen.

Our era needs such wisdom more than bygone ages if the discoveries made by man are to be further humanized. For the future of the world stands in peril unless wiser men are forthcoming. It should also be pointed out that many nations, poorer in economic goods, are quite rich in wisdom and can offer noteworthy advantages to others.

It is, finally, through the gift of the Holy Spirit that man comes by faith to the contemplation and appreciation of the divine plan.

The Dignity of the Moral Conscience

In the depths of his conscience, man detects a law which he does not impose upon himself, but which holds him to obedience. Always summoning him to love good and avoid evil, the voice of conscience can when necessary speak to his heart more specifically: do this, shun that. For man has in his heart a law written by God. To obey it is the very dignity of man; according to it he will be judged. Conscience is the most secret core and sanctuary of a man. There he is alone with God, whose voice echoes in his depths. In a wonderful manner conscience reveals that law which is fulfilled by love of God and neighbor. In fidelity to conscience, Christians are joined with the rest of men in numerous problems which arise in the life of individuals and from social relationships. Hence the more that a correct conscience holds sway, the more persons and groups turn aside from blind choice and strive to be guided by objective norms of morality.

Conscience frequently errs from invincible ignorance without losing its dignity. The same cannot be said of a man who cares but little for truth and goodness, or of a conscience which by degrees grows practically sightless as a result of habitual sin.

The Excellence of Liberty

Only in freedom can man direct himself toward goodness. Our contemporaries make much of this freedom and pursue it eagerly; and rightly so, to be sure. Often, however, they foster it perversely as a license for doing whatever pleases them, even if it is evil.

For its part, authentic freedom is an exceptional sign of the divine image within man. For God has willed that man be left "in the hand of his own counsel" so that he can seek his Creator spontaneously, and come freely to utter and blissful perfection through loyalty to Him. Hence man's dignity demands that he act according to a knowing and free choice. Such a choice is personally motivated and prompted from within. It does not result from blind internal impulse nor from mere external pressure.

Man achieves such dignity when, emancipating himself from all captivity to passion, he pursues his goal in a spontaneous choice of what is good, and procures for himself, through effective and skillful action, apt means to that end. Since man's freedom has been damaged by sin, only by the help of God's grace can he bring such a relationship with God into full flower. Before the judgment seat of God each man must render an account of his own life, whether he has done good or evil. (pp. 210–15)

•

The Help Which the Church Strives to Bring to Individuals

Modern man is on the road to a more thorough development of his own personality, and to a growing discovery and vindication of his own rights. Since it has been entrusted to the Church to reveal the mystery of God, who is the ultimate goal of man, she opens up to man at the same time the meaning of his own existence, that is, the innermost truth about himself. The Church truly knows that only God, whom she serves, meets the deepest longings of the human heart, which is never fully satisfied by what this world has to offer.

She also knows that man is constantly worked upon by God's Spirit, and hence can never be altogether indifferent to the problems of religion. The experience of past ages proves this, as do numerous indications in our own times. For man will always yearn to know, at least in an obscure way, what is the meaning of his life, of his activity, of his death. The very presence of the Church recalls these problems to his mind.

But only God, who created man to His own image and ransomed him from sin, provides a fully adequate answer to these questions. This He does through what He has revealed in Christ His Son, who became man. Whoever follows after Christ, the perfect man, becomes himself more of a man.

Thanks to this belief, the Church can anchor the dignity of human nature against all tides of opinion, for example, those which undervalue the human body or idolize it. By no human law can the personal dignity and liberty of man be so aptly safeguarded as by the gospel of Christ which has been entrusted to the Church.

For this gospel announces and proclaims the freedom of the sons of God, and repudiates all the bondage which ultimately results from sin. The gospel has a sacred reverence for the dignity of conscience and its freedom of choice, constantly advises that all human talents be employed in God's service and men's, and, finally, commends all to the charity of all.

All this corresponds to the basic law of the Christian dispensation. For though the same God is Savior and Creator, Lord of human history as well as of salvation history, in the divine arrangement itself the rightful autonomy of the creature, and particularly of man, is not withdrawn. Rather it is re-established in its own dignity and strengthened in it.

Therefore, by virtue of the gospel committed to her, the Church proclaims the rights of man. She acknowledges and greatly esteems the dynamic movements of today by which these rights are everywhere fostered. Yet these movements must be penetrated by the spirit of the gospel and protected against any kind of false autonomy. For we are tempted to think that our personal rights are fully ensured only when we are exempt from every requirement of divine law. But this way lies not the maintenance of the dignity of the human person, but its annihilation. (pp. 240–41)

Rita Nakashima Brock (b. 1950)

Journeys by Heart (1988)*

Sinfulness, as a category within Christian analyses of humanity, is tied to the reinforcement of patriarchal theology. That reinforcement is hooked to the structure of the patriarchal family with mothers at its center. Sinfulness is aligned with blame, punishment, and guilt, and blame has usually been assigned to woman as the originator of sin, or to our maternal, organic birth which must be transcended by a higher, spiritual birth. While such assignation of blame may absolve individual believers of guilt, it carries undertones of both misogyny and self-hate for it puts persons in inner conflict with themselves....

Modern discussions of sinfulness tend to describe it as alienation which emerges through self-assertion and the denial of the self's dependence on God. Sinfulness is understood to be a state that is prior to the particular relationships that shape human beings. In the face of political oppressions, vast economic inequities, wars, and the current threat of global suicide by nuclear destruction, Christian theologians have stepped back from their nineteenth-century optimism about human nature to a stronger emphasis on the pervasiveness of human sin and on the need for us to acknowledge our sinful state and responsibility for evil. Our sophisticated, intricate society and its technology have enabled us to create increasingly original forms of sin.

Western theology has followed Augustine in identifying the human condition as original sin. Until the last decade feminist studies of patriarchy have not influenced discussions of the human condition. These studies should inform our understanding of the human condition because they provide a new, important perspective useful to theological reflection. While feminists are not naive about human evil and suffering, we understand sin as historically and socially produced, which requires us to take responsibility for understanding and stopping oppression and suffering.

I believe understanding sin as damage enhances responsibility and healing instead of miring us in blame and guilt. I am suggesting that sinfulness is neither a state that comes inevitably with birth nor something that permeates all human existence, but a symptom of the unavoidably relational nature of human existence through which we come to be damaged and damage others. Our attempts to avoid that radically relational nature — a thoroughly contingent existence which embeds us in history and society — emerge from our inability to face our own pain and be healed. If we begin with an understanding that we are intimately connected, constituted by our relationships ontologically, that is, as a basic unavoidable principle of existence, we can understand our brokenness as a consequence of our relational existence. This ontological relational existence, the heart of our being, is our life source, our original grace. But we are, by nature, vulnerable, easily dam-

---

*Reprinted from Rita Nakashima Brock, *Journeys by Heart: A Christology of Erotic Power* (New York, 1988), 6–9, 16–17, 22–24, by permission of the Crossroad Publishing Company.

aged, and that vulnerability is both the sign of our connectedness and the source of the damage that leads us to sin.

Sin emerges because our relationships have the capacity to destroy us and we participate in destruction when we seek to destroy ourselves or others. Hence sin is a sign of our brokenheartedness, of how damaged we are, not of how evil, willfully disobedient, and culpable we are. Sin is not something to be punished, but something to be healed. That we exist at all is a sign that the destructive relationships of our lives have not been final and that we have the responsibility of acknowledging our connectedness to others and our commitment to the creation of right relationships.

While modern discussions of sin are not intended to impart blame or evoke guilt, but are supposed to free us to be self-accepting without the necessity for being good or perfect, feminist discussions of sin assert that our doctrines of sin do not lead to enhanced self-acceptance for women. In addition, the admission of our powerlessness in the face of the magnitude of human evil finally leaves us impotent to take responsibility for our own evil except through dependence on a "higher" power. The acknowledgment of our sinful nature and dependence on divine power have not stopped the church and Christian nations from creating some of the most oppressive societies in history, as theologians are quick to acknowledge. We have found little to pull us out of the increasing velocity of the vortex sucking us into global death.

I take human evil and suffering and their consequences seriously, but I do not believe most doctrines of sin go deep enough to the roots of our ability to hurt ourselves and each other. For all their discussions of pride, evil, alienation, greed, racism, war, and so on, Christians have not been able to deal fully with the presence of evil in our own patriarchal hearts. Hence churches have tended not to initiate actions to understand or stop the evils that lie closest to the heart of society, the family — evils such as child abuse, battering, rape, incest, or forced pregnancy and sterilization. It has taken feminists to call attention, repeatedly, to these issues. Even when Christians have addressed such problems as poverty and oppression, our approach is often benignly paternalistic. It is far safer to identify with victims and want to help them than to look at our own participation in systems of oppression and our responsibility for changing ourselves and the systems from which we benefit. The Christian attitude toward charity is often built on the idea of the superior helping the inferior, which locks paternalism into the relationship. Rather than seeing our capacity to give to the poor as part of a social-economic system that produces poverty and hunger, much Christian charity is designed to help others into the exploitive system. Until liberation, black, and feminist theologians began to speak of the self-empowerment of the oppressed, the oppressed were largely seen as victims to be acted upon rather than as a presence in the church that radically challenged its self-identity.

Through the profound acknowledgment of our primal interrelatedness we can begin to find grace and to embrace and to heal the damage and suffering of our deepest selves and our society. Original grace is this healing gift, a reality that begins at birth. I search for theological images and ideas that will help us embrace the fullest possible life through the ultimate claim relationships make on our very being. I will explore, in the context of original grace, the damage to self, to heart, that is a consequence of patriarchy, damage that can be understood theologically as one major violation of original grace. I believe it is our damage — in which one major factor is patriarchy — that has produced a doctrine of sin as a description of our original human state. The existence of that category requires us to misplace divine incarnation and human redemption in someone else's perfection and heroic action, or in a power outside ourselves that helps us transcend the concrete realities of our lives. Believing in our own goodness does not eliminate our need to take responsibility for our own capacities for evil. In fact, I believe that self-acceptance and attention to all our feelings and impulses empower us to change, to heal ourselves, and to understand the roots of evil. (pp. 6–9)

•

Because the very existence of heart is basic to the structure of human life itself and is the basis of our being broken in relationships, we require connections if we are to acknowledge our own broken heart and be healed. At the earliest part of our lives we are dependent on the loving power of others to nurture us. Their failure to do so has serious consequences. We are broken by the world of our relationships before we are able to defend ourselves. It is not a damage we willfully choose. Those who damage us do not have the power to heal us, for they themselves are not healed. To be healed, we must take the responsibility for recognizing our own damage by following our hearts to the relationships that will empower our self-healing. In living by heart, we are called not to absolve ourselves of the consequences of an inherited flaw. We are called to remember our own brokenheartedness, the extent of our vulnerability, and the depth of our need for relationships. Hence we are called not to dependence on a power outside ourselves, but to an exploration of the depths of our most inner, personal selves as the root of our connections to all others.…

Heart is our original grace. In exploring the depths of heart we find incarnate in ourselves the divine reality of connection, of love. The grace we find through heart reveals the incarnate graciousness, generosity, and love necessary to human life. *But the heart's strength lies in its fragility.* To be born so open to the presence of others in the world gives us the enormous, creative capacity to make life whole. Yet such openness means that the terrifying and destructive factors of life are also taken into the self, a self that then requires loving presence to be restored to grace. Finding our heart requires a loving presence who helps the search, who is not afraid of the painfulness of the search, and who can mirror back our buried and broken heart, returning us to a healing memory of our earliest pain and need for love. This loving presence and healing memory carry the profoundest meanings of forgiveness and remembrance. (pp. 16–17)

•

Neither healing nor liberation of the whole self — body, mind, spirit, and feelings — is possible without memory, a memory that is comprehensive, honest, and discerning. Feminist research on child abuse and incest reveals the extent to which early physical and emotional pain can be forgotten and yet have lasting consequences on adult behavior and self-esteem. Feminist research indicates that women who have been raped as children repress memories of molestation but continue as adults to have very low self-esteem and highly ambivalent relationships with men. Childhood sexual abuse can produce substance abuse, depression, prostitution, self-labeling as bitch or whore, and the attribution of greater danger to male sexuality. I have personally observed instances, with students, some of them male, and with adult women of various ages in supportive contexts, of breaking through the amnesia of their past experiences of molestation in childhood. Their remembering, their *anamnesis*, was frightening, painful, illuminating, and, ultimately, an important opening into healing and empowerment as each struggled to understand this awesome memory of pain. Being part of a community of support that opened space for the memory to surface, that accepted their complex feelings, and that empathized with their struggle to understand what had happened were important aspects of beginning the healing process. Without a safe and nurturing environment for remembering, in which we can reexperience the pain of our own brokenheartedness, we remain lost to ourselves and each other, cut off from the grace that gives us life....

We begin to heal, in remembrance and forgiveness, by allowing anger to surface, by reconnecting to our deepest, most passionate feelings, feelings grounded in the rich complexities of our full embodied experience, and by actively reclaiming memory, memory grounded in our relationships.... Memory that emerges from the heart of ourselves binds us to the suffering of others and provides us the routes to empowerment and self-acceptance. Such memory also makes us hungry for collective memory, for the stories of our own people, and of the truth of the life of the human species.

To act lovingly and ethically, through self-awareness and self-acceptance, does not mean the conquest of our urges and separation from our bodies to gain self-control. To act well, we must be willing to listen to our deepest needs, urges, and feelings and to transform ourselves and our world through the healing energy of heart, which is the only energy capable of touching the hearts of others. In remembering heart we gain an embodied self-acceptance that was taken from us; we reclaim our own fragile original grace and through that our truest human character. With such self-acceptance, we are better able to take on the monumental tasks of transforming patriarchy because our strength comes from heart, a centered energy that radiates outward, giving and receiving love. Original grace allows us to acknowledge our own vulnerability. In living through heart, we can begin to love the world, but we no longer need the world to be fused with us to survive, for we live in connection and beyond separation and dependency. We live in the passionate, impassioned, compassionate world of heart, with courage and integrity.

While confirmation from or with the world no longer becomes necessary for a centered self to survive, the restoration of original grace is difficult because we can only come into flower with connections to other self-accepting selves. This relationality is the terrifying and redemptive grace of the character of being human. Living with self-acceptance, we begin a similar process for other selves. In our fragile interdependence we are powerful. With the arrival of self-acceptance, a new sense of power emerges, one that does not require status and control of others and that does not require using the power of others. (pp. 22–24)

Marjorie Hewitt Suchocki (b. 1933)

The Fall to Violence (1994)*

To restate the problem, original sin defined the human situation as one of universal implication in sin, apart from any conscious consent.[1] Sins arise from the condition of sin. Whether classical theologians dealt with the nature of sin as pride, sloth, unbelief, disobedience, or any other variation, the exercise of all vices depended upon and arose from this original condition. The mechanism used to account for the universal nature of sin was the first humans' misdirected will in deviating from their given good. With this deviation, they corrupted the nature that was passed on to their progeny. Every generation consequently finds itself in the plight that it must deal with an internal inclination to participate in and therefore to perpetuate sin. Original sin begets sinners.

In our contemporary situation we experience an enormity to social and personal evils, but the notion of "original sin" that accounts for them theologically has been brought into question. Issues such as racism, sexism, classism, heterosexism, handicappism, anthropocentrism, anti-semitism, and whatever other "isms" we have devised toward the ill-being of peoples and nature, together with massive machines of organized killing called wars and ever more awesome capacities to destroy our environment, require more than an analysis of individual sin to account for the pervasiveness and depth of the problem. The doctrine of original sin must be reappropriated in such a way that it speaks to our condition, and allows us to name our condition.

As noted in the discussion of Reinhold Niebuhr, anxiety plays a major role in twentieth-century discussions of original sin. In such thinking, all sin stems from the need to secure oneself from the anxieties of existence. Thus the fundamental reason why men rape women, or soldiers commit atrocities, or adults abuse children, is because such people are acting out of an anxiety triggered by their finitude and consequent insecurity.

Yet this seems to put too heavy a burden upon the human phenomenon of finitude, nor does it take into consideration the positive elements of anxiety. In many respects anxiety is an important if painful aspect of our humanity resulting from the vulnerability of relationships. To love a person who is in imminent danger of death, such as one with a terminal illness, is to be subjected to anxiety over the well-being of the loved one. The anxiety also contributes to one's anguish in such a situation, but would it be better to feel no anguish? Surely anguish over the pain of the other and over the impending loss are natural consequences of love. And

---

*Reprinted from Marjorie Hewitt Suchocki, *The Fall to Violence: Original Sin in Relational Theology* (New York, 1994), 82–86, 95–96, by permission of the Continuum Publishing Company.

1. Earlier, Suchocki has written: "Sin as the unnecessary violation of the well-being of any aspect of creation is my primary definition of sin" (48).

far from becoming a direct path to sin, the anxiety that underlies this anguish often becomes the prompting power for acts of kindness and care. Likewise, persons facing their own imminent death often respond to the attendant anxiety not by increased sinning, but by increased albeit anguished value of the beauty of all the ordinariness of life, and by an overflow of love toward those they hold dear. Since Niebuhr and others consider the fragility of life to be the limiting factor causing anxiety, surely the condition of those most directly confronted with death should be illustrations of the power of anxiety as the presupposition of sin. But this is not the case.

As for anxiety over the lack of being a self, is it anxiety that produces the lack of being a self or the other way around? Feminist and minority scholars amply show that society pressures or forces selected groups into pre-established roles that have no necessary relation to the unique capabilities of the persons concerned. Under such conditions, it is eminently difficult to break out of these roles in order to discover and develop one's true being, or, as feminists put it, "one's own voice." Is it not the case that the lack of a "self" imposed by such conditions is itself the cause of anxiety? Furthermore, far from anxiety then becoming a condition influencing one to sin, anxiety can become the catalyst that signals the wrongness of the stereotype into which one is forced. Anxiety can be a first step toward liberation.

It seems specious to argue that those who oppress children and young people . . . do so out of a fundamental anxiety occasioned by their mortality. Is all domination, greed, rapaciousness, and cruelty so reducible to the need to shore up the defenses against death? To the contrary, young persons often (though certainly not always) seem so unaware of their mortality as to be overly incautious, and even the phenomenon of teen-age suicide is tinged with the haunting tragedy that the victims do not really believe in death. Adults also can be marvelously impervious to mortality so long as they are healthy, and the shock of serious illness is often the surprised recognition that "even I am mortal." How, then, is anxiety over fear of death to account for the extent and enormity of sins of oppression?

To be sure, some theologians such as Paul Tillich dismiss anxieties over specific things, such as imminent death or the lack of oneself as being but bare manifestations of a far deeper "existential anxiety" that in fact has no object. This type of anxiety emerges concomitantly with one's finitude, then the scales crash down on the side of sin. Given the insufficiency of experienced anxiety relative to death to account particularly for sin, how can an underlying anxiety over finitude per se be the prompting cause of all human evil? One wonders if such existential anxiety is a phantom called up to save the notion of "rebellion against God" as the primal notion of sin. Anxiety over one's finitude, whether occasioned by nameable situations or by an unnameable existential precondition of human personality, seems a fragile beast to bear the burden of so enormous a problem as human violence.

Rather than looking to a finitude-engendered anxiety as the reason behind human ill-doing, why not look to a violence-engendered anxiety? It might well be that human personality contains a substructure of violent aggression related to survival, and that the effects of this substructure give rise to an anxiety such as Tillich named. Violence rather than finitude per se is the presenting cause of anxiety. This suggestion will be developed more fully [later]; for the present, we explore the issue of the human tendency toward violence as the condition of sin. My thesis is that original sin is created through a triadic structure constituted by a propensity toward violence, by an interrelational solidarity of the human species, and by social structures that shape the formation of consciousness and conscience.

With regard to violence, we are by nature an aggressive species with a history of physical and psychic violence. Killing is violence; greed and verbal abuse are also violence. Violence has many forms existing along a continuum from obvious to subtle, but at its base, violence is the destruction of well-being. The capacity for violence is built into our species through aggressive instincts related to survival. When that violence is unnecessary and avoidable, it is sin.

Under a traditional "rebellion against God" concept, it would be unthinkable to point to aggression, with its easy entailment of violence, as a cause of sin. A tendency toward aggression is built into human nature, so that if this tendency is a cause of sin, then the creator of human nature would be implicated in the fact of human sin. Hence the only creaturely basis of sin that could save the creator from implication was human freedom, for which each human was solely responsible. Since the universal misuse of freedom belied freedom's reality, the original sin of Adam accounted for the distorted conditions of freedom that lead all humans into sin. Thus human responsibility was preserved, and God the creator was kept free from culpability.

But a relational conceptuality posits a situation where the world is creation in a threefold sense, rather than in a unilateral sense. Under a supposition of God as unilateral creator, the cause of sin cannot be located in the finite situation per se. If it were, then God would share the guilt — and perhaps even the greater guilt — for God is presumably unconditioned by any necessity and acts out of the divine freedom and fully in accord with the divine nature. This impossible possibility of the guilt of God was rejected in the Christian tradition not by considering a more complex notion of creation, but by assigning all responsibility for sin to the free will of the creature. There could be nothing in nature itself that predisposes the creature toward sin.

But does the same objection hold if God and the world together share in the creation of the world? Earlier, I argued that every entity in the universe is creation in a threefold sense: It is created by its past, since the past lays down the parameters to which it must in some way conform; the past emits the energy fields from which the new entity emerges. But every entity is also created by its future, mediated to it by God. God, acting out of a fullness of knowledge of the becoming creature's context, and also out of the effect of God's own nature upon that context, offers the becoming creature its best creative possibility for unification of its past world. The third sense in which the world is creation is through each entity's response to past and future. In every standpoint of existence the becoming element of the world integrates its responsive feelings of its past and future; the "how" of this integration finally rests with the entity in question. Thus God is creator of the world *with* the world, overturning the long tradition of creation by divine fiat alone. All three factors — God, the past, and the subject — must be taken into consideration in order to understand the world as creation.

But in this case, one is no longer left with the onerous problem that if there is actually a finite inclination toward sin it must somehow be God the creator's fault. And, if some degree of freedom on a continuum from indeterminism toward at least our own degree of freedom is characteristic of every particle in the world, then creaturely freedom per se, and not simply human freedom, accounts in part for the way the world is. Therefore, if there are factors within the way the world is even prior to the emergence of human beings that can account for the universality of human perversity, then God is not necessarily the one to be held responsible for these factors. Rather, there is a shared responsibility between God and the world.

Creation is a process that takes place between God and the world, apparently unfolding and turning in on itself and moving yet again in an infinite number of ways. Whether the intricate process can be called "story" and treated as directional at all is certainly questionable; the most that can be said is that from our perspective of experienced beginnings and endings, we humans at least turn creation into story, into history.

We understand ourself as coming into existence through a long process; our story emerges from artifacts our ancestors left behind. And if our creation spans a long period of time, and if God is ever a creative God, then are we not still in the process of our creation? What reason have we to think that we as a race are a "finished product," particularly given the raw cruelty to which we are prone? Perhaps our very incompletion in relation to the criterion of well-being is witness to the continual call of God, luring us toward our further creation. (pp. 82–86)

•

The condition of original sin, then, involves aggressive tendencies within our humanity that naturally incline us toward violence. Instincts toward bonding are also primal within us, and self-transcendence through memory, empathy, and imagination makes it possible for bonding rather than aggressiveness to be our dominant mode of being. To the extent that we do not avoid unnecessary violence, we live in sin. To this day, we continue to deal with aggressive tendencies toward violence as the stuff from which our sin is fashioned.

Traditional Christian doctrine has certainly recognized the violence of humankind, but has maintained that first came pride, which was then the cause of violence. This theory suggests that violence came first, which then became the cause of pride as the self-construed justification of violence. Traditional theology still defines pride as the undue exaltation of the self, or the attempt to establish one's own borders, independently of considerations of the good of others. Most typically, these borders were construed psychically rather than physically, as is evident in the classic theme adopted by Christianity of the "overreacher." But the studies above suggest that innate aggression rather than pride leads to the violent defiance of boundaries, and that psychic forms of this violence are transmutations of the more fundamental physical forms related to aggressive territorialism. Thus aggression and violence do not emerge from pride; pride emerges from aggression and its attendant violence.

Pride emerges from aggression as a way of dealing with the tension created by the violation of one's own ability to transcend violence. Violence is disregard of the well-being of the other. When this takes place in the context of transcendence, then a tension is created in the self-understanding, for transcendence relates one empathically to the violated other. How is such a tension resolved? The most common way is a deceptive denial of relationship, which of course entails the denial of the empathic regard for the other as subject. One continues in the primitive mode of regarding the other as object, thus searing the transcendence knowledge sufficiently to allow the violence to continue. One justifies one's continuing actions of violation by assuming the right to such violation. In short, violation engenders a sinful mode of pride as a way of coping with the transcendent consciousness that whispers the knowledge of sin. Through the means of pride, one dulls the very essence of one's humanity — which means, of course, that if pride pretends an exaltation, it does so paradoxically from an actual lessening of the fullness of what it can mean to be human.

This sinful mode of pride is to be sharply distinguished from the holy and healthy strength of ego that facilitates the openness of the self to the other. This, too, is pride in the form of a relationally based esteem of self, and it can well be a means of manifesting truth, love, and beauty. Such pride recognizes the truth of the relational interdependence of the self with all others; it participates in love toward mutual well-being in relationship, and this togetherness of truth and love inexorably weaves the world into yet a new form of beauty. The undue self-exaltation of sinful pride is a perversion of the self-and-other exultation of a reality-based relational pride that is fostered through the esteem of the relational self. (pp. 95–96)

Part Two

THE DOCTRINE OF
THE CHURCH

– 4 –

The Early Period

INTRODUCTION

Telling the story of Christian ideas about the church is an important way to review the history of the church itself, since questions of identity are inseparable from the context in which an entity comes to know and understand itself. The earliest Christian writers were pushed into questions of identity because of their relationship with three other major cultural/religious systems: Judaism, Hellenistic philosophy, and heresy. Challenges of authenticity from these traditions (which were, of course, also emerging themselves) generated a diverse range of Christian documents. Because such documents often devoted attention to defending a Christian perspective, attacking a non-Christian perspective, or resolving disputes among various factions of Christians, a clear articulation of Christian identity defined on its own terms is elusive. Nonetheless, from the variety of texts which offer us insight into early understandings of the church we can identify two sets of issues which occupied many early Christians, but which were not always addressed with equal emphasis or eloquence by our authors.

The first set pertains to the organization of the church: its structure, functions, and organizations. The second set highlights the nature of the church, its place in the cosmological order, and its relationship to God. The practical issues contained in the first set of concerns necessitated larger doctrinal definitions which were often implicit in the earliest documents but which awaited the thought of Irenaeus and Origen for fuller development.

Early theologians took several organizational metaphors from scripture, funneled primarily through Paul. Indeed, the striking absence of concern over "church" in the Gospels indicates, first, Jesus' thorough commitment to the reform of his own religious tradition and, second, the focus of Gospel writers on the meaning of Jesus' life rather than on the communities which survived his death.[1] But Paul's intense interest in missionary activity to the Gentiles caused him both to probe the nature of the church and to develop the concept of the universality of the Christian church, a collective sense of "all his churches" as a larger body. Indeed, although it is perhaps anachronistic, because a consensus on the nature of the church as "one, holy, catholic, and apostolic" awaited the fourth century, these themes are nascent in the first century and developed singly or even at times collectively throughout the early period of Christian history.

---

1. There are only two references to "ecclesia" in all of the Gospels, both of which come from Matthew. See Matthew 16:18 and 18:17.

Christianity's Jewish roots certainly reinforced the notion of "one" and "holy," the church as God's chosen people, a people of the covenant, set apart from the Gentiles but with a prophetic role within the world. The metaphor most borrowed by Christian authors was that coming from the Song of Songs, in which bride and bridegroom take thorough delight in one another. Paul paves the way for the development of the church as the bride of Christ in Ephesians 5:23–32, suggesting that the intimate cherishing of a spouse is an appropriate way to understand the church. Paul's most important contribution to the conceptualization of church, however, lies in his repeated use of the metaphor of the body, most notably in 1 Corinthians 12, but also in Ephesians 4:7–11 and Colossians 1:18, 24–28. The church as Christ's body affirms at once the unity of the church, for as Christ could not be divided neither could the church (see 1 Cor. 1:13 and 12:12, 20–26), its sacramentality, and its universality (1 Cor. 12:13, 27). And, as Paul enumerates the various functions of the members of Christ's body, the apostolic function receives a place of primary importance (see 1 Cor. 12:28).

The themes introduced by Paul take on special importance in the thought of Clement of Rome, the assumed author of *1 Clement,* who, like Paul, used the metaphor of the body to characterize the church in his letter to the Corinthians. This letter, thought to have been written ca. 96, sketches an image of the Christian community in which all of its members participate fully in Christ's body, but their participation is mediated through obedience to their bishop. Clement emphasizes "apostolic" over "one," "holy," or "catholic," suggesting that apostolic orientation is a divinely ordained order. Clement writes: "The apostles received the gospel for us from the Lord Jesus Christ; Jesus, the Christ, was sent from God. Thus Christ is from God, and the apostles from Christ. In both instances the orderly procedure depends on God's will."[2] Thus, in highlighting the authority of the bishop as the successor to the apostles, Clement introduces a notion of the church as monolithic, intimately connected with the person of Jesus Christ since, in representing the apostles, the bishops can transcend time.

As Clement explains at the outset, concern over the unity of the church at Corinth compelled him to compose his letter; the appointed leader of the community faced opposition from a rival candidate. Thus the appeal to the church as Christ's body is used to reinforce the oneness of the community. Concern over Christian unity also motivated another early author to develop metaphors for the church. The letters of Ignatius (d. ca. 107), bishop of Antioch, served many functions, but in them he expressed a similar fear of schism, this one rooted less in discipline than in doctrine. Ignatius had grown concerned that divergent understandings about who Christ was threatened to tear apart the church, and he specifically decried the tendency of some to diminish or even reject the human activity of Jesus, a movement known as Docetism. Eventually orthodox Christianity would teach that Christ was fully human and fully divine, but in the early church many people were unsure that Christ could have been fully human. Indeed, it was easier to see Jesus as a kind of god walking among humans who finally returned to the heav-

---

2. Clement of Rome, *The Letter of the Church of Rome to the Church of Corinth, Commonly Called Clement's First Letter,* in *Early Christian Fathers,* trans. and ed. Cyril C. Richardson (New York: Macmillan, 1970), 62.

ens from which he had come. So the Docetists understood Jesus to have taken on the appearance (*dokesis*) of flesh while still being a spiritual person.

Ignatius argued most forcefully against Docetism in the *Letter to the Smyrnaeans,* in his affirmation of the bodily resurrection.[3] But, for Ignatius, Christ's true incarnation was not merely theoretical. Ignatius's major argument against Docetism was Ignatius's own sacrifice of himself: if Christ were not both human and divine, Ignatius's death would have no meaning. Thus he writes to the Trallians: "And if, as some atheists (I mean unbelievers) say, his suffering was a sham (it's really *they* who are a sham!), why, then, am I a prisoner? Why do I want to fight with wild beasts? In that case I shall die to no purpose. Yes, and I am maligning the Lord too!"[4] This may partially explain Ignatius's fervent desire for martyrdom. He expresses this most clearly in the *Letter to the Romans,* which he writes specifically to "clear the path" toward martyrdom, implying that the church there could have prevented his sacrifice (*Romans* 4).

Ignatius believed that early debate over who Jesus was would divide the church, so he made a bid for unity through emphasis on obedience to the bishop. Ignatius believed in the importance of the bishop primarily to "control" doctrine. He did not base this idea on apostolic succession, however. Instead he identified the function of the bishop with Christ's role as a high priest. He suggested that the hierarchical order developing in the churches was representative of a celestial hierarchy, an assertion he made more striking by using the metaphor of a harp: "Hence you should act in accord with the bishop's mind, as you surely do. Your presbytery, indeed, which deserves its name and is a credit to God, is as closely tied to the bishop as the strings to a harp. Wherefore your accord and harmonious love is a hymn to Jesus Christ. Yes, one and all, you should form yourselves into a choir, so that, in perfect harmony and taking your pitch from God, you may sing in unison and with one voice to the Father through Jesus Christ."[5]

Not all documents of the first and early second centuries reflect the preoccupation with either the authority of the church leaders or its orientation to hierarchical organization. Another document, approximately contemporary with *1 Clement* and Ignatius's letters,[6] known as the *Didache,* reflects a very different ecclesiology, as both W. H. C. Frend and Hans von Campenhausen have observed.[7] In the *Didache* there is an emphasis on the ethical life of the community, the importance of the Eucharist as both a ritual of remembrance and a communal celebration, and a continuing openness to the word of God as expressed through the prophets. Here the word "apostle" is not used to specify the original disciples nor to speak of succession; rather, it is used to refer to the function of the itinerant preacher who makes the word of God come alive for the community.

When comparing the *Didache* to the documents of Clement and the letters of Ignatius, one could argue that the lengthy arguments regarding hierarchical

---

3. See Richardson, *Early Christian Fathers,* 113.

4. Ibid., 100 (*Trallians* 10); italics in original.

5. Ibid., 89 (*Ephesians* 4).

6. Dating the *Didache* is difficult because it is a composite of at least two documents. For a discussion of the dating problems, see introduction to the document below.

7. W. H. C. Frend claims that "in their spirit and in content it is impossible to reconcile the *Didache* with the letters of Ignatius" (*Rise of Christianity* [Philadelphia: Fortress Press, 1984], 145).

authority employed by both Ignatius and Clement represent the justification of novelty in church organization. Certainly the *Didache* sees the prophet as the normative leader of the community, taking the place of the "high priest." That this is an established order within the community is attested by the lack of justification for the custom as well as a discussion of what the community should do if the ordinary system of prophetic authority is abused. What ties all three documents together, despite their differing views of authority and organization, is their orientation to the centrality of the Eucharist. Ritually and doctrinally, the period up to the mid–second century shows a church living out the metaphor of Christ's body.

By the late second century the diversity of church models we have observed had narrowed, and this process of developing hierarchical structures and systems of authority, with a concurrent loss of spontaneity, flexibility, and charismatic orientation, continued to characterize the Christian church throughout the remainder of the early period. As it continued to differentiate itself from Judaism, Christian leaders were confronted with the problem of their nebulous status within the Roman Empire, and the apologist movement was born. Christian apologists combined many tasks: first, they were explaining the basics of the Christian faith as it was evolving, attempting to establish its legitimacy and even superiority to other religions; second, they were synthesizing the Christian tradition with Stoic and Platonic systems to give it philosophical and ethical credibility; and third, they were negotiating for acceptance within the Roman Empire, even suggesting that Christians were exemplary Roman citizens and subjects of the emperor. The combination of these tasks was difficult, and even proved impossible. The example of the early apologist Justin Martyr (d. 165) highlights the irony of a man who wrote of his loyalty to the emperor but died as a martyr after refusing to sacrifice to the Roman gods.

Justin Martyr's case was somewhat exceptional for the second century, a time not marked by deliberate, state-sponsored persecution of Christians. Instructive in this regard is the correspondence between Pliny and Trajan in the early second century. Pliny, a commissioner for the Roman emperor Trajan (reigned 98–117), wrote to Trajan in 112 asking advice about whether or not to prosecute Christians. In their correspondence Trajan revealed that Christians were not inherently criminal and should not be hunted down, but if they were denounced by others and refused to worship Roman gods they should be punished. It was not until the third century that imperial officials initiated action against Christians; Christians were martyred in the second century either in pogrom-like initiatives such as in Lyons in 177, or they were executed as a result of someone's denunciation, as in the case of Justin Martyr.[8]

While second-century persecution did not significantly threaten the spread of Christianity, the unity of the early church did seem threatened by schism over doctrine, practice, and the direction of Christian growth. Concern over the popularity of three significant heretical movements, gnosticism, Marcionism, and Montanism, generated new Christian writings which attempted to clarify orthodox

---

8. Indeed, if Ignatius is a credible witness, martyrdom in the second century may have been difficult to attain. In his *Letter to the Romans*, Ignatius actually begs his readers not to intervene on his behalf to the Roman authorities. See Richardson, *Early Christian Fathers*, 103 (*Romans* 1–2).

positions and also to redefine teaching authority within the church. "Gnosticism" is best understood as an umbrella term, used to identify certain philosophical tendencies among theologians. During the first two centuries of Christian history, distinctions between gnostics and orthodox Christians were not entirely clear. In the period of acute Hellenization (mid- to late second century) the gnostics, associated with philosophical schools in Alexandria, offered Christianity an attractive intellectual framework for the interpretation of its sacred texts. Irenaeus of Lyons, writing about 185, identified gnostic leaders like Basilides and Valentinus as heretics, but other orthodox theologians, such as Clement of Alexandria, were highly indebted to their work. Gnostics moved the words of Jesus into a more abstract realm which could universalize them and set forth a pathway to enlightenment, wisdom, and union with God. The urge to intellectualize was not a movement to co-opt or undermine the practical nature of Jesus' ministry, as rigorists like Tertullian (flourished 190–220) feared. Indeed, the gnostic understanding of the God of knowledge was consistent with the wisdom tradition of the Old Testament as well as the thought of the author of the Gospel of John.

While gnosticism made important contributions to Christian theology, however, it also, by means of differentiation, pushed orthodox theologians toward clarification of doctrinal issues. Important christological questions emerged as the gnostic understanding of Christ as the wisdom of God seemed to disparage Christ's full humanity. Indeed, some gnostics even disputed that Christ had ever truly died. The gnostic emphasis on the saving knowledge of God imparted by Jesus raised questions about the universality of salvation: could all achieve knowledge of God? Was such knowledge not beyond all but the most disciplined? While the gnostics addressed important philosophical questions, the establishment of Christianity hinged upon its ability to make universal claims about God and Christ. Thus, in terms of the understanding of the church and its function as administrator of saving sacraments, gnosticism was a movement to be viewed with some suspicion.

Marcionism, another important heretical movement, emerged with the person of Marcion (ca. 85–160), at first an orthodox Christian, who was exiled from the Christian community at Rome in 144. Marcion's theological questions stemmed from an inability to reconcile the God of the Old Testament with the "Abba" whom Jesus had revealed. The first was an anthropomorphic God of justice; the second was a God of love of whom Jesus could speak with familiarity but whose transcendent love was mysterious and unfathomable. Marcion's insistence that these two gods could not be reconciled led him to reject the allegorical interpretation of scripture being developed, which identified Christ with Old Testament prophecies and figures. Marcion's questions met with sympathy; many important centers of Marcionism existed at the end of the second century, and orthodox theologians agreed that Marcion was the "arch-heretic" of his day. Marcion raised issues of teaching authority which would contribute substantially to the rise of the hierarchical structure of the orthodox church.

The third major heresy of the second century, Montanism, also pushed the issue of teaching authority, although it did so from a different vantage point. Montanus (flourished 170s) and two women prophets emerged in the Phrygian province of Asia Minor around 172. They claimed to be preaching upon the inspiration of the Holy Spirit and called for prayer and fasting to prepare for the imminent second coming of Christ. Montanism did not disappear when the promised parousia did not materialize. In fact, Montanism proved to be one of the most tenacious challenges to orthodox Christianity. Its appeal lay in its dual emphasis on moral behavior and direct access to God through prophetic revelation. As orthodox Christianity moved into the third century, it committed itself to a canon of scriptural texts,[9] thereby asserting that the Word of God had been spoken definitively and had only to be interpreted by qualified teachers. Montanists, on the other hand, looked to the prophetic utterances of its adherents for continuing insight into the will of God. Additionally, in contrast to the direction of orthodox Christianity, the church of the Spirit allowed for the equal participation of inspired men and women.

The writings of Irenaeus (ca. 130–200), bishop of Lyons, took on these heresies explicitly, while at the same time affirming a sense of the unity of the Christian church. This unity was chiefly expressed through general consensus on doctrine. Irenaeus asserts that there is one Christian tradition and that this tradition was universally understood by its adherents and its teachers. The unity of the church is guaranteed by the one Christ, and the authority of Christ's message is safeguarded by the apostles and their disciples. Thus in Irenaeus there is a fully articulated sense of apostolic succession, suggested earlier by Clement of Rome, which vouchsafes a "Rule of Faith" in which the scriptures, as the source of authority about Christ and God, can be taught with one voice by the successors of the first disciples. This Rule of Faith guaranteed that, as he asserted, the faith of Christians from Germany to Libya was the same faith. With Irenaeus, we get a very real sense of the church beginning to understand itself as "one, holy, catholic, and apostolic."

The growth of the church in the third century was disrupted by a brief but significant wave of persecution under the emperor Decius. The response of Christians to this crisis revealed the fragility of the church structures so carefully built and defended in the second century. In October 249, Decius, a military leader, took over the government of the Roman Empire. In his attempts to restore unity to the empire Decius revived the cult of the emperor, and, in January 250, personally performed sacrifices to Jupiter, ordering that such offerings be repeated in the capitols of every city in the empire. Each citizen would have to obtain a certificate stating that the sacrifice had been made. The universal order to offer sacrifices to the Roman gods — the first ever in Christian history — threw the Christian church into disorder. Fabian, bishop of Rome, was executed for refusing to perform the sacrifice in late January of 250. Other bishops were also imprisoned and executed; still others, including Cyprian of Carthage, went into hiding or fled their sees. Among the laity there was a similar range of responses: many made the sacrifice, yet the persecution also produced more Christian martyrs. As the historian W. H. C. Frend explains, the Decian persecution revealed how un-

---

9. The process of determining and codifying the canon of scripture took several decades and was completed by about 200. This listing of texts is known as the Muratorian Canon. It included the Apocalypse of Peter and omitted the Letter to the Hebrews, 1 and 2 Peter, and 3 John.

even converts' commitment to Christian beliefs and practices was: "Throughout the empire the church had been accepting a large number of nominal converts as well as committed individuals. . . . Behind its monolithic exterior all was far from well."[10] Fortunately, the Decian persecution proved brief. Decius's reign ended in 251, leaving the church the tremendous task of restoring order and determining who would be its authentic leaders.

Those who had sacrificed or "lapsed" would have to apply to be restored into the church. They would have to perform acts of penance to prepare themselves for readmittance. But to whom would they apply if their bishop had not himself been a "confessor" of Christianity under fire, as was the case with Cyprian? Cyprian called a council at Carthage to determine the proper procedure for the lapsed. He applied penances differently, depending upon the extent to which a Christian had submitted to the order to sacrifice. Those who had sacrificed willingly received harsher penances; those who had obtained certificates without sacrificing (i.e., by proxy) received lighter penances. After consolidating his position in Carthage, Cyprian wrote *On the Unity of the Church,* a treatise which rooted the unity of the church in the chair of Peter in Rome and supported the candidate for bishop of Rome, Cornelius, over his rival Novatian. With Cyprian we see clearly the ways in which the doctrine of the church became intertwined with the legitimation of its structures. We also see the emergence of a clearer Petrine orientation by the mid–third century.

After recovering from the Decian crisis, the church was becoming more rooted in its structure and increasingly institutionalized in other ways. Cornelius, the bishop of Rome from 251 to 253, had a staff of some 155 clergy at his service. The liturgy had developed regular forms, as described by Hippolytus in about 215. The penitential system survived and solidified after the Decian persecution, and there were clear boundaries between those who formally entered the Christian church, those who had left it, and those who were considering joining (catechumens). These differences were reinforced in the liturgy, in which Christians participated fully only if they were not undergoing penance. Catechumens were invited to be present at the liturgy up to the time of the Eucharist, but were initiated in this mystery only after they had joined the church. A period of growth, peace, and prosperity for the church lasted into the fourth century.

Under the reign of the emperor Diocletian (284–305), however, the church witnessed a systematic persecution, sometimes referred to as the Great Persecution. On February 24, 303, Diocletian promulgated an edict which ordered churches destroyed and Christian scriptures burned. Additionally, Christians were to be removed from public office. Without producing martyrs, Diocletian sought to reduce the secular power of Christians and destabilize them institutionally. A second edict in 303 targeted the leaders of the Christian communities, ordering bishops arrested and forced to sacrifice. Another edict, promulgated in 304 by the man who would become Diocletian's successor, Galerius, extended the order to sacrifice to all Christians. The extent to which Galerius's edict was enforced in the West is unclear; however, the crisis was over in the West by May 305,

---

10. Frend, *The Rise of Christianity,* 322.

when Diocletian abdicated. In the East, however, another edict of sacrifice was issued in 306, and the crisis of the Great Persecution did not end until 311 with an Edict of Toleration extended by Galerius. After Galerius's death in 311 his deputy (technically the senior Augustus) Maximin encouraged popular uprisings against Christians, and the situation was tense until Constantine's military victory at the Milvian Bridge and the Edict of Milan (June 13, 313), extending religious toleration throughout the Roman Empire.

The career of Constantine was extremely significant for the history of Christianity, particularly with respect to the bond forged between church and state. Constantine's reign produced one of the most fruitful and productive relationships among centuries of such bonds. Yet Constantine's support and influence within the church caused a shift in self-understanding that many Christians found dangerous. It is difficult to characterize how "Christian" Constantine was. Like many Christians of his age he was not baptized until shortly before his death, in 337. However, he took an active role in church governance throughout his life and even at times referred to himself as a "servant of God." He made significant contributions to the church in Rome, including his wife's palace on the Lateran, he granted privileges to the Roman clergy, and the jurisdiction of episcopal tribunals was extended into secular matters. Even more important, he convened and presided over the Council of Nicea in 325, a council which addressed the schism in the church provoked by disagreement over the nature of Christ. Constantine's involvement in the Council of Nicea reveals concern for both doctrine and governance issues and set numerous precedents for imperial intervention in church matters. Finally, Constantine moved the imperial capital to Byzantium, dedicating the "new Rome" in 330. Obviously, Christianity had left the margins of the Roman Empire only to wrestle with new understandings of itself as "universal" and as the "soul" of the social body.

The Donatist controversy and the writings of Augustine capture very forcefully these fourth-century issues. To call Donatism a "controversy" is perhaps misleading; it was a pervasive movement which became an alternative Christian tradition with its own leadership. Donatism arose in North Africa in the aftermath of the Great Persecution as Donatus, a "confessor" and rival bishop, began to rebaptize lapsed clergy. The tensions among confessors and lapsed exploded in 311 when the new bishop of Carthage, Caecilian, was consecrated by another bishop who had lapsed. In 312 a local council condemned Caecilian and elected another bishop to the see. Although Miltiades, the bishop of Rome (311–14), defended Caecilian, as did bishops united at the Council of Arles (314), Donatus and his followers refused to accept his authority. In 317 the matter was still not resolved, and the emperor Constantine intervened by issuing an edict against the Donatists, confiscating their property and exiling their leaders. The Donatists easily survived these measures, however, and their influence solidified and extended throughout North Africa over the next several decades, becoming a mass movement despite the eventual exile of Donatus himself.

Whereas the Christian church was truly moving into its previous claims of universality ("catholic"), perhaps without enough reflection on what that would mean for itself, the Donatist movement emphasized an understanding of church as "one" and "holy." It was a body of people committed to ideals and practices, and it could not extend salvation to anyone if it was not itself a model of integrity and authenticity. The rigorist Christian spirit of Montanism reemerged in the rigorism of Donatism, and persecution by the state only confirmed the Donatists' belief that Christians were often called to uphold the faith in the face of unjust suffering.

By the end of the fourth century, however, Donatism's establishment throughout North Africa led to its own undoing. The arrival of the new bishop of Hippo, Augustine, in 391 sealed its fate. Augustine had converted to Christianity in 386 and was baptized the following Easter. A student of rhetoric and philosophy, Augustine turned his attention to ecclesiology only reluctantly and in response to debates with the Donatists. These debates increased in intensity between the years 397 and 412, until Augustine's personal and professional investment in relegating the Donatists to the status of heretics was high. Augustine revisited the theme of unity, accusing the Donatists of schism. Further, he shifted the arguments of the early Donatists, who, by rejecting the authority of lapsed clergy, had asserted that the Christian community could and should hold clergy to ethical standards. Without specifically addressing their concerns about the morality of Christian leaders, Augustine accused the Donatists of undermining the source of Christian unity, the sacraments. He argued that any sacrament when properly administered maintained its divine character regardless of the status of the minister. Finally, Augustine began to articulate a view of the universal church in which the elect and the nonelect lived together within one body.

The theological issues came to a head in 411 when Augustine brought together a conference of Donatists and non-Donatists for a debate before the imperial commissioner. The commissioner ruled against the Donatists, and in 412 an imperial edict banned the Donatist church and confiscated its property. Augustine's experiences with the Donatists led him to justify state intervention in doctrinal questions and established theoretical justification for coercion against heretics and infidels. His stance suggests a remarkable discrepancy between the theory of coexistence within the body of Christ on earth and the practice of invoking temporal punishment of dissidents. On one level in his affirmation of Christians as the "soul of the world," Augustine suggests that the Christian vision of reality allows some transcendence of social structures and certainly generates a refusal to put all of one's hope in human institutions. Yet, as Augustine articulates so critically, the church has a specific function to provide salvation and to serve as the primary channel for grace in the world.

The coercive power of the state to which Augustine had appealed was limited in very practical ways by the disintegration of the Roman Empire. Invasions of the Vandals began in Gaul as early as 406, and the Visigoths settled there in 418. Vandal invasions extended into North Africa in 429, and Hippo fell to them in 431, a year after Augustine's death. Rome was saved only through the intercession of Pope Leo I (pontificate 440–61). What did the church represent during the politically volatile fifth century? In the West, Christianity struggled to survive the political annihilation of the empire, while in the East the Council of Chalcedon, convened in 451, struggled to understand and clarify the dual nature of Christ.

Despite the differing orientations of eastern and western Christendom, the bishop of Rome asserted a doctrinal and political authority determinative for the course of the medieval papacy.

After much debate and even a disputed Second Council of Ephesus (449) in the East over how it was possible for Christ to be fully human and fully divine, some 520 bishops met at the Council of Chalcedon to establish an orthodox statement. The council recognized that in Christ existed two natures "unconfusedly" yet also "indivisibly," a formula proposed by Pope Leo, one among those who had insisted upon distinguishing between the two natures. Once some consensus had been achieved regarding the nature of Christ, other issues came under discussion, including the primacy of Rome and the status of Constantinople, the "New Rome." Canon 28 of the Council of Chalcedon extended "equal privileges" to Constantinople, a move instantly rejected by Leo. Both the council's adoption of Leo's language surrounding the dual nature of Christ and Leo's insistence on the primacy of Rome added to the doctrinal and jurisdictional authority of the papacy. Although Leo's immediate successors would be unable to assert such authority again for some time, by the end of the fifth century a new dedication to the temporal and spiritual sovereignty of the papacy was emerging. The church's movement toward the acquisition of temporal power signals the beginning of the medieval period.

Christianity's movement into the early medieval period is signaled by the papacy of Gelasius (pontificate 492–96) who, in his correspondence to the emperor Anastasius, asserted the superiority of papal power to imperial power in light of the greater pastoral and sacramental responsibilities of the priesthood. Secular power (*potestas*) is compared to the authority (*auctoritas*) of the church and seen as derivative. Although the papacy of the fifth century was unable to put such an ambitious claim to power into practice, missionary expansion throughout Europe and a series of alliances with temporal leaders over the course of the early Middle Ages propelled the church into governance issues that early Christianity could not have imagined for itself.

TEXTS

Clement of Rome (d. ca. 97)

1 Clement (ca. 96)*

Now that this is clear to us and we have peered into the depths of the divine knowledge, we are bound to do in an orderly fashion all that the Master has bidden us to do at the proper times he set. He ordered sacrifices and services to be performed; and required this to be done, not in a careless and disorderly way, but at the times and seasons he fixed. Where he wants them performed, and by

---

*Reprinted from *The Letter of the Church of Rome to the Church of Corinth, Commonly Called Clement's First Letter,* in *Early Christian Fathers,* trans. and ed. Cyril C. Richardson (New York: Macmillan, 1970), 62–64, 70–71, by permission of Westminster/John Knox Press.

whom, he himself fixed by his supreme will, so that everything should be done in a holy way and with his approval, and should be acceptable to his will. Those, therefore, who make their offerings at the time set, win his approval and blessing. For they follow the Master's orders and do no wrong. The high priest is given his particular duties: the priests are assigned their special place, while on the Levites particular tasks are imposed. The layman is bound by the layman's code.

"Each of us," brothers, "in his own rank"[1] must win God's approval and have a clear conscience. We must not transgress the rules laid down for our ministry, but must perform it reverently. Not everywhere, brothers, are the different sacrifices — the daily ones, the freewill offerings, and those for sins and trespasses — offered, but only in Jerusalem. And even there sacrifices are not made at any point, but only in front of the sanctuary, at the altar, after the high priest and the ministers mentioned have inspected the offering for blemishes. Those, therefore, who act in any way at variance with his will, suffer the penalty of death. You see, brothers, the more knowledge we are given, the greater risks we run.

The apostles received the gospel for us from the Lord Jesus Christ; Jesus, the Christ, was sent from God. Thus Christ is from God and the apostles from Christ. In both instances the orderly procedure depends on God's will. And so the apostles, after receiving their orders and being fully convinced by the resurrection of our Lord Jesus Christ and assured by God's word, went out in the confidence of the Holy Spirit to preach the good news that God's Kingdom was about to come. They preached in country and city, and appointed their first converts, after testing them by the Spirit, to be the bishops and deacons of future believers. Nor was this any novelty, for Scripture had mentioned bishops and deacons long before. For this is what Scripture says somewhere: "I will appoint their bishops in righteousness and their deacons in faith...."[2]

Now our apostles, thanks to our Lord Jesus Christ, knew that there was going to be strife over the title of bishop. It was for this reason and because they had been given an accurate knowledge of the future, that they appointed the officers we have mentioned. Furthermore, they later added a codicil to the effect that, should they die, other approved men should succeed to their ministry. In the light of this, we view it as a breach of justice to remove from their ministry those who were appointed either by them [i.e., the apostles] or later on and with the whole church's consent, by others of the proper standing, and who, long enjoying everybody's approval, have ministered to Christ's flock faultlessly, humbly, quietly, and unassumingly. For we shall be guilty of no slight sin if we eject from the episcopate men who have offered the sacrifices with innocence and holiness. Happy, indeed, are those presbyters who have already passed on, and who ended a life of fruitfulness with their task complete. For they need not fear that anyone will remove them from their secure positions. But you, we observe, have removed a number of people, despite their good conduct, from a ministry they have fulfilled with honor and integrity. Your contention and rivalry, brothers, thus touches matters that bear on our salvation. (pp. 62–64)

---

1. See 1 Corinthians 15:23.
2. See Isaiah 60:17.

•

So, then, let us obey his most holy and glorious name and escape the threats which Wisdom has predicted against the disobedient. In that way we shall live in peace, having our confidence in his most holy and majestic name. Accept our advice, and you will never regret it. For as God lives, and as the Lord Jesus Christ lives and the Holy Spirit (on whom the elect believe and hope), the man who with humility and eager considerateness and with no regrets does what God has decreed and ordered will be enlisted and enrolled in the ranks of those who are saved through Jesus Christ. Through him be the glory to God forever and ever. Amen.

If, on the other hand, there be some who fail to obey what God has told them through us, they must realize that they will enmesh themselves in sin and in no insignificant danger. We, for our part, will not be responsible for such a sin. But we will beg with earnest prayer and supplication that the Creator of the universe will keep intact the precise number of his elect in the whole world, through his beloved Child Jesus Christ. It was through him that he called us "from darkness to light," from ignorance to the recognition of his glorious name, to hope on Your name, which is the origin of all creation. (pp. 70–71)

Ignatius of Antioch (ca. 35–ca. 107)

Letter to the Ephesians (ca. 107)*

I do not give you orders as if I were somebody important. For even if I am a prisoner for the Name, I have not yet reached Christian perfection. I am only beginning to be a disciple, so I address you as my fellow student. I needed your coaching in faith, encouragement, endurance, and patience. But since love forbids me to keep silent about you, I hasten to urge you to harmonize your actions with God's mind. For Jesus Christ — that life from which we can't be torn — is the Father's mind, as the bishops too, appointed the world over, reflect the mind of Jesus Christ.

Hence you should act in accord with the bishop's mind, as you surely do. Your presbytery, indeed, which deserves its name and is a credit to God, is as closely tied to the bishop as the strings to a harp. Wherefore your accord and harmonious love is a hymn to Jesus Christ. Yes, one and all, you should form yourselves into a choir, so that, in perfect harmony and taking your pitch from God, you may sing in unison and with one voice to the Father through Jesus Christ. Thus he will heed you, and by your good deeds he will recognize you are members of his Son. Therefore you need to abide in irreproachable unity if you really want to be God's members forever.

If in so short a time I could get so close to your bishop — I do not mean in a natural way, but in a spiritual — how much more do I congratulate you on having

---

*Reprinted from Ignatius of Antioch, *Letter to the Ephesians*, in *Early Christian Fathers*, trans. and ed. Cyril C. Richardson (New York: Macmillan, 1970), 88–89, by permission of Westminster/John Knox Press.

such intimacy with him as the Church enjoys with Jesus Christ, and Jesus Christ with the Father. That is how unity and harmony come to prevail everywhere. Make no mistake about it. If anyone is not inside the sanctuary, he lacks God's bread. And if the prayer of one or two has great avail, how much more that of the bishop and the total Church. He who fails to join in your worship shows his arrogance by the very fact of becoming a schismatic. It is written, moreover, "God resists the proud."[1] Let us, then, heartily avoid resisting the bishop so that we may be subject to God.

The more anyone sees the bishop modestly silent, the more he should revere him. For everyone the Master of the house sends on his business, we ought to receive as the One who sent him. It is clear, then, that we should regard the bishop as the Lord himself.

Ignatius of Antioch, *Letter to the Magnesians* (ca. 107)*

Now, it is not right to presume on the youthfulness of your bishop. You ought to respect him as fully as you respect the authority of God the Father. Your holy presbyters, I know, have not taken unfair advantage of his apparent youthfulness, but in their godly wisdom have deferred to him — nay, rather, not so much to him as to the Father of Jesus Christ, who is everybody's bishop. For the honor, then, of him who loved us, we ought to obey without any dissembling, since the real issue is not that a man misleads a bishop whom he can see, but that he defrauds the One who is invisible. In such a case he must reckon, not with a human being, but with God who knows his secrets.

We have not only to be called Christians, but to *be* Christians. It is the same thing as calling a man a bishop and then doing everything in disregard of him. Such people seem to me to be acting against their conscience, since they do not come to the valid and authorized services. Yes, everything is coming to an end, and we stand before this choice — death or life — and everyone will go "to his own place."[2] One might say similarly, there are two coinages, one God's the other the world's. Each bears its own stamp — unbelievers that of this world; believers, who are spurred by love, the stamp of God the Father through Jesus Christ. And if we do not willingly die in union with his Passion, we do not have his life in us.

I believed, then, that I saw your whole congregation in these people I have mentioned, and loved you all. Hence I urge you to aim to do everything in godly agreement. Let the bishop preside in God's place, and the presbyters take the place of the apostolic council, and let the deacons (my special favorites) be entrusted with the ministry of Jesus Christ who was with the Father from eternity and appeared at the end [of the world].

Taking, then, the same attitude as God, you should all respect one another. Let no one think of his neighbor in a carnal way; but always love one another

---

1. See Proverbs 3:34.

*Reprinted from Ignatius of Antioch, *Letter to the Magnesians,* in *Early Christian Fathers,* trans. and ed. Cyril C. Richardson (New York: Macmillan, 1970), 95–96, by permission of Westminster/John Knox Press.

2. See Acts 1:25.

in the spirit of Jesus Christ. Do not let there be anything to divide you, but be in accord with the bishop and your leaders. Thus you will be an example and a lesson of incorruptibility.

As, then, the Lord did nothing without the Father (either on his own or by the apostles) because he was at one with him, so you must not do anything without the bishop and presbyters. Do not, moreover, try to convince yourselves that anything done on your own is commendable. Only what you do together is right. Hence you must have one prayer, one petition, one mind, one hope, dominated by love and unsullied joy — that means you must have Jesus Christ. You cannot have anything better than that.

The *Didache* (ca. 110)*

Now about the apostles and prophets: Act in line with the gospel precept.[1] Welcome every apostle on arriving, as if he were the Lord. But he must not stay beyond one day. In case of necessity, however, the next day too. If he stays three days, he is a false prophet. On departing, an apostle must not accept anything save sufficient food to carry him till his next lodging. If he asks for money, he is a false prophet.

While a prophet is making ecstatic utterances, you must not test or examine him. For "every sin will be forgiven," but this sin "will not be forgiven."[2] However, not everybody making ecstatic utterances is a prophet, but only if he behaves like the Lord. It is by their conduct that the false prophet and the [true] prophet can be distinguished. For instance, if a prophet marks out a table in the Spirit, he must not eat from it. If he does, he is a false prophet. Again, every prophet who teaches the truth but fails to practice what he preaches is a false prophet. But every attested and genuine prophet who acts with a view to symbolizing the mystery of the Church, and does not teach you to do all he does, must not be judged by you. His judgment rests with God. For the ancient prophets too acted in this way. But if someone says in the Spirit, "Give me money, or something else," you must not heed him. However, if he tells you to give for others in need, no one must condemn him.

Everyone "who comes" to you "in the name of the Lord"[3] must be welcomed. Afterward, when you have tested him, you will find out about him, for you have insight into right and wrong. If it is a traveler who arrives, help him all you can. But he must not stay with you more than two days, or, if necessary, three. If he wants to settle with you and is an artisan, he must work for his living. If, however, he has no trade, use your judgment in taking steps for him to live with you as a Christian without being idle. If he refuses to do this, he is trading on Christ. You must be on your guard against such people.

---

*Reprinted from *The Didache*, in *Early Christian Fathers*, trans. and ed. Cyril C. Richardson (New York: Macmillan, 1970), 176–78, by permission of Westminster/John Knox Press.

1. See Matthew 10:40, 41.
2. See Matthew 12:31.
3. See Matthew 21:9.

Every genuine prophet who wants to settle with you "has a right to his support." Similarly, a genuine teacher himself, just like a "workman, has a right to his support."[4] Hence take all the first fruits of vintage and harvest, and of cattle and sheep, and give these first fruits to the prophets. For they are your high priests. If, however, you have no prophet, give them to the poor. If you make bread, take the first fruits and give in accordance with the precept. Similarly, when you open a jar of wine or oil, take the first fruits and give them to the prophets. Indeed, of money, clothes, and of all your possessions, take such first fruits as you think right, and give in accordance with the precept....

You must, then, elect for yourselves bishops and deacons who are a credit to the Lord, men who are gentle, generous, faithful, and well tried. For their ministry to you is identical with that of the prophets and teachers. You must not, therefore, despise them, for along with the prophets and teachers they enjoy a place of honor among you.

Furthermore, do not reprove each other angrily, but quietly, as you find it in your gospel. Moreover, if anyone has wronged his neighbor, nobody must speak to him, and he must not hear a word from you, until he repents. Say your prayers, give your charity, and do everything just as you find it in the gospel of our Lord.

Irenaeus of Lyons (ca. 130–202)

Against Heresies (ca. 185)*

Now the Church, although scattered over the whole civilized world to the end of the earth, received from the apostles and their disciples its faith in one God, the Father Almighty, who made the heaven, and the earth, and the seas, and all that is in them, and in one Christ Jesus, the Son of God, who was made flesh for our salvation, and in the Holy Spirit, who through the prophets proclaimed the dispensations of God — the comings, the birth of a virgin, the suffering, the resurrection from the dead, and the bodily reception into the heavens of the beloved, Christ Jesus our Lord, and his coming from the heavens in the glory of the Father to restore all things, and to raise up all flesh, that is, the whole human race, so that every knee may bow, of things in heaven and on earth and under the earth, to Christ Jesus our Lord and God and Savior and King, according to the pleasure of the invisible Father, and every tongue may confess him, and that he may execute righteous judgment on all. The spiritual powers of wickedness, and the angels who transgressed and fell into apostasy, and the godless and wicked and lawless and blasphemers among men he will send into the eternal fire. But to the righteous and holy, and those who have kept his commandments and have remained in his love, some from the beginning [of life] and some since their repentance, he will by his grace give life incorrupt, and will clothe them with eternal glory.

---

4. See Matthew 10:10.

*Reprinted from Irenaeus, *Against Heresies,* in *Early Christians Fathers,* trans. and ed. Cyril C. Richardson (New York: Macmillan, 1970), 360–61, by permission of Westminster/John Knox Press.

Having received this preaching and this faith, as I have said, the Church, although scattered in the whole world, carefully preserves it, as if living in one house. She believes these things [everywhere] alike, as if she had but one heart and one soul, and preaches them harmoniously, teaches them, and hands them down, as if she had but one mouth. For the languages of the world are different, but the meaning of the [Christian] tradition is one and the same. Neither do the churches that have been established in Germany believe otherwise, or hand down any other tradition, nor those among the Iberians, nor those among the Celts, nor in Egypt, nor in Libya, nor those established in the middle parts of the world. But as God's creature, the sun, is one and the same in the whole world, so also the preaching of the truth shines everywhere, and illumines all who wish to come to the knowledge of the truth. Neither will one of those who preside in the churches who is very powerful in speech say anything different from these things, for no one is above [his] teacher, nor will one who is weak in speech diminish the tradition. For since the faith is one and the same, he who can say much about it does not add to it, nor does he who can say little diminish it.

Cyprian of Carthage (d. 258)

"Unity of the Catholic Church" (ca. 251)*

The Lord says to Peter: "I say unto thee that thou art Peter, and upon this rock I will build my Church; and the gates of hell shall not prevail against it. I will give unto thee the keys of the kingdom of heaven: and whatsoever thou shalt bind on earth shall be bound in heaven; and whatsoever thou shalt loose on earth shall be loosed also in heaven."[1] He builds the Church upon one man. True, after the resurrection he assigned the like power to all the apostles, saying: "As the Father hath sent me, even so send I you. Receive ye the Holy Ghost: whose soever sins ye remit, they shall be remitted unto him; whose soever ye retain, they shall be retained."[2] Despite that, in order to make unity manifest, he arranged by his own authority that this unity should, from the start, take its beginning from one man. Certainly the rest of the apostles were exactly what Peter was; they were endowed with an equal share of office and power. But there was unity at the beginning before any development, to demonstrate that the Church of Christ is one. This one Church is also intended in the Song of Songs, when the Holy Spirit says, in the person of the Lord: "My dove, my perfect one, is but one: she is the only one of her mother, the choice one of her that bare her."[3] Can one who does not keep this unity of the Church believe that he keeps the faith? Can one who resists and struggles against the Church be sure that he is in the Church? For the blessed apostle Paul gives the same teaching and declares the same mystery of unity when

---

*From Cyprian of Carthage, "Unity of the Catholic Church," chapters 4–7 in *Early Latin Theology*, trans. and ed. S. L. Greenslade (Philadelphia: Westminster Press, 1956), 126–28.

1. Matthew 16:18–19.
2. John 20:21–23.
3. Song of Songs 6:9.

he says: "There is one body and one Spirit, one hope of your calling, one Lord, one faith, one baptism, one God."[4]

It is particularly incumbent upon those of us who preside over the Church as bishops to uphold this unity firmly and to be its champions, so that we may prove the episcopate also to be itself one and undivided. Let no one deceive the brotherhood with lies or corrupt the true faith with faithless treachery. The episcopate is a single whole, in which each bishop's share gives him a right to, and a responsibility for, the whole. So is the Church a single whole, though she spreads far and wide into a multitude of churches as her fertility increases. We may compare the sun, many rays but one light, or a tree, many branches but one firmly rooted trunk. When many streams flow from one spring, although the bountiful supply of water welling out has the appearance of plurality, unity is preserved in the source. Pluck a ray from the body of the sun, and its unity allows no division of the light. Break a branch from the tree, and when it is broken off it will not bud. Cut a stream off from its spring, and when it is cut off it dries up. In the same way the Church, bathed in the light of the Lord, spreads her rays throughout the world, yet the light everywhere diffused is one light and the unity of the body is not broken. In the abundance of her plenty she stretches her branches over the whole earth, far and wide she pours her generously flowing streams. Yet there is one head, one source, one mother boundlessly fruitful. Of her womb we are born, by her milk we are nourished, by her breath we are quickened.

The bride of Christ cannot be made an adulteress. She is undefiled and chaste. She knows but one home, she guards with virtuous chastity the sanctity of one bed-chamber. It is she who keeps us for God and seals for the kingdom the sons she has borne. If you abandon the Church and join yourself to an adulteress, you are cut off from the promises of the Church. If you leave the Church of Christ you will not come to Christ's rewards, you will be an alien, an outcast, an enemy. You cannot have God for your father unless you have the Church for your mother. If you could escape outside Noah's Ark, you could escape outside the Church. The Lord warns us, saying, "He that is not with me is against me; and he that gathereth not with me, scattereth."[5] To break the peace and concord of Christ is to go against Christ. To gather somewhere outside the Church is to scatter Christ's Church. The Lord says, "I and the Father are one," and again, of Father Son, and Holy Spirit it is written: "And the three are one."[6] Can you believe that this unity, which originates in the immutability of God and coheres in heavenly mysteries, can be broken in the Church and split by the divorce of clashing wills? He who does not keep this unity does not keep the law of God, nor the faith of the Father and the Son — nor life and salvation.

In the Gospel there is a proof of this mystery of unity, this inseparable bond of harmony, when the coat of the Lord Jesus Christ is not cut or rent at all. The garment is received whole and the coat taken into possession unspoilt and undivided by those who cast lots for Christ's garment, asking who should put on Christ. Holy Scripture says of this: "But for the coat, because it was not sewn but

4. Ephesians 4:4–6.
5. Matthew 12:30.
6. John 10:30; 1 John 5:7.

woven from the top throughout, they said to each other, Let us not rend it, but cast lots for it, whose it shall be."[7] He showed a unity which came from the top, that is from heaven and the Father, a unity which could by no means be rent by one who received and possessed it. Its wholeness and unity remained solid and unbreakable forever.

Augustine of Hippo (354–430)

"On Baptism, against the Donatists" (401), Book 5, Chapters 27–28*

And in that the Church is thus described in the Song of Songs, "A garden enclosed is my sister, my spouse; a spring shut up, a fountain sealed, a well of living water; thy plants are an orchard of pomegranates, with pleasant fruits" [Song 4:12–13]; I dare not understand this save of the holy and just — not of the covetous, and defrauders, and robbers, and usurers, and drunkards, and the envious, of whom we yet both learn most fully from Cyprian's letters, as I have often shown, and teach ourselves, that they had baptism in common with the just, in common with whom they certainly had not Christian charity. For I would that someone would tell me how they "crept into the garden enclosed and the fountain sealed," of whom Cyprian bears witness that they renounced the world in word and not in deed, and that yet they were within the Church. For if they both are themselves there, and are themselves the bride of Christ, can she then be as she is described, "without spot or wrinkle" [Eph. 5:27], and is the fair dove defiled with such a portion of her members? Are these the thorns among which she is a lily, as it is said in the same Song? So far, therefore, as the lily extends, so far does "the garden enclosed and the fountain sealed," namely, though all those just persons who are Jews inwardly in the circumcision of the heart (for "the king's daughter is all glorious within" [Ps. 45:13]), in whom is the fixed number of the saints predestined before the foundation of the world. But that multitude of thorns, whether in secret or in open separation, is pressing on it from without, above number. "If I would declare them," it is said, "and speak of them, they are more than can be numbered" [Ps. 40:5]. The number, therefore, of the just persons, "who are the called according to His purpose" [Rom. 8:28], of whom it is said, "The Lord knoweth them that are His" [2 Tim. 2:19], is itself "the garden enclosed, the fountain sealed, a well of living water, the orchard of pomegranates with pleasant fruits." Of this number some live according to the Spirit, and enter on the excellent way of charity; and when they "restore a man that is overtaken in a fault in the spirit of meekness, they consider themselves, lest they also be tempted" [Gal. 6:1]. And when it happens that they also are themselves overtaken, the affection of charity is but a little checked, and not extinguished; and again rising up and being kindled afresh, it is restored to its former course. For

---

7. John 19:23–24.

*Reprinted from *A Select Library of the Nicene and Post-Nicene Fathers of the Christian Church*, ed. Philip Schaff, vol. 4: *St. Augustine: The Writings against the Manichaeans and against the Donatists* (Grand Rapids, Mich., 1979), 476–78, by permission of the William B. Eerdmans Publishing Company.

they know how to say, "My soul melteth for heaviness: strengthen thou me according unto Thy word" [Ps. 119:28]. But when "in anything they be otherwise minded, God shall reveal even this unto them" [Phil. 3:15] if they abide in the burning flame of charity, and do not break the bond of peace. But some who are yet carnal, and full of fleshly appetites, are instant in working out their progress; and that they may become fit for heavenly food, they are nourished with the milk of the holy mysteries, they avoid in the fear of God whatever is manifestly corrupt even in the opinion of the world, and they strive most watchfully that they may be less and less delighted with worldly and temporal matters. They observe most constantly the rule of faith which has been sought out with diligence; and if in aught they stray from it, they submit to speedy correction under Catholic authority, although, in Cyprian's words, they be tossed about, by reason of their fleshly appetite, with the various conflicts of fantasies. There are some also who as yet live wickedly, or even lie in heresies or the superstitions of the Gentiles, and yet even then "the Lord knoweth them that are His." For, in that unspeakable foreknowledge of God, many who seem to be without are in reality within, and many who seem to be within yet really are without. Of all those, therefore, who, if I may so say, are inwardly and secretly within, is that "enclosed garden" composed, "the fountain sealed, a well of living water, the orchard of pomegranates, with pleasant fruits." The divinely imparted gifts of these are partly peculiar to themselves, as in this world the charity that never faileth, and in the world to come eternal life; partly they are common with evil and perverse men, as all the other things in which consist the holy mysteries.

Hence therefore, we have now set before us an easier and more simple consideration of that ark of which Noah was the builder and pilot. For Peter says that in the ark of Noah, "few, that is, eight souls, were saved by water. The like figure whereunto even baptism doth also now save us (not the putting away of the filth of the flesh, but the answer of a good conscience towards God)" [1 Pet. 3:20–21]. Wherefore, if those appear to men to be baptized in Catholic unity who renounce the world in words only and not in deeds, how do they belong to the mystery of this ark in whom there is not the answer of a good conscience? Or how are they saved by water, who, making a bad use of holy baptism, though they seem to be within, yet persevere to the end of their days in a wicked and abandoned course of life? Or how can they fail to be saved by water, of whom Cyprian himself records that they were in time past simply admitted to the Church with the baptism which they had received in heresy? For the same unity of the ark saved them, in which no one has been saved except by water. For Cyprian himself says, "The Lord is able of His mercy to grant pardon, and not to sever from the gifts of His Church those who, being in all simplicity admitted to the Church, have fallen asleep within her pale."[1] If not by water, how in the ark? If not in the ark, how in the Church? But if in the Church, certainly in the ark; and if in the ark, certainly by water. It is therefore possible that some who have been baptized without may be considered, through the foreknowledge of God, to have been really baptized within, because within the water begins to be profitable to them unto salvation; nor can

---

1. See Cyprian, *Epistle of Cyprian to Jubaianus* 73:23.

they be said to have been otherwise saved in the ark except by water. And again, some who seemed to have been baptized within may be considered, through the same foreknowledge of God, more truly to have been baptized without, since, by making a bad use of baptism, they die by water, which then happened to no one who was outside the ark. Certainly it is clear that, when we speak of within and without in relation to the Church, it is the position of the heart that we must consider, not that of the body, since all who are within in the heart are saved in the unity of the ark through the same water, through which all who are in heart without, whether they are also in body without or not, die as enemies of unity. As therefore it was not another but the same water that saved those who were placed within the ark, and destroyed those who were left without the ark, so it is not by different baptism, but by the same, that good Catholics are saved, and bad Catholics or heretics perish.

– 5 –

The Medieval and Reformation Period

INTRODUCTION

The papacy of Gregory the Great (590–604) signals a new era in the development of Roman primacy and reflects the orientation of church organization for the medieval period. Under Gregory the church asserted itself as an important temporal and spiritual force, engaging in diplomatic relations, initiating missionary movements, and expanding its pastoral duties within the city of Rome itself. With the breakdown of secular government in Rome, Gregory increasingly stepped in to mediate in the problems of urban life. In addition to managing the growing papal estates, Gregory was concerned about grain distribution to the poor and the expansion of monasticism as a stabilizing force throughout Europe. In 596 he sent a band of monks under a Sicilian Benedictine named Augustine to England, which led to the conversion of King Ethelbert and mass conversions thereafter. Augustine was consecrated a bishop, and slowly Christian churches replaced earlier places of worship. Two key developments for western Europe came out of this period. First, as the papally directed church continued to develop westward, its ties to Constantinople and the East diminished. Second, practically and administratively, the papacy had asserted a new role for itself in Europe, the role of Roman primacy.

While later popes did not always pursue the broad program of Gregory the Great with the same consistency or intensity, the eighth century manifested some further development in papal alliances with secular leaders. During the mid–eighth century there were two important European powers near Rome to whom the papacy looked for military assistance. The Lombards, who had established a kingdom in northern Italy, defended Pope Gregory II (715–31) from attack by the emperor Leo V. Later, an alliance between Pope Zachary (741–52) and the Frankish ruler Pepin provided the royal Frankish house with a legitimacy and divine sanction it had lacked. In 755 the Franks defended the papacy from attack by the Lombards, who were trying to extend their control of Italy. This conflict definitively established papal control over central Italy and set the pope up as an independent monarch.

Pepin's son Charles, known as Charlemagne (reigned 768–814), forever changed the course of European political history, and, thus, the destiny of the church. Massive military victories throughout the 770s allowed him to change the Frankish kingdom into an empire, and Charlemagne was coronated Holy Roman Emperor in 800. There are differing accounts of this coronation, which give the papacy a role of greater or lesser importance; however, it symbolized the

95

emergence of a new order to western Christianity, one in which popes and emperors cooperated or rivaled one another for power, but never ignored one another. Further, the imperial court as Charlemagne developed it gave Christianity a new sphere of influence with regard to intellectual life and culture.

Throughout the rest of the medieval period papal relationships with secular leaders would take up as much time as the internal administration of the church. Assertion of papal power forms a major theme in papal documents of this period, and the historian Brian Tierney characterizes the medieval period as a time when "conflicts between kings and popes...merged into one another in such a fashion that we may regard them all as changing aspects of one long, continuing crisis."[1] The "crisis period" to which Tierney refers begins around 1050, with the establishment of the college of cardinals and the reform and reorganization of other church structures. Prior to that period, ecclesiology was not a major theoretical concern. It was enough for church structures to have been maintained after repeated European invasions by the Vikings and Muslims in the ninth century, and the Magyars throughout the early tenth century. Indeed, ironically, the popes began to reassert their power in the eleventh century only after Emperor Henry III of Germany had traveled to Rome, deposed three rival claimants for the papacy, and installed his own candidate for pope in 1046. Leo IX, pope from 1049 to 1054, introduced a series of reforms which centralized ecclesiastical power and established a reforming party in Rome which would continue to assert papal authority throughout Europe. The major reforms Leo accomplished included stronger attempts to enforce clerical celibacy, elimination of simony (the purchase of ecclesiastical titles), and the establishment of the college of cardinals to advise the papacy. Leo held a series of synods in Rome and traveled throughout Europe to meet with bishops and clergy regarding his reform program.

The papal reform program initiated by Leo IX ran into significant obstacles in the mid–eleventh century during a conflict known as the Investiture Controversy. Under Nicholas II (1059–61) the newly established college of cardinals challenged the emperor's claim to "invest" bishops with a ring and a staff, the symbols of their power, and declared that the cardinals would elect the pope. Wresting this privilege from secular leaders would prove extremely difficult, for the bishops had acquired significant wealth and land. The declarations of this synod were put to the test with the relatively simple election of Alexander II (1061–73) and then, more significantly, during the turbulent pontificate of Gregory VII (1073–84).

In February of 1075 a synod in Rome decreed that no bishop or abbot should receive investiture from any secular leader, and shortly afterward Gregory drew up a set of propositions regarding the nature of papal and imperial power. His ideas, known as the *Dictatus papae,* include claims that the pope can depose the emperor, that the pope is beyond secular judgment, and that the Roman church has never erred nor shall it ever err.[2] The *Dictatus papae* itself appears to be a series of headings for a canonical decree without any of the textual justifications that would have completed the document. If this is the proper genre of the

---

1. Brian Tierney, ed., *The Crisis of Church and State, 1050–1300* (Englewood Cliffs, N.J.: Prentice-Hall, 1980), 1.
2. For a copy of the *Dictatus papae* see ibid., 49–50.

document, it is significant that Gregory never ordered canonists to support the propositions. Perhaps, over the course of his conflict with the emperor Henry IV, Gregory realized that, on a practical level, his theories of papal power could never be achieved. When the two leaders entered into open conflict over who was to become the new bishop of Milan, Gregory threatened to excommunicate Henry, and Henry responded by summoning a synod of German bishops who declared Gregory a "usurper." Gregory's threats became real in February 1076 when he excommunicated Henry and declared him "deposed." In January 1077 Henry approached Gregory in the garb of a penitent, and Gregory lifted the excommunication. But the German princes had already recognized a new king, Rudolph of Swabia, and Gregory spent three years deciding whether or not to endorse Rudolph or Henry. In 1080 Gregory renewed the excommunication and deposition of Henry, but his second decree did not carry the authority of the first. Henry summoned the German bishops, who elected a different pope, Clement III, and went to Rome to install him there. Fierce fighting ensued, and in 1084 Clement did indeed arrive at St. Peter's while Gregory took refuge at the nearby palace of Sant Angelo. Henry and Clement were repelled from Rome by the Normans acting on behalf of Gregory. However, the Norman alliance proved disastrous for Rome, for after liberating the pope, the Normans ransacked the city, taking Gregory with them. Gregory died soon afterward, his claims for papal power thoroughly discredited.

For the next two decades debate over the roots and limits of papal and royal authority continued. The spiritual, pastoral, and temporal power and authority of the church were being defined in theory and policy and eventually involved diplomatic ventures. Compromise over the Investiture Controversy was reached at the beginning of the twelfth century during the pontificate of Pascal II (1099–1118). Bishops were to be elected canonically, then they would receive the feudal estates and secular jurisdiction attached to their office from the king, when he was consecrated. The spheres of church and state had come to an uneasy truce. On a practical level the understanding of the church as a temporal as well as a spiritual authority had been established.

Yet not all were comfortable with the temporal power and wealth of church officials. Indeed Pascal II himself suggested that the solution to the investiture crisis was for the bishops to give up their temporal wealth and power, but there was no way to force bishops to comply. Other voices added theological depth to the critique of the church's appropriation of secular privileges. Without any disloyalty to the ecclesiastical structures or officials, the Cistercian abbot Bernard of Clairvaux (1090–1153) attempted to call the church back to its pastoral functions as he applied his exegesis of the Song of Songs to the relationship between Christ and the church. Bernard spoke of the church as the bride of Christ whose gracefulness consists of love, justice, patience, and the other Christian virtues, which she can then impart in the world. The church is also the heavenly Jerusalem, where God dwells with humanity. For Bernard the nature of the church reinforces the nature of humanity; in sermon 27 on the Song of Songs, he describes how individual humans, imitating the form of the church, also become the bride of Christ. Bernard's sermon ably entwines the individual and church into the metaphor of bride, slipping easily from one signifier to another and using scriptural texts to reinforce the commonality of church and person. For example, just as the church "possesses heaven within her" the soul also "provides avenues spacious enough for the God of majesty to walk in." Both realities are made possible by their shared identity as bride of Christ. Yet to be such a bride, both the church and the human person must move beyond human defects: "She certainly cannot afford to be entangled in law-suits nor by worldly cares; she cannot be enslaved by gluttony and sensual pleasures, by the lust of the eyes, the ambition to rule, or by pride in the possession of power."[3]

The pontificate of Innocent III (1198–1216) brought claims to papal power to their highest point. Innocent brought new language to the understanding of the papacy, including the phrase "vicar of Christ." Prior to this time, the pope had been known as the vicar of Peter. As Innocent understood his term the pope was the temporal representative of Christ and as such embodied Christ's saving power for the world. Innocent also articulated the "sun and moon" theory, in which he likened the pope to the sun and secular rulers to the moon, asserting that, just as the moon derived its light from the sun, so all authority on earth was ultimately derived from the pope. The Fourth Lateran Council, held in 1215, affirmed this understanding of the church, laying out rules for the administration and reception of the sacraments and requiring Christians to receive the Eucharist at least once a year.

Within the universities, theologians developed and analyzed the meaning of the church as the mystical body of Christ, particularly as such an understanding related to salvation. Just as we have seen in the thought of Bernard of Clairvaux, ecclesiology for Thomas Aquinas (1225–74) was a field which bound together several theological perspectives. For Thomas, the doctrine of the church was intertwined with the sacramental theology he was constructing out of the ideas of Augustine and Aristotle. The church on earth derives its being from Christ's suffering, as he explains in the *Summa theologiae*: "From the side of Christ, sleeping on the cross, the sacraments flowed — namely, blood and water — on which the Church was established."[4] And, in his *Exposition on the Apostles' Creed*, Aquinas explains that the second attribute of the church (among the attributes of one, holy, catholic, and apostolic), its holiness, is rooted in the cleansing power of Christ's blood. Another important feature of the church is its function to teach correct doctrine. Both elements, sacraments and doctrine, keep the church holy and unified. Similarly, the apostolic nature of the church is affirmed because the church teaches apostolic truths. Aquinas saw problems of schism similar to those which Cyprian and Augustine confronted, and he revived much of this line of thought, moving ecclesiology away from questions of church and state to explore the pastoral functions of the church and to relate questions of salvation and sanctification directly to discussions of the church's nature.

The early fourteenth century saw another reassertion of papal monarchy under Boniface VIII (1294–1303), but the results were disastrous, and the theory of pa-

---

3. Bernard of Clairvaux, *Sermons on the Song of Songs,* trans. Kilian Walsh (Kalamazoo, Mich.: Cistercian Publications, 1976), 2:83.

4. Thomas Aquinas, *Summa theologiae,* Ia, q. 92, art. 3.

pal monarchy never recovered. Boniface first came into conflict with the king of France, Philip IV, in 1296, when he issued a bull, *Clericis laicos,* forbidding the clergy from paying taxes to the prince without papal approval. Philip's response was to ban the export of gold and silver from France, effectively cutting off an important source of papal revenue. Eventually Boniface capitulated, allowing Philip to tax the clergy in a state of emergency, which the king could declare as he saw fit. However, the two leaders engaged in an extensive conflict beginning in 1301, which led to propaganda campaigns on both sides. In November 1302 Boniface issued a famous bull, *Unam sanctam,* in which he asserted the temporal authority of the church. The bull used the attribute of "oneness" to assert that from the one head of the one church stemmed both material and spiritual power, "the one exercised for the church, the other exercised by the church." Connecting salvation with this one church, Boniface admonished, "It is altogether necessary to salvation for every human creature to be subject to the Roman Pontiff."[5] Boniface's claims fell on deaf ears; in 1303, as he considered excommunicating Philip, Boniface was confronted by some of Philip's supporters outside of Rome. The mob refrained from harming the pope but looted his possessions and held him until nobles intervened. Boniface died shortly after this humiliation at Anagni.

The doctrine of papal sovereignty, particularly as it was expressed in *Unam sanctam,* generated a significant amount of comment and criticism, most notably from Marsilius of Padua (ca. 1275–1342) and William of Ockham (ca. 1285–1347). Marsilius of Padua, who was the rector of the University of Paris, wrote a work called *The Defender of the Peace,* in which he argued that power originated within the human community, through which it was passed on to those who represented the community. Marsilius applied this theory to both the church and the state, arguing that the hierarchical church was a human invention and that the papacy derived its power not from God but from the faithful, who could depose a pope. Marsilius reversed the channel of authority which papal monarchists had asserted; instead of the pope being higher than humanity but lower than God, it was the people who retained that position. In his critique of Boniface VIII, Marsilius asserted that only the general council of Christians, under the guidance of the Holy Spirit, could excommunicate since their judgment could not be "perverted by ignorance or malice."[6] Further, he argued that the papacy had become corrupted by its acquisition of temporal power and ought to return to the simplicity of Christ and the apostles. Pope John XXII condemned Marsilius on October 27, 1327, for his theories on the nature of power. But Marsilius's ideas, once expressed, would not disappear.

The nominalist movement, particularly the thought of William of Ockham, contributed to further developments in ecclesiology. Aquinas's system had established an essential role for the church as mediator of grace in the sacraments, through which God could be experienced and known. But by reinforcing the contingency of the world and the sacramental system Ockham's thought introduced a certain anxiety about salvation. For Ockham, God was not only unknowable

---

5. Boniface VIII, *Unam sanctam,* in Tierney, *Crisis of Church and State,* 189.
6. Marsilius of Padua, *The Defender of the Peace,* trans. Alan Gewirth (Buffalo, N.Y.: University of Toronto Press, 1980), 294.

by definition, but even recourse to the sacraments allowed individuals to respond only to God's ordained will, not God's absolute will, which would not be bound to any ecclesiastical system. Therefore, Ockham disputed both the inerrancy of the papacy and the inerrancy of a council. Ockham was summoned to the papal court in Avignon in 1324; after that point he called upon John XXII (1316–34) to step down from the papacy. Ockham was disturbed by the pope's condemnation of the spiritualist Franciscan position, which held to a more rigorist view of poverty, understanding it to be a critical sign of apostolic (and therefore ecclesial) authenticity. In 1323 John XXII had issued a bull, *Cum inter nonnullos,* which declared that Jesus and the apostles had not lived in poverty and had possessed goods both privately and in common. John XXII's bull invalidated the Spiritualists' interpretation of poverty, although it had been previously recognized by Gregory IX and Nicholas III. In Ockham's view John XXII had abused his authority as pope and had demonstrated that not even the pope was immune from heterodoxy. Ockham was excommunicated by John XXII in 1328.

Although few Christians called upon the pope to resign his office, many were concerned about the corrupted state of the church and its ability to minister credibly. Mystics and reformers like Bridget of Sweden (1302–72) and Catherine of Siena (1347–80) appealed to the papacy to move the papal curia back to Rome, believing that this move was necessary to establish its pastoral authenticity. In letters and treatises they described direct revelations they had received from God which expressed what they claimed was God's will for the church. In her *Dialogue* Catherine of Siena denounced in no uncertain terms what she called the selfishness of the clergy, which had "poisoned the whole world as well as the mystic body of holy Church and made the garden of this bride a field overgrown with putrid weeds."[7] In January 1377 Gregory XI returned to Rome, but the return alone would not accomplish the ecclesiastical reforms people like Catherine of Siena advocated. Indeed, when Gregory died in 1378, the papal curia, sharply divided, elected an Italian prelate, breaking with the pattern of previous decades of electing French candidates. When the new pope, Urban VI, announced his intention to reform the curia, the French cardinals withdrew from Rome and declared that they had elected Urban under duress; indeed, during the election in 1377 the cardinals had been surrounded by an Italian mob and had been told by Roman officials that their safety could not be guaranteed if they elected a Frenchman. Thus they announced that the election of Urban VI was invalid, and they elected a French candidate, Clement VII, in his place. Clement took up residence in Avignon, and a thirty-nine-year papal schism began.

The crisis of the papal schism spurred further reflection on the nature of the church, but this reflection had an urgent, practical focus: what could be done to move the church back to the unity that was one of its essential hallmarks? The clearest theoretical solution was to emphasize that Christ, not his vicar, was the single head of the church and, on a practical level — once appeals to rival popes failed to persuade them to give up their claim to the papal office — to establish a council as the governing body of the church during the crisis. However, the first

---

attempt to resolve the papal schism by means of a council, the Council of Pisa, resulted in the emergence of three popes. As the crisis worsened, treatises were written to address the problem.

Two important thinkers to express conciliarist perspectives were Jean Gerson (1363–1429) and Dietrich of Niem (ca. 1340–1418). Gerson, chancellor of the University of Paris, wrote several treatises on the church and was an important figure at the Council of Constance (1414–18). In 1391 Gerson wrote *The Union of the Church,* and in 1409 he wrote *The Unity of the Church.* In 1410 Dietrich of Niem wrote *The Ways of Uniting and Reforming the Church in a Universal Council.* While both theorists advocated a speedy resolution of the schism, they also argued that the oneness of the church could not be destroyed by the current lack of union within the church. Thus they rooted the oneness of the church in its universality as represented by the general councils of the church. For Dietrich of Niem, such councils kept the pope from usurping the power which belongs only to the universal church.

Others were articulating views of the church which challenged the traditional understanding of the church's oneness. John Wycliffe (ca. 1330–84), the English theologian, in reflecting upon the ecclesiastical situation, revived a version of the Donatist position, in which corrupt and sinful church officials lost their ability to exercise power within the church. Wycliffe's positions derived from two premises: first, that there existed a true church contained within the larger church, and second, that church offices were not divinely instituted, nor was the church, as it currently was structured, of divine origin. The true church consisted of the predestined, and it existed simultaneously with the larger church. Only those who were part of the true church could have any sacramental or jurisdictional authority, since those who knowingly violated God's will could not presume to exercise power on God's behalf. Wycliffe's ideas were particularly influential in Bohemia and at the University of Prague. There Jan Hus (ca. 1373–1415), the Czech reformer condemned to execution at the Council of Constance, wrote *On the Church* in 1413.

The Council of Constance succeeded in ending the papal schism by deposing John XXIII, the second Pisan pope, recognizing the abdication of the Roman pope, Gregory XII, and deposing the Avignon pope, Benedict XIII. They elected Martin V on November 11, 1417. The council was less successful in enacting its decree *Frequens,* which declared that church governance required the frequent convocation of councils. Although councils were called in Pavia (1423), Basel (1431), and Ferrara/Florence (1438–39), these councils struggled to assert their jurisdiction over the papacy. As historian Steven Ozment describes the church's situation in the early fifteenth century: "A few decades earlier there had been schismatic popes; now there were schismatic councils. When schismatic popes reigned, a council of the church proved supreme; now, when there were schismatic councils, the pope would prove supreme."[8] By 1460 Pope Pius II had condemned conciliar theories in his bull *Execrabilis.*

---

8. Steven Ozment, *The Age of Reform, 1250–1550: An Intellectual and Religious History of Late Medieval and Reformation Europe* (New Haven: Yale University Press, 1980), 175.

One effect of the tension between council and popes was a marked decline in papal revenues.[9] Concurrently, the penitential system was developing into a papally directed indulgence system, whereby Christians could apply to the pope or his representative for pardon for sins.[10] When such "indulgences" (pardons) were granted it was common for the applicant to make a donation to the church in gratitude. During the pontificate of Pope Sixtus IV (1471–84) the potential for increased papal revenue expanded enormously, because Sixtus declared that indulgences would be effective even in purgatory. This move allowed Christians to purchase pardons for their relatives suffering in purgatory. Increased papal revenues helped finance the famous Sistine Chapel in Rome. Many of these late-fifteenth-century developments, coupled with a series of popes who sought temporal rewards through their office, left the authority of the institutional church in a vulnerable state as it faced rising nationalistic orientation in the sixteenth century.

The figure of Martin Luther brought the tensions between the temporal and spiritual orientation of the church to a situation of crisis in the second decade of the sixteenth century. A German Augustinian, Luther's preparation of sermons from the Pauline epistles and his reflection on the nature of justification caused him to react strongly against the sale of indulgences during a 1517 campaign to rebuild the basilica of St. Peter in Rome. Luther rejected the idea that the pope could control the status of someone who was already dead. Reflecting on the nature of indulgences, Luther drafted his Ninety-five Theses, which he sent to the archbishop of Mainz to stimulate discussion. As a result of Luther's theses a public debate between Johann Eck (1486–1543) and Luther's colleague at the University of Wittenberg, Andreas von Carlstadt, was scheduled in Leipzig from June 27 to July 19, 1519. Luther was admitted to the debate after intervention by Eck. As a result of their debate, Luther moved from advocating the reform of the church to attacking its constitution. He soon became a national hero, having articulated about the papacy and the indulgence campaign what many Germans had already thought. In January of 1521 Luther was formally excommunicated; many of his ideas about indulgences had already been declared heretical in the papal bull *Exsurge Domine* of June 1520.

Luther's reflections on the nature of the church emerged from his experience of excommunication from the Roman Catholic Church and his understanding of the process of justification by faith alone. For Luther the hierarchical church existed apart from the true church, which is an invisible, spiritual priesthood of all believers. However, the church could be identified by concrete signs, particularly its preaching of the word of God and its practice of the sacraments of baptism and the Eucharist.

During the 1520s, as Germans debated the ideas of Luther and other reformers, several other positions emerged. Followers of Ulrich Zwingli (1484–1531)

---

9. Ibid., 174: "The plight of popes in the conciliar age is illustrated by the fact that between 1427 and 1436 papal revenues declined by almost two-thirds."

10. It was Pope Clement VI (1342–52) who declared in his bull *Unigenitus* (1343) that the pope could avail himself of the treasury of merit bestowed upon humanity by Christ's death, applying this merit to anyone who requested it.

and many Radical Reformers parted company with Lutheran doctrine and worship. When, in 1530, the Holy Roman Emperor Charles V returned to Germany to unite the empire and to present a solid front against the threat of invasion by the Turks, he called a Diet to review Luther's positions. In preparation, Luther's colleague Philip Melanchthon (1497–1560) prepared a confession of faith, now known as the Augsburg Confession, which answered many of the charges Catholic theologian Johann Eck had leveled against Luther. The Augsburg Confession succinctly synthesized much early Lutheran thought. In Article 7 the confession characterizes the church as the assembly of believers in which the gospel is preached and the sacraments are administered. No hierarchical structure is acknowledged, but rather the elements of gospel, sacraments, and human community signal its authenticity. In a move which reflected how far his years in Spain had taken him from the perspectives of his German subjects, Charles V ordered the Lutherans to return to Catholicism. The Lutherans refused and formed the League of Schmalkald, a group of electors who rejected Charles's authority and formed their own political body. By 1532 the League of Schmalkald was powerful enough to negotiate a pact with Charles: in exchange for their military support in the campaign against the Turks, Protestants were tolerated.

Another important form of Protestantism emerged in the 1530s with the emergence of John Calvin (1509–64). Calvin's studies in Paris and Orleans put him in contact with humanists and reformers. By 1534 he was a vocal proponent of Protestant reform and fled to Basel out of fear of persecution. Influenced by Swiss reformers there, Calvin composed the first version of his *Institutes of the Christian Religion* in 1536; other versions were printed in 1539 and 1559. In the *Institutes* Calvin described the church as the elect, emphasizing their oneness in the body of Christ. These elect are made visible by their "confession of faith, an exemplary life, and participation in the sacraments."[11] Calvin rejected the organization of the Roman church, proposing instead four church offices: pastors, teachers, elders, and deacons. The tasks of these officials rested in preaching the word of God. These ministers represent Christ and are given significant authority, although they are also held to considerable moral accountability.

Another branch of the reform movement, known as the Radical Reformers, developed in opposition both to Roman Catholicism and to the established Protestant churches. Also called Anabaptists, these groups shared many (but not all) of the following characteristics: they were committed to the baptism of mature adults who could affirm their commitment to their faith; they were committed to personal and communal standards of morality; they sought to return to the practices of the New Testament church; and they found most forms of religious and temporal power inconsistent with Christianity. A diverse group, many of their ideas were set down at a meeting of Swiss and German Anabaptists in 1527 in a document known as the Schleitheim Articles. These articles do not address the need for a conscious commitment to the Christian community before baptism can be administered, and they propose a ban on members of the community who fail to live up to the promises they made at baptism. Both of these ideas support the

---

11. Calvin, *Institutes;* see text below.

fourth article, regarding the need for separation from the world. Because individuals entered and remained in the church due to their personal commitment to a moral lifestyle and to the support of other members, the world outside the church was by definition immoral and a source of danger. If the Anabaptists had lost a sense of the universality of the church, they could clearly assert the holiness of the church. Because the Anabaptists posed a threat to Catholic leadership and magisterial reformers alike, they often met with persecution. Jacob Hutter, who emerged as an important Anabaptist leader in the Tirol, eventually sought refuge for himself and his congregation in Moravia but was captured in the fall of 1535 and burned at the stake in 1536 in Innsbruck. While not all Anabaptist groups espoused nonviolence, the communities which endured and remained influential after the sixteenth century did. The Mennonites and Hutterites, in particular, offered attractive ways of being church which saw the church as an intentional community of adults which shared its goods, and through simplicity, pacifism, and charity daily proved its holiness.

In light of the many Protestant developments in northern Europe, Roman Catholicism found itself primarily on the defensive, attempting to reaffirm its traditional ecclesiological perspectives. Although the Council of Trent, which met in three separate sessions from 1545 to 1563, did not discuss ecclesiology explicitly, it affirmed the hierarchical nature of the church and submitted its decrees to the pope for his approval. However, the catechism developed to teach Tridentine decrees did address the doctrine of the church. The church is the body of Christ, a communion of sacraments; it contains the church triumphant (the blessed) as well as the church militant, the faithful who are at "eternal war with those most implacable enemies, the world, the flesh, and the devil."[12] The church militant contains both the wheat and the chaff; it is governed by the Holy Spirit and therefore "cannot err in delivering the discipline of faith and morals."[13] The defensive posture of the Roman Catholic Church through the Council of Trent was indicative of the sixteenth-century tendency to assert and maintain confessional perspectives.

Such confessional allegiances spawned political divisions and played a significant role in civil wars and revolutions. As the sixteenth century came to a close, the oneness of the church could only be affirmed in a spiritual sense, its holiness had been examined and found wanting, its universality was threatened by schisms of many types, and its apostolicity had been interpreted in significantly different ways. The church was passing on to the modern period a diverse and troubled tradition.

---

12. In Eric G. Jay, *The Church: Its Changing Image through Twenty Centuries* (Atlanta: John Knox Press, 1980), 198.
13. Ibid., 200.

T E X T S

Bernard of Clairvaux (1090–1153)

"Sermon 27 on the Song of Songs" (ca. 1145)*

The bride's form must be understood in a spiritual sense, her beauty as something that is grasped by the intellect; it is eternal because it is an image of eternity. Her gracefulness consists of love, and you have read that "love never ends" (1 Cor. 13:8). It consists of justice, for "her justice endures forever" (Ps. 111:3). It consists of patience, and Scripture tells you "the patience of the poor shall not perish forever" (Ps. 9:19). What shall I say of voluntary poverty? Of humility? To the former an eternal kingdom is promised, to the latter an eternal exaltation. To these must be added the holy fear of the Lord that endures for ever and ever; prudence too, and temperance and fortitude and all other virtues; what are they but pearls in the jeweled raiment of the bride, shining with unceasing radiance? I say unceasing, because they are the basis, the very foundation of immortality. For there is no place for immortal and blissful life in the soul except by means and mediation of the virtues. Hence the Prophet, speaking to God who is eternal happiness, says: "Justice and judgment are the foundation of your throne" (Ps. 88:15). And the Apostle says that Christ dwells in our hearts, not in any and every way, but particularly by faith. When Christ, too, was about to ride on the ass, the disciples spread their cloaks underneath him, to signify that our Savior, or his salvation, will not rest in the naked soul until it is clothed with the teaching and discipline of the apostles. Therefore the Church, possessing the promise of happiness to come, now prepares for it by adorning herself in cloth of gold, girding herself with a variety of graces and virtues, in order to be found worthy and capable of the fullness of grace.

Though this visible, material heaven, with its great variety of stars, is unsurpassingly beautiful within the bounds of the material creation, I should not dare to compare its beauty with the spiritual and varied loveliness she received with her first robe when being arrayed in the garments of holiness. But there is a heaven of heavens to which the Prophet refers. "Sing to the Lord who mounts above the heaven of heavens, to the east" (Ps. 67:33-34). This heaven is in the world of the intellect and the spirit; and he who made the heavens by his wisdom, created it to be his eternal dwelling-place, You must not suppose that the bride's affections can find rest outside of this heaven, where she knows her Beloved dwells: for where her treasure is, there her heart is too (see Matt. 6:21). She so yearns for him that she is jealous of those who live in his presence; and since she may not yet participate in the vision that is theirs, she strives to resemble them in the way she lives. By deeds rather than words she proclaims: "Lord, I love the beauty of your house, the place where your glory dwells" (Ps. 25:8).

---

*Reprinted from Bernard of Clairvaux, *Sermons on the Song of Songs*, trans. Kilian Walsh (Kalamazoo, Mich., 1976), 2:76–80, by permission of Cistercian Publications.

She has no objection whatever to being compared to this heaven, made glorious by the marvelous and manifold works of the Creator, that reaches out like a curtain, not over mighty spaces but over the hearts of men. Any distinctions that exist there do not consist of colors but of degrees of bliss. Among its inhabitants we find Angels, Archangels, Virtues, Dominations, Principalities, Powers, Thrones, Cherubim, and Seraphim. (See 1 Cor. 12:28; Eph. 4:11.) These are that heaven's sparkling stars, these are that curtain's shining glories. We are dealing with only one of the curtains of my Solomon, but the one that surpasses all in the radiance of its multiform glory. This immense curtain contains within itself many other curtains of Solomon, for every blessed and saint who dwells there is indeed a curtain of Solomon. They overflow with kindness, their love reaches out till it comes down even to us. Far from begrudging us the glory they enjoy, they want us to share it, and hence find it no burden to accompany us for that purpose, sedulously watching over us and our concerns. They are all spirits whose work is service, sent to help those who will be the heirs of salvation. Therefore, since the multitude of the blessed, taken as a unit, is called the heaven of heavens, so, when taken individually, they are called the heavens of heavens, because each is a heaven, and we may apply to each the words: "You have spread out heaven like a curtain" (Ps. 103:2). You now see, I hope, what these curtains are to which the bride so assuredly compares herself, and to which Solomon they belong.

Contemplate what a glory is hers who compares herself to heaven, even to that heaven who is so much more glorious as he is divine. This is no rashness, taking her comparison from whence her origin comes. For if she compares herself to the tents of Kedar because of her body drawn from the earth, why should she not glory in her likeness to heaven because of the heavenly origin of her soul, especially since her life bears witness to her origin and to the dignity of her nature and her homeland? She adores and worships one God, just like the angels; she loves Christ above all things, just like the angels; she is chaste, just like the angels, and that in the flesh of a fallen race, in a frail body that the angels do not have. But she seeks and savors the things that they enjoy, not the things that are on the earth. What can be a clearer sign of her heavenly origin than that she retains a natural likeness to it in the land of unlikeness, than that as an exile on earth she enjoys the glory of the celibate life, than that she lives like an angel in an animal body? These gifts reveal a power that is more of heaven than of earth. They clearly indicate that a soul thus endowed is truly from heaven. But Scripture is clearer still: "I saw the holy city, the new Jerusalem, coming down out of heaven from God, prepared as a bride adorned for her husband. And I heard a great voice from the throne saying 'Behold the dwelling of God is with men. He will dwell among them'" (Rev. 21:2-3). But why? In order to win a bride for himself from among men. How wonderful this? He came to seek a bride, but did not come without one. He sought a bride, but she was with him. Had he then two brides? Certainly not. "My dove is only one," he says. (See Song 6:8.) Just as he wished to form one flock of the scattered flocks of sheep, that there might be one flock and one shepherd, so, although from the beginning he had for bride the multitude of angels, it pleased him to summon the Church from among men and unite it with the one from heaven, that there might be but the one bride and one Bridegroom. The one from heaven perfects the earthly one; it does not make two. Hence he says: "My perfect one is only one" (Song 6:8). Their likeness makes them one, one now in their similar purpose, one hereafter in the same glory.

These two then have their origin in heaven — Jesus the Bridegroom and Jerusalem the bride. He, in order to be seen by men, "emptied himself taking the form of a servant, being born in the likeness of men" (Phil. 2:7). But the bride — in what form or exterior loveliness, in what guise did St. John see her coming down? Was it perhaps in the company of the angels whom he saw ascending and descending upon the Son of Man? It is more accurate to say that he saw the bride when he looked on the Word made flesh, and acknowledged two natures in the one flesh. For when that holy Emmanuel introduced to earth curriculum of heavenly teaching when we came to know the visible image and radiant comeliness of that supernal Jerusalem, our mother, revealed to us in Christ and by his means, what did we behold if not the bride in the Bridegroom? What did we admire but that same person who is the Lord of glory, the Bridegroom decked with a garland, the bride adorned with her jewels? "He who descended is he also who ascended" (Eph. 4:10), since "no one has ascended into heaven but he who descended from heaven" (John 3:13), the one and same Lord who as head of the Church is the Bridegroom, as body is the bride.

Thomas Aquinas (1225–74)

"Exposition on the Apostles' Creed" (1273)*

As in one single human being there is one soul and one body but many members, so the Catholic Church has one body but many members. The soul animating this body is the Holy Ghost. Hence the Creed, after bidding us believe in the Holy Ghost, adds, the Holy Catholic Church.

Church means congregation. Holy Church is the congregation of believers of which each Christian is a member: draw near to me, ye unlearned; and gather yourselves together into the house of discipline. [Ecclus. 51:23]

The Church has four marks, being one, holy, catholic or universal, and strong or lasting. Heretics lack the first, for because they have invented a variety of sects and are split into factions they do not belong to the Church, which is one: one is my dove; my perfect one is but one. This unity has a threefold cause; it comes from agreement of faith, of hope, of charity. Of faith, for all Christians who belong to the body of the Church believe the same truths: now I beseech you, brethren, by the name of our Lord Jesus Christ, that you all speak the same thing, and that there be no schisms among you. And again, one Lord, one faith, one baptism. Unity of hope, for all are comforted by the same confidence of coming to life eternal: one body and one spirit; as you are called in one hope of your redemption. Unity of charity, for all are bound together in the love of God and

*Reprinted from Thomas Aquinas, "Exposition on the Apostles' Creed," in *Theological Texts,* trans. Thomas Gilby (New York: Oxford University Press, 1955), 340–43. Permission requested.

of one another: the love which thou hast given me, I have given them; that they may be one, even as we are one. The genuineness of this love is shown when the members of the Church care for one another and are compassionate together: doing the truth in charity, we may in all things grow up in him who is the head, even Christ; from whom the whole body, being compacted and fully joined together by that which every joint supplieth, according to the effectual working in the measure of every part, maketh increase of the body unto the edifying of itself in love. According to the grace granted him, each should serve his neighbor; nobody should be despised, nobody should be treated as an outcast, for the Church is like the Ark of Noah, outside of which nobody can be saved.

Then the Church is holy: know you not that you are the temple of God. A church when consecrated is washed — so are the faithful cleansed by the blood of Christ: he hath loved us and washed us from our sins in his own blood. A church is anointed too — so also the faithful receive a spiritual unction for their sanctification, otherwise they would not be Christians. The Christ means the Anointed One. And his unction is the grace of the Holy Spirit: now he that confirmeth you in Christ and hath anointed us in God, who also hath sealed us and given us the pledge of the Spirit in our hearts. Moreover, the Church is holy by the indwelling of the Blessed Trinity: this is the place of awe, none other but the house of God and gate of heaven. There, also, is God invoked: thou, O Lord, art in the midst of us, and we are called by thy name; leave us not. So then, let us guard against defiling our soul with sin: for if any man violate the temple of God, him shall God destroy.

The Church is catholic, that is, universal. First with regard to place: we have received grace and apostleship for obedience to his faith, in all nations. Our Lord commanded us, Go ye into the whole world and preach the gospel to every creature. The Church has three parts, one on earth, a second in heaven, a third in purgatory. The Church is universal with regard to all conditions of human beings; nobody is rejected, whether they be masters or slaves, men or women: there is neither Jew nor Greek, neither bond nor free, neither male nor female. It is universal in time, and those are wrong who allow it a limited span of time, for it began with Abel and will last even to the end of the world: behold, I am with you always, even to the consummation of the world. And even after, for the Church remains in heaven.

Fourthly, the Church is firm, solid as a house on massive foundations. The principal foundation is Christ himself: for other foundation no man can lay but that which is laid, which is Christ Jesus. Secondary foundations are the Apostles and apostolic teaching: hence the Church is called apostolic: the walls of the city had twelve foundations; and in them the names of the Apostles of the Lamb. Its strength is signified by Peter, or Rock, who is its crown. A building is strong when it can never be overthrown though it may be shaken. The Church can never be brought down. Indeed it grows under persecution, and those who attack it are destroyed: whosoever shall fall on this stone shall be broken; but on whomsoever it shall fall, it shall grind him to powder. Nor can the Church be destroyed by errors: men corrupted in mind, reprobate concerning the Faith, but shall proceed no farther, for their folly shall appear to all men. Nor by the temptations of demons, for the Church will stand, a secure place of refuge: the name of the Lord is a strong tower. Though he strives to undermine it, the devil will never succeed: the gates of hell shall not prevail. Only the Church of Peter, to whose lot fell all Italy when the disciples were sent out to preach, has always stood fast in the Faith. While the Faith has disappeared or has partly decayed in other regions, the Church of Peter still flourishes in faith and free from heresy. This is not to be surprised at, for our Lord said to Peter, I have prayed for thee that thy faith fail not, and thou, when thou art converted, confirm thy brethren.

Catherine of Siena (1347–80)

The Dialogue (ca. 1378)*

You will recall that I already told you I would fulfill your desires by giving you refreshment in your labors, that I would satisfy your anguished longings by reforming holy Church through good and holy shepherds. I will do this, as I told you, not through war, not with the sword and violence, but through peace and calm, through my servants' tears and sweat. I have set you as workers in your own and your neighbors' souls and in the mystic body of holy Church. In yourselves you must work at virtue; in your neighbors and in the Church you must work by example and teaching. And you must offer me constant prayer for the Church and for every creature, giving birth to virtue through your neighbors. For I have already told you that every virtue and every sin is realized and intensified through your neighbors. Therefore, I want you to serve your neighbors and in this way share the fruits of your own vineyard.

Never cease offering me the incense of fragrant prayers for the salvation of souls, for I want to be merciful to the world. With your prayers and sweat and tears I will wash the face of my bride, holy Church. I showed her to you earlier as a maiden whose face was all dirtied, as if she were a leper. The clergy and the whole of Christianity are to blame for this because of their sins, though they receive their nourishment at the breast of this bride! But I will tell you about those sins in another place. (pp. 159–60)

•

Now listen well, dearest daughter, for I want to show you the wretchedness of their [my ministers'] lives, so that you and my other servants will have the more reason to offer me humble and constant prayer for them. No matter where you turn, to secular or religious, clerics or prelates, lowly or great, young or old, you see nothing but sin. All of them pelt me with the filth of deadly sin. But their filth harms only themselves, not me.

Up to now I have told you about the excellence of my ministers and the virtues of the good, both to refresh your soul and to make you better appreciate the

---

*Reprinted from Catherine of Siena, *The Dialogue*, trans. Suzanne Noffke (New York, 1980), 159–60, 231–35, by permission of Paulist Press.

wretchedness of these wicked ones and see how deserving they are of greater rebuke and more intolerable punishment. By the same token, my chosen and loved ministers, because they have virtuously used the treasure entrusted to them, deserve a greater reward, deserve to stand as pearls in my sight. It is just the contrary for these wretched ones, for they will reap a cruel punishment.

Do you know, dearest daughter — listen with grieving bitterness of heart — do you know where these have set their principle and foundation? In their own selfish self-centeredness. There is born the tree of pride with its offshoot of indiscretion. So, lacking in discernment as they are, they assume honor and glory for themselves by seeking higher office and adornments and delicacies for their bodies, repaying me with abuse and sin. They take to themselves what is not theirs and give me what is not mine. To me should be given glory and my name should be praised; to themselves is due contempt for their selfish sensuality. They ought to know themselves enough to consider themselves unworthy of the tremendous mystery they have received from me. But they do just the opposite, for, bloated with pride as they are, they never have their fill of gobbling up earthly riches and the pleasures of the world, while they are stingy, greedy, and avaricious toward the poor.

Because of this wretched pride and avarice born of their sensual selfishness, they have abandoned the care of souls and give themselves over completely to guarding and caring for their temporal possessions. They leave behind my little sheep, whom I had entrusted to them, like sheep without a shepherd. They neither pasture nor feed them either spiritually or materially. Spiritually they do administer the sacraments of holy Church (the power of which sacraments can neither be taken away nor lessened by any sin of theirs) but they do not feed them with sincere prayers, with hungry longing for their salvation, with holy and honorable living, nor do they feed their poor subjects with temporal assistance.

I told you they were to distribute their material goods in three portions: one for their own needs, one for the poor, and one for the use of the church. But these do the opposite. Not only do they not give what they are in duty bound to give to the poor, but they rob them through simony and their hankering after money, selling the grace of the Holy Spirit. Some are so mean that they are unwilling to give to the needy the very things I have given them freely so that they might give them to you — unless their hands are filled [with money] or they are plentifully supplied with gift [in return]. They love their subjects for what they can get from them, and no more. They spend all the goods of the Church on nothing but clothes for their bodies. They go about fancily dressed, not like clerics and religious, but like lords or court lackeys. They are concerned about having grand horses, many gold and silver vessels, and well-adorned homes. They have and keep what they ought not, all with huge vanity. Their heart babbles out its disordered vanity, and their whole desire is feasting, making a god of their bellies, eating and drinking inordinately. So they soon fall into impure and lustful living.

Woe, woe to their wretched lives! For what the gentle Word, my only-begotten Son, won with such suffering on the wood of the most holy cross they spend on prostitutes. They devour the souls who were bought with Christ's blood, eating them up in so many wretched ways, and feeding their own children with what belongs to the poor. O you temples of the devils! I appointed you to be earthly angels in this life, but you are devils who have taken up the devils' work! The devils dispense darkness from what is theirs, and administer excruciating torments. With their vexatious temptations they lure souls away from grace to drag them down to the guilt of deadly sin. They exert every effort they can in this. Although no sin can touch the soul who does not want it, they nevertheless do all they can. Thus these wretches, unworthy of being called ministers, are devils incarnate, for by their sins they have patterned themselves after the devils. They perform their task of administering me, the true Light, out of the darkness of deadly sin, and they administer to their subjects and to others the darksomeness of their perverted and evil lives. They are the cause of confusion and suffering to the consciences of those they succeed in dragging down from the state of grace and the way of truth, for by leading them into sin they make them walk in the way of falsehood.

But those who follow them do not in fact have an excuse for their sin, for no one can be forced into deadly sin either by these visible devils or the invisible ones. No one ought to give attention to their lives or copy what they do. Still, as my Truth admonished you in the holy Gospel, you should do as they tell you. This is the teaching given you in the mystic body of holy Church, borne in Holy Scripture, and brought to you by my trumpeters, the preachers whose duty it is to proclaim my word. But the woe that is their just desert, and their evil lives, you are not to imitate. Nor are you to punish them, for in that you would offend me. Leave them their evil lives and take for yourselves their teaching. And leave their punishment to me, for I am the gentle eternal God, and I reward everything good and punish every sin.

Their dignity in being my ministers will not save them from my punishment. Indeed, unless they change their ways, they will be punished more severely than all the others, because they have received more from my kindness. Having sinned so miserably, they are deserving of greater punishment. So you see how they are devils, just as I told you that my chosen ones are angels on earth and do the work of the angels.

I told you that the pearl of justice was luminous in those chosen ones. Now I tell you that the jewel these puny wretches wear over their heart is injustice. This injustice proceeds from and is mounted in their self-centeredness, for because of their selfishness they perpetrate injustice against their own souls and against me, along with their dark lack of discernment. They do not pay me my due of glory, nor do they do themselves the justice of holy and honorable living or desire for the salvation of souls or hunger for virtue. Thus they commit injustice against their subjects and neighbors, and do not correct them for their sins. Indeed, as if they were blind and did not know, because of their perverse fear of incurring others' displeasure, they let them lie asleep in their sickness. They do not consider that by wishing to please creatures they are displeasing both them and me your Creator.

Sometimes they administer correction as if to cloak themselves in this little bit of justice. But they will never correct persons of any importance, even though they may be guilty of greater sin than more lowly people, for fear that these might retaliate by standing in their way or deprive them of their rank and their way of living. They will, however, correct the little people, because they are sure these cannot harm them or deprive them of their rank. Such injustice comes from their wretched selfish love for themselves.

This selfishness has poisoned the whole world as well as the mystic body of holy Church and made the garden of this bride a field overgrown with putrid weeds. That garden was well cultivated when it had true workers, that is, my holy ministers, and it was adorned with an abundance of fragrant flowers, because good shepherds whose own lives were honorable and holy kept their subjects from living evil lives. But that is not the case today. In fact, it is just the opposite, because evil shepherds are causing their subjects to be evil. So this bride is full of thorns, full of a multitude of different sins.

Not that she can herself be infected with the filth of sin or that the power of her holy sacraments can suffer any damage. But those who feed at the breast of this bride imbibe filth into their souls when they surrender the dignity to which I appointed them. Their dignity is not lessened in itself, but only in relation to themselves. Thus because of their sins the blood is disgraced, for laypeople lose the reverence they ought to have for them because of the blood, even though this should not be so. And if they are irreverent, their guilt is not lessened because of their shepherds' sins. It is only that these wretches have become mirrors of wickedness, whereas I had appointed them to be mirrors of virtue. (pp. 231–35)

Martin Luther (1483–1546)

"Sermons on the Catechism" (1528)*

The Christian church is your mother, who gives birth to you and bears you through the Word. And this is done by the Holy Spirit who bears witness concerning Christ. Under the papacy nobody preached that Christ is my Lord in the sense that I would be saved without my works. There it was an evil and human spirit that was preaching. That spirit preaches Christ, it is true, but along with it, preaches works, that through them a man is saved. The Holy Spirit, however, sanctifies by leading you into the holy church and proclaiming to you the Word which the Christian church proclaims.

"The communion of saints." This is one piece with the preceding. Formerly it was not in the Creed. When you hear the word "church" understand it means group [Haufe], as we say in German, the Wittenberg group or congregation [Gemeine], that is a holy, Christian group, assembly, or, in German, the holy, common church, and it is a word which should not be called "communion" [Gemeinschaft], but rather "a congregation" [eine Gemeine]. Someone wanted to explain the first term, "catholic church" [and added the words] *communio sanctorum*, which in German means a congregation of saints, that is, a congregation made up only of saints. "Christian church" and "congregation of saints" are one and the same thing. In other words: I believe that there is a holy group and a con-

---

*From *Luther's Works*, vol. 51: *Sermons: I*, ed. and trans. John W. Doberstein (Philadelphia: Muhlenberg Press), 162–93, as reprinted in *Martin Luther: Selections from His Writings*, ed. John Dillenberger (New York: Doubleday, 1961), 212–14.

gregation made up only of saints. And you too are in this church; the Holy Spirit leads you into it through the preaching of the gospel. Formerly you knew nothing of Christ, but the Christian church proclaimed Christ to you. That is, I believe that there is a holy church [*sanctam Christianitatem*], which is a congregation in which there are nothing but saints. Through the Christian church, that is, through its ministry [*officium*], you were sanctified; for the Holy Spirit uses its ministry in order to sanctify you. Otherwise you would never know and hear Christ.

Then, in this Christian church, you have "the forgiveness of sins." This term includes baptism, consolation upon a deathbed, the sacrament of the altar, absolution, and all the comforting passages [of the gospel]. In this term are included all the ministrations through which the church forgives sins, especially where the gospel, not laws or traditions, is preached. Outside of this church and these sacraments and [ministrations] there is no sanctification. The clerics are outside the church, because they want to be saved through their works. Here we would need to preach about these individually.

The third point is that the Holy Spirit will sanctify you through "the resurrection of the flesh." As long as we live here [on earth] we continue to pray, "Forgive us our trespasses, as we forgive those who trespass against us"; but after death sin will have completely passed away and then the Holy Spirit will continue his work and then my sanctification will be complete. Therefore it will also be life and nothing but life.

This is a brief explanation of the third article, but for you it is obscure, because you do not listen to it. The third article, therefore, is that I believe in the Holy Spirit, that is, that the Holy Spirit will sanctify me and is sanctifying me. Therefore, from the Father I receive creation, from the Son redemption, from the Holy Spirit sanctification. How does he sanctify me? By causing me to believe that there is one, holy church through which he sanctifies me, through which the Holy Spirit speaks and causes the preachers to preach the gospel. The same he gives to you in your heart through the sacraments, that you may believe the Word and become a member of the church. He begins to sanctify now; when we have died, he will complete this sanctification through both "the resurrection of the body" and "the life everlasting." When we [Germans] hear the word "flesh," we immediately think that what is being spoken of is flesh in a meat market. What the Hebrews called "flesh," we call "body"; hence, I believe that our body will rise from death and thus live eternally. Then we will be interred and buried "in dishonor," as 1 Cor. 15[:43] says, but will be raised "in glory."

These latter clauses show the ways in which he sanctifies me, for the Holy Spirit does not justify you outside of the church, as the fanatics, who creep into corners, think. Therefore immediately after the Holy Spirit is placed the Christian church, in which all his gifts are to be found. Through it he preaches, calls you, and makes Christ known to you, and breathes into you the faith that, through the sacraments and God's Word, you will be made free from sin and thus be totally free on earth. When you die, remaining in the church, then he will raise you up and sanctify you wholly. The apostles called him the Holy Spirit because he makes everything holy and does everything in Christendom and through the church. On the other hand, an evil spirit does the opposite. The creation we have had long since and Christ has fulfilled his office; but the Holy Spirit is still at work, because the forgiveness of sins is still not fully accomplished. We are not yet freed from death, but will be after the resurrection of the flesh.

John Calvin (1509–64)

Institutes of the Christian Religion (1559)*

First, we believe in the Holy Catholic Church, that is, the number of the elect, whether they be angels or men (Eph. 1:9–10; Col. 1:16); of men, whether dead or now living; of the living, in whichever lands they dwell or wherever they are scattered throughout the world. There is one Church and society and one people of God, of which Christ our Lord is leader and prince and, as it were, the head of one body; according as they have been chosen in him by virtue of the divine goodness before the foundation of the world, they are all gathered together into the kingdom of God. Now this society is catholic, that is, universal, because one may not find two or three such societies. But all the elect of God are thus united and joined together in Christ, so that just as they depend upon one head, so they may grow together as in one body. By means of this arrangement they band together among themselves as members of the same body. Truly, they are made one, who live at the same time in one faith, hope, love, in the same Spirit of God, having been called to the same inheritance of eternal life (Rom. 12:4–5; 1 Cor. 10:16–17, 12:12–27; Eph. 4:4–6). The Church is also holy because as many soever as have been chosen by the eternal providence to be members of the Church, are sanctified by the Lord (John 17:17–19; Eph. 5:25–32). And so, indeed, this order of the mercy of God is described to us by Paul (Rom. 8:30), that those whom he elected from among men, he might call; that those whom he called, he might justify; that those whom he justified, he might glorify. He calls when he draws to himself his own, manifesting himself to them to be known as their God and Father. He justifies, when he clothes them with the righteousness of Christ, by which also they are adorned for their perfection and they cover their imperfection. And he refreshes them with the blessings of the Holy Spirit by means of which day after day they are cleansed from the corruption of the flesh and regenerated to newness of life, until they appear in his presence entirely holy and immaculate. He will glorify, when the majesty of his kingdom shall be manifested in all and by all. And so when the Lord calls, justifies, glorifies them, he declares nothing else than their eternal election to which he had determined them to be born. Wherefore, no one will ever enter into the glory of the celestial kingdom who has not been called and justified in this way, since, without any exception he has chosen them out of all men, the Lord shows forth and manifests in this way their election....

But since the Church is the people of God's chosen ones, it is not possible that those who truly are members of it should perish in the end, or should be

*Reprinted from *John Calvin: Selections from His Writings*, ed. John Dillenberger (Missoula, Mont., 1975), 295–97, 299–300, 301–2, by permission of Scholars Press.

lost by evil destruction (John 10:28). For their salvation rests upon a support
so certain and solid that even though all the machinery of the universe should
be violently shaken, it could not destroy it or overthrow it. In the first place, it
stands with the election of God, and it can neither fall nor change except with
that eternal wisdom. Therefore, they can stagger and vacillate, they can even fall,
but they cannot be broken, because the Lord interposes his hand: that is what
Paul says (Rom. 11:29). "The gifts and calling of God are without repentance."
Then, those whom the Lord elected he handed over to the faithful protection and
care of Christ his Son, so that "he should not lose one of them but raise them
all at the last day" (John 6:39–40). Under such good care the elect can both
err and fall, but they certainly cannot be lost. Besides, this must be established:
there was no period from the foundation of the world in which the Lord did not
have his Church upon the earth, and there certainly will be no time, even to the
consummation of the world, in which he is not going to have it, just as he himself
promised (Joel 3:20; Ps. 89:29, 35–37; 132:12–18). For although immediately
from the beginning of the human race, on account of Adam's sin, it was corrupted
and marred, from it, however, like as from a polluted mass, God always sanctifies
certain vessels to honor so that there would not be any generation which would
not experience his mercy. Finally, we must believe in the Church in such a way
that resting our trust on the divine goodness, we may be certain that we belong
to it. We trust that we shall be perfectly justified and glorified with the rest of the
elect of God, with whom we have been called and have already been justified in
part. We cannot, of course, comprehend the incomprehensible wisdom of God,
nor does it belong to us to discuss it that we may ascertain who by his eternal
counsel may have been chosen and who may have been rejected (Rom. 11:1–36).
But this is not the task of our faith which is repaid abundantly with this secure
promise, to wit, that God acknowledges as sons those who will receive his only
begotten Son (John 1:12). Who could be so depraved by cupidity that he is not
content to be a son of God and should desire to be something else? (pp. 295–97)

•

But although we cannot know with the certainty of faith who are chosen,
nevertheless since the Scripture describes to us certain infallible distinguishing
marks, as was said before, by means of which we may distinguish the elect and
the sons of God from the reprobates and foreigners, insofar as he wills that we
should know, all those who by a confession of faith, an exemplary life, and participation in the sacraments, confess with us the same Christ and God, ought to
be considered with a certain charitable consideration as elect and members of the
Church. Even though some imperfection should remain in their manners (as no
one on earth is seen to be perfect) provided that they do not caress and please
themselves too much in their vices and expect something favorable from them, it
will happen that under the guidance of God they will continuously make progress
until divested of every imperfection they arrive at the eternal blessedness of the
elect. For by means of these distinguishing marks and signs the Scripture defines
for us the elect of God, the sons of God, the people of God, the Church of God,
so that we might know them. But those who do not agree with us in the same

faith or, even if they hold the confession with their lips nevertheless deny with their actions the God whom they confess with their mouth (as we see them in every aspect of life accursed and lost, drunk with the desire to be sinning, asleep and unaware of their evil deeds), they thus signify clearly that they are not, for the present, members of the Church. For this purpose excommunications have been established, by which those are disowned and expelled from the community of the faithful who falsely plead the faith of Christ, those who because of the wantonness of their life, and their unbridled passion in sinning, are not anything else than that scandal of the Church and unworthy, therefore, to glory in the name of Christ (1 Cor. 5:1–5; Matt. 18:15–19; 1 Tim. 1:20). In the first place, it would be outrageous to God, if they were named among Christians; it would be as if his holy Church were all together a conspiracy of evil and reprobate men. In the second place, they must be excommunicated lest by the example of their perverse life they should corrupt others because of frequent intercourse. Finally, that they themselves, confused by this disgrace, may begin to repent of their baseness, and from this repentance learn at last to know themselves. (pp. 299–300)

•

But although it is not lawful to judge individually who belongs to the Church and who does not, since we do not yet know the judgment of God, nevertheless wherever we see the word of God is sincerely preached and heard and the sacraments instituted by Christ administered, it is not to be doubted in any way that there is a Church of God, since his promise cannot fail: "Wherever two or three are gathered in my name there I am in the midst of them" (Matt. 18:20). We cannot even have on earth a more certain knowledge of God's Church, nor can we otherwise discern those who are outside the Church, not by any means! Yes, indeed, not one of these things is understood except by faith, because we say that when we say: we believe in the Church. For these things are believed which cannot be seen by our present eyes. Wherefore, it is clear that the Church is not a carnal thing which ought to be present to our senses, or circumscribed in a certain place, or fixed in any See.

We also believe in the Communion of the Saints, that is, that in the Catholic Church there is a mutual communication and participation of all goods by all the elect, who at the same time worship God with true faith. Wherefore, it is not denied that the graces of each one are different (as Paul teaches that the gifts of the Spirit are diverse and distributed in different ways) (1 Cor. 12:4–11); it is not denied that each one should rightly and orderly hold his own property, because they possess this right from the civil constitution (as it is necessary under the first principles of the world that possessions should be distinct among men); but the community of the faithful observe this point: that they share among themselves, generously and with the love which they owe to each other, every kind of possessions, whether of the spirit or of the body, insofar as it is fair and experience demands it. And, indeed, whichever of God's gifts fall to one's lot, they are truly participants of it, although by the dispensation of God this gift is given particularly to one, not to the others (Rom. 12:4–8; 1 Cor. 12:12, 26); likewise, the members of the body share all things among themselves by a certain mutual participation, nevertheless each one has its own particular gifts and distinct functions; for, as has been said, they are gathered and fitted together in one body. This is the Catholic Church, the mystical body of Christ (Eph. 1:22–23). Thus in the last section we have testified that we believe in the Church. In this we truly declare that this is the kind of Church in which we believe. I know, indeed, that this part has been omitted by some, interpreted in another sense by others; but I have interpreted it with the best faith and to the best of my ability. (pp. 301–2)

– 6 –

The Modern Period

INTRODUCTION

While in the sixteenth century churches had worked hard to produce broad confessional statements, defending such statements entailed political and military campaigns into the seventeenth century. The years 1618 through 1648, a period known as the Thirty Years' War, represent the height of such conflicts. The Peace of Augsburg (1555) had not protected the rights of Calvinists; as their influence grew, the Catholic League of Princes, organized by Maximilian I of Bavaria in 1609, tried to oppose their attempts gain political power. Over the course of the conflict, concerns over religion became secondary and even symbolic of the political struggle between nations and territories; by the end of the war church structures had been seriously weakened. In 1648 the Peace of Westphalia established a general tolerance along the lines of the earlier Peace of Augsburg in which the political head of the region determined its religion. Throughout Europe, not only in Germany, a significant amount of ecclesiastical property was secularized, and the church lost much of its economic and temporal power. Louis XIV in 1682 enacted the Gallican Articles, which limited the power of the pope throughout France. In Russia, Peter the Great brought the Russian Orthodox Church under state control.

As a result of these religio-political tensions, reflection on the nature of the church took a turn toward introspection; the role of the church in the world, and particularly the defense of its temporal power, was acted out more in military campaigns than in treatises. The Anabaptist approach to church, which stressed the importance of each individual member, his/her intention to become part of the Christian community, and the community's witness of pacifism, charity, and simplicity to the outside world, became an appealing option.

Anabaptist ideas of the church emerged powerfully in the seventeenth century through George Fox (1624–91) and his circle of friends, known as the Quakers. The Quakers emphasized the importance of direct revelation from God, translating such revelations into concrete commitments to social equality. They affirmed the presence of Christ in all people and organized themselves in communities dedicated to fostering and nurturing expressions of Christ's presence. This understanding of the church was established in Pennsylvania in the eighteenth century and in utopian communities of the nineteenth century. When, in 1681, Charles II paid a debt owed to the family of William Penn (1644–1718) with a grant of land, the Quakers had the space and freedom to enact their "holy experiment," guaranteeing religious freedom to all who settled in Pennsylvania and maintaining pacifist principles. Other religious groups were attracted by that colony's religious toleration, and Mennonites, Moravians, Brethren, and Amish settled there as well. With the Quakers they urged moral purity, practiced pacifism, and maintained a simple lifestyle. However, in contrast to the Quakers, many of these groups upheld a rigid separation from the predominant culture and deliberately perpetuated their German cultural heritage.

The trends toward secularization already apparent in the seventeenth century continued throughout the eighteenth century. An epistemological shift was also occurring, in which many of the great thinkers sought to understand the nature of the universe and reality on their own terms, within a framework of natural law which, many argued, could ultimately be separated from God. In the eighteenth century one turns to philosophers (many of whom were religious) for the kinds of speculative treatises theologians, monks, or mystics would have produced in earlier centuries. As a result, broad statements about the nature of the church were replaced by practical experiments of various communities.

In the eighteenth century several such communities contribute to an understanding of the church rooted primarily in intentional communities. The example of the Shakers shows both the desire to affirm the immediate reality of God in the world so common in the revivalism of the seventeenth century, as well as the tendency to understand Christianity as a commitment to intentional, moral living which often necessitated some sort of separatism from worldly influences. The earliest Shakers were English Quakers who had broken from the Society of Friends in 1747. They were oriented to the imminent second coming of Christ, a coming they saw in the person of Ann Lee (1736–84), who seemed to lead the small community into an experience of union with Christ. Through Mother Ann the Shakers believed they had been ushered into the unitive presence to become the living Christ today. Shaker ecclesiology was well articulated in the nineteenth century, but even in the 1780s, as communities formed in America throughout New England and the Midwest, a view of the church as dynamic, transformative, and persecuted was emerging. For the Shakers, their societies were a way of participating fully in the body of Christ, understood as the true resurrection body come again. As part of their commitment to this body, Shakers took a vow of celibacy, shared their belongings, and worked to promote peace and equality.

Shaker documents on the nature of their societies stressed their desire to return to "primitive Christianity," a total form of community which did not allow for divisions among members. The behavior of the community was an important witness to the reality of Christ. In a treatise written in 1818, John Dunlavy, an important leader of the Ohio-Kentucky Shaker Societies, explained the Shaker vision of the church: "Christians are united by one Spirit into one body, as the habitation or temple of God. And as like causes produce like effects, the unity of the Spirit within produces unity of operation without, for as is the fountain, so are the streams. Therefore it is that believers are united in a manner and degree which the world cannot imitate, and the rule of Christ is proved true by experiment."[1]

---

1. John Dunlavy, *The Manifesto, or a Declaration of the Doctrine and Practice of the Church of Christ* (New York: Edward O. Jenkins, 1847), in Robley Edward Whitson, ed., *The Shakers: Two Centuries of Spiritual Reflection* (New York: Paulist Press, 1983), 190.

Throughout Shaker writings the identity of the church as Christ, an unfolding event all humans can experience, is stressed.

The thought of Friedrich Schleiermacher (1768–1834) moved ecclesiology into an even more sophisticated theological realm, while still stressing the primacy of human experience and feeling. Advocating the importance of separation of church and temporal concerns, Schleiermacher in *The Christian Faith* defines the church as "nothing but a communion of association relating to religion or piety," a community which forms as people become conscious of their need for redemption and the possibility of redemption in Christ.[2] The church has a salvific function, which is connected to its role in revitalizing and affirming the individual consciousness of Christ. In other words it reifies the divine reality already experienced.

The nineteenth century saw an important movement toward revivalism, missionary work, and intense experiences of religious conversion known as the Second Great Awakening. While this movement is generically Protestant in its orientation, the phenomenon of revivalism and missionary work entered each denomination and also characterized Roman Catholicism. Throughout the nineteenth century, the United States was considered "missionary territory" by the Vatican; much of the American Catholic experience of the nineteenth century was rooted in the home, with little access to regular liturgy or sacraments except in urban environments. Even for Catholics, a local, community-based understanding of church was normative. The Second Great Awakening added a personal dimension to that experience in which individuals pondered how their moral choices should reflect their internal experience of God.

The Second Great Awakening and the religious enthusiasm it generated gave rise to considerable educational developments. Colleges, secondary schools, and primary schools were founded with the explicit aim of directing students' moral growth in a religious context. Within Catholicism there was an explosive growth of religious orders (often female) which ran hospitals, schools, orphanages, and all manners of social services. Within Protestantism, the emphasis on personal revelation reinforced by the revivalist movement also encouraged the development of women's role as ministers but opened the question of ordaining women. While some religious traditions continued to maintain and perpetuate the cult of domesticity, others supported women taking on leadership positions within the church. Contributing to this movement, Oberlin College, the nation's first coeducational school, graduated women with theological degrees soon after its founding in 1833. In one of her *Letters on the Equality of the Sexes and the Condition of Women* (1837), Sarah Grimke reviewed the Christian tradition from its scriptural roots to the nineteenth century, demonstrating ample precedent for women's leadership within Christian communities.[3]

Official Roman Catholicism's response to nineteenth-century intellectual trends was definitive during the pontificate of Pius IX (1846–78). In 1854 Pius IX declared as Catholic dogma the immaculate conception of Mary. In 1864 his "Syllabus of Errors" condemned rationalism, communism, and Bible societies. The

2. Friedrich Schleiermacher, *The Christian Faith* (Edinburgh: T. & T. Clark, 1976), 5.
3. See Sarah Grimke, *Letters on the Equality of the Sexes and the Condition of Woman* (New York: Source Book Press, 1970), 98–114.

practical effects of the "Syllabus of Errors" are difficult to assess, but the document reflects the continued assertion of Roman authority in a world which had come to embrace the intellectual superiority of nonreligious ways of reasoning. Such a bid for authority reached a zenith during the First Vatican Council (1869–70), which defined the universal episcopacy of the papacy and papal infallibility. These developments involved the jurisdictional power of the pope over the whole church and the infallibility of the pope in doctrinal matters when speaking "ex cathedra."

Within the United States the demographics of religion were shifting substantially over the course of the nineteenth century, as streams of European immigrants shifted the ratios of Catholics, Protestants, and Jews. From an overwhelmingly Protestant culture, the United States struggled with its emerging diversity, a creative tension religious historian Martin Marty has termed "the one and the many." The increase of the "many" reflects both previously underrepresented denominations of Christians as well as the development of new traditions, such as the Mormons, Seventh-Day Adventists, Jehovah's Witnesses, and Christian Scientists.

The growing diversity of America's immigrant population, coupled with the rise of industrialization and growing economic disparities, led to further reflection about how the church should respond to its environment. The movement known as the Social Gospel, which developed in the late nineteenth century, further propelled many Christians into issues of social injustice arising with increased industrialization. Perhaps the most important exponent of this movement, Walter Rauschenbusch (1861–1918), saw firsthand the conditions of factory workers and became convinced that the church must take an active role in social reforms. The church, he wrote, "does not exist for her own sake; she is simply a working organization to create the Christian life in individuals and the kingdom of God in human society."[4] In the encyclical *Rerum Novarum*, Pope Leo XIII (1878–1903) recommended economic and social reform, paralleling the orientation of the Social Gospel Movement and leading Roman Catholicism into a new phase in ecclesiology.

The turn of the century also saw another important movement within ecclesiology: the rise of ecumenism. As a century of intense missionary work came to a close, many of the churches reflected upon the disparity between the nature of the church and the partisan way it was so often represented to people outside the Christian tradition. The truth of Christianity appeared to be undermined by denominational differences which new Christians could not comprehend. Responding to this problem, individual missionary societies began to meet in international gatherings, first in London (1878 and 1888), then in New York (1900), and then in Edinburgh (1910). Understanding missionary activity as a common endeavor, these discussions attempted to promote cooperation and unity among the various denominations. However, no Roman Catholic representatives were present at these early conferences. Over the course of the twentieth cen-

---

4. Walter Rauschenbusch, *Christianity and the Social Crisis*, ed. Robert D. Cross (New York: Harper, 1964), 185.

tury the conferences urged a single council of all the churches; however, this was not accomplished until after World War II, when the World Council of Churches (WCC) was inaugurated in 1948. Individuals participate in the WCC as members of their own denominations, and the unity for which the WCC strives is not predicated on any particular doctrine. Instead, the WCC stresses the commonality of Christians in their commitment to their faith, in their recognition of the truth of the gospel, their breaking of one bread, their dedication to prayer, and their obligation to service.[5]

The WCC indicated the direction of the second half of the twentieth century, a century in which warfare had driven technological development, raising new ethical questions and heightening the need for organized religious response and direction. The social, political, and economic currents after the Second World War called for a radical reassessment of church policies and their rationales. Such was the context for the Second Vatican Council, which sought to revitalize Roman Catholicism. Vatican II was an intense effort involving major discussion about many key issues in the church and much preparation. John XXIII announced his intentions to convoke a general council in 1959 and instituted a commission to consult with bishops and theologians to recommend the subjects to be considered. This commission worked for three years before the actual council was held. In 1960 John XXIII established ten commissions to prepare issues: for matters relating to scripture, traditions, and faith and morals; for the governance of dioceses; for the role of the clergy and laity; for religious; for the discipline of the sacraments; for the liturgy; for seminaries; for the eastern churches; for missionary activity; and for the laity. The council met during four periods from 1962 to 1965.

Two documents of the council highlight its ecclesiological developments, *Lumen Gentium* and *Gaudium et Spes*. *Lumen Gentium* reviews the Christian tradition for a synthetic understanding of the church and ends by moving the church into greater concern for the social experience of its members. The "call of the church to holiness" is understood as entailing not a retreat from the world, but a dedication to a fullness of life and grace currently denied many by unjust social and political structures. *Gaudium et Spes* picks up where *Lumen Gentium* leaves off, asserting that the church must interpret carefully the "signs of the times" in light of the gospel and serve as a source of hope for the downtrodden.

The theology of Karl Rahner both undergirds and develops the ecclesiology of Vatican II. He was a member of the commissions which drafted both *Lumen Gentium* and *Gaudium et Spes*. Assessing the significance of the Second Vatican Council shortly before his death, Rahner said: "The Second Vatican Council is the first council of a World Church that really wants to be a World Church and not a Church with European exports to all parts of the world. And the Church of the Second Vatican Council has begun to become that World Church."[6] Rahner reinforces the social nature of Christianity, explaining that a personal approach to

---

5. See W. A. Visser 't Hooft, ed., *The New Delhi Report: The Third Assembly of the World Council of Churches, 1961* (New York: Association Press, 1962), 116.

6. Karl Rahner, *I Remember: An Autobiographical Interview with Meinold Krauss,* trans. Harvey D. Egan (New York: Crossroad, 1985), 89.

religion negates the gospel, since "love of neighbor cannot merely mean a private relationship to another individual, but also means something social and political, and implies responsibility for social and political structures within which love for one's neighbor can or cannot be practiced" (see text below).

While one would expect ecclesiology today to have lost much of its polemical character, the post–Vatican II church continues to struggle with its self-understanding. Several of the recent disciplinary silences issued by the Vatican to Roman Catholic theologians such as Leonardo Boff have been over the issue of the nature of the church. Much of this concern, it seems, is over the link between the identity of the church and the political and social issues which surround the church. Cardinal Joseph Ratzinger's "Instruction on Certain Aspects of 'Liberation Theology'" (1984), which associated liberation theology with Marxism, also suggested that liberation theology's nearly exclusive focus on the reign of God prevents the church from having an identity separate from its current context. Yet, as Ratzinger himself acknowledges, the emergence of a world church presents "unprecedented problems."[7]

Theologian Leonardo Boff has probably accomplished the most in terms of attaching liberation theology to ecclesiological issues. In his *Church: Charism and Power* he addresses the need to establish the proper prioritization of the elements of the reign of God, the world, and the church "in such a way that the Church is always seen as a concrete and historical sign (of the Kingdom and of salvation) and as its instrument (mediation) in salvific service to the world" (see text below). This task calls for a "new way of being church," as Brazilian bishop Pedro Casaldáliga asserts, in which the church puts itself at the service of the reign of God: "To spend itself, and wear itself out, for the Reign of God, even if this takes its life, this is the purpose and deepest meaning of the church" (see text below).

The most important contribution of liberation theology to our contemporary understanding of the church has been its emphasis on the primary mission of the church to promote the reign of God. As Gustavo Gutiérrez, often called the "father" of liberation theology, writes, "Since the church is not an end in itself, it finds its meaning in its capacity to signify the reality in [virtue] of which it exists.... this reality is the Kingdom of God which has already begun in history."[8] Such a definition requires the church to take on a prophetic role in any and all situations of injustice, continually affirming the dignity of all individuals, since they share in the image of God. Solidarity with the oppressed and advocacy on their behalf is, however, the most authentic witness to the gospel, as José Comblin concludes: "We find that the rights of the human person are the very nucleus, the center of the Christian message."[9]

Language about the reign of God takes on less prominence in the thought of many feminist liberation theologians, because they often focus on how the underlying principles of the reign of God must be enacted at the level of commu-

7. See discussion in Harvey Cox, *The Silencing of Leonardo Boff: The Vatican and the Future of World Christianity* (Bloomington, Ind.: Meyer Stone Books, 1988), 70–76, at 72.

8. Gustavo Gutiérrez, *A Theology of Liberation*, trans. Sr. Caridad Inda and John Eagleson (Maryknoll, N.Y.: Orbis Books, 1973), 261.

9. José Comblin, *The Church and the National Security State* (Maryknoll, N.Y.: Orbis Books, 1979), 106.

nities in order to be transformative. Thus Rita Nakashima Brock emphasizes the ways in which the Christian community sustains life-giving power for its members through healing them of a brokenheartedness that leads to sinful behavior. And Elisabeth Schüssler Fiorenza describes the true *ekklesia* as a community of equals committed to the kind of discipleship Jesus modeled, "his healings and exorcisms, his promise to the poor and challenge to the rich, his breaking of religious law and his table community with outcasts and sinners" (see text below). The most significant contributions of feminist liberation theology to ecclesiology involve drawing the necessary links between sinful social structures and ruptured interpersonal relationships. Feminist ecclesiology asserts that communities of support and nurturance are the context which makes possible any authentic embodiment of or witness to the reign of God. These authors have focused previous discussions of power by understanding charisma as primarily relational.

Reading the contemporary documents on the nature of the church one immediately observes how the question of the church's identity is understood very differently depending upon where one is located within the church. The debates of the medieval period about the church's role in the world have been translated into the postmodern world as we continue to define what it means to be a sacramental sign, an authentic witness to the Word of God, and the embodiment of Jesus Christ. Liberation theologians have alerted us to the need for these questions to be worked out within a world permeated with injustice.

While in some circles there is a residual backlash against the so-called forces of secularization, this question has been taken over by a more immediate sense of socioeconomic crisis. Indeed, discussion about the nature of the church could be characterized by two overarching questions: How does the church today continue to be relevant and meaningful in the lives of its members? And how can the church today embody Christ in a meaningful way in light of so much suffering and injustice? As Albert Nolan has shown in *Jesus before Christianity,* the sense of social and spiritual crisis which many Christians feel in our century is not unlike the context of Jesus' own life. How the church, as a community of believers and an institutional force, witnesses to the reality of Christ in light of such "signs of the times" remains a critical theological question today.

TEXTS

Friedrich Schleiermacher (1768–1834)

The Christian Faith (1830–31)*

In reckoning the two expressions — the fellowship of believers and the Christian Church — as equivalent, our proposition seems to be in opposition to the Roman Symbol; but neither earlier versions of the latter nor the Nicene Creed know anything of using the two side by side with a distinction. What is evident

---

*Reprinted from Friedrich Schleiermacher, *The Christian Faith* (Edinburgh, 1976), 525–26, 527–28, 578–81, by permission of T. & T. Clark.

is that fellowship may be taken in a narrower or a wider sense. For, if the regenerate find themselves already within it, they must have belonged to it even before regeneration, though obviously in a different sense from actual believers. If this were not so, no accession to or extension of the Church could be imagined except by an absolute breach of continuity — that is, in a way unknown to history. But the truth is that the new life of each individual springs from that of the community, while the life of the community springs from no other individual life than that of the Redeemer. We must therefore hold that the totality of those who live in the state of sanctification is the inner fellowship; the totality of those on whom preparatory grace is at work is the outer fellowship, from which by regeneration members pass to the inner, and then keep helping to extend the wider circle. It would, however, be quite a novel and merely confusing use of terms to try to assign the two expressions in question respectively to the two forms of fellowship.

Further, no particular form of fellowship is here definitely asserted or excluded; every form, perfect and imperfect, that has ever been or that may yet appear, is included. This, and this only, is assumed, that wherever regenerate persons are within reach of each other, some kind of fellowship between them is bound to arise. For if they are in contact, their witness to the faith must in part overlap, and must necessarily involve mutual recognition and a common understanding as to their operation within the common area. What was stated at the beginning of our treatment of the consciousness of grace, namely, that it always proceeds from a common life, was meant exclusively in this far-reaching sense; but now that very statement finds for the first time its full explanation. For if, when regenerate, we did not find ourselves already within a common life, but had to set out to discover or constitute it, that would mean that just the most decisive of all the works of grace was not based on a life in common. (pp. 525–26)

•

The Christian self-consciousness expressed in our proposition is the general form, determined by our faith in Christ, taken by our fellow-feeling with human things and circumstances. This becomes all the clearer if we combine with it the corresponding negative expression. For if, leaving redemption out of the account, the world is, relatively to humanity, the place of original perfection of men and things which yet has become the place of sin and evil; and if, with the appearance of Christ a new thing has entered the world, the antithesis of the old; it follows that only that part of the world which is united to the Christian Church is for us the place of attained perfection, or of the good, and — relatively to quiescent self-consciousness — the place of blessedness. This is so, not in virtue of the original perfection of human nature and the natural order, though of course it is thus conditioned, but in virtue solely of the sinless perfection and blessedness which has come in with Christ and communicates itself through Him. With this goes the converse, that the world, so far as it is outside this fellowship of Christ, is always, in spite of that original perfection, the place of evil and sin. No one, therefore, can be surprised to find at this point the proposition that salvation or blessedness is in the Church alone, and that, since blessedness cannot enter from without, but can be found within the Church only by being brought into existence there, the

Church alone saves. For the rest, it is self-evident that the antithesis between what is realized in the world by redemption and all the rest of the world is acute in proportion to the completeness with which the peculiar dignity of Christ and the full content of redemption is apprehended. It disappears or loses itself in a vague distinction between better and worse only where the contrast between Christ and sinful man is similarly obliterated or toned down.

This, too, affords the best proof that our proposition is simply an utterance of the Christian self-consciousness. For if the Christian Church were in its essential nature an object of outside perception, that perception might be passed on without involving attachment to the fellowship. But the fact is that those who do not share our faith in Christ do not recognize the Christian fellowship in its antithesis to the world. Wherever the feeling of need of redemption is entirely suppressed, the Christian Church is misconstrued all round; and the two attitudes develop *pari passu*. With the first stirrings of preparatory grace in consciousness, there comes a presentiment of the divine origin of the Christian Church; and with a living faith in Christ awakens also a belief that the Kingdom of God is actually present in the fellowship of believers. On the other hand, an unalterable hostility to the Christian Church is symptomatic of the highest stage of insusceptibility to redemption; and this hostility hardly admits even of outward reverence for the person of Christ. But faith in the Christian Church as the Kingdom of God not only implies that it will ever endure in antithesis to the world, but also — the fellowship having grown to such dimensions out of small beginnings, and being inconceivable except as ever at work — contains the hope that the Church will increase and the world opposed to it decrease. For the incarnation of Christ means for human nature in general what regeneration is for the individual. And just as sanctification is the progressive domination of the various functions, coming with time to consist less and less of fragmentary details and more and more to be a whole, with all its parts integrally connected and lending mutual support, so too the fellowship organizes itself here also out of the separate redemptive activities and becomes more and more co-operative and interactive. This organization must increasingly overpower the unorganized mass to which it is opposed. (pp. 527–28)

•

Fixing our attention on the Redeemer in the maturity of His human life, we see in the totality of His powers an organism adequate to the impulses proceeding from the being of God within Him. The individual as regenerate can never in this respect be regarded even as an image of Him, because the condition of varied sinfulness in which divine grace found him does not permit of an exact correspondence in the relationship of his psychical capacities to the impulses of the Spirit. But if the Christian Church is a true common life, a unified or, as we say, a moral personality though not indeed an inherited or natural one, it cannot on this latter account be the same as a personality arising from the person-forming activity of Nature, for in the two cases growth and decay are related in very different fashion; but nonetheless it can and must be an image of such a personality. For since the Divine Essence is one and everywhere self-identical, then, even if its mode of being in the individual, Christ, and in the common life is not the same, it follows that the impulses proceeding from it must be the same in both cases. Hence the modes both of comprehension and of action are the same in the Church as in the Redeemer, because there are present in every member, and therefore in the whole, the very same powers which in Christ's case were taken up into unity with the divine principle. Such an aggregate of human powers in a certain sense exists in every organized mass of people, where the most important contrasts which human life offers are ordinarily found side by side. In the primitive Church, too, in spite of its limited size, the same truth was exemplified by the fact that it very quickly spread among Jews and pagans, and thus included what in this respect was the most significant contrast of all, with the result that thus every further development through the inclusion of minor contrasts was prepared for and introduced. If, however, we are seeking the image in its true perfection, we must regard the Church in its absolute purity and integrity. Manifestly we see its purity only if what we view as an element of the Church is not the entire life of regenerate individuals, even subsequently to regeneration, but only that in their life which constitutes its good works, and not that which belongs to its sins. It follows at once that the absolute integrity of the Church is only to be seen in the totality of the human race. For just as in the first pair (viewed as the common ancestors of all) there can be imagined no distinct differences of temperament or constitution simply because it was from them that all differences, whether climatic or more individual, were to develop, and therefore their perfect image is found only in the fundamental types of all human races taken together, and of all the tribes into which they are subdivided — which tribes again are completely represented only by the totality of all the individual beings belonging to them — so too is it in regard to Christ as the actually given spiritual archetype and original. If we recall our explanations regarding His sinless perfection on the one hand and the basis of the sinfulness of all others on the other hand, it follows that each individual is not merely in each of his individual characteristics an imperfect image; even considered as a whole he is an image of a one-sided and partial kind, which requires to be supplemented on every side. From this it follows of itself that the perfect image of Christ is only to be found in the sum-total of all the forms of spiritual life based on the varieties of natural foundation; for it is only so that one-sided tendencies fully supplement each other, and the imperfections compatible with one are canceled by the others. We reach the same result if we regard the work of Christ rather than His Person, and in that relation view the Church as an organic body, equipped for a sum-total of activities in which the perfection of each vital function is conditioned by the integrity of the various members. For various functions can be properly apportioned only if the apportionment is based on a variety of gifts, and this again, if it is to arise in a natural way, presumes a variety present in the personal living unity. In this way the two facts harmonize well, that the Church is called the body of Christ, ruled by the Head, and that the more it becomes externally complete and inwardly perfect, the more it is also said to become the image of Christ.

>From this there now follows the second half of our proposition. In reference to this last point it can be said without hesitation that everything any single

person contributes by his activity to the maintenance and growth of the whole can only be replaced by the concurrence of several others, else Christ would have been wrong in saying of each that he was all the same an unprofitable servant. Yet, in reference to what was said earlier, in spite of all his imperfection and one-sidedness every individual, as a subordinate unit in the whole, is a part irreplaceable by any other. For even in the sphere of the new man there are several ties in the natural man; and each of these fundamental types includes a multitude of subordinate varieties which we can neither count nor measure, but which nevertheless our Christian sentiment (just as in the natural sphere our race-consciousness does) compels us to regard as integral and each a whole by itself. And for this we find a justification not only in the Biblical figures already cited, but also in the recognition we are commanded to give all such peculiarities, without limit or exception. Accordingly, we must say also of the development of the Christian fellowship in time that nothing would happen in the Church as it does, unless each individual were what he is. With this is connected the fact that everything in it is common action and common work, therefore common merit and common guilt; not manifested in individuals, however, in quite the same ways. Accordingly, the Church only gradually attains to be the perfect image of Christ, and the divine ordinance seen in the gradual addition of individual members and the widening compass of the whole can be expressed in the formula that the advance comes about in such a way that only is the whole, at every particular moment viewed by itself, as complete and inclusive as possible, but also each moment contains within itself a basis for the largest possible integration in the moment succeeding. At the same time this is only grasped by faith and can never be proved by experience. (pp. 578–81)

Vatican II (1962–65)

Vatican II, *Lumen Gentium* (1964)*

In the human nature which He united to Himself, the Son of God redeemed man and transformed him into a new creation (cf. Gal. 6:15; 2 Cor. 5:17) by overcoming death through His own death and resurrection. By communicating His Spirit to His brothers, called together from all peoples, Christ made them mystically into His own body.

In that body, the life of Christ is poured into the believers, who, through the sacraments, are united in a hidden and real way to Christ who suffered and was glorified. Through baptism we are formed in the likeness of Christ: "For in one Spirit we were all baptized into one body" (1 Cor. 12:13). In this sacred rite, a union with Christ's death and resurrection is both symbolized and brought about: "For we were buried with him by means of Baptism into death." And if "we have been united with him in the likeness of his death, we shall be so in the likeness of his resurrection also" (Rom. 6:4–5).

---

*From *The Documents of Vatican II*, ed. Walter M. Abbott (New York: Guild Press, 1966), 20–24.

Truly partaking of the body of the Lord in the breaking of the Eucharistic bread, we are taken up into communion with Him and with one another. "Because the bread is one, we though many, are one body, all of us who partake of the one bread" (1 Cor. 10:17). In this way all of us are made members of His body (cf. 1 Cor. 12:27), "but severally members one of another" (Rom. 12:5).

As all the members of the human body, though they are many, form one body, so also are the faithful in Christ (cf. 1 Cor. 12:12). Also, in the building up of Christ's body there is a flourishing variety of members and functions. There is only one Spirit who, according to His own richness and the needs of the ministries, distributes His different gifts for the welfare of the Church (cf. 1 Cor. 12:1–11). Among these gifts stands out the grace given to the apostles. To their authority, the Spirit Himself subjected even those who were endowed with charisms (cf. 1 Cor. 14). Giving the body only through Himself and through His power and through the internal cohesion of its members, this same Spirit produces and urges love among the believers. Consequently, if one member suffers anything, all the members suffer it too, and if one member is honored, all the members rejoice together (cf. 1 Cor. 12:26).

The Head of this body is Christ. He is the image of the invisible God and in Him all things came into being. He has priority over everyone and in Him all things hold together. He is the Head of that body which is the Church. He is the beginning, the firstborn from the dead, so that in all things He might have the first place (cf. Col. 1:15–18). By the greatness of His power He rules the things of heaven and the things of earth, and with His all-surpassing perfection and activity He fills the whole body with the riches of His glory (cf. Eph. 1:18–23).

All the members ought to be molded into Christ's image until He is formed in them (cf. Gal. 4:19). For this reason we who have been made like unto Him, who have died with Him and been raised up with Him, are taken up into the mysteries of His life, until we reign together with Him (cf. Phil. 3:21; 2 Tim. 2:11; Eph. 2:6; Col. 2:12; etc.). Still in pilgrimage upon the earth, we trace in trial and under oppression the paths He trod. Made one with His sufferings as the body is one with the head, we endure with Him, that with Him we may be glorified (cf. Rom. 8:17).

>From Him, "the whole body, supplied and built up by joints and ligaments, attains a growth that is of God" (Col. 2:19). He continually distributes in His Body, that is, in the Church, gifts of ministries through which, by His own power, we serve each other unto salvation so that, carrying out the truth in love, we may through all things grow up into Him who is our head (cf. Eph. 4:11–16, Greek text).

In order that we may be unceasingly renewed in Him (cf. Eph. 4:23), He has shared with us His Spirit who, existing as one and the same being in the head and in the members, vivifies, unifies, and moves the whole body. This he does in such a way that His work could be compared by the holy Fathers with the function which the soul fulfills in the human body, whose principle of life the soul is.

Having become the model of a man loving his wife as his own body, Christ loves the Church as His bride (cf. Eph. 5:25–28). For her part, the Church is subject to her Head (cf. Eph. 5:22–23). "For in him dwells all the fullness of the Godhead bodily" (Col. 2:9). He fills the Church, which is His Body and His fullness, with His divine gifts (cf. Eph. 1:22–23) so that she may grow and reach all the fullness of God (cf. Eph. 3:19).

Christ, the one Mediator, established and ceaselessly sustains here on earth His holy Church, the community of faith, hope, and charity, as a visible structure. Through her He communicates truth and grace to all. But the society furnished with hierarchical agencies and the Mystical Body of Christ are not to be considered as two realities, nor are the visible assembly and the spiritual community, nor the earthly Church and the Church enriched with heavenly things. Rather they form one interlocked reality which is comprised of a divine and a human element. For this reason, by an excellent analogy, this reality is compared to the mystery of the incarnate Word. Just as the assumed nature inseparably united to the divine Word serves Him as a living instrument of salvation, so, in a similar way, does the communal structure of the Church serve Christ's Spirit, who vivifies it by way of building up the body (cf. Eph. 4:16).

This is the unique Church of Christ which in the Creed we avow as one, holy, catholic, and apostolic. After His Resurrection our Savior handed her over to Peter to be shepherded (John 21:17), commissioning him and the other apostles to propagate and govern her (cf. Matt. 28:18ff.). Her He erected for all ages as "the pillar and mainstay of the truth" (1 Tim. 3:15). This Church, constituted and organized in the world as a society, subsists in the Catholic Church, which is governed by the successor of Peter and by the bishops in union with that successor, although many elements of sanctification and of truth can be found outside of her visible structure. These elements, however, as gifts properly belonging to the Church of Christ, possess an inner dynamism toward Catholic unity.

Just as Christ carried out the work of redemption in poverty and under oppression, so the Church is called to follow the same path in communicating to men the fruits of salvation. Christ Jesus, "though He was by nature God…emptied himself, taking the nature of a slave" (Phil. 2:6), and "being rich, he became poor" (2 Cor. 8:9) for our sakes. Thus, although the Church needs human resources to carry out her mission, she is not set up to seek earthly glory, but to proclaim humility and self-sacrifice, even by her own example.

Christ was sent by the Father "to bring good news to the poor, to heal the contrite of heart" (Luke 4:18), "to seek and to save what was lost" (Luke 19:10). Similarly, the Church encompasses with love all those who are afflicted with human weakness. Indeed, she recognizes in the poor and the suffering the likeness of her poor and suffering Founder. She does all she can to relieve their need and in them she strives to serve Christ. While Christ, "holy, innocent, defiled" (Heb. 7:26), knew nothing of sin (2 Cor. 5:21), but came to expiate only the sins of the people (cf. Heb. 2:17), the Church, embracing sinners in her bosom, is at the same time holy and always in need of being purified, and incessantly pursues the path of penance and renewal.

The Church, "like a pilgrim in a foreign land, presses forward amid the persecutions of the world and the consolations of God,"[1] announcing the cross and

---

1. See Augustine, *City of God*, book 18, 51:2.

death of the Lord until He comes (cf. 1 Cor. 11:26). By the power of the risen Lord, she is given strength to overcome patiently and lovingly the afflictions and hardships which assail her from within and without, and to show forth in the world the mystery of the Lord in a faithful though shadowed way, until at the last it will be revealed in total splendor.

Vatican II, *Gaudium et Spes*, "The Role of the Church in the Modern World" (1965)*

The Church and the World as Mutually Related

Coming forth from the eternal Father's love, founded in time by Christ the Redeemer, and made one in the Holy Spirit, the Church has a saving and an eschatological purpose which can be fully attained only in the future world. But she is already present in this world, and is composed of men, that is, of members of the earthly city who have a call to form the family of God's children during the present history of the human race, and to keep increasing it until the Lord returns.

United on behalf of heavenly values and enriched by them, this family has been "constituted and organized in the world as a society"[1] by Christ, and is equipped with "those means which befit it as a visible and social unity."[2] Thus the Church, at once a visible assembly and a spiritual community, goes forward together with humanity and experiences the same earthly lot which the world does. She serves as a leaven and as a kind of soul for human society as it is to be renewed in Christ and transformed into God's family.

That the earthly and the heavenly city penetrate each other is a fact accessible to faith alone. It remains a mystery of human history, which sin will keep in great disarray until the splendor of God's sons is fully revealed. Pursuing the saving purpose which is proper to her, the Church not only communicates divine life to men, but in some way casts the reflected light of that life over the entire earth.

This she does most of all by her healing and elevating impact on the dignity of the person, by the way in which she strengthens the seams of human society and imbues the everyday activity of men with a deeper meaning and importance. Thus, through her individual members and her whole community, the Church believes she can contribute greatly toward making the family of man and its history more human. (pp. 238–39)

The Help Which the Church Strives to Give to Society

Christ, to be sure, gave His Church no proper mission in the political, economic, or social order. The purpose which He set before her is a religious one. But out of this religious mission itself comes a function, a light, and an energy which can serve to structure and consolidate the human community according to

---

*From *The Documents of Vatican II*, ed. Walter M. Abbott (New York: Guild Press, 1966), 238–39, 241–43.

1. *Lumen Gentium*, chap. 1, art. 8.
2. *Lumen Gentium*, chap. 2, art. 9.

the divine law. As a matter of fact, when circumstances of time and place create the need, she can and indeed should initiate activities on behalf of all men. This is particularly true of activities designed for the needy, such as the works of mercy and similar undertakings.

The Church further recognizes that worthy elements are found in today's social movements, especially an evolution toward unity, a process of wholesome socialization and of association in civic and economic realms. For the promotion of unity belongs to the innermost nature of the Church, since she is, "by her relationship with Christ, both a sacramental sign and an instrument of intimate union with God, and of the unity of all mankind."[3]

Thus she shows the world that an authentic union, social and external, results from a union of minds and hearts, namely, from that faith and charity by which her own unity is unbreakably rooted in the Holy Spirit. For the force which the Church can inject into the modern society of man consists in that faith and charity put into vital practice, not in any external dominion exercised by merely human means.

Moreover, in virtue of her mission and nature, she is bound to no particular form of human culture, nor to any political, economic, or social system. Hence the Church by her very universality can be a very close bond between diverse human communities and nations, provided these trust her and truly acknowledge her right to true freedom in fulfilling her mission. For this reason, the Church admonishes her own sons, but also humanity as a whole, to overcome all strife between nations and races in this family spirit of God's children, and in the same way, to give internal strength to human associations which are just.

This Council, therefore, looks with great respect upon all the true, good, and just elements found in the very wide variety of institutions which the human race has established for itself and constantly continues to establish. The Council affirms, moreover, that the Church is willing to assist and promote all these institutions to the extent that such a service depends on her and can be associated with her mission. She has no fiercer desire than that, in pursuit of the welfare of all, she may be able to develop herself freely under any kind of government which grants recognition of the basic rights of person and family and to the demands of the common good.

The Help Which the Church Strives to Give to Human Activity through Christians

This Council exhorts Christians, as citizens of two cities, to strive to discharge their earthly duties conscientiously and in response to the gospel spirit. They are mistaken who, knowing that we have here no abiding city but seek one which is to come, think that they may therefore shirk their earthly responsibilities. For they are forgetting that by the faith itself they are more than ever obliged to measure up to these duties, each according to his proper vocation.

---

3. *Lumen Gentium*, chap. 1, art. 1.

Nor, on the contrary, are they any less wide of the mark who think that religion consists in acts of worship alone and in the discharge of certain moral obligations, and who imagine they can plunge themselves into earthly affairs in such a way as to imply that they are altogether divorced from the religious life. This split between the faith which many profess and their daily lives deserves to be counted among the more serious errors of our age. Long since, the prophets of the Old Testament fought vehemently against this scandal and even more so did Jesus Christ Himself in the New Testament threaten it with grave punishments.

Therefore, let there be no false opposition between professional and social activities on the one part, and religious life on the other. The Christian who neglects his temporal duties neglects his duties toward his neighbor and even God, and jeopardizes his eternal salvation. Christians should rather rejoice that they can follow the example of Christ, who worked as an artisan. In the exercise of all their earthly activities, they can thereby gather their humane, domestic, professional, social, and technical enterprises into one vital synthesis with religious values, under whose supreme direction all things are harmonized unto God's glory. (pp. 241–43)

Hans Urs von Balthasar (1905–88)

Church and World (1967)*

Mary's special role as regards the new people of God in the history of salvation gives part of the answer to the question "Who is the Church?" It cannot give the whole answer, but what it can do is usher in the complete answer, since it is the infinite disponibility of her attitude of faith ("be it done unto me according to thy word") that makes her the ideal (moral) and real (physical) womb of the Church. Her own person, in its faith, love, and hope, has become so supple in the hand of the Creator that he can extend her beyond the limits of a private consciousness to a Church consciousness, to what the older theology since Origen and Ambrose is accustomed to call *anima ecclesiastica*.

This *"ecclesiasticizing" of the individual consciousness* is, however, available on a different level to everyone regenerated from the private existence of the natural state and the still more cramped bounds of sin-consciousness estranged from God, regenerated, that is, to the Church through the death of the old man, and endowed with the consciousness of the new man. The truths propounded here are such as the "old man" cannot grasp, eluding the subtlest philosophical dialectic of alternation with its progressive broadening out of consciousness into the Absolute. The fact is that the dying and burial of the old man has already taken place "en Christo," and so likewise the resurrection of the new, who lives "en Christo," ontologically, and so, of necessity, also consciously. "Therefore if any

---

*Reprinted from Hans Urs von Balthasar, *Church and World*, trans. A. V. Littledale with Alexander Dru (New York: Herder and Herder, 1967), 137–44. Permission requested.

one is in Christ, he is a new creation; the old has passed away, behold, the new has come" (2 Cor. 5:17).

The newness in question consists not in a diminution, still less in an extinction of personal consciousness, but in its being taken along in faith into the consciousness of Christ: "[I]t is no longer I who live, but Christ who lives in me; and the life I now live in the flesh I live by faith in the Son of God, who loved me and gave himself for me" (Gal. 2:20). "And he died for all, that those who live might live no longer for themselves but for him who for their sake died and was raised" (2 Cor. 5:15). "If we live, we live to the Lord, and if we die, we die to the Lord; so then, whether we live or whether we die, we are the Lord's" (Rom. 14:8). This constantly renewed and variously expressed expropriation of man, in which he dies to himself, is, in its positive aspect, his appropriation by God, to "obtain salvation" (1 Thess. 5:9). The expression is never used in a singular sense, however: it always refers to God's own people (1 Pet. 2:9), and only as such are they called to "obtain the glory of our Lord Jesus Christ" (2 Thess. 2:13). This taking up of the "I" and the "we" through God into Christ is often described by Paul as a changeover from consciousness of one's own action to consciousness of God's action taking place within us: "Not that I have already obtained this or am already perfect; but I press on to make it my own, because Christ Jesus has made me his own" (Phil. 3:12). "But if one loves God, one is known by him" (1 Cor. 8:3). "...what we are is known to God" (2 Cor. 5:11). "...you have come to know God, or rather to be known by God" (Gal. 4:9). And, eschatologically: "Now I know in part; then I shall understand fully, even as I have [now already] been fully understood" (1 Cor. 13:12).

What kind of consciousness this is of the new man, according to Paul (and also, of course, John, Peter, and James), comes out most clearly from his use of the personal pronouns. Paul makes copious use of the first person singular. His "I" has astonishing vitality, diversity, agility: in fact, with regard to the community, it has a kind of omnipresence beyond space and time — *absense corpore, praesens spiritu* ("absent in body...present in spirit" — 1 Cor. 5:3). He uses "I" in speaking of such a commonplace thing as the plan of a journey which he propounds, but also in speaking of the vertiginous height of his solitary calling in God's plan of salvation: "...you have heard of the stewardship of God's grace that was given to me for you, how the mystery was made known to me by revelation, as I have written briefly. When you read this you can perceive my insight into the mystery of Christ" (Eph. 3:2–4). His "I" is of such unique character, is so patterned on Christ and imitative of him as to be recommended, in its turn, for imitation. It had its beginning at Damascus. It is the "I" of Christ's mission, the "I" transformed into the servant of Christ, from flesh become spirit. It is ecclesiastical, and manifests itself — brings out its own anatomy before the eyes of all — only because it is a paradigm of the mission, the functional side of the Church, of membership in the body of Christ. It knows itself as utterly divested of ownership of itself; belonging wholly to Christ and the communion of saints, it would prefer to die so as to be with Christ, that being by far the best — but it no longer knows any personal preference: what is best for Paul is what serves the Church best, and for her sake he continues to live (Phil. 1:23–25).

We can see from this that to attempt to write a psychology of Paul is no less absurd, in principle, than to do the same of Christ. The personal reality that drives forward with such impetus cannot, by its very nature, be contained in these categories, although it does not destroy them (which is what tantalizes the onlooker so much), but makes sovereign use of them. It is because the "I" of Christ harbors the Father and the Spirit in circumincession[1] that he can release out of himself the mystical body with all his personal members, their missions of sanctification and functions of love. And because the Trinitarian "I" of Christ wills to dwell in those who love him (John 14:23), the "I" of Paul is not only entirely dominated by this divine life, but harbors, for its part, the communities entrusted to him, which he brings forth in travail out of himself (Gal. 4:19), and to which he is father, mother, and nurse....

This "I" — explicable in terms of the mission, and not of psychology — which the Church bears in herself, and which as expanded to become the *anima ecclesiastica,* is now able to think and to say things about the Church, quite beyond the reach of a personal "I." This occurs when, in the course of its official function, it has to contrast itself with the "you" of those in its charge and can, therefore, include with its own content the content of the churches and communities — and so, also, the content of the "you." In such cases, it can use the ecclesiastical "we" in statements bearing on salvation, which none of the individuals addressed could presume to do. Take the beginning of the Letter to the Ephesians, where the Father's eternal plan of salvation is as absolute as that of the Church herself (which prevents neither him nor the actual Church from supporting this assurance by fervent prayer and penance — "lest, while I preach to others, I myself become a castaway"). But he absolutely includes within it the community of which he has actual charge, not in a vague, rhetorical "we," but in the "we" of the father, of the responsible apostle, who gathers his children around him as a hen gathers her brood under her wings (Matt. 23:38); yet the parrhesia[2] for doing so he derives from his mission and office. It is only when admonishing and censuring in his function as educator that he opposes himself to the community, or, at any rate, excludes himself from it *ad teptus;* while in his preaching office he includes himself; and his consciousness of the Church can compensate for any lack of parrhesia in the utterance of others. " ...become as I am, for I also have become as you are" (Gal. 4:12). That is, you too must allow yourselves to be formed by the Church: "And we exhort you, brethren, admonish the idle, encourage the fainthearted, help the weak, be patient with them all. See that none of you repays evil for evil, but always seek to do good to one another and to all" (1 Thess. 5:14–15). It is clear from this that the "Church of the saints" not only "represents" the Church of sinners, of the imperfect, the struggling, but also carries them and is responsible for them before God. With Christ it empties itself, so as, in weakness and shame, to bring in the least member, and to be able to represent each such, not only in word, in reprimanding, but in deed and in truth.

---

1. *Circumincession* is a reference to the mutual indwelling of the persons of the Trinity and to the flow of divine energy among them, sometimes called *interpenetration.*
2. In other words, the sense of confidence or assurance, even authority.

Thus the opposition between "I" and "you" ("Thou") is always reconciled by the "we" which joins them together, and the transition from one to the other is smooth and imperceptible.

"We" can mean: (1) the person of Paul in his office. The plural, then, expresses the neutralization of the person by his office, but, at the same time, emphasizes the function, which, as such, is always represented by a plurality of subjects. The transition from this "official" to the "theological" (carrying and including) plural remains imperceptible (see 1 Thess. 3:1, 3–4, 6f., where, in verse 5, the "I" suddenly emerges from the "we"); (2) the hierarchs, for instance Paul with Timothy and Silvanus as joint authors of the letter, where Paul either purposely includes the others or, forgetting them for the moment and speaking from the fullness of his own heart, includes them only implicitly. The "party of the hierarchs" can also pass over, without a break, into the "party of the Church," since the teachers have confidence in it manifesting what is taught in its mode of life; (3) of this account, "we" can simply mean the Christians in the Church, Paul and the community together.

"You" is either (1) the individual community spoken to, or (2) a considerable section of the Church, for instance the Gentile Christians, to whom Paul speaks as a Jew from the other side, or alternatively, the Jewish Christians, whom Paul appeals to as the apostle of the Gentiles. But it can also be (3) simply "you Christians," you baptized, dead and risen in Christ; and then its scope is coincident with the "we" in the last signification. In this case, it is indifferent whether Paul uses "you" or "we": he is carrying on the inner colloquy of the Church with herself; he gives utterance to her self-consciousness, either as he is authorized to do so, or (which comes to the same thing) as the voice of the whole. This applies equally to questions of fact and of obligation. Consequently, it does not matter if the instruction proceeds from the "we" to the "you" (1 Thess. 4:1f.), and then again comprises both in a common "we" (4:14), continuing in the "you" only again to include the "you" in the "we," and to establish a rigid exclusion from those not belonging to the Church and from their conduct (5:5–10). In Galatians 6:1–10, "I" alternates with "you," "thou," and "we"; all facets of the Church-consciousness that never impairs the person, but protects and elevates it to a superior order.

This analysis shows that the birth of the new man, belonging specifically to the Church in the grace of baptism, in the outpouring of faith, hope, and love through the Holy Spirit (Rom. 5:1–5), means the extension of the narrow limits of the individual sinful subject as compared with the subject of the Church. This does not imply that the believer becomes Christ substantially, nor does it mean a direct participation in the hypostatic union; nor, indeed, a progressive pantheism according to Eckhart, or as Hegel teaches in such an extreme sense. On the other hand, the mysteries of the *communio sanctorum,* the degree of the mutual circumincession of the members, their mutual power of representation before God, their community of goods even of the most inward, the monadic power to love to draw everything on itself and into itself (as described in particular by Tauler), and, as a result, to extend itself over everything and, while remaining a single heart, to become one *cor mundi:* these mysteries cannot be adequately mastered by means of purely philosophical distinctions ("*entitative* singular, *intentionaliter* universal"). The theological paradoxes are sharper; and it is simply a question of preserving their sharpness and not reducing one side to the other. They are paradoxes that thrust themselves on our attention from the indwelling of the Trinity in the Church: for the Church is uniquely the sphere which binds God and creature together. Therefore, where the most improbable event must necessarily occur, where, that is, the individual person, penetrated by God's dwelling in him, is both elevated and sublimated in his personality and opened to and made the portion of the community. Here too the mysteries of the Trinitarian relations and of their opposition in identity cannot fail to impinge; and the mystery of Christ himself, who in the Church is at once himself (his body) and another (his bride), works out in the Christian's life of grace in the Church. But with all this, the fundamental law of the creaturely status is not to be held superseded and overborne by the divine paradoxes to which man is raised. On the contrary, his elevation is what brings out clearly, confirms and fulfills the ultimate end of the created being as such (*gratia perficit naturam*). Looked at in this way, the laws of the *corpus mysticum* are commendable to reason, and that is why Paul could borrow his image of the body from Romans. It is reasonable that the member should sacrifice itself for the *bonum commune,* as Cicero says, and after him Caiaphas (John 11:50), unconsciously prophesying, that is, not suspecting how truly he spoke. And it is equally in accord with any rational social order that the strong should care for the weak, and so bring about a balance (Rom. 15:1f.; 1 Cor. 8). But just how far this law can go is made manifest only in the Church.

Karl Rahner (1904–84)

Foundations of Christian Faith (1976/78), Chapter 7: "Christianity as Church"*

In the period before the resurrection Jesus Christ knew himself to be the "absolute mediator of salvation," the inauguration of God's kingdom, and the eschatological climax of salvation history. The historical continuation of Christ in and through the community of those who believe in him, and who recognize him explicitly as the mediator of salvation in a profession of faith, is what we call church. And if the period before Christ was already encompassed by God's salvific will and by his self-communication, and hence if it was a history of hope, although it was hope in a future which was open and ambivalent from the perspective of man's freedom and mankind's freedom, then the period after Christ is all the more encompassed by and bears the stamp of an explicit profession and knowledge of the fact that this Jesus Christ is the salvation of the world, and that in him God has offered himself to the world *irrevocably.* Consequently, hope does indeed still remain because, in spite of the closeness of God's king-

*Reprinted from Karl Rahner, *Foundations of Christian Faith: An Introduction to the Idea of Christianity,* trans. William V. Dych (New York: Seabury Press, 1978), 322–23, 342–43, 347–48, 389–90, by permission of the Crossroad Publishing Company.

dom which has come in Christ, man does not lose the responsibility of his own freedom. This hope however has acquired a quite different and "eschatological" character in view of God's irreversible offer of himself to the world. But if the period after Christ is also the "Christian age" on the level of an explicit profession of faith, and in the dimension in which the irreversibility of God's salvific self-expression becomes historically and institutionally tangible, then it is the period of the church.

Looked at from the perspective of the Christian understanding of existence, what we are calling church, that is, the institutional constitution of the religion of the absolute mediator of salvation, is obviously not accidental to man's essence as a being orientated towards God. If man is a being of interpersonal communication not just on the periphery, but rather if this characteristic co-determines the whole breadth and depth of his existence, and if salvation touches the whole person and places him as a whole and with all of the dimensions of his existence in relationship to God, and hence if religion does not just concern some particular sector of human existence, but concerns the whole of human existence in its relationship to the all-encompassing God by whom all things are borne and towards whom all things are directed, then this implies that the reality of interpersonal relationship belongs to the religion of Christianity. But by man's very nature such interpersonal relationships may not be seen merely as a matter of the feelings or of a purely personal and spiritual relationship between two persons, but rather they must also be interpersonal relationships which are concretized in society. If salvation history as the history of God's transcendental self-communication to man is a history which can be experienced in time and space, then it follows from this perspective too that in the Christian understanding religion is necessarily ecclesial religion.

In addition to this there is the characteristic which stems from our own particular epoch and which characterizes us for today and for tomorrow. >From the eighteenth century until the first half of the twentieth century it might perhaps have looked as though a person could appropriate his religion in a private kind of interiority. People tried to situate religion someplace where they might escape the rigors of their concrete historical and social nature. But if today we are moving more and more towards the unity of a single history of the world and towards the development of the human community into a closer social network, and if we see that a person cannot discover his personhood and his uniqueness by looking for them as something absolutely contrary to his social nature, but can only discover them *within* his social nature and in function of this social nature; and if there is a relationship of mutual conditioning between love of God and love of neighbor, and hence if love for one's neighbor is not merely a secondary moral consequence of a proper relationship to God; and if, beyond this, love of neighbor cannot merely mean a private relationship to another individual, but also means something social and political, and implies responsibility for social and political structures within which love for one's neighbor can or cannot be practiced, then it also follows from all of this that basically it would be a late bourgeois conception to think that religion has nothing essential to do with society and with church. We are aware today in a quite new and inescapable way that man is a social being, a being who can exist only within such intercommunication with others throughout all of the dimension of human existence. And from this perspective we acquire a new understanding of Christian religion as an ecclesial religion. (pp. 322–23)

•

The church is more than a social organization for religious purposes, even if these purposes would be Christian and would bear the stamp of Christianity. Wherever there are human beings there is "church" in the sense of a religious organization. Wherever any religious attitudes and any religious practices at all are found, even among those who protest against church, they form a community from the viewpoint of the sociology of religion and constitute something like a "church" in this very broad and provisional sense even if they call themselves a "free religion." When we say that Christianity must be constituted as church, we mean that this ecclesial community belongs to the religious existence of man as such, quite independently of the question how it must be constituted more precisely in the concrete. It is part of man's question about salvation and it is fundamentally co-constitutive of his relationship to God. It is in this sense that we are maintaining that church has something to do with the essence of Christianity, and that it is not merely an organization for the practice of religion, which in its real meaning would also be conceivable independently of such a religious organization.

When we say that church exists only when the question of religious organization itself is part of the real essence of what is Christian and what is religious, and hence when it acquires salvific significance itself, this does not mean that anyone who does not belong to such an ecclesially constituted Christianity loses his salvation, nor that he cannot have the ultimate and decisive relationship to God which is grounded in the grace of Christ. But the fact that God's salvific work is offered in principle to all people, and that in principle it effects the salvation of every person if it is accepted in obedience to one's moral conscience, this does not exclude the fact that the full and historically actualized Christianity of God's self-communication is an ecclesial Christianity.

The question about the church is not merely a question of human expediency, but rather it is a question of faith in the proper sense. By the very nature of Christianity, church must be understood in such a way that it springs from the very essence of Christianity as the supernatural self-communication of God to mankind which has become manifest in history and has found its final and definitive historical climax in Jesus Christ. Church is a part of Christianity as the very event of salvation. We cannot exclude communal and social intercommunication from man's essence even when he is considered as the religious subject of a relationship to God. If basically God is not a particular reality alongside all other possibilities, but rather is the origin and the absolute goal of the single and total person, then the whole person including his social and interpersonal dimension is related to this God. By the very nature of man and by the very nature of God, and by the very nature of the relationship between man and God when God is understood correctly, the social dimension cannot be excluded from the essence of religion. It belongs to it because man in all of his dimensions is related to the one God who saves the whole person. Otherwise religion would become merely a private affair of man and would cease to be religion. (pp. 342–43)

•

As we have already said, Christianity is essentially ecclesial, and not just in a secondary way or from the viewpoint of the social or pedagogical aspects of religion. The church as such belongs to Christianity, at least when Christianity really becomes conscious of itself and when it intends to maintain the continuity of a real history of salvation and has to prolong this continuity. Church is more than merely a practical and humanely unavoidable organization for fulfilling and satisfying religious needs. Christianity, as ultimate self-communication, is ecclesial. We tried to show this from man's ultimate salvific situation and from the fact that Christianity claims the whole person for the salvation of the whole person. For man is essentially a being of intercommunication and community, and therefore he is also a historical and social being. We also tried to acquire a further understanding of this by saying that no matter how this works out more exactly in the concrete, a Christian has to anticipate an authoritative church. He has to anticipate a church which is more than his own social organization if and to the extent that Christianity is essentially more than an affair of his own subjective and pious dispositions and his own religious consciousness, and is more than the objectification of this. From this perspective church means the church which makes a claim upon me, the church which is the concreteness of God's demands upon me. Basically this concreteness is to be expected precisely if Christianity is not a religion which I create, but rather is the event of salvation which God bestows upon me by his own incalculable initiative. And if this salvific event as an act of God is not merely to come to me in the ultimate depths of conscience, but rather in the concreteness of my existence, then the concreteness of this God, who makes demands upon me and who is not my discovery or my creation, is Jesus Christ and his concrete church which makes demands upon me in the same way.

The same thing follows from the fact that, insofar as Christianity is the personal self-communication of the mystery of God, it comes to us in such a way that there is a real history of God's self-communication to us. God's supernatural and transcendental self-communication is necessarily mediated historically. If, then, there is a history of salvation, and indeed one which ultimately has unfolded to its absolute and irreversible climax in the history of Jesus, the crucified and risen one, then the concreteness of salvation history as the concrete mediation of my supernatural and transcendental relationship to God in grace must continue to exist, and this means that church has to exist. (pp. 347–48)

•

There has to be a church in the Christian understanding of faith and of human existence. Christianity is not the ideological creation of a religious enthusiasm, nor of the religious experience of an individual. It comes to the individual rather by the same route from which he receives the rest of his life, including his intellectual and spiritual life: it comes from history. No one develops and unfolds from out of the purely formal and antecedent structure of his essence. Rather he receives the concreteness of his life from a community of persons, from intercommunication, from an objective spirit, from a history, from a people, and from a family, and he develops it only within this community, and this includes what is most personal and most proper to himself. This is also true for salvation and for the Christian religion, and for the Christianity of an individual.

Obviously a Christian is a Christian in the innermost depths of his divinized essence. Nor would he ever be or ever become a Christian if he were not to live from out of the innermost center of his essence as divinized by grace. But the very thing which he is in his innermost depths and in the origins of his most individual existence, and is by the grace of God whose domain he cannot leave, this very thing comes from the concrete history of salvation to meet him in the concrete as his very own: it comes in the profession of faith of Christians, in the cult of Christians, in the community life of Christians, in a word, it comes in the church. An absolutely individual Christianity in the most personal experience of grace and ecclesial Christianity are no more radically opposed than are body and soul, than are man's transcendental essence and his historical constitution, or than are individuality and intercommunication. The two condition each other mutually. The very thing which we are from God is mediated in the concreteness of history by what we call church. And it is only in and through this mediation that it becomes our own reality and our own salvation in full measure. For this reason church exists and has to exist. It is simply taken for granted by Christians of every denomination, and is taken for granted as something which is a necessary dimension of their Christian existence....

For ultimately it is true, and this is an element in the new experience and understanding of the church in the Catholic church of the Second Vatican Council: we ourselves are the church, we poor, primitive, cowardly people, and together we represent the church. If we look at the church from outside, as it were, then we have not grasped that we are the church, and basically it is only our own inadequacies which are looking at us from the church. Not only does a Christian not have a right to idealize his church in a false way. He is also obliged by his faith to recognize the church of God and the assembly of Jesus Christ in this concrete church with its inadequacies, with its historical dangers, with its historical refusals, and with its false historical developments. For the victory of God's grace in us men who together are the church is won right here in the form of this servant and under the cross of its Lord, and under the ongoing shadow of the powers of darkness. It is won inside it and not outside. This church always continues to be a living church not only because there really takes place within it faith, hope, and love, not only because the Lord's Supper is celebrated and his death is proclaimed, but also because the real thing which constitutes the church does become manifest again and again in a way which is sufficient for anyone who looks at the church with an open heart and with the eyes of faith. (pp. 389–90)

Leonardo Boff (b. 1938)

Church: Charism and Power (1981)*

More and more, the Church in Latin America occupies the attention of religious analysts, owing primarily to its numerical importance, to the ecclesiological studies being developed there, to the new positions of the episcopacy on various social problems, and to the emergence of a Church that is being born out of the grassroots, the *base*. What are the tendencies that describe this church today, and what kind of future is projected by each of them? True ecclesiology is not the result of textbook analysis or theological hypotheses; it comes about as a result of ecclesial practices at work within the institution. Thus, if we want to identify the principal tendencies emerging in the Latin American Church, we must analyze the various practices in effect and from there arrive at the theoretical premises and formulations behind these practices. This will enable us clearly to outline those aspects that apply not only to the Church in Latin America but also to a new ecclesiology of the universal Church.

In order to go beyond mere phenomenological analysis, we must identify the theological poles that enter into our understanding of what it is to be Church. The Church cannot be understood in and of itself because it is affected by those realities that transcend it, namely, the Kingdom and the world. World and Kingdom are the two pillars that support the entire edifice of the Church. The reality of the Kingdom is that which defines both the world and the Church. Kingdom — the category used by Jesus to express his own unique intention (*ipsissima intentio*) — is the utopia that is realized in the world, the final good of the whole of creation in God, completely liberated from all imperfection and penetrated by the Divine. The Kingdom carries salvation to its completion. The world is the arena for the historical realization of the Kingdom. Presently the world is decadent and stained by sin; because of this, the Kingdom of God is raised up against the powers of the anti-Kingdom, engaged in the onerous process of liberation so that the world might accept the Kingdom itself and thus achieve its joyous goal.

The Church is that part of the world that, in the strength of the Spirit, has accepted the Kingdom made explicit in the person of Jesus Christ, the Son of God incarnated in oppression. It preserves the constant memory and consciousness of the Kingdom, celebrating its presence in the world, shaping the way it is proclaimed, and at the service of the world. The Church is not the Kingdom but rather its sign (explicit symbol) and its instrument (mediation) in the world.

These three elements — Kingdom, world, and Church — must be spelled out in their proper order. First is the Kingdom as the primary reality that gives rise to the others. Second is the world as the place where the Kingdom is concretized and the Church is realized. Finally, the Church is the anticipatory and sacramental realization of the Kingdom in the world, as well as the means whereby the Kingdom is anticipated most concretely in the world.

---

*Reprinted from Leonardo Boff, *Church: Charism and Power: Liberation Theology and the Institutional Church*, trans. John W. Diercksmeier (New York, 1985), 1–2, 7–11, by permission of the Crossroad Publishing Company.

There is the danger of too close an approximation, or even identification, of the Church and the Kingdom that creates an abstract and idealistic image of the Church that is spiritualized and wholly indifferent to the traumas of history. On the other hand, an identification of the Church and the world leads to an ecclesial image that is secular and mundane, one in which the Church's power is in conflict with the other powers of the world. And there is the danger of a Church centered in on itself, out of touch both with the Kingdom and the world, such that it becomes a self-sufficient, triumphal, and perfect society, many times duplicating the services normally found in civil society, failing to recognize the relative autonomy of the secular realm.

These dangers are theological "pathologies" that cry out for treatment; ecclesiological health depends on the right relationship between Kingdom-world-Church, in such a way that the Church is always seen as a concrete and historical sign (of the Kingdom and of salvation) and as its instrument (mediation) in salvific service to the world. (pp. 1–2)

A New Model: A Church from the Poor

In the 1970s arose a growing consciousness of the true causes of underdevelopment as a problem that is not simply technical or political. It is the consequence of capitalistic development in the countries of the North Atlantic which, in order to maintain current levels of growth and accumulation, need to establish unbalanced relationships with those countries that are technologically backward, though rich in raw materials. These latter countries are *kept* in underdevelopment, that is, the other side of development. This dependency creates oppression on economic, political, and cultural levels. In view of this, the long-range Christian strategy is to achieve a liberation that guarantees a self-sustained development that meets the real needs of the people, and not the consumerist needs of rich countries and groups associated with those countries.

A Political and Religious Liberation

The historical subjects of this liberation are the oppressed who must develop a consciousness of their oppressed situation, organize themselves, and take steps that will lead to a society that is less dependent and less subject to injustices. Other classes may, and should, join this project of the oppressed, but without trying to control it. In this way, beginning in the early seventies, countless young people, intellectuals, and a whole range of movements arose to make such a liberation viable. They made an option for the people: they began to enter the world of the poor, embracing the culture, giving expression to their claims, and organizing activities that were considered subversive by the forces of the status quo. More than a few took on the violence of urban guerrillas and campesinos, and were violently repressed.

Countless Christians and organizations took part in this process. They were generally individuals and groups of middle-class extraction, full of idealism but lacking political sense in terms of the concrete viability of such a popular liberation.

Later, after years of harsh repression, the bases of the Church took on exceptional importance both ecclesiologically and politically. The people themselves took responsibility for their destiny. This generally began with reading the Bible and proceeded to the creation of small base or basic ecclesial communities (*comunidades eclesiales de base*). Initially, such a community serves to deepen the faith of its members, to prepare the liturgy, the sacraments, and the life of prayer. At a more advanced stage these members begin to help each other. As they become better organized and reflect more deeply, they come to the realization that the problems they encounter have a structural character. Their marginalization is seen as a consequence of elitist organization, private ownership, that is, of the very socioeconomic structure of the capitalist system. Thus, the question of politics arises and the desire for liberation is set in a concrete and historical context. The community sees this not only as liberation from sin (from which we must always liberate ourselves) but also a liberation that has economic, political, and cultural dimensions. Christian faith directly seeks the ultimate liberation and freedom of the children of God in the Kingdom but it also includes historical liberation as an anticipation and concretization of that ultimate liberation.

A Church Born of the People's Faith

How do individuals move from the religious to the political? In general the two realities come together as one. To begin, the religious points out the injustices that God does not desire. Later the people proceed to an understanding of the true structures that produce such injustices, realizing that it is imperative to change those structures in order to keep them from generating such social sin.

Political commitment is born of the reflection of faith that demands change. Faith is never absent from an analysis of the mechanisms of oppression; faith provides a means of understanding, a powerful spirituality for action, and a focal point for human activity. The base ecclesial community does not become a political entity. It remains what it is: a place for the reflection and celebration of faith. But, at the same time, it is the place where human situations are judged ethically in the light of God. The Christian community and the political community are two open spheres where what is properly Christian circulates. The community celebrates and is nourished by its faith; it hears the word of God that engenders a commitment to one's brothers and sisters. In the political community one works and acts side by side with others, concretely realizing faith and salvation, listening to God's voice which is fully expressed in the Christian community. Both spheres are clothed in the reality of the Kingdom of God which is being realized (under different signs) in both the political and religious community.

Primarily, the base ecclesial community is more than an instrument by which the Church reaches the people and evangelizes them; it is a new and original way of living Christian faith, of organizing the community around the Word, around the sacraments (when possible), and around the new ministries exercised by lay people (both men and women). There is a new distribution of power in the community; it is much more participatory and avoids all centralization and domination. The unity of faith and life, of Gospel and liberation, is given concrete form without the artificiality of institutional structures. It makes possible the rise of a rich ecclesial sacramentality (the entire Church as sacrament), with much creativity in its celebrations and a deep sense of the sacred — all belonging to the people. A true "ecclesiogenesis" is in progress throughout the world, a Church being born from the faith of the poor.

The base ecclesial community is also the place where a true democracy of the people is practiced, where everything is discussed and decided together, where critical thought is encouraged. For a people who have been oppressed for centuries, whose "say" has always been denied, the simple fact of *having a say* is the first stage in taking control and shaping their own destiny. The *comunidad eclesial de base* thus transcends its religious meaning and takes on a highly political one.

The formation of these small communities is based on an ecclesiology that is grounded in the categories of People of God, *koinonia* (communion), prophecy, and *diakonia* (service). This type of Church presupposes what was crystallized at the Latin American bishops' meeting at Puebla in 1979: a preferential option for the poor. The exact meaning of this option is to recognize the privileged status of the poor as the new and emerging historical subject which will carry on the Christian project in the world. The poor, here, are not understood simply as those in need; they are in need but they are also the group with a historical strength, a capacity for change, and a potential for evangelization. The Church reaches out to them directly, not through the state or the ruling classes. Thus, we are no longer speaking of a Church *for* the poor but rather a Church *of* and *with* the poor. From this option for and insertion among the poor the Church begins to define its relationship with all other social classes. It does not lose its catholicity; its catholicity becomes real and not merely a matter of rhetoric. The Church is directed toward all, but begins from the poor, from their desires and struggles. Thus arise the essential themes of the Church: social change creating a more just society; human rights, interpreted as the rights of the poor majority; social justice and integral liberation, achieved primarily through sociohistorical freedom and concrete service in behalf of the disinherited of this world; and so on.

A Church Rising to Human Challenges

The categories People of God and church-communion call for a better distribution of *potestas sacra* (sacred power) within the Church and so demand a redefinition of the roles of bishop and priest while allowing for new ministries and a new style of religious life incarnated in the life of the people. The hierarchy is functional and is not an ontological establishment of classes of Christians. (This is not the place to develop the ecclesiology present in the practices of this type of Church; it is already found in an advanced stage in the theology being done in Latin America.)

This type of Church allows for a proper dialectic of the relationship of Kingdom-world-Church. The Kingdom is certainly the Christian utopia that lies at the culmination of history. But it must be repeated that this Kingdom is found in the process of history wherever justice and fraternity are fostered and wherever the poor are respected and recognized as shapers of their own destiny. All individuals, institutions, and activities directed toward those ideals favored by the historical Jesus are bearers of that Kingdom. The category of world takes on a historical meaning: the world of the poor, the "subworld" that must be transformed into the world of mutual human sharing; the Kingdom and the anti-Kingdom (the "subworld" of misery) that exist together in the world. The Kingdom is built above and against the anti-Kingdom, whose agents must be denounced. The Church proposes, in this mode, to enter into the subworld of the "nonhuman" to aid in the process of integral liberation, carrying with it its special character: its reference to the religious and its reading of the Kingdom of God already in process.

It seems that through the Church's pact with the poor (the greatest symbol of which was Pope John Paul II's gift of the pontifical ring to the *favelados* of Rio de Janeiro in July 1980) a new path for the Church has opened up. Ever since Theodosius founded the Christian state in A.D. 380 the Church has been a Church *for* the poor but it never became a Church *of* the poor. Today the poor are not looked upon simply from a charitable perspective but from a political one. This new historical subject, the poor, will decide the shape of future society. They are growing in their level of consciousness, organizing their activities, and demanding a more participatory and less elitist society. The Church in its reflection and praxis (at least in Latin America) is meeting these demands. It has let go of inadequate models and is rising to the challenge of the present. It would seem that future society will be structurally marked by Christian and gospel elements, owing to a Church that is giving birth to that future. This fact is so overwhelming that in Latin America some analysts state that any society that does not possess a high level of Christian participation will be antipopular and elitist. The model followed by the people is a Christian one; this model is being expressed in a structure that responds to the demands of history. Now is the time to demonstrate its strength and truth. It is in this light that the most promising future of the Church will be defined.

A Call to the Universal Church

In conclusion, we can say that there are distinct pastoral practices in the church, each with its latent image of what it means to be Church. Some prolong the tradition of colonial Christianity, others adapt themselves to new historical realities, especially to the need to explore the capitalist system more deeply and critically, advocating changes that are contrary to dominant social trends but that are nevertheless linked to a deep current of desire for the liberation of the poor. This multiplicity of images makes up the vitality of the Church of Christ, living and suffering its paschal mystery on the periphery of the powerful societies and the venerable churches of Europe. But the voice of this new Church speaks out more and more loudly and can be heard in the heart of the centers of power. This is a call to the whole Church to be more evangelical, more at service, and more of a sign of that salvation that penetrates the human condition. The various pastoral practices outlined above incarnate what they are called to incarnate, and this has invincible historical power. (pp. 7–11)

Congregation for the Doctrine of the Faith

"Notification to Father Leonardo Boff" (1985)*

On Feb. 12, 1982, Leonardo Boff, OFM, took the initiative of sending the Congregation for the Doctrine of the Faith his answer to the archdiocesan commission for the doctrine of the faith at Rio de Janeiro, which had criticized his book *Church: Charism and Power.* He declared that the criticism contained grave errors of reading and of interpretation.

The doctrinal congregation studied the text of the book under its doctrinal and pastoral aspects, and expressed a number of reservations to the author in a letter of May 15, 1984, which invited him to accept them and at the same time offered him the possibility of a dialogue for the sake of clarification. However, considering the influence which the book was having on the faithful, the congregation informed L. Boff that the letter would be made public in any case, account being eventually taken of the position which he might assume during the dialogue.

On Sept. 7, L. Boff was received by the cardinal-prefect of the congregation, who was assisted by Msgr. Jorge Mejia (as notary). Included in the conversation were a number of ecclesiological problems, arising from a reading of the book *Church: Charism and Power,* which were pointed out in the letter of May 15, 1984. The conversation was carried on in a fraternal atmosphere and offered the author the opportunity to present his clarifications, which were also conveyed by him in writing. All of that was noted in a final communique issued and drawn up in accord with L. Boff. At the end of the talk, the eminent Cardinals Aloisio Lorscheider and Paulo Evaristo Arns, who were in Rome for the occasion, were received by the cardinal-prefect in another place.

According to its practice, the congregation examined the oral and written clarifications furnished by L. Boff, while it noted the good intentions and repeated testimonies of fidelity to the church and the magisterium he expressed, it stated however that the reservations raised in regard to the volume and indicated in the letter could not be considered substantially overcome. It therefore considers it necessary, as was provided, to make the doctrinal content of the aforesaid letter public in its essential parts.

Doctrinal Premise

The ecclesiology of the book *Church: Charism and Power* is intended to meet the problems of Latin America, particularly Brazil (cf. p. 1),[1] through a series of studies and views. Such an intention demands on the one hand serious and

---

*Issued by the Vatican Congregation for the Doctrine of the Faith on March 11, 1985.

1. Pages cited refer to *Church: Charism and Power* unless otherwise noted.

thorough attention to the concrete situations to which the book refers; on the other hand — in order really to achieve its purpose — it requires a concern to enter into the universal church's great task, which is aimed at interpreting, developing, and applying under the guidance of the Holy Spirit the common inheritance of the unique Gospel, entrusted once and for all by the Lord to our fidelity.

In such fashion the one single faith in the Gospel creates and builds up the Catholic Church over the centuries, and the church remains one throughout the diversities of times and the differences of situations proper to the many particular churches. The universal church develops and lives in the particular churches, and these form a church, while remaining expressions and realizations of the universal church in a determined time and place so that the universal church grows and progresses in the growth and development of the particular churches; whereas the particular church would diminish and decay if unity diminished.

Therefore, true theological reasoning ought never to be content only to interpret and animate the reality of a particular church, but rather should try to penetrate the contents of the sacred deposit of God's word entrusted to the church and authentically interpreted by the magisterium. Praxis and experience always rise out of determined and limited historical situations; they aid the theologian and oblige him to make the Gospel accessible in his time. However, praxis neither replaces nor produces the truth, but remains at the service of the truth consigned to us by the Lord. The theologian has therefore to decipher the language of the various situations — the signs of the times — and to open this language up to the understanding of the faith (cf. *Redemptor Hominis*, 19).

When examined in the light of the criteria of an authentic theological method — which has just been briefly outlined — certain options in L. Boff's book appear to be unsustainable. Without claiming to analyze all of them, here are the ecclesiological options which seem decisive: the structure of the church, the concept of dogma, the exercise of sacred power, and the prophetic role.

The Structure of the Church

L. Boff, according to his own words, sets himself inside an orientation where it is affirmed that "Jesus did not have in mind the church as institution but rather that it evolved after the resurrection, particularly as part of the process of de-eschatologization" (p. 74). Consequently, for him the hierarchy is "a result" of "the powerful need to organize" and the "assuming of societal characteristics" in "the Roman and feudal style" (p. 40). Hence the necessity arises for permanent "change in the church" (p. 64); today a "new church" must arise (p. 62 and *passim*), which will be "an alternative for the incarnation of new ecclesial institutions whose power will be pure service" (p. 63).

It is in the logic of these affirmations that he also explains his interpretation of the relations between Catholicism and Protestantism: "It would appear that Roman Christianity (Catholicism) is distinguished by its valiant affirmation of sacramental identity while Protestant Christianity has fearlessly affirmed nonidentity" (p. 80; cf. pp. 84ff).

In this view, both confessions would be incomplete mediations, pertaining to a dialectical process of affirmation and negation. In this dialectic "Christianity is manifested.... What is Christianity? We do not know. We only know what is shown in the historical process" (p. 79).

This relativizing concept of the church stands at the basis of the radical criticisms directed at the hierarchic structure of the Catholic Church. In order to justify it, L. Boff appeals to the constitution *Lumen Gentium,* of the Second Vatican Council. From the council's famous statement, *Haec ecclesia (sc. unica Christi ecclesia)... subsistit in ecclesia Catholica* ("this church [that is, the sole church of Christ]... subsists in the Catholic Church"), he derives a thesis which is exactly the contrary to the authentic meaning of the council text, for he affirms: "In fact it (i.e., the sole church of Christ) may also be present in other Christian churches" (p. 75). But the council had chosen the word *subsistit* — subsists — exactly in order to make clear that one sole "subsistence" of the true church exists, whereas outside her visible structure only *elementa ecclesiae* — elements of church — exist; these — being elements of the same church — end and conduct toward the Catholic Church (*Lumen Gentium* 8). The decree on ecumenism expresses the same doctrine (*Unitatis Redintegratio* 3–4), and it was restated precisely in the declaration *Mysterium Ecclesiae* (no. 1, AAS LXV [1973], pp. 396–98).

Turning upside down the meaning of the council text on the church's subsistence lies at the base of L. Boff's ecclesiological relativism, which is outlined above; a profound misunderstanding of the Catholic faith in the church of God in the world is developed and made explicit.

Dogmas and Revelation

The same relativizing logic is found again in the conception of doctrine and dogma expressed by L. Boff. The author criticizes in a very severe way the "doctrinal" understanding of revelation (p. 42). It is true that L. Boff distinguishes between dogmatism and dogma (cf. p. 85), admitting the latter and rejecting the former. However, according to him, dogma in its formulation holds good only "for a specific time and specific circumstances" (p. 76). "In the later stages of the process, the text must be able to give way to a new text of faith proper to today's world" (p. 77).

The relativism resulting from such affirmations becomes explicit when L. Boff speaks of mutually contradictory doctrinal positions contained in the New Testament (cf. p. 77). Consequently, "the truly Catholic attitude" would be "to be fundamentally open to everything without exception" (p. 77). In L. Boff's perspective, the sole authentic Catholic conception of dogma falls under the verdict "dogmatism." "As long as this type of dogmatic and doctrinaire understanding of revelation and salvation continues, there inevitably will be repression of the freedom of thought within the church" (p. 42).

In this regard it must be pointed out that the contrary of relativism is not literalism or immobility. The ultimate content of revelation is God himself, Father, Son, and Holy Spirit, who invites us to communion with him; all the words refer to the word or, as St. John of the Cross says: "In his Son... he told everything to all of us and at one time in that sole word, and he has no more to say" ("Ascent of Mount Carmel," 11, 22). But the truth on God and man is expressed in a way deserving belief in the always analogical and limited word of Scripture and the authentic belief of the church, based on Scripture. The permanent necessity of interpreting the language of the past, far from sacrificing this truth, renders it accessible and develops the richness of the authentic texts. Walking under the guidance of the Lord, who is the way and the truth (John 14:6), the church, teaching and believing, is sure that the truth expressed in the words of faith not only does not oppress man, but liberates him (John 8:32) and is the sole instrument of real communion among people of various classes and opinions, whereas a dialectical and relativistic conception exposes man to arbitrary decision making.

Already in the past this congregation has had to point out that the sense of the dogmatic formulas always remains true and coherent, determined and unalterable, although it may be further clarified and better understood (cf. *Mysterium Ecclesiae*, pp. 403–4).

In order to go on with its function of being the salt of the earth which never loses its savor, the *depositum fidei* (the deposit of faith) must be loyally preserved in its purity, without falling along the line of a dialectical process of history and in the direction of the primacy of praxis.

Exercise of Sacred Power

A "grave pathology" from which, according to L. Boff, the Roman church ought to liberate itself is constituted by the hegemonic exercise of the sacred power which, besides making the Roman church an asymmetrical society, has also deformed it.

L. Boff takes it for granted that the organizational axis of a society coincides with the specific mode of production proper to it, and he applies this principle to the church. Thus he affirms that there has been a historical process of expropriation of the means of religious production on the part of the clergy and to the detriment of the Christian people; the latter would then have seen itself deprived of its capacity to decide, to teach (cf. pp. 43; 133ff.; 138–43). Moreover, after having suffered this expropriation, the sacred power would also have been gravely deformed, thereby falling into the same defects as profane power in terms of domination, centralization, triumphalism (cf. pp. 72, 56, 60ff.). In order to remedy these unbefitting features, a new model of the church is proposed in which power is conceived without theological privileges, as pure service, articulated according to the community's needs (cf. pp. 161, 63).

One ought not impoverish the reality of the sacraments and the word of God by reducing them to the "production and consumption" pattern, thus reducing the communion of faith to a mere sociological phenomenon. The sacraments are not "symbolic material," their administration is not production, their reception is not consumption. The sacraments are gifts of God, no one "produces" them, all receive the grace of God in them, which are the signs of the eternal love. All that lies beyond any production, beyond every human doing and fabrication. The sole measure corresponding to the greatness of the gift is utmost fidelity to the will of the Lord, according to which all — priests and laity — will be judged, all of them being "useless servants" (Luke 17:10). Certainly the danger of abuse always exists. The problem is always present of how access by all the faithful to full participation in the church's life and its sources, the Lord's life, can be guaranteed. But interpreting the reality of the sacraments, of the hierarchy, of the word, and the whole life of the church in terms of production and consumption, of monopoly, expropriation, conflict with the hegemonic bloc, rupture, and the occasion for an asymmetrical method of production is equivalent to subverting religious reality, and that, far from contributing to the solution of various problems, leads rather to the destruction of the authentic meaning of the sacraments and of the word of faith.

Role in the Church

The book *Church: Charism and Power* denounces the church's hierarchy and institutions (pp. 3–34; 57; 154–56). By way of explanation and justification of this attitude, it makes primary the role of the charisma, particularly of prophecy (cf. pp. 33–34; 57; 154–56; 162). The hierarchy would have the mere function of "coordinating," of "making way for unity and harmony among the various services," and keeping flowing and impeding all division and impositions, therefore eliminating from the prophetic function "immediate subordination of the members to those in the hierarchy" (p. 164).

There is no doubt that the whole people of God takes part in the prophetic office of Christ (cf. *Lumen Gentium* 12). Christ fulfills his prophetic office not only by means of the hierarchy but also by means of the laity (cf. ibid.). But it is equally clear that, in order to be legitimate, prophetic denunciation in the church must always remain at the service of the church itself. Not only must it accept the hierarchy and the institutions, but it must also cooperate positively in the consolidation of the church's internal communion; furthermore, the supreme criterion for judging not only its ordinary exercise but also its genuineness pertains to the hierarchy (cf. ibid., 12).

Conclusion

In making the above publicly known, the congregation also feels obliged to declare that the opinions of L. Boff analyzed here endanger the sound doctrine of the faith, which this congregation has the task of promoting and safeguarding.

The supreme pontiff John Paul II, in the course of the audience granted to the undersigned prefect, approved the present notification, decided upon in the ordinary meeting of this congregation, and ordered its publication.

Rome, from the seat of the Congregation of the Doctrine of the Faith, March 11, 1985

Cardinal Joseph Ratzinger, prefect
Archbishop Albert Bovone, secretary

John Macquarrie (b. 1919)

Principles of Christian Theology (1977)*

In the preceding sections of this chapter, we have tried to set forth some basic characteristics of the Church. The time has now come to gather these together in a more coherent scheme, and also to bring them down to earth, as it were, by considering the actual visible structure in which they find expression. For up till now, we have (quite justifiably) been looking for the essence of the Church in terms of its highest manifestations and in relation to those theological doctrines which determine its direction and destiny. But if we lay too much stress on these ways of conceiving the Church, we can come out with that mistaken understanding of the Church which gives to it a premature glory and confuses it with the eschatological kingdom of God. If indeed we believe that the Church is a theological entity as well as a sociological one, then we should expect to see even in the dustiest epochs of "the church militant here on earth" some glimmerings of the glory which, as we hope, shall yet be revealed in it. But the treasure is very much in earthen vessels, and the Church is a mixed phenomenon. It unfolds creation and ministers reconciliation, but it falls short of consummation.

Our discussion may be conveniently organized around the four traditional notes of the Church, as the one, holy, catholic, and apostolic Church. Unity, holiness, catholicity, and apostolicity will be found to sum up those essential characteristics of the Church which have emerged in the earlier discussions. We shall see how in the actual historical Church these notes may be more or less visible, according as the essence of the Church is emerging more or less purely. The Christian hope is that these notes will come through more and more clearly as the Church moves toward consummation. But at any given time, we see them only "more or less." Moreover, each of them needs some visible or institutional structure for its embodiment and protection, but, as with all "earthen vessels," while these are quite indispensable, they are never perfect.

We have first to say something about the *unity* of the Church, though this is such an inclusive concept that it can hardly be separated from the other three marks of the Church. In its fullest sense, the unity of the Church implies its holiness, catholicity, and apostolicity. However, there is a basic unity which can be discussed at the outset.

The basic unity has at its center Jesus Christ himself. The Christian community of faith is at one in confessing that Jesus Christ is Lord, and the unity which he establishes extends through and holds together the many Christian groups. We have seen already that the most appropriate of all the titles of the Church is the "body of Christ." Christ is the head of the body, and therefore the source of its unity. It is he who makes it a body, a unitary coordinated organism, rather than a collection of individual entities. Yet this very metaphor of the body also stresses the diversity in unity. St. Paul declares: "The body does not consist of one mem-

---

*Reprinted from John Macquarrie, *Principles of Christian Theology* (New York: Charles Scribner's Sons, 1977), 401–13, by permission of Simon and Schuster.

ber, but of many,"[1] and he is at pains to show the diversity of gifts and functions that are necessary to the life of the body. We see that the richer is the diversity, the stronger is the unity and interdependence. We are reminded also by this picture that the Church is a microcosm, for this diversity in unity we recognize as the end of creation itself; and while the Church is the fellowship of the Holy Spirit, the same Spirit is "unitive Being," that movement in Being which builds up ever larger and richer unities. So we see too that the Church has indefinite edges — it merges into the wider community of faith, and eventually into the whole divine work of creation-reconciliation-consummation. But the Christian sees it as the spearhead of this work, though its ultimate destiny may be to lose itself and transcend itself in the still wider unity of the consummated kingdom.

The problem of the Church's unity — as of the wider unity of mankind, to which it is closely related — is rightly to balance the unity against the diversity. A unity that flattens out all diversity falls far below that free kind of unity which we saw to be at once the glory and the risk of creation. The first is the unity of a machine, the second a unity of persons. Cardinal Bea has well said: "A unity that does not respect the principle of freedom may eventually create a certain form of unity, but not a human one; it is not a unity of free and responsible men, but of slaves."[2] But if there is a unity that swallows up freedom, there is also a diversity that breaks up unity rather than contributing to it. The member lives to itself in a false autonomy, eventually destroying itself and perhaps the whole body with it.

It is important to remember that in his great prayer for his disciples, Christ asked "that they may be one," and immediately went on to indicate that this unity should be like the unity of the Father and the Son.[3] The ultimate model for the Church's unity is therefore the unity of the triune God, a unity embracing the richest diversity and thus one in which there is neither stifling absorption nor damaging division.

The historical Church has sometimes more, sometimes less manifested something like a genuine unity in Christ. Even in New Testament times, there was destructive divisiveness and factionalism, and no period of the Church's history has been without its schisms, heresies, and dissensions. But although we hear a lot about "our unhappy divisions," we ought to remember that just as offensive to true unity has been the false unity that has characterized other phases of the Church's history — the outward uniformity that has suppressed legitimate differences and has been imposed by force. The genuine diversity-in-unity of the body of Christ needs to be defended against uniformity just as much as against divisiveness. . . .

The most obvious visible sign of the Church's unity is the Bible. If indeed the center of the Church's unity is Jesus Christ, as the head of the body, then the Bible is the embodiment of that unity because it is the written word, testifying to the manifestation of the living Word in the flesh. The Bible is also the most widespread visible sign of the unity of faith that belongs to the whole body of Christians, for some groups that do not even have the sacraments (Quakers, Sal-

---

1. 1 Corinthians 12:14.
2. Augustin Bea, *Unity in Freedom* (New York: Harper and Row, 1964), 6–7.
3. John 17:11.

vation Army) and yet which are undeniably Christians, have the Bible. The Bible therefore stretches out as far as what we have called the "indefinite" borders of the Church. More than this, however, the Bible links the Church with the wider community of faith, for the Bible contains not only the distinctively Christian New Testament but also the Hebrew scriptures; and although to the Christian theologian this is the "Old Testament" and is read in a Christian perspective, no reasonable person would deny that in and by themselves, the Hebrew scriptures have been produced out of the experiences of faith and revelation, and still function as vehicles of revelation in Judaism. Hence the Bible links Christianity with Judaism and so eventually with the faith adventure of the world's religions.

Because of its universal acceptance among Christians, the Bible already constitutes a remarkable foundation for unity, and any ecumenical theology must be firmly rooted in the Bible. But this is certainly not meant to imply that such an ecumenical theology must be narrowly biblicist. The kind of theology that has been produced in Protestant ecumenical circles has up till now been too much dominated by the somewhat narrow idea of a "biblical" theology, free from external cultural influences, such as was fashionable in the earlier days of the Barthian movement. Far more allowance has to be made — as the later Barth seems to recognize — for subsequent development in the Church, that is to say, for tradition. The canon of the Bible itself, after all, was fixed by the Church. In doing this, the Church set up a visible embodiment to protect the unity of its faith. At the same time, however, it erected a standard to which it submits itself. So we come back to the idea of a division of authority. This reminds us too that the note of unity in the Church has an inclusiveness that spills over into the other notes, and the full conception of unity and its visible embodiment cannot be reached until we have talked also of the remaining three notes.

Next among the notes comes *holiness*. Here it is very much a case of "more or less," and to many it will seem that the Church has often been less rather than more holy. We have to be clear, however, about what the "holiness" of the Church means. It cannot mean an otherworldly holiness that keeps its hands clean, so to speak, by avoiding contamination with earthly things. In our discussion of the saints, stress was laid on the variety of gifts and vocations. The "holiness" of the saints is not an escape from the world (though there will always be some whose vocation is to protest against materialistic preoccupations by a life of withdrawal), but obedience in a particular situation. "Let it be to me according to your word."[4] In again quoting these words of the Virgin, I am trying to make the point that holiness means being an agent of the incarnation, letting Christ be formed in the Church and in the world. Or in the more ontological language that we have used from time to time, holiness is cooperation with the letting-be of Being, it is the strengthening and promoting of the beings as against the threat of dissolution. But normally this can be done only by the maximal participation and involvement in the life of the world.

The Church is the communion of saints, and the achievements of the saints remain as a constant testimony and encouragement to the reality of grace in the

4. Luke 1:38.

Church. But here again we must be careful not to form an exaggerated idea of the Church as it is *in via*. It has innumerable blind spots and lapses. We may believe in its ultimate indefectibility and that holiness, in the sense explained, is making headway, so that the Church and indeed all humankind is being sanctified by God's reconciling work. But we have already distinguished indefectibility from infallibility. In many particular instances, the Church utterly falls short of holiness, and may even, through its support of wrong causes or a reactionary politico-social *status quo,* or sometimes through the idolizing of its own structure, work against sanctification. Yet one would hope — and legitimately, since this is simply part of the eschatological Christian hope — that these lapses would be episodes which would be eventually overcome in the total life of the Church.

The visible embodiment of the Church's holiness is its sacramental life. Since the sacraments will be discussed in detail in a later chapter, only some brief remarks need to be made here; but in any case, the whole basic philosophy of this book, with its stress on how Being becomes present and manifest in and through the beings, lends itself readily to the sacramental and incarnational principle. The sacraments may be understood as the growing points, as it were, at which the divine grace sanctifies the Church and conforms its life to Christ. They are also the ways by which the existence of the individual is incorporated into the body of Christ. Yet once again, as in the case of the Bible, we must avoid rigidity. In both cases, one can develop a "fundamentalism" that mistakes the earthen vessel for the treasure that it contains. We have seen that there are some Christian groups that have discarded the commonly accepted sacraments. It is not to be denied that grace operates in them too, for the operation of the divine Spirit is not confined to the recognized sacraments, any more than it is confined to the Christian religion. It may even be that these groups constitute a warning against the overprizing of sacramental forms. Yet even such groups have sacraments of a sort, whatever they may call them, for the grace of Being cannot reach us save through the beings in which it is present and manifest. We must not idolize particular sacramental forms, yet on the other hand the forms which are rooted in the Bible and which have been developed in the Church's tradition and proved of value in her devotional life are bound to command a very special respect and reverence. These are the institutional forms, suited to our embodied existence, that protect and foster the growth of holiness, first in the Church and then in all humanity.

We pass to the third note of the Church — *catholicity*. There are two distinct but related ideas implied in this third note. "Catholicity" means, first of all, universality. The Church is for all men, for what goes on in the Church, as we have seen, is simply the spearhead of what is going on in the creation as a whole. The end of the Church cannot be complete until the whole creation is complete, and then of course the distinction between the Church and the rest of creation will have disappeared. This means that the Church must be an open rather than a closed society. In its catholic outreach, it abolishes the divisive demarcations that set one segment of society against another, though it does not obliterate the variety of human beings but enriches the unity of the whole by giving scope to many kinds of gifts and vocations. St. Paul affirms that "in Christ" there is "neither Jew nor Greek, there is neither slave nor free, there is neither male nor female";[5] but he is equally clear that "there are varieties of gifts...varieties of service...varieties of working."[6] It is this inclusive unity-with-diversity that constitutes the catholicity of the Church as universality. But "catholicity" also means authenticity, that is to say, authenticity of belief and practice in the Church. This second meaning is related to the first, for it has in view the consensus of the Church. The authentic faith is to be learned by considering the universal faith. So from New Testament times onward, we find that when some weighty matter is to be decided, this is done by summoning a council and ascertaining the consensus of the Church.

The structures in which the catholicity of the Church gets embodied are primarily the catholic creeds, especially the Apostles' and Nicene; and also the pronouncements of the universally recognized councils of the Church, such as those of Nicaea and Chalcedon. They give considered expression to the mind of the universal Church, speaking, as it believes, under the guidance of the Spirit.

The creeds are catholic in both senses of the word. They set forth the authentic faith, but they are not to be thought of as sets of propositions to be intellectually received. We have insisted from the beginning of this study that faith is more than belief; it is an existential attitude. This comes out clearly in the reciting of the creeds by the Christian community. The creeds express the identity of the community. The only qualification required for joining the community is to share its faith, and to join with the members of the community in the creed is to identify with them, to participate in their attitude toward Christ, toward existence, toward Being.

Perhaps relatively few Christians understand fully on the intellectual level the contents of the ancient creeds. In any case, the creeds and the pronouncements of the ancient councils were aimed at excluding errors, and were certainly not intended to exclude further study. They leave plenty of room for freedom and development in theological discussion. The attempt to define too many doctrines too precisely is an error, for it overestimates the importance of the visible structure and forgets that this structure has not been produced for its own sake but in order to protect and foster a living faith, which cannot be completely transcribed into words.

If we remember the double meaning of catholicity, we shall not be in danger of confusing it with correct doctrine. There may be churches which stick to the letter of correct doctrine and which yet offend against catholicity because they deny the universality of the Church. We do in fact hear from time to time about churches which exclude from their membership and even from their worship persons of a different race from the members; and often enough, such churches pride themselves on their orthodoxy and their conservative (not to say reactionary) theology. No matter how orthodox these congregations may be, they have cut themselves off from true catholicity by denying the universal character of the Church. They can no longer have any part in that ever-widening fellowship which cannot stop short of all creation, and which will be transformed into the kingdom when it

---

5. Galatians 3:28.
6. 1 Corinthians 12:4–6.

coincides with creation — and only then. Such so-called churches are moving in the opposite direction into isolation and disintegration, like branches that have been severed from the vine. This is true even if (as one must charitably hope) their attitude springs from ignorance rather than from malice against their human brethren.

Thus the case with catholicity is like those we have already met in connection with unity and holiness. There is a structural form within the world that both expresses and protects the truly catholic being of the Church, but we must again hold the balance between inner and outer, between spontaneity and the fixity of forms. The creeds and the ancient christological formulae are so built into the Church that they express its very identity and let its members experience their solidarity in this universal community; but they are meaningless if they do not protect and enhance a faith that reaches into all the dimensions of existence.

The last note that we have to consider is *apostolicity*, and this one perhaps gives rise to the greatest controversy. Apostolicity is not too sharply distinguished from catholicity, especially in the second of the two senses of "catholicity." The apostolic Church is the authentic Church, continuing the teaching and practice of the apostles, who had been "eyewitnesses" of the events proclaimed in the Church's message, and who had been commissioned by Christ himself. Faithfulness to the apostles appears as a mark of the New Testament Church in its earliest period: "[T]hey devoted themselves to the apostles' teaching."[7] Before long, many heretical sects were springing up, as the Christian teaching coalesced with Gnostic and other religious ideas of the time. The authentic Christian community had to distinguish itself and its message from the heterodox groups, and it sought to do this by establishing its continuity with the apostles. The respect in which the apostles were held is attested by the well-known fact that there are several books in the New Testament written by anonymous authors but ascribed to leading apostles, so as to gain for them an authority that they could not otherwise have. But of course, the heretics played the same game, and we have many apocryphal writings that also bear the names of apostles. Eventually the Church, as we have already noted, decided which books were to be regarded as authoritative, and the canon was formed. But since there were, both inside and outside the canon as it was eventually formed, books claiming to be written by apostles, the matter was not settled just by the question of authorship, but by the Church's own living continuity with the apostles. Even in ancient times, there were doubts as to the authorship of some of the New Testament documents, and in modern times these doubts have crystallized in some cases into virtual certainty. But this does not in the slightest degree alter the Church's attitude toward these documents, for whether or not their actual authors were apostles, their teaching is in accordance with apostolic tradition, as this was received and continued among the first generations of Christians.

Whereas "catholicity" indicates the authenticity of the Church's practice and teaching by pointing to the consensus of Christians throughout the world, "apostolicity" has to do rather with the extension of the Church through time, its

---

7. Acts 2:42.

continuity and identity through the ages. Though it must indeed change in many ways, it can claim to be the Church of Jesus Christ only if it has retained at least a minimal degree of continuity with Christ, first through his apostles and then through the generations of their successors. Again, we can make a comparison between the Church and a self. As the commitment of faith plays an important part in unifying a self, so that we can recognize it as the same self as it moves through time, so too the community of faith is united by the same faith that has spanned the centuries. The formulations of that faith have changed and will change, but the existential attitude which constitutes the core of the faith has remained constant. So the inner meaning, if we may so speak, of the apostolicity of the Church is its constancy in the faith of the apostles.

As with the other notes of the Church, the note of apostolicity has its own embodiment or institutional form to protect it. This form is the episcopate. This office, publicly transmitted by the apostles to their successors and then on through the generations, is the overt, institutional vehicle for ensuring the continuity of that heritage of faith and practice which was likewise transmitted by the apostles.

There will be a discussion of the ministry of the Church and its various orders and functions in the next chapter, so I do not propose to embark here on any lengthy remarks about the office of a bishop. Let me simply draw attention to the parallel between the episcopate and the other "embodiments" (the canon of Scripture, the sacraments, the creeds) which we met when considering the first three notes of the Church. The episcopate, like the others, protects by an outward institution the inner life of the Church. In all the threats of heresy and perversion to which it has been exposed, not only in the early centuries but later, the Church has held to its apostolic heritage and this has been in no small measure due to the specific office of the bishop, as the guardian of that heritage, and also, let it be said, to the qualities of most of those who have held this office. The episcopate cannot be treated as if it were on a different footing from the other embodied forms associated with the fundamental notes of the Church.

The case has been put so well and clearly by John Knox that I can do not better than summarize his argument. He shows how the various features of the early Catholic Church were intended to establish its unity and integrity, and were not only *ad hoc* responses to the Gnostic threat but developments of the New Testament understanding of the Church. In particular, he draws an analogy among the canon, the creeds, and the episcopate. All came to be regarded as "apostolic," which means "that the early Catholic Church, which in reality established these forms (or in whose experience they were first established), thought of itself as doing no more than recognizing what had been established by the apostles themselves." It is not a question of whether, as a matter of historical fact, the apostles wrote the books ascribed to them in the New Testament, or whether the Apostles' Creed was actually composed by the apostles, or whether the apostolic ministry in the form of the historic episcopate was plainly and universally present from the beginning. We are to think of these rather in the context of the Church as a "visible, historical community," possessing an identity and yet developing in response to new demands and opportunities. The point about the various forms is that although they required time before they developed to the point where they clearly emerge in history, they express the mind and character of the Church as it had been since the apostles.

The argument summarized here is entirely compatible with the views developed in this book of embodied existence in the world, of community as extending through time in a manner analogous to selfhood, and of the Church as a community of faith which must express and protect its being through specific institutional forms that have now become part of its identity. For these reasons, we have to agree with John Knox when he says: "I for one have no hesitancy ascribing the same status to episcopacy as to canon and creed."[8]

It is time for us to draw together the findings of this section on the notes of the Church. As a historical association, the Church exhibits "more or less" the unity, holiness, catholicity, and apostolicity which will fully belong to it only when it gives itself up in order to become the kingdom of God. It exhibits unity the more it is obedient to Christ as its head; holiness, the more the divine Spirit is immanent and active within it; catholicity and apostolicity, the more it manifests the authentic Christian faith that brings men into community across the barriers of geography, race, culture, or even time. Because it is embodied in an earthly existence, the Church has its treasures in earthen vessels that are not to be despised, and we have listed as the four most vital to it: the Holy Scriptures, the sacraments, the catholic creeds, and the historic episcopate....

It must be remembered too that no claim is made that only churches which have this fourfold structure are "true" churches. It was already conceded that even Christian groups that do not have the sacraments are not to be thought of as "excluded," and it has also been maintained that the Church merges at its borders into the wider community of faith and eventually into the world. God's Spirit is not confined to particular institutional channels. On the other hand, the Church cannot live without an institutional structure, and the four forms that have been described may be said to constitute the normative shape of the Church, a shape that has proved its value in most of its provinces throughout most of its history.... Within the framework of the "quadrilateral," there is endless scope for variety and experiment, though stability and continuing identity are likewise assured. We should indeed expect that in our changing world, new forms of church life must be developed. What, in detail, these might be, is not our business to say, but we can well envisage that house-churches, industrial missions, vocational groups, *ad hoc* actions in critical situations and the like may all be required and in some cases may prove much more effective than some of the cumbrous machinery that has come down to us. Actually, the demands are very different in different areas of the Church. For instance, they are one thing where the Church suffers from the danger of popularity, but quite another where the danger is persecution. It is always worth remembering that in the most glorious period of all in its history, the first three centuries, the Church had hardly any of the "apparatus" or "plant," still less of the appalling bureaucracy, that now seems to be taken for granted. Yet it must also be remembered that it was precisely in that early period that the Church protected and stabilized her life and mission by firmly basing

8. John Knox, *The Early Church and the Coming Great Church* (London: Epworth, 1957), 152.

herself on that fourfold foundation which bodied itself forth in the canon, the sacraments, the creeds, and the apostolic ministry.

Rita Nakashima Brock (b. 1950)

Journeys by Heart (1988)*

The remembrance of Jesus' death is a call to decision and action. The Gospel of Mark insists that those who would travel in the territories of erotic power must risk living their new vision. This risk is the process of being on the way, not to a goal at the end of history or time, but always on the journey of expectation that comes from the courage of living by heart. The church claimed the defeat of death by placing salvation in spiritualized form and went on to reproduce unilateral forms of power in its own systems and theology, blaspheming erotic power. The death of Jesus, remembered in its complexity in Mark, provides us with evidence that our reliance on unilateral powers will cause us to betray our own original grace and perpetuate suffering and destruction. No one heroic or divine deed will defeat oppressive powers and death-delivering systems. We cannot rely on one past event to save our future. No almighty power will deliver us from evil. With each minute we wait for such rescue, more die.

The power that gives and sustains life does not flow from a dead and resurrected savior to his followers. Rather, the community sustains life-giving power by its memory of its own brokenheartedness and of those who have suffered and gone before and by its members being courageously and redemptively present to all. In doing so, the community remains Christa/Community and participates in the life-giving flow of erotic power. No one person or group exclusively reveals it or incarnates it. In thinking that a single person, a savior, or even one group can save us, we mistake the crest of a wave for the vast churning beneath it.

Jesus is like the whitecap on a wave. The whitecap is momentarily set off from the swell that is pushing it up, making us notice it. But the visibility of the whitecap, which draws our attention, rests on the enormous pushing power of the sea — of its power to push with life-giving labor, to buoy up all lives, and to unite diverse shores with restless energy. That sea becomes monstrous and chaotically destructive when we try to control it, and its life-giving power is denied. Jesus' power lies with the great swells of the ocean without which the white foam is not brought to visibility. To understand the fullness of erotic power we must look to the ocean which is the whole and compassionate being, including ourselves.

No one else can help us avoid our own pain. No one else can stop the suffering of brokenheartedness in our world but our own courage and willingness to act in the midst of the awareness of our own fragility. No one else can die for us or bring justice, liberation, and healing. The refusal to give up on ourselves and our willingness to struggle with brokenheartedness involve us in healing the powers of destruction, which must be taken into our circle of remembrance and healing if we

---

*Reprinted from Rita Nakashima Brock, *Journeys by Heart: A Christology of Erotic Power* (New York, 1988), 105–8, by permission of the Crossroad Publishing Company.

are to understand and love the whole of life. Our heartfelt action, not alone, but in the fragile, resilient interconnections we share with others, generates the power that makes and sustains life. There, in the erotic power of heart, we find the sacred mystery that binds us in loving each other fiercely in the face of suffering and pain and that empowers our witness against all powers of oppression and destruction.

In facing the ambivalent realities of our own lives and of the patriarchal societies in which we live, we are led to heal ourselves and each other. In the self-acceptance and wholeness that come with healing, we are empowered to live by heart, to reach out to each other and to the whole aching and groaning cosmos in acts of honest remembrance and heartfelt connection. We are called to find the courage to find the destructive forces of brokenheartedness in solidarity with all those who suffer....

Evocations of an honest, healing memory that returns us to heart can happen in unexpected places. The journey into the territories of erotic power like the women's journey to Jesus' tomb is a journey with surprises and no definite goals. It can only be followed as our hearts lead us. It is like Nelle Morton's description of the journey of a metaphor: trying to control it toward a predetermined outcome thwarts the process. The mystery of the journey's way stations and the unexpected twists and turns that startle, frighten, inspire, enliven, and heal us are the gifts of its grace. Those gifts are always available, even when we do not expect them. The fundamental question for our civilization and for all life as we know it on our planet is will we have the courage to give ourselves to the call of that mystery, to the active, forbearing, passionate gentleness that will not let life go.

Christa/Community is found in unexpected and expected places. Vast as the ocean, that community stretches far into the unexplored territories of erotic power. It is alive in the daily actions of those who, in small acts and large ones, live with courage, with heart.

We stand as witnesses against those who seek to dominate others and objectify and disconnect life. We also stand as witnesses against all theologians that continue to affirm divine power as paternalism and dominance. Erotic power is the only life-giving power. Our ability to live in its grace and to risk acting to stop the forces that crush it is what continually creates salvific acts. Spirit-Sophia and humanity as Christa/Community journey together into the territories of erotic power where we discover our love for the whole and compassionate being, the incarnation of divine love.

Pedro Casaldáliga (b. 1928)

"A New Way of Being Church" (1993)*

The subject of the church in the spirituality of liberation is crucial, and it often involves conflict, because it challenges not merely individuals, but the in-

*Reprinted from Pedro Casaldáliga and José-María Vigil, *Political Holiness: A Spirituality of Liberation* (Maryknoll, N.Y., 1994), 181–83, by permission of Orbis Books.

stitution itself. The vision, the conception, the perspective, the attitude, the love, the spirit, with which the spirituality of liberation envisages the mystery and the fact of the church enable us to talk of a "new sense of the church," or of a new spirituality in living the mystery of the church in Latin America. Typical phrases often used — quite legitimately — in Latin America to describe this development are "the conversion of the church," "a new way of being church," and even "a new life-style for the whole church, communal from top to bottom," which is particularly associated with the base communities of Brazil.

The most important point to understand in order to appreciate the essence of this spirituality is the relationship between the church and the Reign. There was a time when the church was identified with the Reign of God on earth, and was described as a "perfect society." The first draft of the Dogmatic Constitution on the Church prepared for the First Vatican Council said: "We teach and declare that the church has all the marks of a perfect society. It is so perfect in itself that this is what distinguishes it from all other human societies and places it above them." In our time, however, we are much more conscious of the centrality of the Reign of God and see the church as an instrument in the service of the Reign.

The church is not the Reign, but the "seed and beginning" of the Reign. It is an instrument. It is at the service of the Reign. Its only purpose is to serve the Reign and prepare for its coming, hasten its coming, be a channel for it, encourage it. This is a constant theme of the documents of the Second Vatican Council: "The church receives the mission to proclaim and establish among all peoples the Kingdom of Christ and of God" (*Lumen Gentium* 5); "Its goal is the Kingdom of God, which has been begun by God himself on earth and is to be further extended" (*Lumen Gentium* 9); "For this the church was founded, [to spread] the Kingdom of Christ everywhere" (*Apostolicam Actuositatem* 2); "The church has a single intention, that God's Kingdom may come" (*Gaudium et Spes* 45). It is entirely dependent on the Reign. Everything in the church, including its very existence, has to be at the service of the Reign, at the service of God's cause, which is also the cause of human beings: "Christians cannot yearn for anything more ardently than to serve the people of the modern world ever more generously and effectively" (*Gaudium et Spes* 93); "The church claims no other authority than that of ministering to people" (*Ad Gentes* 12); "The church has declared itself, as it were, the servant of humanity. The idea of service occupied a central place. All this wealth of teaching leads in one direction: serving human beings."[1] To spend itself, and wear itself out, for the Reign of God, even if this takes its life, this is the purpose and deepest meaning of the church. This takes us far away from any "church-focus" such as existed in the past: "Unfortunately it has happened that (the church) became more interested in its own problems, in its own advantage, and did not concern itself with the problems of justice and freedom unless they affected the church, its structures, or its internal ecclesiastical structure. As late as the time of Pius IX, the church of the clergy was more interested in itself than

---

1. Paul VI, closing speech of the Second Vatican Council, in *Concilio Vaticano II* (Madrid: Editorial Católica, 1966), 1028.

in the world's problems, which it often did not react to or discuss."[2] The Reign is the absolute, and everything else is relative (*Evangelii Nuntiandi* 8). Everything in the church (its organization, its resources, its assets, its law) must be always at the service of the Reign.

The Reign is Jesus' cause, which is justice, love, freedom, mercy, reconciliation, direct contact with God. Whenever human beings work for the victory of these causes, they are making the Reign, and carrying forward Jesus' cause. On the other hand, when people say that they believe in the name of Jesus or belong to his church, it does not always mean that they are carrying forward his cause. The most important thing is the Reign, not the church. The church is important too, but its importance is rooted in its continually building the Reign until it comes to fruition.

In this new sense of what the church is, as in the other elements of our spirituality, we do not rely on a "new theological theory," but on our eagerness to be guided by Jesus. Jesus' aim was not "to found a church," but to serve the Reign. No church would be really the church of Jesus if it did not, like him, place its life at the service of the Reign as an absolute. We believe in a church that is a "sacrament" (*Lumen Gentium* 1), the flesh of Jesus in every time and place, the visible, incarnate, and inculturated sign of the presence of Jesus: "It is the function of the church, led by the Holy Spirit who renews and purifies her ceaselessly, to make God the Father and his incarnate Son present and in a sense visible" (*Gaudium et Spes* 21).

This becomes as tangible as Jesus' own flesh. To be the church, to be "the church of Jesus," for us can be nothing other than to live and fight for Jesus' cause, for the Reign of God, that is, to transform this world by bringing it closer to the utopia that God has shown to us so that we may build it in history: the Reign of God, which is "life, truth, justice, peace, grace, love, reconciliation, forgiveness, knowledge of God."

Elisabeth Schüssler Fiorenza

Discipleship of Equals (1993)*

It is usually assumed that spirituality has something to do with the life of the "soul," with prayer-life and worship, with meditation and mystical union, with "waiting" for God's will to come to pass and religious experience of the divine. In this understanding spirituality concentrates above all on prayer and meditation, on "spiritual" direction and Christ's indwelling of the soul, on ascetic and religious exercises as the precondition for progress on the spiritual journey of the soul from one level to another. In a similar fashion feminist spirituality can

---

2. Yves Congar, "Iglesia y mundo en la perspectiva del Vaticano II," in *La Iglesia del mundo de hoy, III: Reflexiones y Perspectivas*, ed. Yves Congar and Pierre Peuchmaurd (Madrid: Editorial Católica, 1970), 4.

*Reprinted from Elisabeth Schüssler Fiorenza, *Discipleship of Equals: A Critical Feminist Ekklesia-logy of Liberation* (New York, 1993), 197–201, 204–5, by permission of the Crossroad Publishing Company.

be occupied with meditation and incantations, spells and incense, womb chant and candle gazing, feminine symbols for the divine and trance induction. Such an understanding of spirituality in terms of religious rituals and practices is found in all religions and not limited to Christianity. Therefore, it does not capture the specific vision of Jesus and the movement initiated by him.

The gospel is not a matter of the individual soul; it is the communal proclamation of the life-giving power of Spirit-Wisdom. It is God's vision of an alternative community and world. The experience of the Spirit's creative power releases us from the life-destroying powers of structural sin and sets us free to choose an alternative life for ourselves and for each other. The focal point of early Christian self-understanding was not a holy book or a cultic rite, not mystic experience and magic invocation, but a set of relationships: the experience of God's presence among one another and through one another. To embrace the gospel means to enter into a community; the one cannot be obtained without the other. The gospel calls into being the *ekklesia* as a discipleship of equals that is continually being re-created in the power of the Spirit. Jesus' ministry, his healings and exorcisms, his promise to the poor and challenge to the rich, his breaking of religious law and his table community with outcasts and sinners, made experientially available God's new world, not, as we used to think, *within* us but *among* us. God's presence is found in the "midst of us" (Luke 17:21). The name of Jesus is Emmanuel, "God with us." The God of Jesus is divine Wisdom-Spirit whose power is gentle and whose yoke is light.

Like Jesus' own ministry so the community called forth by Jesus, the messenger of Divine Wisdom, is not an end in itself. In the power of the Spirit the disciples are sent to do what he did: to feed the hungry, heal the sick, liberate the oppressed, and announce the inbreaking of God's intended world and humanity here and now. In every generation Divine Wisdom commissions prophets — women and men — and makes them friends and children of God. To embrace the gospel means to enter a movement, to become a member of God's people who are on the road that stretches from Christ's death to Her return in glory. *Ekklesia* — the Greek term for church — expresses this dynamic reality of Christian community. It is not a local, static term; it is not even a religious expression; it means the *actual* gathering of people, the assembly of free citizens in a town called together in order to decide matters affecting their own welfare.

In the First Testament *ekklesia* means the "assembly of the people of Israel before God." In the Second Testament *ekklesia* comes through the agency of the Spirit to visible, tangible expression. It is realized in and through the gathering of God's people around the table, eating together a meal, breaking the bread and sharing the cup in memory of Christ's passion and resurrection. *Christian* spirituality means eating and drinking together, experiencing God's presence through each other, and in doing so proclaiming the gospel as God's alternative vision for everyone, especially for those who are poor, outcast, and battered, the majority of whom are women and children dependent on women. As long as Christian women are excluded from breaking the bread and deciding their own spiritual welfare and commitment, *ekklesia* as the discipleship of equals is not realized and the power of the gospel is greatly diminished. The true spiritual person according to St. Paul is the one who *walks* in the Spirit. It is she who brings about the alternative world and family of God over and against all oppressive powers of this world's enslaving patriarchal structures.

A feminist Christian spirituality therefore calls us to gather together the *ekklesia of women* who in the angry power of the Spirit are sent forth to feed, heal, and liberate their people who are women. It unmasks and sets us free from the structural sins and alienation of sexism, racism, and exploitation, and propels us to become children and spokeswomen of God. It rejects the idolatrous worship of maleness and articulates the Divine Image in female human existence and language. It sets us free from the internalized demands of altruism and self-sacrifice, from a mind-set that is concerned with the welfare and work of men first to the detriment of our own and other women's welfare and calling. It enables us to live "for one another" and to experience the presence of God in the *ekklesia* as the gathering of wo/men. Those of us who have heard this calling respond by committing ourselves to the liberation struggle of women and all peoples, by being accountable to women and their future, and by urging solidarity within the *ekklesia* of women. Commitment, accountability, and solidarity in community are the hallmarks of our calling and struggle.

Two major objections are usually raised at this point: The first is that the *ekklesia* of women does not share in the fullness of church. This is correct, but neither do male-dominated hierarchical assemblies as the actual gathering of the people of God. Such women's religious communities have always existed within the Catholic tradition. They were generated as soon as local church structures became patriarchal and hierarchical and relegated women to subordinate roles or eliminated them from church offices altogether. The male hierarchical church in turn has always sought to control these communities by colonizing them through male theology, liturgy, law, and spirituality, but was never quite able to do so. By abolishing these religious communities of women the Protestant Reformation strengthened the patriarchal church structures and intensified male clerical control of women's communities in modern times. In the last centuries, however, there have arisen again and again women leaders of their people who have sought to gather communities of women free from clerical and monastical control. A Catholic feminist spirituality claims these communities of women and their history as our own heritage and seeks to transform them into the *ekklesia* of women by claiming our own spiritual powers and gifts, by deciding our own welfare, by standing accountable for our decisions, in short, by rejecting the patriarchal structures of lay-women and nun-women, which deeply divide us along sexual lines.

The second objection made to the expression "*ekklesia* of women" is the charge of reverse sexism and the appeal to "mutuality with men" whenever women gather together as the *ekklesia* of women in Her name. However, such an objection does not sufficiently realize the gravity of the issues of patriarchal oppression and power. It looks too quickly for easy grace after having paid lip-service to the structural sin of sexism. Do we call it "reverse imperialism" if the poor of South and Central America gather together as a people? Or do we call it "reverse colonialism" whenever Africans or Asians gather together as a people?

We do not do so because we know too well that the coming together of those who are exploited does not spell the oppression of the rich or that the oppressed are gaining power over white Western men and nations; rather it means the political bonding of oppressed people in their struggle for economic and cultural survival. Why do men then feel threatened by the bonding of women in the struggle for liberation? Why then can churchmen not understand and accept that Christian women gather together for the sake of our spiritual survival as Christians and as women? It is not over and against men that we gather together but in order to become *ekklesia* before God, deciding matters affecting our own spiritual welfare and struggle. (pp. 197–201)

•

Women as the *ekklesia* of God have a continuous history that can claim Jesus and the early Christian movement as its roots and beginnings. This history of women as the people of God must be exposed as a history of oppression and reconstructed as a history of conversion and liberation. When I speak of the *ekklesia* of women, I have in mind women of the past and of the present, women who acted and act in the power of the life-giving Spirit-Wisdom. Such an understanding of Catholic sisterhood that spans all ages, nations, and continents does not need to claim salvific powers for women or to narrow its understanding of sisterhood to those women who are the elect and the holy. It need not expect salvation from women because it knows that women have also internalized the structural sin of sexism and therefore can act against our own spiritual interests and leaders. It calls us to solidarity with all women of the present and the past. Such a solidarity in sisterhood allows us to treasure and recover our heritage as Christian women and as Catholic Christians. As Judy Chicago has pointed out: All the institutions of our culture seek to persuade us that we are insignificant by depriving us of our history and heritage. "But our heritage is our power."

Finally, a feminist Christian spirituality is rooted in the *ekklesia* of women as the "body of Christ." Bodily existence is not detrimental or peripheral to our spiritually becoming *ekklesia* but constitutive and central to it. Not the soul or the mind or the innermost self but the body is the image and model for our being church. How can we point to the eucharistic bread and say "this is my body" as long as women's bodies are battered, raped, sterilized, mutilated, prostituted, and used for male ends? How can we proclaim "mutuality with men" in the Body of Christ as long as men curtail and deny reproductive freedom and moral agency to us? As in the past so still today men fight their ideological-religious wars on the battlefields of our bodies, making us the targets of their physical or spiritual violence. Therefore, the *ekklesia* of women must reclaim women's bodies as the "image and body of Christ." It has to denounce all violence against women as sacrilege and to maintain women's moral power and accountability for deciding our own spiritual welfare that encompasses body and soul, heart and womb.

The *ekklesia* of women gathers together to reject the idolatry of maleness in ourselves and to call the Christian brotherhood to repentance. Yet our primary task is to nurture and support one another. In breaking the bread and sharing the cup we celebrate not only the passion and resurrection of Christ but also that of women. (pp. 204–5)

Avery Dulles (b. 1918)

The Catholicity of the Church (1985)*

Since the Reformation it had become common in Roman Catholic apologetics to assert that the Church of Christ, with its four marks of unity, holiness, catholicity, and apostolicity, was simply identical with the Roman Catholic communion, and that catholicity, consequently, belonged to it alone. In opposition to the Anglo-Catholics, the Holy Office declared in 1864: "No other Church is catholic except that which is built on the one individual Peter, and which grows up into one body closely joined and knit together [see Eph. 4:16] in the unity of faith and love."[1]

Vatican Council II, without directly contradicting this doctrine, nuanced it in a remarkable way. In its Constitution on the Church it predicated catholicity not directly of the Roman Catholic Church but rather of the Church of Christ, which the council depicted as "subsisting" in the Catholic Church (*Lumen Gentium* 8), so that the fullness of catholicity was not obtainable except in communion with Rome (*Unitatis Redintegratio* 4). But the Church of Christ was held to be present in some measure in other Christian communities, which could participate in catholicity to the extent that they continued to accept and live by the authentic Christian heritage. The Decree on Ecumenism could therefore teach that the "entire heritage of spirituality and liturgy, of discipline and theology" in the various traditions of the Orthodox churches "belongs to the full catholic and apostolic character of the Church" (*Unitatis Redintegratio* 17), and that "some Catholic traditions and institutions continue to exist in certain Western communities, such as the Anglican Communion" (*Unitatis Redintegratio* 13). Vatican II's concept of catholicity may therefore be called cautiously ecumenical rather than narrowly confessional.

The council's vision of the Church, moreover, was not limited to the Christian arena. While acknowledging that the Church may at times appear as a "little flock," the council asserted that Christ, the universal Savior, continues to use it as an instrument for the redemption of all (*Lumen Gentium* 9). "All are called to be part of this catholic unity of the People of God" (*Lumen Gentium* 13). The Constitution on the Church goes on to assert that all human beings, even those to whom the gospel has not as yet been preached, are related to the Church of Christ (*Lumen Gentium* 16). This general statement is then specified with respect to four groups: Jews, Muslims, adherents of other religions, and atheists. None of these groups is excluded from the redemptive influence of Christ, which impels

---

*Reprinted from Avery Dulles, *The Catholicity of the Church* (Oxford: Clarendon Press, 1985), 20–25, 167–70. Permission requested.

1. The Letter of the Holy Office to the Bishops of England, September 16, 1864 (Denzinger-Schönmetzer 2888).

its recipients toward the catholic unity of the Church. The grace of Christ thus operates in a secret way in all persons of good will, ordering them toward salvation and disposing them to accept the gospel if and when they hear it credibly proclaimed (*Lumen Gentium* 16–17).

The Church, according to Vatican II, achieves its catholicity in a historically palpable way by evangelizing all peoples. Missionary activity is therefore seen both as an expression and as an intensification of the Church's catholicity. By evangelizing the world the Church can become in manifest actuality what in principle it has been from its origins — the universal communion of all men and women with God in Christ. "It is plain, then," we read in the Decree on Missionary Activity, "that missionary activity wells up from the Church's innermost nature and spreads abroad her saving faith. It perfects her Catholic unity by expanding it" (*Ad Gentes* 6). The New Covenant, according to the same Decree, calls for a Church that speaks all tongues and "thus overcomes the divisiveness of Babel" (*Ad Gentes* 4). Inspired by this vision, the Church "prays and labors in order that the entire world may become the People of God, the Body of the Lord, and the Temple of the Holy Spirit" (*Lumen Gentium* 17).

At various points in its documents, Vatican II acknowledged that the catholicity of the Church is in fact limited. One reason has already been indicated: the failure of Christian missionary activity to have effectively reached all peoples and all individuals with the good news of Jesus Christ. A second reason, chiefly treated in the Decree on Ecumenism, is the inner dividedness of Christianity itself. To overcome this, the Church is under grave obligation to pursue the apostolate of Christian unity. "The divisions among Christians," says the Decree, "prevent the Church from effecting the fullness of catholicity proper to her in those of her children who, although joined to her by baptism, are yet separated from full communion with her" (*Unitatis Redintegratio* 4). This renders it "difficult for the Church to express in actual life her full catholicity in all its aspects" (ibid.). In other words, the Catholic Church itself is a less splendid expression than it ought to be of Christ's universal redemptive power.

A third obstacle to catholicity is the failure of Catholics themselves to realize in their own household the kind of unity God wills for the Church. In this connection the Decree on Ecumenism insists on the importance of preserving a healthy freedom and diversity in styles of spirituality, discipline, and liturgy, and in the formulation of revealed truth (*Unitatis Redintegratio* 16–17). The council at this point echoes the axiom popularized by Pope John XXIII: unity in necessary matters, freedom in others, and charity in all. As we shall see more in detail..., this principle has important applications to the local church. "The variety of local churches with one common aspiration," says the Constitution on the Church, "is particularly splendid evidence of the catholicity of the undivided Church (*Lumen Gentium* 23). Elsewhere the Constitution asserts that legitimate differences, far from impeding catholic unity, can actually enrich and strengthen it (*Lumen Gentium* 13).

In summary, Vatican II presents catholicity not as a monotonous repetition of identical elements but rather as reconciled diversity. It is unity among individuals and groups who retain their distinctive characteristics, who enjoy different spiritual gifts, and are by that very diversity better equipped to serve one another and thus advance the common good. Individual Christians and local churches are bound to one another in mutual service and mutual receptivity. This relationship is founded not upon domination but on a free exchange of trust and respect. Thanks to Christ's faithfulness to his promise to be with his people, catholicity is never lacking to the Church. But it is dynamic and expansive; it continually presses forward to a fullness and inclusiveness not yet attained. It is a ferment at work in the Catholic Church and in every authentic Christian community. Even beyond the borders of explicit Christianity, the grace of Christ, working in the hearts of all who are open to it, brings individuals and groups into a saving relationship with the Church catholic, the God-given sign and sacrament of the ultimate unity to which the entire human race is called. Thus the Catholic Church is, according to the teaching of Vatican II, "a lasting and sure seed of unity, hope, and salvation for the whole human race" (*Lumen Gentium* 9).

Vatican II's doctrine of catholicity is not, to be sure, a totally new invention. It is for the most part a selection and recombination of elements taken from the tradition. It draws heavily on the New Testament and on ancient theologians such as Irenaeus and Eusebius, Augustine and Aquinas. Here and there one can perhaps detect the influence of a Johann Adam Möhler, a John Henry Newman, a Henri de Lubac, and especially an Yves Congar. Although securely rooted in the tradition, the council's teaching on catholicity is attuned to the new situation that became evident after World War II. It takes cognizance of the plurality of cultures, the other Christian churches, the non-Christian religions, and atheism. Optimistic without being overweening, modest without being abject, this treatment of catholicity is serene and attractive. In comparison with papal teaching of the nineteenth century, Vatican II shows a remarkable respect for freedom and diversity, both without the Church and in the larger sphere of human relations. (pp. 20–25)

•

To bring this study to a close it may be helpful to summarize some of our principal findings and to reflect on the difficulties and opportunities facing catholicity in the contemporary world.

The concept of catholicity, being analogous rather than univocal, does not admit of any precise definition, but it can be distinguished from other similar concepts such as fullness and universality. Unlike universality, catholicity is a concrete term: it is predicated not of abstract essences but of particular, existing realities. Furthermore, it always implies intensity, richness, and plenitude. Unlike fullness, it implies a unitive relationship among things that are diverse. "Catholic," writes Henri de Lubac, "suggests the idea of an organic whole, of a cohesion, of a firm synthesis, of a reality which is not scattered but, on the contrary, turned towards a center which assures its unity, whatever the expanse in area or the internal differentiation might be.[2]

---

2. Henri de Lubac, "Particular Churches," in *The Motherhood of the Church* (San Francisco: Ignatius Press, 1982), 173–74.

Catholicity, far from excluding differences, demands them. In all the instances of catholicity we have considered — Trinity, Incarnation, Church, and world — we have found a union of opposites that might, in themselves, seem incompatible.

Finally, catholicity is a dynamic term. It designates a fullness of reality and life, especially divine life, actively communicating itself. This life, flowing outwards, pulsates through many subjects, draws them together, and brings them into union with their source and goal. By reason of its supreme realization, which is divine, catholicity assures the ultimate coherence of the whole ambit of creation and redemption.

In the widest sense of the term, catholicity may be predicated of the universe as a whole. The entire cosmos has in Christ its center of unity, coherence, and fulfillment (cf. Col. 1:17). Nature is essentially good and perfectible; it is, as Bonhoeffer said, "directed to the coming of Christ,"[3] who is at work recapitulating the cosmos under his universal headship (cf. Eph. 1:10).

The catholicity of the Church is a more intense participation in the divine catholicity. The Church has her catholicity not from herself but from God, who makes himself present in her. Catholicity, however, is not attributed to the Church merely by extrinsic denomination, for Christ is truly present in the Church through the Holy Spirit. The Church, therefore, is a real representation of Christ. She is his new presence, not under his own proper form, but in the community of believers. Having in himself the plenitude of divine life and grace, Christ communicates this to be the Church. The transformative and expansive power of the Church, as well as her continuity in time, derive from the divine source of her being. The catholicity of the Church, as we have seen, may be explicated in terms of height, depth, breadth, and length.

When in the creed we designate the Church as catholic we are going beyond the empirical data. Although something of the catholicity of the Church appears in history, we perceive only the external signs of a far deeper reality, apprehended in faith, which alone can affirm the divine dimension of the Church's life. The adjective "catholic" in the creed does not express a mere hope of ideal, but a present, though imperfect, reality. The catholicity of the Church, coming from God as its source and tending to him, as its goal, is always incomplete and in quest of its own completion.

The Church, as a real symbol, charged with the power of the divine life within her, may be called, in a true but analogous sense, a sacrament. Her catholicity achieves a certain visibility through signs that express and sustain her essential reality. The Church as sacrament is endowed with certain visible or social structures usually considered under the heading of Catholicism. Among these structures are the sacraments, all of which have a social or ecclesial significance, as we have seen in particular with regard to baptism, penance, and the Eucharist. The hierarchical ministry is likewise a Catholic structure, sacramental in its own way. This ministry is, in its highest exercise, episcopal. The bishop of Rome, as head and center of the college of bishops, has a uniquely Catholic ministry, with special responsibility for the unity and mission of the universal Church.

---

3. Dietrich Bonhoeffer, *Ethics* (London: Collins, 1964), 144.

The adjective "catholic" may in some measure be predicated of every Christian church, for all participate in the reality of the Church which they confess as one, holy, catholic, and apostolic. All, moreover, have certain Catholic structures, such as canonical scriptures, creeds, sacraments, and ordained ministry. In a more specific sense, the term Catholic (usually with a capital C) is predicated of those churches which are conspicuous for their sacramental, liturgical, hierarchical, and dogmatic features, and those which stress continuity with the institutional and doctrinal developments of the patristic and medieval periods. In a still more specific sense, the term Catholic refers to that Church which, at Vatican II, called itself "the Catholic Church," and which alone insists on communion with Rome as the touchstone of unity.

It has sometimes been suggested that the Church of Christ, as a complex reality, may appropriately be realized in two contrasting forms, Protestant and Catholic. This view can be misleading, at least if it is taken as implying that the Catholic features are not essential to the Church. According to the analysis given in the preceding chapters, these features belong to the Church of Christ by her very nature, for they are required to actualize, express, and safeguard her catholicity. According to Vatican II, the Catholic Church has no essential features over and above those of the Church of Christ. She claims to be the organization in which that Church subsists. The essence or idea of Catholicism is the same as that of the Church of Christ, viewed in terms of its structures of mediation and continuity.

The Catholic principle, as we have used the term, justifies and protects the mediatory structures of the Church. This principle inculcates respect for the divine presence in the cosmic and natural means whereby God communicates himself. More especially, it arouses reverence for, and confidence in, the ecclesial structures by which, in accordance with God's free promises, the grace of Christ is symbolized and transmitted. The Catholic principle defends the individual Christian and the church from the inroads of skepticism, irreverence, and sectarian pride.

The Catholic principle, however, does not fully express the nature of the Church. It focuses on the visible and social structures of mediation rather than on the immediacy of the Holy Spirit, who animates the body and all its members. Without attention to the immediacy of grace, the Catholic structures could be alienating. There is need for a complementary principle that prevents the structures from being unduly absolutized, from becoming opaque and oppressive. Idolatry must be precluded; false and inopportune developments must be detected and pruned away. This correlative principle of immediacy and criticism corresponds to what Tillich and others have called the Protestant principle. Tillich's terminology could be misleading, since it suggests that Protestantism is essentially negative in nature, but his observations convey an important truth and one which, we have argued, is necessary for the health of Catholicism. The Protestant principle, as Tillich understands it, is not intended to dissolve the Christian substance, but to shield it against distortions. But the Protestant principle, as we have seen, can be misused to erode the Christian heritage. To protect it against its own excesses, it musts be held in check by what we have called the Catholic principle.

Though the Church of Christ, according to Vatican II, "subsists" in the Catholic Church, Catholicism does not claim perfection for itself. On the contrary, the council stated that the Church is in continual need of purification and reform. Even in her catholicity, she is deficient. Her actual, lived catholicity would be enhanced if she were holier, more faithful, more widely diffused, more deeply implanted in human cultures, and more internally unified. Catholicity, therefore, is both a gift and a task. It designates not only a present reality but also a programme for action. (pp. 167–70)

Edward Schillebeeckx (b. 1914)

Church: The Human Story of God (1989)*

According to the biblical admonition, "judgment begins at the house of God," in Israel and the church (1 Pet. 4:17–18). Therefore Vatican II took over the Reformation concern for the *Ecclesia semper reformanda* almost literally, *Ecclesia semper purificanda*. For of the church on the way, the mystery of which is described in the first chapter of *Lumen Gentium*, the same council says: "Advancing through trials and tribulations the church is comforted (in the biblical sense, strengthened) by God's grace, promised to her by the Lord so that she may not waver from perfect fidelity, but remain the worthy bride of the Lord, ceaselessly renewing herself through the action of the Holy Spirit until, through the cross, she may attain to that light which knows no setting."[1] The conquest of weakness takes place only "through the power of Christ and love."[2] Here in its own way the council is accepting a Reformation view when it says that the church is *sancta simul et purificanda*: it is holy, but must constantly be purified; it must arrive at *metanoia*, repentance and renewal.

This promise does not rest only on the church as a whole but on a particular, i.e., ministerial, way of ministerial service in the church, especially — in both its function as proclamatory teaching — of cultic and sacramental healing through presiding in prayer and sacrament — and finally in its function of pastoral guidance.

However, given that the biblical admonition constantly to renew oneself in the Spirit in the weakness of the flesh is addressed to the people of God as a whole, even before there is any mention (in this Dogmatic Constitution) of the functional or ministerial or official differences between believers and ministers, both the hierarchy and believers stand under the constant admonition to incessant renewal and a Christian "return to the sources."

>From this it may be concluded that the church as the community of salvation and as a saving institution stands under the powerful promise of the Lord, who will not tolerate its becoming unfaithful. Nevertheless this church must constantly renew itself in the power of the Spirit.

---

*Reprinted from Edward Schillebeeckx, *Church: The Human Story of God* (New York, 1994), 195–98, 210–13, by permission of the Crossroad Publishing Company.

1. *Lumen Gentium*, chap. 2, no. 9.
2. See *Schema Constitutionis de Ecclesia*, 1964, *Relationes de singulis numeris*, Relatio in no. 8, 23.

The synchronic affirmation of the *Ecclesia indefectibilis* (i.e., a church which cannot fall away from its basic inspiration or cannot come loose from its original roots) and the *Ecclesia semper purificanda* (the church which must always purify itself) poses serious and delicate problems. Precisely on the basis of the support promised it by the Lord, "The gates of hell shall not prevail against it" (Matt. 16:18), and thus on the basis of the Lord's powerful promise, the firm stand of the church on its indefectibility takes the historical form of a constantly renewed *metanoia*, renewal and self-correction. It already emerges from this that this is an indefectibility not in triumphalism, but in weakness in which God's grace triumphs. This implies that there is no indefectibility *despite* weakness; i.e., automatic indefectibility, but in and through constant renewal in faith, hope, and love.

The indefectibility of the church is therefore not a static, as it were fixed, essentialist property of the church which could bypass the constantly precarious, existential faith of the church in obedience to God's promise. The promised indefectibility becomes effective only in the faith, trust, and constant self-correction of the church. The term "divine guarantee" does not fit in with this. It is at least misleading, though it can be used as an extrapolation of the overwhelming power of grace into the juridical sphere, grace so powerful that it is at work *in* the response of the church in faith. But a juridical objectification of this indefectibility at work in faith and in believing self-correction is impossible, because the nature of the church called to life through the career of Jesus Christ implies the existential experience of the community of salvation, precisely as the fruit of redemption.

We must also see the so-called four marks of the church in this perspective. With the creed of the Council of Constantinople in 381 (often wrongly called the Nicene Creed), all Christian churches confess: "I believe the one, holy, catholic, and apostolic *ecclesia* or community of faith." In the Second Vatican Council this is said of each local church in which, also living in community with the other local churches, the universal church is present. But we know that this unity does not exist: the Christian churches are divided. We all suffer under our own sinfulness and that of our churches. So the four marks do not describe our real churches in their historical forms, while on the other hand no church can achieve a mystical distillation of the essence "church": churches exist only in historical forms.

This does not mean on the other hand that the four marks of the church are purely eschatological, a reality of the final kingdom. It means that all the Christian churches now already contain elements which call for this unity, particularly the church's belief in one God and one Lord, one baptism and one table. Because these four marks are present in all churches defectively and in a mediocre way, in particular or restrictive compartmentalization, they are nevertheless internal imperatives of change within all the churches: a summons really to go on the way to the final ecumenical fulfillment. The dynamic of these structural elements in all the churches does not call for this break. The gospel does not legitimize mediocrity. And the message that is proclaimed is in no way the basis for shutting oneself off in different hiding places to provide protective security from "the other"! The four "properties" of the church issue a summons for conversion to all Christian churches. One cannot just ask for the conversion of other Christian churches. All local and confessional churches are "church" to the degree that they can affirm, encourage, and further *communio*, communication, with other local churches.

The scandal is not that there are differences but that these differences are used as an obstacle to communion (though on the other hand people rightly do not want to make a comedy of unity; they take the differences seriously). But richly diverse unity-in-communion in no way calls for a formal, institutional, and administrative unity, nor a super-church. Even for the Roman Catholic Church the four "properties" confessed are not a description of the specific form of the church but an imperative for it, as they are for other churches. The ecumene [or ecumenical community] is not a private annexation of the gospel by any confessional church, but the "self-dispossession" of each and every Christian church. Although there is historical plurality as a system of exclusion, there is also multiplicity which need not arouse opposition and can be experienced within communion and mutual recognition. Difference is positive only within communion with the other: in respect of the other who is other and yet not alien to us.

There can be no authentic ecumene without the attempt to understand and experience the plurality of churches theologically: we must be able to experience and understand it . . . in mutual difference. There is no eternally valid model of unity to which all churches must convert themselves. We need all Christian churches for the ecumene as the true church of Jesus, the Christ. All Christians must strive for a unity the model for which does not fully exist in any single church. Unity is future for all the Christian churches, not a return to any old situation. Moreover there is no community without internal conflicts except in utopia (i.e., nowhere, except in wishful thinking) and eschatologically, in heaven. But this final consummation judges our present by the human and Christian revolt against the unredeemed present of the churches and the world. (pp. 195–98)

•

In recent times, use, but above all much misuse, has been made of the deep insight that the church is a "mystery." This misuse is supported by a tenacious, dualistic misunderstanding.

It is obvious to all of us that the church of Jesus Christ, like any other community, never lives in a socio-historical and political-cultural vacuum. The community of the "church" is either opposed to that world environment around it or, whether for evangelical and pastoral or from ideological motives, critically or uncritically accepts it. So in the course of time it has taken on many faces. In its historical manifestations it has sometimes shown very attractive and often not very sympathetic aspects, sometimes bleak and at other times non-committal or neutral. Sometimes there was nothing in the church to feel warm about or to overwhelm one; believers then speak of a "lukewarm" church, as the book of Revelation already says to the church of Laodicea: "I know your deeds, you are neither cold nor hot. Would that you were either cold or hot!" (Rev. 3:15). There were also times when we cannot regard the empirical churches in their local or even their world-wide setting as having been other than sinful, sinful above all through neglect, while their saints, those who continued to be faithful to the gospel, at the same time led a hidden life or underwent a martyr death.

Precisely because the concrete church is a reality which can be discussed from many standpoints, a certain ecclesiology often proves to be alien to reality. Many people already have a spontaneous experience of communities in general. These can also be analyzed scientifically in more specific terms. So among other things the sociology of knowledge has shown *how* structures of authority come into being in a community and *why* they arise, and thus how the particular experiential wisdom of which a particular culture is the real vehicle in the long run nevertheless develops towards the specialization and protection (through individuals from the community) of its own values and views which are close to the heart of all.

The specialized subject of authority in a particular cultural tradition of experience, and thus the specialized subject of this protection, defense, and exposition of particular popular values and wisdom, can sometimes coincide. But on the basis of the content of the specific direction of the two, through social differentiation and the distribution of tasks the manifold interests of this particular cultural tradition will ultimately be encouraged within this community by various authorities. All this can be analyzed in sociological terms and also tested historically, and in this way one can also trace the sociological rules of developments and conflicts between different instances within a cultural community.

All this equally applies to religious communities of faith, including the church as a society which in the religious language of faith is called a "community of God." Moreover it will also be necessary to speak in a "second discourse," namely in the religious language of faith, about the same secular religious and social reality. What is described in human experiential terms and sociologically analyzed must ultimately also be expressed in the language of faith. This means that the religious language of faith becomes empty and meaningless unless it contains a recognizable reference to real human experiences and the autonomous structures implied in them. On the other hand, talk in the language of faith about a social, empirically accessible reality such as the church is not in fact a superfluous luxury nor (at least in itself) ideological talk about an event which could already be understood adequately on a purely secular basis. The saving revelation of God, offered to us through and in the Christian experiential tradition of the church community of faith, is indeed a grace, but a grace mediated through and in the structure of historical experiences. Anyone who forgets that begins for example to split up the mystery of the church as it were gnostically and dualistically into a "heavenly part" (which then, in this hypothesis, falls outside all sociological approaches and ideological criticism) and an earthly part, about which (in the same hypothesis) evidently all the bad things may be said. By contrast, Vatican II says: "The earthly Church and the Church endowed with heavenly riches are not to be thought of as two realities."[3]

There is also an extremely urgent need to investigate these historical mediations of the grace of God scientifically (with the help of the humane, behavioral, and semiotic sciences), above all at a time which (in all religions) is tending to-

---

3. *Lumen Gentium*, chap. 1, no. 8.

wards religious fundamentalism, dualism, and flight from its own insecurity and ignorance into the arms of a guru or self-assured and omniscient leader.

However, if anywhere in theology there is any question of pseudo-problems piling up, then it is precisely in the field of the relationship to all these cases in which human reality and the reality of grace — like, for example, freedom and grace; emancipatory self-liberation and Christian redemption; the humanity and divinity of Jesus — are set side by side and alongside each other as two different realities which on this presupposition must subsequently be reconciled dialectically by all kinds of theological devices. Above all we have here the pseudo-problem that one and the same reality which can be discussed in different languages (e.g., scientific and religious) is wrongly regarded as two different opposed or parallel realities. This is to overlook the fact that this one reality, because of its riches, is fully accessible (and then still in a limited human way) only from two (or more) different perspectives, questions, and language games.

Anyone who loses sight of the different perspectives either has grace working only where men and women cease to have active responsibility and then calls that the area of "mystery" or passes over the reality that one can receive God's grace in very different ways, even to the point of actually rejecting this grace to which reference is made. Creation and redemption, christology and ecclesiology, are then proclaimed at the expense of autonomous human and historical experience and reality. Instead of grace in the structure of historically mediating human experiences and praxis, we then get a stereophony of laborious human activity on the one hand and blessings direct from heaven on the other. These latter are then called the real mystery, which can no longer be approached in scientific terms. However, the real mystery lies in the human reality itself, as a mystery of justice or faithfulness to the grace in human acts of government and decision leave aside the mediating organs of the Holy Spirit or interpret them in terms of their own interests.

However, what in fact stands directly over against this is, for example, human freedom *as thought* and grace *as thought*. In other words, at the level of the concepts and their linguistic expression both terms — human freedom and divine grace — are indeed thought of as being next to and alongside each other, but in truth they are one and the same thing, a text to be deciphered in different language games. God and the creature can never be added together or written on one line or captured in one proposition. Where this happens nevertheless, two language games are being jumbled up and the ace of trumps is thrown onto the board in the middle of a chess game, on the assumption that the game can be won with this card. This is often literally the case when particular bishops make an immunizing reference to the "mystery of the church" as opposed to what social and behavioral scientists say about this same church.

The language of faith and empirical, descriptive language always relate to one and the same reality, so we do not have to reconcile two competing realities, however dialectically. There is fidelity and infidelity to grace, half-hearted trust and half-trust, good will and barely good will, or just mistrust — in many shades. Here, too, *sancta, sed semper purificanda* holds.

The charge that is often heard from particular episcopal and sometimes also

theological quarters of the Christian churches, namely that contemporary theologians go too much in their teachings by human sciences and so (the dualism
is already betrayed by this "so") think too horizontally and thus overlook the
"vertical" mystery of the church, in fact goes back either to a dualistic and supra-
naturalistic or a fideistic view of religious realities. It bears witness to a kind of
religious positivism which, either out of anxiety or short-sightedness, gives itself
immunity from scientific clarification, ideological criticism, or theological hermeneutics by referring to "mystery." In other words, it is a form of fundamentalism
which is spreading everywhere at present, even in the Catholic Church, which has
always thought that this is an erroneous characteristic of some Protestantism.

The church community as mystery cannot be found behind or above concrete,
visible reality. The church community is to be found *in* this reality which can be
demonstrated here and now. We too, along with everyone in the base communities, are part of this living mystery. What happens in these communities is at the
same time part of what we call the mystery of the church. The experiments and
explorations, the mistakes and perhaps even follies and the finding, are parts of
the phenomenon of the one great Catholica, which is found precisely as Christian
communities of faith, more watered down or more strongly concentrated. It is to
be found in the meetings of base communities, of some house communities, of
men and women, who come together in the name of Jesus, confessed by them as
the Christ. Among them are many people who suffer from and over the present-
day world and their own church and oppose the suffering which God does not
will. They too are part of the mystery of the church, they too celebrate and bear
witness to that mystery, and they do not allow themselves to be banned from this
mystery by a church government with a short-sighted policy.

Together, these men and women of God are a real and true segment of the
"people of God" — an honorific title which was given by the Second Vatican
Council to "the Catholica": *subsistit in!* We too, along with all those in the
base communities, are contained in this (= *subsistit in*), even when for reasons
of church politics (for this is what they are — nothing to do with the gospel and
theology) bishops do not want to enter into dialogue with what for them are
nuisances at the grass roots. We too are nevertheless part of "the mystery of the
church," *sancta et semper purificanda.* (pp. 210–13)

Part Three

BIOGRAPHICAL AND TEXTUAL INFORMATION

Augustine of Hippo (354–430)

Augustine of Hippo was born in Thagaste, Algeria, of relatively poor but well-patronized parents. Education was his ticket out of a difficult agricultural economy, and his father, Patricius, ensured Augustine's education through the patronage of a local landowner named Romanianus. In 371 Augustine went to Carthage to study. Soon after he began to live with a woman of unknown name, although their common-law marriage lasted some fifteen years, and the two had a son, Adeodatus, probably in 373. About this same time Augustine experienced a growing maturity in his studies, what many scholars interpret to be the "first stage" of his conversion journey to Christianity. Through his reading of Cicero's *Hortentius,* described in book 3 of the *Confessions,* Augustine gave himself over to pursue a love of wisdom, a quest which was at least as much religious as philosophical. Augustine was particularly drawn to probe the nature of the human soul and the question of good and evil. For the next ten years he would become part of the Manichean sect, a dualist religion which sought the illumination of the soul, through which the soul was gradually awakened to its own goodness despite being weighed down at the same time by its passions, its corrupt body, and its attachment to evil within the world.

The 380s signal a new stage in Augustine's life, demarcated by his arrival in Milan in 384 where he had been appointed professor of rhetoric. There he came under the influence of the bishop, Ambrose, whose extensive background in Greek philosophy certainly overshadowed Augustine's own training. Listening to Ambrose's sermons compelled Augustine to revisit questions of human nature through the lens of a refined, baptized Platonism in which the return of the soul to God was placed within what Augustine understood to be a more sophisticated cosmology than that of the Manicheans. Augustine's intellectual advancements were coupled with a new orientation to social climbing, perhaps facilitated by his mother, Monica, who had accompanied Augustine's family to Milan. A legitimate marriage was arranged, and Augustine's common-law wife was sent back to northern Africa.[1] Augustine's famous "conversion" in 386 was the final step in his integration of the pursuit of wisdom with Christian asceticism. Retiring to Cassiciacum, Augustine reflected on providence, the spiritual life, and Christian education, writing *Against the Academicians, The Happy Life, Divine Providence and the Problem of Evil,* and his *Soliloquies.* He was baptized in 387.

In 391 Augustine arrived in Hippo to found a monastery. He was ordained a priest, and he became increasingly involved in questions of orthodoxy. He wrote several treatises against the Manicheans, then turned his attention to the Donatists. The orthodox church in northern Africa was challenged by the immense popularity of Donatism, an approach to the church which had arisen in the face of earlier persecutions of Christianity. After the Diocletian persecution of 303–5, a group of Christians rejected the authority of an African bishop who had been a *traditor* to the church when he handed over sacred documents to Roman authori-

---

1. See *Confessions,* book 6, 15:25.

ties. In 311 eighty Numidian bishops elected a replacement. Conflict over the rival candidates escalated, eventually involving Miltiades, the bishop of Rome, and the Emperor Constantine himself. Repeated interventions did not keep the Donatists from organizing their own church leaders, and eventually they established a parallel church tradition in North Africa.

As their own ecclesiology developed, the Donatists came to espouse a view of church as a religious body which must form an alternative community to society, a way of life which would call others to holiness because of its own dedication to purity. The Donatists venerated the early martyrs and strove to maintain, through their ritual practices and pursuit of virtue, a covenantal relationship with God. In 395 Augustine was consecrated bishop of Hippo and dedicated himself to a thorough campaign against the Donatists. His major concern was to establish that the rites of the church were valid and real independent of their subjective qualities. Thus the moral behavior of a priest was not relevant to the establishment and maintenance of any individual's Christian life through the sacraments of the church.

Augustine affirmed a notion of church which, while it was two-tiered (made up of both serious and nominal Christians), did not exclude anyone from the sacraments, the earthly vehicle for salvation. Using the image of Noah's Ark, Augustine suggested a view of predestination not fully articulated until his arguments with Pelagius: the church is the resting place of the saved and unsaved through which both groups receive the sacraments. The foreknowledge of God separates the two groups, and neither being outside the church harms the saved nor does being inside the church save the damned.

Conflicts with the Donatists grew in intensity, and the imperial court intervened, removing Donatist bishops from their posts and ordering orthodox bishops to replace them. Augustine's defense of the intervention of the state in matters of heresy, while it would have troublesome implications for the later church, served to propel Augustine into his public position as bishop. He had evolved from a reader and speculative thinker into an administrator who devoted his time to theological controversies.

Augustine of Hippo's doctrine of the church was highly influential in the history of Christianity. His personal experiences as bishop, specifically the conflict with the Donatists in North Africa, as well as his tendency toward a theory of predestination informed his ecclesiology.

In addition to trouble with the Donatists, Augustine addressed another theological controversy which emerged in 411, that of the Pelagians. Pelagius, a native of Britain who had settled in Rome, was troubled by the popularity of Augustine's *Confessions*, a book which seemed to minimize the human contribution to Christian holiness. A monk devoted to the pursuit of Christian perfection, Pelagius found Augustine's notion of original sin, which made it impossible for humans not to continue to sin, to be problematic. His followers, notably Julian of Eclanum, were particularly disturbed that Augustine would have God find innocent infants guilty of inherited sin and condemn them to punishment. Augustine, fresh from his problems with the Donatists, saw in Pelagianism some of the same problems he had been battling for over a decade. The pursuit of Christian perfection, when applied to the community of believers as a whole, might exclude some from the church itself and the healing power of the sacraments. Augustine's response to Pelagianism included his reflection on the absolute dependence of humanity on God, whereas the Pelagian school emphasized that humans were adults capable of making responsible choices about their behavior. As the debate grew more intense, Augustine committed more of his rhetorical skills into synthesizing his theological vision. From 414 to 420 Augustine hit a most fruitful period as a theologian: he finished *On Nature and Grace* and *On the Trinity* in 415 while he continued to generate books of the *City of God* through 425. Commentator Peter Brown describes this period of Augustine's life as the one which he dedicated to the *causa gratiae*, or "making the case for grace," and he explains that this endeavor proved to be "the high-water mark of Augustine's literary career."[2]

It is difficult to overestimate the influence of Augustine's understanding of human nature within the Christian tradition. That said, however, his anthropological views are complex enough to have initiated many distinct strands of debate within the tradition. In his debate with the Pelagians, Augustine articulated a position first expressed in the *Confessions,* that every moment of life was guided by the providence and grace of God, which humans experience as an internal force through the movement of their own wills. Augustine stated clearly that the human will needed grace to enable it to delight in doing good. The absolute dependence of humanity upon God led him to a position of predestination which later commentators pushed to extremes. However, in *On the Trinity* Augustine developed a view of the human soul as the resting place of the trinity. This view is rooted in the text of Genesis 1:27 that humanity is created in the image and likeness of God, and thus embodies a similar trinitarian unity of memory, understanding, and will. The image of God in the soul is not wholly blotted out through the Fall.

The turn in the human will toward its tendency to evil is a profound mystery to Augustine and one of the questions which he simply cannot answer, but recognizes as human reality. "Seek not to find the efficient cause of an evil will. It is not a matter of efficiency, but of deficiency.... To defect from the one who is the highest being to something that has less being, this is to begin to have an evil will. To seek the causes of such a defect — deficient causes, not efficient ones — is like trying to see darkness or to hear silence" (*City of God,* 12:7).

Augustine was widely influential in his day, both through his capacity as bishop and in his capacity as a writer. In his final years he reviewed his works, compiling a list of them and commenting on his own ideas in his *Retractions*. In a sense this self-critique pulled Augustine's ideas out of the immediate context of their polemical debates, allowing him to make clear theological statements from his perspective as an older man and to identify issues on which he had changed his position. However, on some doctrines he never reached a definitive position.[3] His understanding of original sin continued to trouble him, as he expressed in his letter

---

2. Brown, *Augustine of Hippo,* 354. For more detailed information on sources see the bibliography at the end of each biographical essay.

3. For some interesting examples of Augustine's changes in position, see Norman L. Geisler, ed., *What Augustine Says* (Grand Rapids, Mich.: Baker Book House, 1982).

to Jerome: "Tell me what we are to answer about the children."[4] The changes in Augustine's thought over the course of his life have challenged later commentators to represent accurately the complexity of this most influential Christian theologian.

Bibliography

Brown, Peter. *Augustine of Hippo.* Berkeley: University of California Press, 1967.

Kristo, J. G. *Looking for God in Time and Memory: Psychology, Theology, and Spirituality in Augustine's "Confessions."* New York: University Press of America, 1991.

Miles, Margaret. *Desire and Delight: A New Reading of Augustine's "Confessiones."* New York: Crossroad, 1992.

O'Donnell, James J. *Augustine.* Boston: Twayne Publishers, 1985.

Bernard of Clairvaux (1090–1153)

Bernard of Clairvaux, the highly influential Cistercian abbot, is a critical figure in the history of theology. A member of the Burgundian nobility, Bernard joined the recently established Cistercian order at age twenty-three and became the abbot of Clairvaux at the young age of twenty-five. His auspicious writing career, then, developed within the context of his role as teacher, preacher, and pastor within a monastic order dedicated to simplicity and contemplation. Particularly noteworthy are his mystical treatises, including *The Steps of Humility and Pride, On Grace and Free Choice,* and *On Loving God,* all produced during the 1120s. His cycle of eighty-six sermons, *Sermons on the Song of Songs,* is a highly developed commentary on the mystical life.

Although committed to the monastic life, Bernard took public stances on many issues outside the cloister. He supported the pontificate of Innocent II against the claims of Anacletus II during a period of schism. He engaged in polemical debates against the scholastic Peter Abelard. And in 1146–47 he preached a cycle of sermons in support of the Crusades. Bernard's ecclesiastical and theological influences are extensive. He was canonized in 1174 and declared a doctor of the church in 1830.

Bernard's reflections on the nature of humanity involve a characterization of God's image and likeness as they have been made manifest in human persons (see Gen. 1:26). While there are some variations in Bernard's presentation of image and likeness, some aspect of the image of God remains indestructibly in the soul as a result of God's creation. It is the likeness to God which has been diminished through sin, although the likeness, too, is restored by grace, partially in human life and completely in glory. The restoration of God's likeness, a process enabled by grace, is the reformation of the human person through gradual union with Christ. This process begins with self-knowledge, an understanding of human sinfulness which also provokes compunction and the desire for a change in our condition, a lifelong, deepening conversion to the Word of God incarnate in us.

In his *Sermons on the Song of Songs* Bernard of Clairvaux's identification of the

---

4. See Augustine, Letter 166.16, in *Letters,* vol. 4, trans. Wilfred Parsons (New York: Fathers of the Church, 1955), 21.

bride is twofold: the bride is both the church as the collective embodiment of Christ and the individual soul as it participates in that body of Christ. This exegetical move is consistent with earlier commentaries on the Song of Songs, especially that of Origen. As Bernard explains, "No one among us would dare to claim for himself the title of Bride of Christ for his soul, but because we belong to the church which justly glories in this name and its reality, we not unjustly appropriate a share in this glory" (sermon 12). In sermon 27, Bernard uses the metaphor of the bride for the church and the soul almost interchangeably, moving smoothly back and forth between the two referents. Bernard's sermons represent a revival of the doctrine that Christ and the church are wholly united, as in the sacrament of marriage. Indeed, the union of the bride and bridegroom is reminiscent of the union between God and humanity expressed in Christ. Bernard's notion of the preexistence of the heavenly Jerusalem (the form of the church) reinforces the idea that, through the church, Christ's spouse, the human person can be restored to full union with God. Consistent with Bernard's christology, the church is both bride and mother: her union with Christ bears fruit in offspring who need her tender care.

Bibliography

Elder, E. Rozanne, and John R. Sommerfeldt. *The Chimaera of His Age: Studies on Bernard of Clairvaux*. Kalamazoo, Mich.: Cistercian Publications, 1980.

Gilson, Etienne. *The Mystical Theology of Saint Bernard*. Trans. A. H. C. Downes. New York: Sheed & Ward, 1940.

Leclercq, Jean. *Bernard of Clairvaux and the Cistercian Spirit*. Trans. Claire Lavoie. Kalamazoo, Mich.: Cistercian Publications, 1976.

McGinn, Bernard. *The Growth of Mysticism*. Vol. 2 of *The Presence of God: A History of Western Christian Mysticism*. New York: Crossroad, 1994.

Pennington, M. Basil. *Saint Bernard of Clairvaux: Studies Commemorating the Eighth Centenary of His Canonization*. Kalamazoo, Mich.: Cistercian Publications, 1977.

Leonardo Boff (b. 1938)

Leonardo Boff was born in 1938 in Concórdia, Brazil, one of eleven children. He entered the seminary at ten and was ordained to priesthood as a Franciscan in 1964. He completed his education in Munich, where in 1971 he submitted his doctoral dissertation, "The Church as Sacrament in the Horizon of World Experience," to his professor Joseph Ratzinger and it was regarded highly. Returning to parish work in Brazil, Boff's theology increasingly was informed by the experience of radical poverty. His pastoral responses to the needs of his parishioners dovetailed with his interests in analyzing the role of the church in the world. Turning his attention to the nature of the institutional church, Boff wrote many individual pieces which applied principles of liberation theology to the structures of the church. A collection of these essays was published in Portuguese, Spanish, and Italian in 1981, under the title *Church: Charism and Power*. A subsequent English translation was published in 1985.

Controversy over the nature of hierarchical power soon emerged as the ideas of *Church: Charism and Power* were debated. On May 15, 1984, Boff received a summons to Rome from Joseph Cardinal Ratzinger, prefect of the Sacred Congregation for the Doctrine of the Faith. On September 2, 1984, Boff arrived in Rome, taking with him a lengthy response to the theological questions Ratzinger had raised in his letter. Ratzinger released his "Instruction on Certain Aspects of 'Liberation Theology' " on September 3, which, while highly critical of liberation theology, nonetheless affirmed its basic premises by condemning social injustices in Latin America.

On May 9, 1985, Boff received notice from the Vatican that he must observe an "obedient silence," a disciplinary measure which involved suspending his work as editor of the Brazilian journal *Revista Eclesiastica Brasileira* and halting his writing and lectures. This silence lasted a year and was lifted in 1986. Shortly after the silencing Bishop Pedro Casaldáliga composed the poem, "The Blessing of St. Francis on Friar Leonardo Boff," which posed the question, "What would my compadre St. Francis say to his son Leonardo Boff in this hour of his provocation?" Casaldáliga suggested that Boff "partake of the profound mystery of the poor, who have no voice anyway either in the church or in society."[1]

Bibliography

Boff, Leonardo. *The Lord's Prayer: The Prayer of Integral Liberation.* Maryknoll, N.Y.: Orbis Books, 1983.

———. *Church, Charism and Power: Liberation Theology and the Institutional Church.* New York: Crossroad, 1985.

———. *Introducing Liberation Theology.* With Clodovis Boff. Maryknoll, N.Y.: Orbis Books, 1987.

———. *Trinity and Society.* Maryknoll, N.Y.: Orbis Books, 1988.

Ferm, Deane William. "Leonardo Boff," in *Profiles in Liberation: 36 Portraits of Third World Theologians,* 124–28. Mystic, Conn.: Twenty-third Publications, 1988.

Maduro, Otto. "Leonardo Boff," in *A New Handbook of Christian Theologians,* ed. Donald W. Musser and Joseph L. Price, 74–84. Nashville: Abingdon Press, 1996.

Bonaventure (ca. 1221–74)

Giovanni di Fidanza, known as Bonaventure, was born sometime between 1217 and 1221 in the Tuscany region of Italy. His father Giovanni was a physician and his mother was Maria of Ritella. As a young boy, he became seriously ill. But he was saved from death, according to his own testimony, by the intercession of Francis of Assisi, the founder of the Franciscan movement. Giovanni studied at the University of Paris, earning a master of arts degree in 1243. At about the same time he joined the Franciscans and took the name Bonaventure. He continued his studies of theology at Paris until 1248, where one of his teachers was Alexander of Hales, an important Franciscan theologian of the early thirteenth century. With the completion of his theology studies, Bonaventure began to lecture, first on the Bible and then (1251–53) on Peter Lombard's *Sentences.* In 1254 he received his master of theology degree and continued to teach in Paris until 1257.

---

1. See Harvey Cox, *The Silencing of Leonardo Boff: The Vatican and the Future of World Christianity* (Bloomington, Ind.: Meyer-Stone Books, 1988), 32.

His defense of the right of Franciscans to teach in the university context and his high moral character won such respect from his fellow Franciscans that he was elected minister general of the order in 1257. He assumed leadership of the order at a time when it was troubled by conflict between the Spiritual Franciscans, who insisted on strict adherence to a rigorous understanding of apostolic poverty, and the Conventual Franciscans, who held a more relative view of poverty. By personal example and careful diplomacy, Bonaventure was able to steer a middle course and to preserve the unity of the order.

Bonaventure was clearly very impressed by the spiritual life of Francis of Assisi. He spent much time reflecting on Francis's life and developed an orderly exposition of the course of Francis's spiritual growth. Like many of his contemporaries, Bonaventure believed that Francis had achieved mystical union with Christ, and that this union was made manifest in Francis's reception of the stigmata, or wounds of Christ, during a vision on Mount Alverna, where he saw Christ crucified borne up by a six-winged seraph.

In his best-known work, *The Soul's Journey into God* (1259), Bonaventure lays out the path by which the mind may ascend to God. The treatise begins as a meditation upon the vision of the seraph that Francis had on Mount Alverna. Through six stages, the soul proceeds through the world of the senses, then turns inward to itself, and finally ascends to the level of apprehending God beyond the human mind. In the tradition of Augustine, Bonaventure finds vestiges of the trinity stamped within creation and the human person, created in God's image. Like Augustine, he believes that divine illumination can gradually make these vestiges of God in the world clearer. At the highest level of contemplation, one comes to see in Christ those things "which exceed all the insight of the human intellect." When the mind is elevated beyond itself through prayerful contemplation and God's grace, "all intellectual operations should be abandoned, and the whole height of our affection should be transferred and transformed into God" (chap. 7). The ultimate goal is mystical wisdom and union with God.

During his lifetime Bonaventure was respected by many. Dante mentions him as a saint in his *Paradiso*. Pope Gregory X named him bishop of Albano (Italy) in 1273 and consecrated him as cardinal in 1274, shortly before his death. Bonaventure died during the course of the Second Council of Lyons (1274). Pope Sixtus IV formally declared Bonaventure a saint in 1482, and Pope Sixtus V in the subsequent century declared him to be a doctor of the church. He is often referred to as the Seraphic Doctor. This is probably a reference to his preoccupation with the vision of the seraph, described in *The Soul's Journey into God* and other works.

Bibliography

Bougerol, Jacques Guy. *Introduction to the Works of Bonaventure*. Paterson, N.J.: St. Anthony Guild Press, 1964.

Gilson, Étienne. *The Philosophy of St. Bonaventure*. New York: Sheed & Ward, 1938.

Hayes, Zachary. *The Hidden Center: Spirituality and Speculative Christology in St. Bonaventure*. New York: Paulist Press, 1981.

Rout, Paul. *Francis and Bonaventure*. Liguori, Mo.: Triumph Books, 1997.

Shahan, Robert W., and Francis J. Kovach. *Bonaventure and Aquinas: Enduring Philoso-phers*. Norman: University of Oklahoma Press, 1976.

Tavard, George H. *Transiency and Permanence: The Nature of Theology according to St. Bonaventure*. St. Bonaventure, N.Y.: Franciscan Institute, 1954.

Tracy, David, ed. *Celebrating the Medieval Heritage: A Colloquy on the Thought of Aquinas and Bonaventure*. Chicago: University of Chicago Press, 1978.

Rita Nakashima Brock (b. 1950)

Rita Nakashima Brock is a leading scholar in the field of women's studies and feminist theology. Her life reflects a broad range of interests and an ability to bridge the academic world with concern for issues of global justice, particularly those involving women and human rights. Born in Fukuoka, Japan, on April 29, 1950, to a Japanese mother and a U.S. soldier of Puerto Rican descent, Brock came to the United States at the age of six. She received her bachelor's degree in religion and psychology from Chapman University and a doctorate in the philosophy of religion and theology from the Claremont Graduate School.

>From 1985 to 1989 she directed the women's studies program at Stephens College in Columbia, Missouri. From 1990 to 1997 Brock held an endowed chair in the humanities and was director of the humanities program at Hamline University in St. Paul, Minnesota. She has lectured widely throughout the United States in such places as Princeton Theological Seminary, Yale University Divinity School, the University of Chicago Divinity School, and Harvard Divinity School. She was a founding member of the Committee on the Status of Women in the Profession, a committee of the American Academy of Religion (AAR), and has also served on the AAR Board of Directors. In 1993 the National Council of Churches selected her to represent them on an international peace delegation to Guatemala and El Salvador.

Brock's first book, *Journeys by Heart: A Christology of Erotic Power*, won the 1988 Crossroad/Continuum Press award for the most outstanding manuscript in women's studies. She coedited a collection of essays on feminist theology, *Setting the Table: Women in Theological Conversation*. Her most recent book, coauthored with Susan Thistlethwaite, is *Casting Stones: Understanding Prostitution in Asia and the United States*. This book won first place in the 1997 Catholic Press Awards for gender studies. On September 1, 1997, Brock became the director of the Mary Ingraham Bunting Institute at Radcliffe College, a multidisciplinary center of advanced studies for women.

In *Journeys by Heart: A Christology of Erotic Power*, Rita Brock has developed a christology rooted in the Gospel of Mark, in which Jesus' healing miracles often involve an exchange of power between Jesus and the healed person. Brock characterizes this power to heal and transform as erotic power, and she argues that, rather than seeing this power as originating solely in Christ, we should understand it to be part of the nature of loving, healing relationships, in which Christ is always a part. Brock introduces a sense of the dynamic, transformative nature of erotic power with her use of the phrase Christa/Community, which, from the perspective of ecclesiology, reinforces the sacramental presence of Christ in the church when it is performing the same healing, restorative function as Christ did. Erotic power opposes unilateral power; it cannot be used to dominate or coerce; instead, it is a salve addressing the points of vulnerability or "woundedness" within each individual, restoring them to the strength of their created state.

Thus, for Brock, church as an institution has no real place unless or until it can rid itself of its patriarchal structures, which reinforce the unilateral approach to power which often characterizes its operation. Brock looks directly to the community of people who seek to witness to the transformative power of healing relationships in Christ to be the true church.

John Calvin (1509–64)

John Calvin, one of the most influential Protestant reformers and theologians, was born in Noyon, France, on July 10, 1509. Strongly influenced by Luther, his thought took several turns from Lutheranism, and he formulated a more systematic statement of belief in his *Institutes of the Christian Religion*. The *Institutes* was a "work in progress" which Calvin revised repeatedly. First published in 1536, he addressed the work to Francis I of France. Shortly after writing it, Calvin settled into Geneva and began to put the ideas of his work into practice. He wrote a *Confession of Faith* and *Catechism* to promulgate his theology. In Geneva his reforms provoked opposition, and he settled in Strasbourg in 1538, where he published a new version of the *Institutes* in 1539. Calvin played a role at the colloquies of Worms and Regensburg, the unsuccessful attempts made by Holy Roman Emperor Charles V to end religious schisms. He returned to Geneva in 1541 and established a new constitution for the city called the *Ecclesiastical Ordinances*. These provided for a form of theocracy, or civil rule of church authority, with four offices — pastors, teachers, elders, and deacons — who had doctrinal and disciplinary roles.

Heavily oriented to the Bible and widely familiar with medieval exegetical theory, Calvin drew on the thought of medieval thinkers like Anselm, Peter Lombard, Aquinas, Duns Scotus, and William of Ockham. Calvin developed a position on the sovereignty of God and the depravity of humanity which moved him outside the medieval framework and even pushed him beyond some of the ideas of Martin Luther. Humanity's task is to achieve self-knowledge, available only in the light of the knowledge of God through the visible universe and through scripture. All humanity is enslaved by sin and is saved by faith in God's mercy. However, God's mercy is extended to those intended to receive it, those who with God's grace respond to the operation of the Holy Spirit and who through faith are justified. This justification consists in the forgiveness of sins and the imputation of Christ's righteousness. Calvin's understanding of the irresistibility of God's grace led him to understand that the process of justification was foreordained, a part of God's foreknowledge. Redeemed humanity, then, responds to the strength of God's desire. Condemned humanity is overcome by its will to do evil, and, isolated from the grace of God, is rightly condemned as a sign of the absolute sovereignty of God. In other words, since all things tend toward the glory of God, anyone who perpetuates sin in the world, and thus who does not subsist in God, can have no part in God's eternal glory.

The church houses and ministers to the righteous, and there is no salvation outside the church. The church administers the two sacraments of baptism and the Eucharist, and has both visible and invisible aspects. The visible aspect is the Christian community which includes the condemned. The invisible aspect consists of the elect, who are known to God. The two aspects coexist and are separable only from the divine perspective.

Calvin's thought was most influential in France, the Netherlands, and Scotland, but he was also widely read in England, parts of Germany, and central Europe.

Bibliography

Battles, Ford Lewis. *Analysis of the "Institutes of the Christian Religion" of John Calvin.* Grand Rapids, Mich.: Baker Book House, 1980.

———. *Interpreting John Calvin.* Ed. Robert Benedetto. Grand Rapids, Mich.: Baker Books, 1996.

Calvin, John. *John Calvin on God and Political Duty.* Ed. John T. McNeill. New York: Liberal Arts Press, 1956.

Crampton, Gary. *What Calvin Says: An Introduction to the Theology of John Calvin.* Jefferson, Md.: Trinity Foundation, 1992.

Dowey, Edward A. *The Knowledge of God in Calvin's Theology.* Grand Rapids, Mich.: Eerdmans, 1994.

Gamble, Richard C. *Articles on Calvin and Calvinism: A Fourteen-Volume Anthology of Scholarly Articles.* New York: Garland Publications, 1992.

Garrish, B. A. *Grace and Gratitude: The Eucharistic Theology of John Calvin.* Minneapolis: Fortress Press, 1993.

Garrish, B. A., and Robert Benedetto, eds. *Reformatio Perennis: Essays on Calvin and the Reformation in Honor of Ford Lewis Battles.* Pittsburgh: Pickwick Press, 1981.

George, Timothy, ed. *John Calvin and the Church: A Prism of Reform.* Louisville: Westminster/John Knox Press, 1990.

McDonnell, Kilian. *John Calvin, the Church, and the Eucharist.* Princeton, N.J.: Princeton University Press, 1967.

McGrath, Alister F. *A Life of John Calvin: A Study in the Shaping of Western Culture.* Oxford: Blackwell, 1993.

Richard, Lucian. *The Spirituality of John Calvin.* Atlanta: John Knox Press, 1974.

Steinmetz, David. *Calvin in Context.* New York: Oxford University Press, 1995.

Tamburello, Dennis F. *Union with Christ: John Calvin and the Mysticism of St. Bernard.* Louisville: Westminster/John Knox Press, 1994.

Wyatt, Peter. *Jesus Christ and Creation in the Theology of John Calvin,* Allison Park, Pa.: Pickwick Publications, 1996.

Pedro Casaldáliga (b. 1928)

Pedro Casaldáliga, bishop of São Felix do Araguaia (Mato Grosso, Brazil), is one of the most important representatives of the church of the poor in Latin America. He was born in Barcelona, Spain, in 1928. In 1968 he left Spain for Brazil. He was one of the founders of the Indigenous Missionary Council and the Brazilian Pastoral Commission on the Earth. A poet and the author of more than thirty books on theology, spirituality, and of original poems, Casaldáliga is one of the most important voices of liberation theology. He has worked within the difficult context of the Roman Catholic Church in Brazil, where for decades church workers have been the targets of human rights violations, including torture. Hierarchical representatives of the church have not been excluded from such treatment, including Helder Camara, Waldyr Alheiros, Antonio Fragoso, Hypolito Adriano, and Pedro Casaldáliga himself. Other bishops have been charged with being communists because of their support of farm workers and Indians. Within this repressive context, Casaldáliga's life and theology stands as a testimony to the continued presence of God among the suffering.

Bibliography

Primary

Casaldáliga, Pedro. *Fire and Ashes to the Wind: Spiritual Anthology.* Quezon City, Philippines: Claretian Publications, 1984.
———. *I Believe in Justice and Hope.* Notre Dame: Fides-Claretian, 1978.
———. *In Pursuit of the Kingdom: Writings, 1968–88.* Maryknoll, N.Y.: Orbis Books, 1990.
Casaldáliga, Pedro, and José-María Vigil. *Political Holiness: A Spirituality of Liberation.* Maryknoll, N.Y.: Orbis Books, 1994.

Secondary

Cabestrero, Teófilo. *Mystic of Liberation: A Portrait of Bishop Pedro Casaldáliga of Brazil.* Maryknoll, N.Y.: Orbis Books, 1981.
Puleo, Mev. *The Struggle Is One: Voices and Visions of Liberation.* Albany: State University of New York Press, 1994.

Catherine of Siena (1347–80)

Catherine of Siena was born Caterina di Giacomo di Benincasa, the twenty-fourth of twenty-five children. Her father was a wool dyer in Siena. She was drawn to the church and cloister of San Domenico, a center of Dominican learning and preaching, and at fifteen she cut off her hair in defiance of her family's efforts to get her to marry. At eighteen she received the habit of a Dominican tertiary and by age twenty-one she was engaged in nursing activities outside her home. At the age of twenty-three she experienced a sort of "mystical death" and she redoubled the austerities of her life (almost complete fasting and sleep deprivation). She acquired a following and spent time composing letters which offered both spiritual counsel and political observations. By 1374 she was more involved in intercession among political factions in Siena, Pisa, and Florence. In 1375 she received the stigmata, visible only to herself, and in 1376 she had an audience with Pope Gregory XI attempting to convince him to return the papacy back to Rome. In 1377 she wrote her *Dialogue,* a book constructed as a mystical dialogue between God and the soul. Catherine remained in Siena at a reformed Dominican convent she had founded, until summoned to Rome in 1378 by Urban VI. There she set up her household, met with popes and cardinals, dictated letters,

and counseled her disciples. Weakened by intense fasting and penitential practices, Catherine died in Rome two years later at the age of thirty-three. She was
canonized in 1461 and declared a doctor of the Roman Catholic Church in 1970.

In the text of *The Dialogue* in Part One, Catherine develops many positions
on human nature, the efficacy of the sacraments, and the redemptive process. In
agreement with Augustine's arguments articulated against the Donatists, Catherine affirms that the sacraments are efficacious for the recipient despite the
unworthiness of the minister. Yet she points to the great responsibility of sacramental ministers to conduct themselves with high moral standards. Recipients of
the sacraments, too, once they have been strengthened by the elements, share that
responsibility for ethical behavior; indeed, God has harsh words for those who
continue to approach the sacraments without having done penance for sins.

In terms of original sin Catherine develops the Augustinian position by describing human nature as wounded. The salvation of humanity in Christ is
accomplished with respect to both God's justice and God's mercy, within a system
roughly parallel to that of Anselm. Unique to Catherine, however, is the sense of
God's intense desire to restore humanity to its original state. This process is not
merely part of the divine plan; rather, God's longing impels God to produce the
remedy for the Fall. Christ takes on the role of wet nurse in the restoration of humanity, a metaphor which, again, emphasizes love and service over Christ's *ability*
to redeem.[1] The healing power of Christ so transforms the soul that, although it
remains "scarred," it is able to resist its own tendency to sin. As Catherine notes,
"The inclination to sin, which is the trace that remains from original sin, is a
weakness as I have said, but the soul can keep it in check if she will."

In the text in Part Two, Catherine develops the metaphor of the mystic body of
the church, a body which is "given over to sensuality" and must be reformed. Because many of its leaders have proven to be corrupt, God tells Catherine that the
church will be reformed through the work of virtuous people setting examples.

In the thought of Catherine of Siena the doctrines of human person and church
are intertwined; both the metaphors of the nursing female body and the emphasis
on that body as the temple of virtue form the core of what it means to be a Christian. The metaphor of the church as a garden may well have influenced Teresa of
Avila's discussion of the human soul.

Bibliography

Catherine of Siena. *The Dialogue*. Trans. Suzanne Noffke. New York: Paulist Press, 1980.
———. *The Letters of St. Catherine of Siena*. Trans. Suzanne Noffke. Binghamton, N.Y.:
    Center for Medieval and Early Renaissance Studies, 1988.
Raymond of Capua. *The Life of St. Catherine of Siena*. Trans. George Lamb. New York: P. J.
    Kennedy, 1960.

---

1. Cf. Anselm, *Why God Became Human*, book 2, chap. 6: "If then, as is certain, that celestial city
must be completed from among men, and this cannot happen unless the aforesaid satisfaction is made,
while no one save God can make it and no one save man ought to make it, it is necessary for a God-
Man to make it" (quoted in Eugene R. Fairweather, ed., *A Scholastic Miscellany: Anselm to Ockham*
[Philadelphia: Westminster Press, 1956], 151).

Clement of Rome (d. ca. 97)

The *First Letter of Clement* is a document ascribed to Clement of Rome, identified by Irenaeus as the third bishop of Rome.[1] According to Eusebius, it was commonly read and used in the churches of the fourth century. The letter is usually dated to ca. 95–96 because of the reference at the beginning of the letter to a period of persecution, generally taken to be the Domitian persecution of 95. The letter appears to respond to a crisis of authority within the Corinthian church in which the Corinthian community was divided in its recognition of presbyters. That the Roman church, through Clement, intervened in such an organizational question suggests that it understood itself to have authority over the church in other geographical regions.

Organizationally, the letter is heavily dependent upon Paul's First Letter to the Corinthians, but the understanding of the role of law, authority and hierarchy in the life of the Christian has shifted considerably. As Hans von Campenhausen observes: "[Clement] draws repeatedly on 1 Corinthians, making extensive use of its exhortations to humility, of the imagery of the body and its members, and of the hymn in praise of love. In fact, however, the meaning of all these passages has been shifted to make them support a particular moral and social demand. The miracle of the new life is now understood as the fulfillment of order and law: 'The one who with humility of mind and constant gentleness, without altering his resolve, fulfills the decrees and commandments given by God, is enrolled and numbered among those who are saved by Jesus Christ.' "[2] For Clement, order has turned into a piece of sacred knowledge which touches the essence of the church, a fundamental, exalted truth, which he makes the content of his whole sermon. In practice, this means that Christians ought not to disturb the existing situation in the church; their task is to fit into its beautifully articulated and organized community, and by patience and docility to maintain harmony, peace, and universal order.

Although von Campenhausen argues that Clement moves apostolic authority and the need for order into a new position of importance within the Christian tradition,[3] we should be careful in our approach to the term "presbyter-bishop." Scholars of the subapostolic period believe that the functions of bishops, presbyters, and deacons were emerging slowly throughout this period and were probably subject to local variations. The later meaning of the word "bishop" is not applicable to the church of the first or early second century. Thus *1 Clement* should be understood as an early suggestion of "apostolic succession," a concept which does not reach any clear articulation until Cyprian of Carthage. Yet for Clement, appointment by an apostle is the guarantor of authority, more important than the qualifications of the bishop and more attuned to the will of God than any

---

1. The so-called *Second Letter of Clement* was almost certainly penned by another author.
2. Hans von Campenhausen, *Ecclesiastical Authority and Spiritual Power in the Church of the First Three Centuries*, trans. J. A. Baker (Stanford, Calif.: Stanford University Press, 1969), 87.
3. See ibid., 92.

other criterion. In this document Clement devotes more time to the justification of this structure than to any other aspect of church life.

Cyprian of Carthage (d. 258)

Cyprian of Carthage was a teacher of rhetoric who experienced a conversion to Christianity in 246. Shortly afterward, in 249, he became bishop of Carthage. Cyprian's ascent to the position of bishop without much life experience as a Christian caused some initially to reject his authority, and his ecclesiology is directly related to the challenges he faced as bishop. During the Decian persecution (250–51) Cyprian vacated his post as bishop, returning after Decius's reign. During Cyprian's absence lay leaders who had remained faithful to Christianity (called "confessors") had emerged as leaders of the community. Cyprian's return caused a crisis of authority. Additionally, there were many Christians who had made the imperial sacrifice (called "lapsed") and had to be restored back into the church. To whom would they apply for such readmission, to the confessors who had remained faithful or to Cyprian, who retained apostolic authority, but had left the see? The penitential system itself was burdened by the numbers of lapsed Christians; someone or some group with authority had to act decisively to move the Christian community through this crisis.

In light of these circumstances, Cyprian penned *On the Unity of the Catholic Church*, in which he developed the position that Christian unity is modeled in many areas, including in doctrine, organization, and sacraments — all of which reside in and are upheld through the episcopacy. Unity comes from oneness and the ability to trace one's origins back to a single source, Cyprian argued, which for the church was Peter. Cyprian thus emphasized that the Roman See was the source of episcopacy, and the unity of the church grew out of one apostle, Peter. Of course, in a derivative way, Cyprian's ideas justified his own authority within a difficult disciplinary situation. Returning to Carthage after his exile in 250, Cyprian held a council in 251 to implement a penitential system for the lapsed: each case would be examined by the clergy, but lapsed clergy would not be readmitted to their orders. Those who had sacrificed to the Roman gods would be readmitted to the church only on their deathbeds. The council consolidated Cyprian's power within Carthage, as well as that of the clergy. By the mid–third century the Christian church had made a decisive turn toward hierarchical organization, with the doctrine of apostolic succession and Petrine supremacy serving as theoretical cornerstones.

Bibliography

Hinchliff, Peter Bingham. *Cyprian of Carthage and the Unity of the Christian Church.* London: G. Chapman, 1974.
Laurance, John D. *Priest as Type of Christ: The Leader of the Eucharist in Salvation History according to Cyprian of Carthage.* New York: Peter Lang, 1984.
Raven, Susan. *Rome in Africa.* New York: Routledge, 1993.

Rives, J. R. *Religion and Authority in Roman Carthage: From Augustus to Constantine*. New York: Oxford University Press, 1995.

Robeck, Cecil M. *Prophecy in Carthage: Perpetua, Tertullian, and Cyprian*. Cleveland: Pilgrim Press, 1992.

The *Didache* (ca. 110)

The document known as the *Didache* offers insight into the early practices of some Christian communities. Scholars have compared the *Didache* with early Jewish instructions and have located the "two ways" section of the *Didache* in the text of a Jewish baptizing community near Qumran, associating it with the community described by the Dead Sea Scrolls. At least the first section is probably Syrian, from the same community as the Gospel of Matthew and the letters of Ignatius. W. H. C. Frend dates it to ca. 70; Richardson dates it at least to ca. 90 because of the influence of Matthew and Barnabas, or even to ca. 110 because of the influence of the *Shepherd of Hermas*.[1] Scholar Henry Chadwick places it in the niche between 70 and 110.[2]

The *Didache* suggests that early Christians used the ritual of the Eucharist and certain forms of moral behavior to reinforce their identity as a social group. The emphasis in the text of maintaining a moral life implies that Christian doctrine itself was less important to this community than ethical behavior. Passages regarding the Eucharist suggest that it was celebrated as a communal meal and was a cherished part of community life. Tithes collected as part of the Eucharist were divided among the needy in the community.

With respect to the organization of the community, the *Didache* mentions no bishops or figureheads within the Christian communities, even when describing the Eucharist. The author of the *Didache* certainly does not say that only the bishop can lead it. And when it comes to local leadership, the author suggests that the communities ought to select their own bishops and deacons. In contrast, Clement implies that the laity lack the power to do so and Ignatius implies that they lack the insight to choose wisely. Bishops and deacons are chosen "to carry out the ministry of the charismatists and teachers for you";[3] thus they are secondary figures. If they embody God, they do so not by virtue of the office they hold but by virtue of living out and encouraging the word of God.[4] The document uses the term "apostles" in the text above not to refer to the twelve apostles but rather to itinerant preachers in general who fulfill the function of apostles.

---

1. See Cyril C. Richardson, ed., *Early Christian Fathers* (New York: Macmillan, 1970), 162–63. Richardson claims an Alexandrian scribe compiled the *Didache* around 150; he claims this because the document had canonical authority in Alexandria through the third century.

2. See Henry Chadwick, *The Early Church* (New York: Penguin Books, 1985), 46–47: "But the situation regarding Church order presupposed in the *Didache* makes it hard to find any plausible niche for it in early Christian history other than the period between about 70 and 110. It may be odd there, but it is much odder anywhere else."

3. *Didache*, paragraph 15.

4. Commenting on this document, W. H. C. Frend remarks, "The *Didache* accepts the existence of bishops, but regards them as 'meek men,' hardly the sort of people to dominate a congregation" (*The Rise of Christianity* [Philadelphia: Fortress Press 1984], 145).

Given the emphasis on charismatic authority, it is not surprising that the document also offers insight into a communal discernment of the spirit of the true prophet. The inclusion of such material suggests that the author(s) of the document believed that the Christian community as a whole (as opposed to a single leader) was able to distinguish true from false prophets and that these kinds of decisions sprang from the lived experience of the community. The document's attention to the proper conduct of the prophet can be understood as an affirmation of the importance of prophecy and continued revelation; indeed, the author speaks highly of charismatists, calling them "your 'High Priests' nowadays," a bid for the primacy of the prophet within the Christian community.

Avery Dulles (b. 1918)

Avery Dulles was born on August 24, 1918, in Auburn, New York, the son of John Foster Dulles and Janet (Avery) Dulles. He was educated at Harvard and received his doctorate at the Gregorian Institute in Rome. After serving in the U.S. Navy Reserves from 1942 through 1946, he entered the Society of Jesus in 1946 and was ordained a Roman Catholic priest in 1956. He began his teaching career at Fordham University in the department of philosophy in 1951. In 1960 he began teaching at Woodstock College (Maryland), where he continued through 1974. He served as a member of the Catholic Bishops' Advisory Council from 1969 to 1974. Very interested in both the nature and the governance of the Roman Catholic Church, Dulles published widely in ecclesiology, culminating in his 1974 book *Models of the Church*. In it Dulles proposed various ways of understanding the church, and his work, revised in 1987, has served as an important introduction to the field of Catholic ecclesiology.

In 1974 Dulles joined the faculty at the Catholic University of America. He served on the advisory board of the Ethics and Public Policy Program at the Kennedy Institute at Georgetown University from 1977 to 1980. In 1988 he returned to Fordham University, where he currently occupies the Laurence J. McGinley Chair in Religion and Society.

Dulles's bibliography reflects his desire to blend theology and faith. He is committed to theological service within the church and has a continuing interest in dogmatic theology. He has lectured widely as a visiting professor at such institutions as the Weston School of Theology, Boston College, Union Theological Seminary, Princeton Theological Seminary, and the University of Notre Dame. In recent years Dulles's lectures have addressed specific issues relevant to the identity and future of the Roman Catholic Church. In 1995 Dulles took an unpopular stand in support of *Ordinatio Sacerdotalis* (1994), a statement made by Pope John Paul II in which the pope asserted that the Catholic Church lacks the authority to ordain women and declared that the issue was not to be discussed as a theological matter. The Congregation for the Defense of Faith (CDF) then asserted that *Ordinatio Sacerdotalis* represented an infallible teaching of the church. In defending *Ordinatio Sacerdotalis* Dulles appealed to the pope's previous statement *Mulieris Dignitatem* (1988) in which it was argued that a priest at the altar acts in the person of Christ the Bridegroom, and thus the image or icon of a woman prevents her from acting symbolically as the person of Christ. Theological consensus within the academy, however, does not support Dulles's stance, as evidenced by the 1997 Catholic Theological Society of America (CTSA) document "Tradition and the Ordination of Women," which challenged CDF's ability to close debate on the question of women's ordination and advocated further inquiry into the theological validity of *Ordinatio Sacerdotalis*. Within Catholic circles Dulles often lectures on issues affecting the contemporary life of the church.

Bibliography

Primary (Select)

Dulles, Avery. *The Assurance of Things Hoped For: A Theology of Christian Faith* New York: Oxford University Press, 1994.
———. *A Church to Believe In: Discipleship and the Dynamics of Faith*. New York: Crossroad, 1982.
———. *The Craft of Theology: From Symbol to System*. New York: Crossroad, 1992.
———. *Models of the Church*. New York: Doubleday, 1974.

Ignatius of Antioch (d. 110)

Little is known of the life of Ignatius, who claimed to be the third bishop of Antioch. He was born in Syria and is known primarily through the seven letters he wrote to various churches on his way from Smyrna to be martyred in Rome. On his journey he was received by Polycarp, bishop of Smyrna, who later attested to his actual martyrdom. Ignatius used the circumstances of his impending death to exhort the faithful on the Christian life. His letters reveal concerns over orthodoxy, the doctrinal authority of the bishop, and the unity of the universal church. Against Docetism, a tendency to see in Christ only the appearance of a real human, Ignatius argued for the divinity and humanity of Christ. Concurrently he taught that Christ was present in the Eucharist, and that he was resurrected in the body. Ignatius understood his martyrdom to be the imitation of Christ and a witness to the doctrinal truth of Jesus' full humanity, actual death, and bodily resurrection.

The church, for Ignatius, was the body of Christ, headed by the bishops who represented the mind of God. Thus, through the church, humanity had access to divine wisdom. The Christian life consisted in the celebration of the Eucharist, obedience to the bishop, and an acceptance of suffering and possibly martyrdom. Yet these aspects of Christian life were neither mindless nor disembodied. For Ignatius, doctrine was not merely teaching but wisdom, and thus it had a transformative power in the individual as well as the community. His letters constitute a personal call to holiness as well as an admonition to other Christians to uphold the church as the body of Christ.

Irenaeus of Lyons (ca. 130–202)

Irenaeus, bishop of Lyons, was born in Asia Minor where he became a disciple of Polycarp of Smyrna. He migrated to Rome, where he may have studied with Justin Martyr, and then moved to Gaul. He survived persecutions there in 177 and replaced the martyred bishop Eleutherus. In response to a gnostic movement in Gaul he penned five books entitled *Against Heresies,* written ca. 180–85. He further defended orthodox Christianity in *The Proof of the Apostolic Preaching.*

The emphasis of Irenaeus's theology is the oneness of God, represented on earth by the one true church. Thus unity in the church was critical, and such unity could only be maintained with fidelity to the tradition of the Gospels as they were handed down through the apostles. It was this direct relation to the apostles, through apostolic succession, that authenticated the church and made it an efficacious sign. Further, Irenaeus understood the church's primary function to be the salvation and education of each individual member. His orientation to instruction gave Irenaeus an important perspective on human nature: that it was essentially immature and needed to be taught by word and example. Irenaeus applied the metaphor of infancy and childhood development to adult Christians, individually and collectively, who need to be fed their faith slowly. Humanity at large is not completely developed; the human race at its infancy was unable to preserve the perfection within which it had been created and was to regain it slowly, through the example of Christ and the church. This educational process involves mistakes as well as successes, and the human task is to be a humble and patient student, offering God "a soft and malleable heart; then keep the shape in which the Master molds you." Rebelling against the process results in damnation, but cooperating with it enables us to become "God's perfect work" (see text in Part One).

Irenaeus developed his understanding of the church within the context of conflict against gnostic groups in Gaul. As bishop, Irenaeus wanted to present a forceful, orthodox statement of the Christian faith which asserted the authority of the apostolic tradition over whatever other interpretations of the nature and meaning of Christ's life might exist. The oneness of the church is exhibited in its doctrinal unity ("she believes these things [everywhere] alike"), and this unity is rooted in the faithful witness of the apostles to the one God. Yet this truth is also manifestly open to all, not a hidden mystery, as the gnostics claimed. Indeed, the witness of scripture made the faith immediately accessible. Thus the major function of the church, as Irenaeus understood it, was to bear witness to the one, true faith, and to adopt the position of teacher to the world. Church teachings were not primarily speculative but salvific; they reinforced a closed system of doctrine, organization, and worship, in something of a self-perpetuating circle. Baptism and the Eucharist were important elements of unity, as was obedience to those who had succeeded the apostles, since they had been blessed by the Holy Spirit to perform their ministerial functions.

Julian of Norwich (1342–ca. 1423)

Julian of Norwich was an anchoress associated with the parish church of St. Julian in Norwich. Few details of her life remain; much of what we know of her has been gleaned from her works and from records of bequests made to her. As a young girl, she lived through the entrance of the plague into England; it reached Norwich in January 1349. Subsequent outbreaks in 1359 and 1369 provide some context for Julian's reflection on physical suffering and death, the very real suffering which people often experience out of love for others, the mercy of God, and her own pastoral orientation to those who had experienced suffering. The papal schism, which began in 1377, provides another contextual arena for understanding Julian's relationship to the church, and, particularly, to the bishop of Norwich. Henry Despenser, the bishop of Norwich, supported the Italian claimant, Urban VI, and went on crusade against supporters of the French claimant, Clement. Henry's dedication to garnering social and political support for the papacy may well have been at odds with the pastoral needs of the laity, to which Julian clearly was oriented. Sprinkled throughout her work in interesting passages, Julian professes allegiance to the church as an institution but describes a more profound vision of Christian life than contemporary ecclesiastical leaders exemplified.

Julian's pastoral gifts were expressed through spiritual counsel which she offered to her contemporaries. If we are to judge from *The Book of Margery Kempe,* Julian acquired a reputation for wisdom and holiness which led many to consult with her on spiritual and theological matters. It is not clear when she enclosed herself as an anchoress; some scholars suggest she wrote the second version of the *Showings* (completed in 1393) as an anchoress, and the first bequest to her is dated 1393/94. Other bequests indicate that she lived past 1416. Julian's *Showings* is a remarkable text, although it did not enjoy wide circulation until relatively recently. The reason for its obscurity probably rests in the suspicions of heresy after the prosecution of the Lollards in the early fifteenth century. Contemporary interest in Julian reflects the fact that her theological insights continue to provide meaning to Christians today.

In her work *Showings,* or *The Revelations of Divine Love,* as it became known, she describes that, on May 13, 1373, at the age of thirty, she received a series of revelations as she lay close to death. These revelations were the source of decades of theological reflection resulting in two versions of the text of *Showings.* Edmund Colledge and James Walsh, who authored the definitive modern translation of the *Showings,* believe that Julian concluded the second version of the text in 1393, and that this second version represents nearly two decades of theological maturation following the first version. Indeed, in the second version of the *Showings* Julian admits that she did not completely understand the revelations when she first received them. The absence of the parable of the lord and servant (chapter 51 of the longer text) is indicative of Julian's theological maturation.

Sin, which reflects our separation from God, manifests its power only through the pain it causes us. Julian is in no way disturbed by the power of sin over humanity, nor, indeed, does she devote much attention to humanity's weakness. "Sin has no substance, no share in being, nor can it be recognized except by the pain caused by it.... It is true that sin is the cause of all this pain, but all will be well, and every kind of thing will be well."[1] Moving far away from Anselm's notion of God's honor, which made it "unfitting" for God to restore humanity without the sacrifice of Christ, Julian claims that God does not blame us for sin: "And God showed that sin will be no shame, but honor to humanity, for just as there is indeed a corresponding pain for every sin, just so love gives to the same soul a bliss for every sin."[2] Sin does, however, impede us from union with God.[3]

For Julian, humanity is made for union with God. This is not simply a question of its potential, realized in some state of mystical experience, but of the soul's ontology. She writes: "Our natural will is to have God, and God's good will is to have us, and we can never stop willing or loving until we possess God in the fullness of joy."[4] Thus, the human and divine wills are united in their mutual desire for one another, and their very union is predicated upon their similarity in loving. Since the soul's substance is in God, it is able, in God, to be as God is; that is to love as God loves, accepting suffering as part of the reality of loving. As the soul moves into a way of being which manifests the loving nature of God, it experiences greater joy, a joy which overcomes the inevitable suffering of love relationships.

Julian's understanding of the shared substance of creator and creature is underscored by her continued reference to God and Christ as our mother. These doctrines of Christ and God are explored independently of one another and yet are interrelated through the metaphor of motherhood. The development of God's and Christ's maternal nature is certainly not unique to Julian,[5] but Julian's reflections on God, Christ, and human nature reveal unique sensitivities to human experience. Grounded in the insights of her tradition, they also provide new directions for some of the most essential and urgent theological questions.

Bibliography

Baker, Denise Nowakowski. *Julian of Norwich's "Showings": >From Vision to Book*. Princeton, N.J.: Princeton University Press, 1994.

Jantzen, Grace M. *Julian of Norwich: Mystic and Theologian*. New York: Paulist Press, 1988.

Julian of Norwich. *Showings*. Trans. Edmund Colledge and James Walsh. New York: Paulist Press, 1978.

Nuth, Joan M. *Wisdom's Daughter: The Theology of Julian of Norwich*. New York: Crossroad, 1991.

---

1. Julian of Norwich, *Showings*, 225.
2. Ibid., 243.
3. Ibid., 320.
4. Ibid., 186.
5. For examples of other medieval theologians who develop notions of Christ as mother, see Caroline Walker Bynum, "Jesus as Mother and Abbot as Mother: Some Themes in Twelfth-Century Cistercian Writing," in idem, *Jesus as Mother: Studies in the Spirituality of the High Middle Ages* (Berkeley: University of California Press, 1982), 110–69.

Martin Luther (1483–1546)

Martin Luther was born on November 10, 1483, in Eisleben (Thuringia) to parents of peasant stock, Hans and Margareta. In 1490 Martin began attending the Latin school at Mansfeld, and in 1501 he matriculated at the University of Erfurt. By the fall of 1502 Luther had completed his bachelor of arts, and by the beginning of 1505 he had earned the master of arts and entered the Augustinian cloister in Erfurt. Legend holds that a summer storm, in which Luther was almost struck by lightning, precipitated his desire to enter the monastery. If he had died at the time of the storm, Luther was not sure that he would have been granted eternal life. Leading the life of a good monk was a time-honored way to improve one's chances for a happy destiny.

Luther's years as a monk were not happy. Although he was committed to study and prayer, Luther was overcome by a pervasive sense that he ought to do more. He felt that God was displeased with him, and he lacked the sense of tranquility he had expected monastic life to grant him. In later life, he wrote: "I was a good monk, and I kept the rule of my order so strictly that I may say that if ever a monk got to heaven by his monkery it was I. All my brothers in the monastery who knew me will bear me out. If I had kept on any longer, I should have killed myself with vigils, prayers, reading, and other work."[1]

Between the years 1505 and 1509 Luther devoted himself to a study of the later scholastic theologians, such as William of Ockham, Pierre D'Ailly, and Gabriel Biel. From them he learned to distrust the speculative flights of reason that went beyond revelation. At the same time, Luther began preparations for the priesthood, despite his father's objections. He celebrated his first Mass in May of 1507. By 1510, Luther's study of Augustine and of the late medieval Augustinians had led him to a rapidly growing hostility toward the dominance of Aristotle in theology and toward nominalist theology as a new form of Pelagianism. In 1512 he completed his doctorate in theology and, in the following year, he began his professorial duties at the University of Wittenberg.

Some time after beginning to lecture at the university on the Psalms and the letters of Paul, Luther experienced a new religious insight: God's "righteousness" is not the justice by which God measures people and declares them sinners, but the righteousness that God gives to people freely (Rom. 1:17). Scholars disagree about when Luther had this experience. Much recent scholarship prefers a later date, suggesting that it probably occurred in early 1518. Whether Luther's experience of the gracious righteousness of God occurred suddenly in a given moment or over a longer period of time, it is clear that this experience became the key to all his theology. This insight into the nature of "justification" became the starting point of Luther's career as a reformer. To know that the basis of his justification was not his own holiness, but God's mercy and grace, transformed Luther's despair about attaining salvation into peace and assurance.

The sale of the Saint Peter indulgence in 1517 was the occasion that trans-

---

1. Bainton, *Here I Stand*, 34.

formed Luther's personal insight about justification into the driving force behind his steps for reform of the church. Indulgence sellers such as Johann Tetzel easily won customers with their claim that the purchase of an indulgence entailed the total remission of the temporal punishments for the sins of the purchaser or for his or her dead relatives. To believe that the salvation of souls could be bought by indulgence certificates, the profit from which was being used to rebuild Saint Peter's Basilica, was to Luther a perversion of the notion of grace as a free gift of God. Moreover, forgiveness of sin and guilt depends upon God's authority, not the pope's. At best, the pope could confirm by a subsequent declaration that a sin has already been remitted by God, but he could not make such a declaration about the status of those who had already died. Luther summarized his thoughts about indulgences and the pope's authority to grant them in the Ninety-five Theses, which he sent to Archbishop Albrecht of Mainz and which, according to the testimony of Philip Melanchthon, he posted on the door of the Castle Church in Wittenberg on October 31, 1517. Although Luther did not intend at this time to cause a break with the church of Rome, that date has become in retrospect the "birthday" of the Protestant Reformation. Thanks to the recently invented printing press, Luther's theses were quickly disseminated throughout Germany. Luther even popularized their main ideas in a vernacular "Sermon on Indulgences and Graces" (1517).

In reaction, a heresy investigation against Luther began. In 1518 Luther was summoned to the imperial Diet at Augsburg for interrogation by the pope's legate, Cardinal Cajetan. Refusing to recant his position, Luther secretly left Augsburg before he could be arrested. He then made an appeal for the convocation of a general council to determine the legitimacy of his arguments. Instead of a council, Luther was given the opportunity to debate Johann Eck. Eck wrested from Luther an admission that Jan Hus had been right on some matters and that the general council of Constance had been wrong to condemn him. The effect of this admission was dramatic. Luther was publicly branded as a sympathizer of Hus, whom the authorities of the universal church had condemned. In the papal bull *Exsurge Domine* of June 1520, forty-one of Luther's statements were declared heretical and he was threatened with excommunication. In December, Luther burned the papal bull. He was officially excommunicated on January 3, 1521. In the Edict of Worms (May 1521) Emperor Charles V added his condemnation and made Luther and his followers outlaws in the Holy Roman Empire.

Due to the intervention of Duke Frederick the Wise, Luther was kept free from imprisonment. While hidden away in the Wartburg castle (1521–22), he completed his translation of the New Testament into German. In the fall of 1524 he abandoned his religious habit. Eight months later, Luther married Katharina von Bora. By 1534 Luther had completed his German translation of the entire Bible, which made the scriptures accessible to more Christians. Luther died on February 18, 1546, secure in the knowledge that the work of the Reformation continued.

Luther was not the first of the major reformers of the Christian tradition, but his challenges to the church certainly set the Reformation movement of the sixteenth century ablaze. He gave classic expression to the most important "Protestant principles": First, justification is by grace through faith, not by faith and good works (*sola gratia, sola fide*). Second, scripture, not scripture and tradition, is the sole authority in the church's life and practice (*sola scriptura*). Third, all Christians, by virtue of their baptism, have equal access to God; each should be a "priest" to the others (priesthood of all believers). There is not a qualitative difference between the spiritual state of the clergy and the spiritual state of the laity. These principles were articulated in the three treatises Luther wrote between August and November 1520, the *Address to the Christian Nobility of the German Nation, The Babylonian Captivity of the Church*, and *On the Freedom of the Christian*.

Luther's new understanding of the gospel gave theology a new orientation and the church a new structure. Luther changed the meaning of some familiar terms of medieval theology, such as grace, faith, and law. And he displaced the scholastic "theology of glory," which claimed to know God on the basis of reason, with his "theology of the cross," which claimed to know God authentically only in Christ crucified, proclaimed in the gospel. Instead of speaking abstractly of God "in himself," Luther spoke concretely about God "for us." Instead of speaking about the capacity of human beings to earn merit from God, he spoke of human beings as "simultaneously righteous and sinful" (*simul justus et peccator*). Instead of speaking about the church as a hierarchical and bureaucratic institution, he spoke of the church as the community of believers. Instead of speaking of the sacraments as rituals that caused the transfer of grace almost mechanically, he spoke of the sacraments as promises of Christ and signs of faith. In short, Luther articulated an understanding of Christian faith that, despite its continuities with the previous tradition of the church, was both fresh and distinctive.

The life and integrity of the church was of real concern to Martin Luther. The controversy over indulgences which his ideas generated reflects this preoccupation. In Proposition 13 at the Leipzig Debate (1519) he denied the claim of papal rule by divine right, and after his excommunication in 1521 began to view the papacy as a source of sin. A more constructive approach to ecclesiology, rooted in 1 Corinthians 12:15, was his concept of the priesthood of all believers, in which the spiritual priesthood of all Christians replaced the hierarchical division between clergy and laity. Understanding the priesthood as spiritual rather than temporal led to a primary focus on the invisible church rooted in a communion of faith, not in institutional structures. This invisible church could be known by its signs, especially baptism, the Eucharist, and the Word of God. In a larger sense, the church is the congregation of the faithful who gather together to receive the Holy Spirit through the preaching of the Word of God. The church that preaches the gospel also has the power to forgive sins and to sanctify through God's grace (not through works). Thus the holiness of the church is maintained through fidelity to the Word of God.

Bibliography

Bainton, Roland H. *Here I Stand: A Life of Luther.* New York: Mentor Books, 1950.

Lull, Timothy F., ed. *Martin Luther's Basic Theological Writings.* Minneapolis: Fortress Press, 1989.

Oberman, Heiko A. *Luther: Man between God and the Devil*. Trans. Eileen Walliser-
    Schwarzbart. New Haven: Yale University Press, 1989.
Pelikan, Jaroslav, and Helmut T. Lehmann, eds. *Luther's Works*. 56 vols. Philadelphia:
    Fortress Press, 1955.
Todd, John M. *Luther: A Life*. New York: Crossroad, 1982.

John Macquarrie (b. 1919)

John Macquarrie was born on June 27, 1919, in Renfrew, Scotland. He was
educated at the University of Glasgow where he received a masters in 1940 and
a Ph.D. in 1954. He received a doctorate in divinity in 1981 from Oxford University. In 1963 Macquarrie joined the Anglican communion and was ordained
a priest in the Episcopal church in 1965. He has served as a parish minister, an
army chaplain, and as a canon of Christ Church. Additionally, he was on the
faculty of Union Theological Seminary in New York from 1962 through 1970.
In 1970 he became Lady Margaret Professor of Divinity at Oxford University. A
widely respected voice of the Episcopal church, he has received numerous hon-
orary degrees throughout England and the United States and has an extensive list
of publications.

A philosophical theologian, Macquarrie has approached theology with a number of questions about the nature of being and human nature. His major concern
has been the shift from conceptions of human existence to conceptions of God.
Within the framework of natural theology, wherein one arrives at the knowledge
of God through human reason, Macquarrie has sought to shift the question away
from proofs for the existence of God to connecting forms of discourse — scientific
and theological — with the ordinary discourse of human experience. As his career
progressed, he began to propose a systematic theology rooted in this method. His
Principles of Christian Theology, first published in 1966 and again in 1977, was
a systematic outline of a natural theology in dialectical relationship with dogmatic theology. Rather than seeing doctrine as a priori informing what humans
can know, Macquarrie believes that both faith and human experience mutually
inform one another. This method emerges clearly in his reflections on the nature
of the church, in which he explores the sacramental nature of the church without
either taking that assumption for granted (our human experience must confirm it)
or ignoring historical examples of injustice within the church.

Bibliography

Primary

Macquarrie, John. *Christian Unity and Christian Diversity*. Philadelphia: Westminster Press,
    1975.
———. *Existentialism*. Philadelphia: Westminster Press, 1972.
———. *The Faith of the People of God: A Lay Theology*. New York: Scribner, 1972.
———. *God-Talk: An Examination of the Language and Logic of Theology*. New York:
    Harper, 1967.
———. *God and Secularity*. Philadelphia: Westminster Press, 1967.

———. *In Search of Humanity: A Theological and Philosophical Approach.* New York: Crossroad, 1982, 1985.

———. *Paths in Spirituality.* New York: Harper and Row, 1972.

———. *Principles of Christian Theology.* New York: Scribner, 1966; London: SCM, 1977.

———. *Studies in Christian Existentialism.* Philadelphia: Westminster Press, 1965.

———. *Theology, Church, and Ministry.* New York: Crossroad, 1986.

———. *Thinking about God.* New York: Harper, 1975.

———. *Twentieth-Century Religious Thought: Frontiers of Philosophy and Theology.* New York: Harper, 1963; New York: Scribner, 1981.

Secondary

Jenkins, David. *The Scope and Limits of John Macquarrie's Existential Theology.* Uppsala, Sweden: Acta Universitatis Upsaliensis, 1987.

Long, Eugene T. *Existence, Being, and God: An Introduction to the Philosophical Theology of John Macquarrie.* New York: Paragon House, 1985.

Reinhold Niebuhr (1892–1971)

Niebuhr, one of the most important Protestant theologians and ethicists of the twentieth century, was educated at Yale. An ordained minister, he served as a pastor in Detroit until joining the faculty at Union Theological Seminary in New York in 1928. He established and was editor of the journal *Christianity and Crisis*. His early tendency toward social idealism was tempered by his speculation about original sin. Both his observations of contemporary society and his appreciation of contemporary psychology informed his theological anthropology. Consideration of the human tendency to grasp and wield power, reinforced by the totalitarianisms and warfare of the 1930s and 1940s, led him to develop an understanding of human sin as an egocentric assertion of power. This quest for power, he suggested, originated in human anxiety over finitude and fragility. Humanity is also characterized by the experience of tension between potentiality and finitude. Our desire to reach our potential often causes us to deny our finitude and leads us to the primary sin of pride. Our exacerbated sense of self also leads us to perpetuate injustice in the world.

Niebuhr revives the very traditional notion of sin as pride, found in Augustine, Gregory the Great, and many others within the medieval tradition. Yet he understands pride to have important consequences in the realm of social sin, exploring this category with a new sensitivity more germane to the modern period. His reflection on the experience of finitude incorporates both the concrete realities of the twentieth century and the effects of existentialism. Feminist commentators on Niebuhr have questioned whether or not his emphasis on pride as the primary sin is relevant to women. Patriarchal cultures, they assert, deny women full personhood; in this context, to assert one's selfhood is not an act of pride leading *to* injustice but rather an act of courage and a prophetic stance *against* injustice.

Bibliography

Primary

Niebuhr, Reinhold. *Man's Nature and His Communities: Essays on the Dynamics and Enigmas of Man's Personal and Social Existence.* New York: Charles Scribner's Sons, 1965.
————. *Moral Man and Immoral Society: A Study in Ethics and Politics.* New York: Charles Scribner's Sons, 1932.
————. *The Nature and Destiny of Man.* Vols. 1 and 2. New York: Charles Scribner's Sons, 1941, 1943.

Secondary

Fox, Richard W. *Reinhold Niebuhr: A Biography.* New York: Pantheon Books, 1985.
Harries, Richard, ed. *Reinhold Niebuhr and the Issues of Our Time.* Grand Rapids, Mich.: Eerdmans, 1986.
Plaskow, Judith. *Sex, Sin, and Grace: Women's Experience and the Theologies of Reinhold Niebuhr and Paul Tillich.* Washington: University Press of America, 1980.
Scott, Nathan A., ed. *The Legacy of Reinhold Niebuhr.* Chicago: University of Chicago Press, 1975.
Vaughan, Judith. *Sociality, Ethics, and Social Change: A Critical Appraisal of Reinhold Niebuhr's Ethics in the Light of Rosemary Radford Ruether's Works.* Lanham, Md.: University Press of America, 1983.

Origen (ca. 185–ca. 254)

Origen is one of the most vibrant and original Christian thinkers in history. He was born in Alexandria and educated in Platonic thought by Ammonius Saccas (who was also the teacher of Plotinus). Committed to Platonism and scriptural exegesis, Origen achieved a synthesis of the two idioms, which both illuminated and challenged Christian theology. In 204 he was appointed the head of the catechetical school. His fame as a teacher spread, and he was often consulted to settle theological disputes. He was ordained in Caesarea in 230 and apparently lost the favor of the Alexandrian bishop. He settled in Caesarea and produced some of his most important treatises there, including *On Prayer, Commentary on the Song of Songs,* and *On First Principles.* During the Decian persecution (250–51) Origen put into practice the ideals he had developed in his *Exhortation to Martyrdom* (235), as he was arrested and tortured but not put to death. He died in 253 or 254.

For over a century after his death, Christian theologians discussed his ideas, generating more controversy than agreement. Points of contention included Origen's views on resurrection and the preexistence of souls as well as his trinitarian thought. Origen's thought was not formally condemned until 543 at a synod in Constantinople. Some theologians would argue that this condemnation moved Origen's ideas out of their larger theological context; the complexity of Origen's thought, they argue, makes it difficult to address concrete questions outside of the framework in which they are developed.

As a theologian Origen is appreciated both as a sensitive exegete and as the first "systematic" theologian. However, Origen's thought might well be characterized as a narrative rather than a system. His trinitarian thought in particular indicates the problems inherent in embracing Neoplatonism wholeheartedly within Christian systematic thought, and later thinkers push his christology into troublesome areas. For Origen, Christ as the Word of God mediates between God and rational creation, being both identical with God and identical with souls who participate in the mind of God. The Word is both the same as and other than God, eternally generated by God. While Rowan A. Greer argues that Origen "is less concerned with pursuing the ontological implications of the view he has constructed" than developing an understanding of the role of Christ as Mediator,[1] some of Origen's contemporaries understood him to be suggesting that the Word was subordinate to God.

Origen's real contribution to Christian theology was his ability to blend Platonic notions of emanation and return with his exegetical method, resulting in a systematic theology which rivaled any of the philosophical or religious systems of his contemporaries. Although he did not make definitive theological statements, Origen provided Christianity with a speculative framework for theological inquiry which sparked questions for generations after his death.

Bibliography

Crouzel, Henri. *Origen.* Trans. A. S. Worrall. San Francisco: Harper and Row, 1989.
Kannengiesser, Charles, and William L. Petersen, eds. *Origen of Alexandria: His World, His Legacy.* Notre Dame, Ind.: Notre Dame University Press, 1988.

Karl Rahner (1904–84)

Karl Rahner was born into a middle-class family in Freiburg, Germany, on March 5, 1904. His father was a professor at the local teachers' college, and his mother was a homemaker. He entered the Jesuit novitiate at age eighteen in Feldkirch, Austria (1922). He studied philosophy with Thomists Joseph Marechal and Pierre Rousselot. Rahner studied theology at the Jesuit school of theology in Valkenburg, Holland, beginning in 1929. In addition to learning the strict Neoscholasticism that permeated Catholic seminaries in the wake of the condemnation of Modernism, Rahner learned patristic theology and Ignatian spirituality. After ordination to the priesthood in 1932 and further theological studies, Rahner returned to Freiburg in 1934 for doctoral studies in philosophy. There he attended the seminars of Martin Heidegger. After his dissertation on Aquinas was rejected (although it was published in 1939 and translated as *Spirit in the World* in 1968), Rahner moved to Innsbruck, where he completed his doctorate in 1936. Before teaching theology at Innsbruck in the fall of 1937 he delivered a series of lectures in Salzburg, in which he applied the philosophy of knowledge he had developed in his philosophical dissertation to the question of knowing God through a historical revelation. These lectures were subsequently published as *Hearers of the*

---

1. Rowan A. Greer, "Introduction," in Origen, *Exhortation to Martyrdom,* trans. Rowan A. Greer (New York: Paulist Press, 1979), 9.

Word (1941). *Spirit in the World* and *Hearers of the Word* were the foundational works upon which Rahner was to develop his philosophical theology.

Rahner's initial appointment at Innsbruck did not last long. In the wake of Germany's annexation of Austria in 1938, the theology faculty was abolished and the Jesuits were banished from Innsbruck. Rahner spent most of the war years in Vienna as a member of the diocesan Pastoral Institute. With the war over, Rahner returned to the reconstituted theology faculty in Innsbruck in 1948 and began a very prolific period of writing and publishing. The first three volumes of collected articles, *Schriften zur Theologie,* appeared in 1954–56. Ultimately, Rahner's articles filled sixteen volumes in German and twenty-two volumes in English, where they were published under the title *Theological Investigations.*

Rahner's attempt to think about the tradition of the church in new and creative ways sometimes led him into conflict with Roman Catholic officials. During the pontificate of Pope Pius XII, Rahner was refused permission to publish an article concerning problems in the contemporary Catholic understanding of Mary, and he was forbidden to discuss the possibility of Mass concelebration. Even after Pius's death, the Holy Office carefully scrutinized Rahner's theological writings. In 1962 Rahner was told that everything he wrote had to be submitted to Rome for prior censorship. Thanks to the intervention of the three German-speaking cardinals and several hundred German professors, the special censorship was dropped the following year.

At the same time, preparations were underway for the Second Vatican Council. At the council Rahner was able to exercise significant influence through his role as private adviser to Cardinal Konig of Vienna and Cardinal Dopfner of Munich, as well as through his addresses outside council sessions to the German-speaking bishops and other regional bishops. There is no doubt that by the time the council ended in December 1965 Rahner had exercised enormous influence on the final shape of many of the conciliar documents. Traces of his thought can be found in the council's teaching on the church, papal primacy, and the episcopate, the relationship between scripture and tradition, the inspiration of the Bible, the sacraments and the diaconate, and the possibility of salvation outside the church even for atheists. As William V. Dych notes, "It is ironic that the ideas of a theologian who only recently had been highly suspect and subject to special censorship had now become part of the Church's official teaching. Not only did the Second Vatican Council end Rahner's official difficulties with Rome, but it also gave him international stature as one of the Church's leading theologians."[1]

>From 1964 to 1967 Rahner taught philosophy of religion at the University of Munich. He then accepted a position as professor of dogmatic theology at the University of Münster in 1967. Four years later, with his physical strength declining, Rahner retired from the university and returned to live in Munich. During this so-called retirement he remained busy with writing and lecturing in Germany and abroad. In 1981 he returned to Innsbruck, where he had spent his most productive years from the mid-1940s to the mid-1960s. He died on March 30, 1984.

---

1. Dych, *Karl Rahner,* 13.

Rahner wrote about virtually every area of theology. The bibliography of his books, articles, sermons, and prayers numbers between three thousand and four thousand titles. Rahner also influenced Catholic theology through initiatives such as the series *Quaestiones Disputatae,* which began in 1958 and provided a forum for the scholarly discussion of contemporary theology, and the international journal *Concilium,* which Rahner helped to found and whose first number he edited together with Edward Schillebeeckx in 1965.

Rahner's theological thought is both "transcendental" and "anthropological." That is to say, Rahner sought answers to the question of the possibility of a revelation from God in the transcendental, or given, structures of the human subject. Rahner's theology does not begin with God, scripture, or official church teachings, but with the person who is presupposed by Christianity as the hearer of the gospel. This attention to the meaning of the human person, this "anthropological" focus, is distinctive in Rahner's theology. For Rahner the fundamental experience in which we become conscious of ourselves as selves is that of questioning. In opening ourselves to the unlimited horizon of questioning, we have already transcended ourselves and have moved beyond the limits of any particular explanation. In short, we discover that we are oriented to the Infinite. This orientation, which Rahner called the "supernatural existential," marks the person as a potential hearer of God's word. The radical experience of this unlimited horizon of knowing, this experience of "transcendence," can be ignored or unnoticed. Nonetheless, the basis of all our conscious thinking and activity, Rahner insists, lies in this deeper, prereflective consciousness of infinite reality, toward which we are directed by the very structures of our being as free and knowing subjects. In this sense, even the atheist "knows" God, albeit not consciously as an object of thought, but prereflectively as the source of his or her freedom and the goal of his or her ever striving to know more.

>From Rahner's perspective, then, human life and Christian existence presuppose each other. Human life opens out toward the fulfillment of which the gospel speaks. Christian existence not only presupposes certain human structures, but is their ultimate source: the natural structures of human life as we know them are created by God. "Thus there is an intrinsic point of contact between the human and the Christian dimensions in life, and between philosophy and theology, a unity within their abiding distinction."[2] This approach to theology means that human existence itself is created by and for the Christian message, that human life in its fundamental structures as intelligent and free is, at its core, a personal world intended for response to God's call. In the context of this specific theological anthropology, Rahner can speak of the "anonymous Christianity" of those who are not members of the Christian church. The universal human orientation to God (supernatural existential) is already a share in God's grace or divine self-communication. God communicates God's own being definitively through the Word, who enters into human history, and through the Spirit, who transforms human subjectivity so that it may receive and rejoice in the Word. Through this act of self-communication, God is ultimately revealed to us as a trinitarian God.

---

2. Anne E. Carr, "Starting with the Human," in O'Donovan, *A World of Grace,* 18.

Karl Rahner was influential in the discussions of the nature of the church at the Second Vatican Council but reflected independently on the church in his *Foundations of Christian Faith*. In this text he asserts that the church is a spiritual reality as well as a religious organization, which is a necessary part of every individual's commitment to follow Christ. Rahner asserted that human experience led to transcendent experience, and his dedication to the universal validity of human experience did not cause him to undervalue individual freedom; rather, within the church individual perspectives and insights are seen to make positive contributions to the church community. Rahner represents the new spirit of ecumenism and appreciation of diversity that Roman Catholic circles were embracing. Finally, Rahner argues that the concrete reality of the church mirrors the concrete reality of God in our human experience. Both affirm one another and, coupled with an understanding of selfhood, serve as the proper context in the search for meaning and relevance in today's world.

Bibliography

Dych, William V. *Karl Rahner*. Outstanding Christian Thinkers. Collegeville, Minn.: Liturgical Press, 1992.

Imhof, Paul, and Hubert Biallowons, eds. *Faith in a Wintry Season: Conversations and Interviews with Karl Rahner in the Last Years of His Life*. New York: Crossroad, 1990.

———. *Karl Rahner in Dialogue: Conversations and Interviews, 1965–82*. New York: Crossroad, 1986.

O'Donovan, Leo J., ed. *A World of Grace: An Introduction to the Themes and Foundations of Karl Rahner's Theology*. New York: Seabury Press, 1980.

Rahner, Karl. *Foundations of Christian Faith: Introduction to the Idea of Christianity*. New York: Seabury Press, 1978.

———. *Theological Investigations*. 22 vols. London: Darton, Longman & Todd, 1961–; New York: Seabury Press, 1974–.

Vorgrimler, Herbert. *Understanding Karl Rahner: An Introduction to His Life and Thought*. New York: Crossroad, 1986.

Edward Schillebeeckx (b. 1914)

Edward Schillebeeckx was born on November 12, 1914, in Antwerp, Belgium, the sixth of fourteen children. He was educated by Jesuits, but at the age of nineteen he decided to become a Dominican. He spent his novitiate (1934) in Ghent, then studied philosophy and theology at the University of Louvain. He was ordained a priest in 1941. After World War II he went to Paris for two years for his doctoral work. In 1947 he returned to Louvain to lecture and served as a prison chaplain and spiritual director to university students. In 1958 he went on to teach theology at the University of Nijmegen. As preparations for Vatican II commenced, Schillebeeckx worked closely with the Dutch bishops. Invited to Rome during the council he played a valuable role in critical interpretation of the conciliar documents.

In 1966, after his first lecture tour across the United States, Schillebeeckx grew more interested in hermeneutics and immersed himself in scriptural interpretation. These years of study bore fruit in the trilogy on christology and the life of the church, known as *Jesus, Christ,* and *Church,* arguably Schillebeeckx's best-known works. However, the texts generated controversy. In 1974 the Congregation for the Doctrine of Faith (CDF) began a secret investigation of Schillebeeckx's theological views. In 1976 he was sent a questionnaire, asking him to explain his theological method and his understandings of Jesus as a human person, the doctrine of the incarnation, and the doctrine of the trinity. In 1979 Schillebeeckx went to Rome for an official inquiry. In November of 1980 the CDF asked for further clarification of issues but did not condemn his theological views. Another procedure examined Schillebeeckx's book on the ministry, but again there was no official action against him.

In his conversations with Francesco Strazzari (published as *I Am a Happy Theologian*) Schillebeeckx reflects on his activities and identity as a theologian:

> As a believer I am rational, and look for rational arguments. In that way I feel myself one hundred percent a believer. That is not a contradiction, as some people have remarked to me. To be a believer does not mean that one is irrational. Faith is the confession of a rational person. The rationality of faith must always be explored and clarified. All my theology is the theology of a believer: *fides quarens intellectum,* faith in search of understanding. Human reason is used one hundred percent in the field of faith. To bring in obedience and shut your eyes is neither Christian or Catholic.... There is more and more need for rationality, above all to react against the fundamentalism which is increasingly threatening the churches. The fundamentalism which is also present today in some Christian communities leads to obscurantism.[1]

Schillebeeckx writes "for the men and women of today who are in a particular historical situation. I try to respond to their questions. So my theology has a date; it is contextual, but at the same time I want to go beyond the situation as such."[2] In describing his life's work, he concludes:

> My academic work still represents for me, in a very meaningful way, a form of apostolate and in particular a form of Dominican preaching of the Good News: the gospel of Jesus, the Messiah of the liberating God, chosen in advance by the Spirit. However, in the meantime I have learned by experience that if religion is the greatest good of human beings and for human beings, it is often used completely to humiliate and even to torture people (in body and spirit). So above all, in most recent years, in my theological thought I have preferred to defend human beings, men and women, against the dehumanizing demands of religion, rather than defend religion against the illusory demands of the sinful men and women that we are. In these two aspects, the critical and constructive aspects of my theological thought, I have sought to bear testimony to others about the hope and joy within me. I am truly a happy man.[3]

---

1. Schillebeeckx, *I Am a Happy Theologian,* 79–80.
2. Ibid., 80.
3. Ibid., 81.

Bibliography

Primary (Select)

Schillebeeckx, Edward. *Christ: The Christian Experience in the Modern World.* 1977. English
     translation, New York: Crossroad, 1980.
————. *Christ the Sacrament.* 1959. English translation, New York: Sheed & Ward, 1963.
————. *God the Future of Man.* New York: Sheed & Ward, 1969.
————. *I Am a Happy Theologian: Conversations with Francesco Strazzari.* New York:
     Crossroad, 1994.
————. *Jesus: An Experiment in Christology.* 1974. English translation, New York: Cross-
     road, 1979.
————. *Mary, Mother of Redemption.* 1955. English translation, New York: Sheed & Ward,
     1964.
————. *World and Church.* 1965. English translation, New York: Sheed & Ward, 1971.

Secondary

Bowden, John. *Edward Schillebeeckx: In Search of the Kingdom of God.* New York:
     Crossroad, 1983.
Kennedy, Philip. *Schillebeeckx.* Collegeville, Minn.: Liturgical Press, 1993.

Friedrich Schleiermacher (1768–1834)

Friedrich Ernst Daniel Schleiermacher was born at Breslau on November 21, 1768. His father Gottlieb was a Reformed chaplain in the Prussian army. His mother, Katharina-Maria Stubenrauch, came, like his father, from a family of Reformed pastors. At the age of fourteen Friedrich experienced a spiritual conversion among the Moravian Brethren. He was educated in a Moravian school in Niesky, where he was exposed to the pietist tradition. At the Moravian seminary in Barby, Schleiermacher became familiar with the poetry of Goethe and was exposed to Enlightenment philosophy. In 1787 Schleiermacher entered the University of Halle, where he was influenced by more Enlightenment philosophers and the historical-critical approach to scripture. Although he eventually left the Moravian pietists, Schleiermacher credited his experience among the Brethren with the first germination of his "mystical tendency." In 1802 Schleiermacher wrote to a friend that he had again become a Moravian, only of a higher order.

Schleiermacher was ordained in 1804. Shortly thereafter he was appointed Reformed preacher at the Charite hospital in Berlin. In Berlin, Schleiermacher became familiar with the Romantic movement in its philosophical and literary forms. His first book, *On Religion: Speeches to Its Cultured Despisers* (1799), reflects that influence, but as the title itself suggests, the book did not simply adopt the worldview dominant among his circle of friends. Schleiermacher was the only clergyman in his circle. He used his first book to "issue both a critique of his friends' world view and an apology for his own identity and vocation as a preacher by expounding the mood and themes of Romanticism — especially the idea of individuality — in such a way as to argue that the life uninformed by the cultivation of personal religion and religious community is artificially sterile and out of joint with universal being."[1] The *Speeches* brought Schleiermacher immediate acclaim.

In 1804 Schleiermacher was made professor of theology at Halle, where he lectured on philosophical ethics, hermeneutics, and dogmatic theology. There he also began work on his *Brief Outline of the Study of Theology,* which attempted to describe the nature and proper relationship of the major theological disciplines. Napoleon's invasion of Germany led to the occupation of Halle by the French army and the closing of the university in 1806. Without a salary, Schleiermacher was forced to return to Berlin. There King Friedrich Wilhelm III made him a preacher at Trinity Church in 1809. He shared the pulpit with a Lutheran minister. In the same year, at the age of forty-one, he married Henriette von Willich, the twenty-year-old widow of a close friend. In 1810 he assumed a chair of theology at the University of Berlin.

In 1821–22 Schleiermacher produced his mature publication on dogmatic theology, entitled *The Christian Faith, Presented in Its Inner Connections according to the Fundamentals of the Evangelical Church.* While a professor at the university, Schleiermacher continued to hold his pulpit. His dual career as preacher and professor enabled a balance between the academic and the pastoral, which Schleiermacher believed to be essential. As he noted in his *Brief Outline for the Study of Theology,* academic theological studies were not intended to make one an academic expert in a specialized subdiscipline of theology, but rather to make one an effective leader in the church. Schleiermacher also desired to awaken a social concern among the upper classes (by, for example, shortening working hours). His concern for social justice made him popular beyond educated circles and was another way of integrating his theology with the world around him. After a distinguished career at Berlin, Schleiermacher died on February 12, 1834. According to historian Leopold von Ranke, between twenty and thirty thousand people, drawn from all classes and professions, followed Schleiermacher's coffin to the funeral.

Friedrich Schleiermacher is regarded by many as the father of modern theology. He exercised a profound effect on later theology by highlighting the experiential component in theological reflection, by insisting on the historical character of theology, and by placing theology in the service of helping the church to continue to develop as it ought. Schleiermacher endorsed the Kantian turn to the subject without endorsing Kant's reduction of religion to morality. Theologians today still need to reckon with him above all other nineteenth-century Christian thinkers as "the progenitor of the spirit of modern religious understanding."[2]

As Brian Gerrish has suggested, "liberal evangelical" is perhaps the best label for Schleiermacher's theology.[3] His program was "evangelical" because it made evangelical, experiential Protestant consciousness its object of inquiry. For Schleiermacher "feeling" (*Gefühl*) or religious experience is the primary element in religion. From this perspective, the church's doctrines are secondary elements that attempt to describe adequately the primary religious experiences. Schleier-

---

1. Richard R. Niebuhr, "Friedrich Schleiermacher," in *A Handbook of Christian Theologians,* ed. Dean G. Peerman and Martin E. Marty (Cleveland and New York: World, 1965), 19.
2. Ibid., 18.
3. Gerrish, *A Prince of the Church,* 31–33.

macher's program was also "liberal" because it did not feel bound to the old expressions of Protestant consciousness. Schleiermacher took seriously the scientific and philosophical knowledge of the day. The core of religion, Schleiermacher insisted, is piety. By this he did not mean an anti-intellectual emotionalism, but a sense and taste for the infinite, an awareness that the infinite is immediately present in the finite self. Religious feeling involves a sense of harmony with the All. Schleiermacher argued that all human activity — whether artistic, scientific, or moral — was incomplete without such religious feeling.

In *The Christian Faith* Schleiermacher defines the Christian as the person who is possessed by the feeling of his or her dependence upon God as manifested in Jesus Christ. These two elements are inseparable in the life of the Christian: a general awareness of God and a special relation to Christ. The general awareness of God is, according to Schleiermacher, an "original revelation." Schleiermacher believed that this general awareness of God was part of human nature. All that it takes to recognize it is a little introspection. This was a bold assertion at the beginning of the nineteenth century. Developments in science and rationalist philosophy had made the reality of God less obvious to many educated people. In the wake of such developments, some had come to endorse Deism and other forms of pantheism. Schleiermacher, however, "knew perfectly well that one no longer has the Christian God either if one says with Deism that some events fall outside the divine activity, or if one says with pantheism, as is commonly understood, that talk of divine activity adds nothing to talk of natural events."[4]

Schleiermacher's *The Christian Faith* influenced in some degree all the theologians of the nineteenth century, even his opponents. His advocacy of the experience of the community of faith as the starting point for theological reflection offered a new model for theology, one whose effects are still seen today. But Schleiermacher has not always been a fashionable theologian. Karl Barth (1886–1968), despite some initial excitement, became a sharp critic of Schleiermacher and his legacy. *The Christian Faith* was not translated into English until 1928, more than a hundred years after its first publication in German. Nonetheless, it is right to regard Schleiermacher as "the paradigmatic theologian of modernity"[5] and to hold *The Christian Faith* as one of the masterpieces of Protestant thought.

In his views on the church, Schleiermacher extends his understanding of faith as God-consciousness, applying this idea to a community of believers which comes together because it has such a consciousness. The church here, while universal, is in radical opposition to those who lack such a consciousness. Salvation is possible only within the church, for it is the community within which we are born anew, and it communicates to us the "sinless perfection and blessedness of Christ" (see text in Part Two). The Christian community's consciousness of Christ's presence and the process of redemption distinguish it from the rest of the world. Here Schleiermacher even introduces the concept of the church becoming gradually aware that it is participating in the kingdom of God "actually present in the fellowship of believers."

---

4. Ibid., 59–60.
5. Hans Küng, *Great Christian Thinkers* (New York: Continuum, 1994), 182–84.

The redemptive nature of the church reinforces its identity as the body of Christ. Schleiermacher rejects an association of individuals with the person of Christ but asserts that within the totality of the human race the image of Christ is present, and the church, in inspiring the human consciousness of that reality, therefore "gradually attains to be the perfect image of Christ." Since Christ's image is to be found only in collectivity, Schleiermacher also asserts that no church official can embody Christ and that church offices derive solely from the body of the faithful. He notes that "the formation of the clergy into a self-contained and self-propagating corporation has no Scriptural basis of any kind."[6] Schleiermacher uses his orientation to subjectivity to reaffirm major themes in ecclesiology by articulating their reality based in human experience. The advantages and disadvantages to his system are clear: truths about the church (and whatever other aspect of Christian doctrine) are not demonstrable, but must be experienced in faith; however, once experienced, they become an undeniable reality for the individual and the community.

Bibliography

Gerrish, B. A. *A Prince of the Church: Schleiermacher and the Beginnings of Modern Theology.* Philadelphia: Fortress Press, 1984.

Niebuhr, Richard R. *Schleiermacher on Christ and Religion.* New York: Scribner's, 1964.

Redeker, Martin. *Schleiermacher: Life and Thought.* Trans. John Wallhausser. Philadelphia: Fortress Press, 1973.

Schleiermacher, Friedrich. *The Christian Faith.* Ed. H. R. Mackintosh and J. S. Stewart. Translated from the second German edition (1830–31). Philadelphia: Fortress Press, 1976.

———. *On Religion: Speeches to Its Cultured Despisers.* Trans. John Oman. New York: Harper and Brothers, 1958.

Elisabeth Schüssler Fiorenza (b. 1938)

Born on April 17, 1938, Elisabeth Schüssler Fiorenza received her master of divinity from the University of Würzburg in 1962 and her doctorate in theology from the University of Münster in 1970. She came to the United States in 1970 and taught at the University of Notre Dame until relocating to Boston. Her major areas of expertise are in New Testament exegesis and early church history; in her research she applies feminist theory and feminist theological methods to questions of Christian origins and identity. She is currently Krister Stendahl Professor of Divinity at Harvard Divinity School.

Bibliography

Schüssler Fiorenza, Elisabeth. *Bread Not Stone: The Challenge of Feminist Biblical Interpretation.* Boston: Beacon Press, 1984.

———. *In Memory of Her: A Feminist Theological Reconstruction of Christian Origins.* New York: Crossroad, 1982.

---

6. Friedrich Schleiermacher, *The Christian Faith* (Edinburgh: T. & T. Clark, 1976), 615.

————. *Jesus: Miriam's Child, Sophia's Prophet: Critical Issues in Feminist Christology.* New York: Continuum, 1994.

Marjorie Hewitt Suchocki (b. 1933)

Marjorie Hewitt Suchocki was born on August 13, 1933, in Winthrop, Massachusetts. She received her bachelor of arts from Pomona College and her master of arts and Ph.D. (1974) from Claremont Graduate School. After working on the thought of Alfred North Whitehead, Suchocki applied her understanding of process theology to all the major areas in systematic theology, developing an understanding of God, Christ, and humanity through a notion of relational theology. Her many articles and six books include *God, Christ, Church: A Practical Guide to Process Theology; The Fall to Violence: Original Sin in Relational Theology;* and *Trinity in Process: A Relational Theology of God,* coedited with Joseph Bracken.

Suchocki is currently vice president for academic affairs and Ingraham Professor of Systematic Theology at the Claremont School of Theology in Claremont, California.

Bibliography

Primary

Suchocki, Marjorie Hewitt. *The Fall to Violence: Original Sin in Relational Theology.* New York: Continuum, 1994.
————. *God, Christ, Church: A Practical Guide to Process Theology.* New York: Crossroad, 1982.
Suchocki, Marjorie Hewitt, and Joseph Bracken, eds. *Trinity in Process: A Relational Theology of God.* New York: Continuum, 1996.

Teresa of Avila (1515–82)

Teresa of Avila is one of Christianity's most beloved mystics. Increasingly appreciated as a theologian, she was also an important monastic reformer and continues to be an inspirational figure. Less is known about Teresa's early life than one might like, leading many biographers to rely heavily on the sketchy information Teresa supplies in her *Life,* which she wrote around the age of fifty. As recent scholarship has demonstrated, however, Teresa's works are somewhat encoded; the rhetorical skill which enabled her works to survive severe scrutiny during and after her life hides as much as earlier scholars thought her "clear and candid style" revealed.[1]

Born on March 28, 1515, into a merchant-class family of Jewish origin, and educated in an Augustinian convent, Teresa entered the local Carmelite convent

---

1. For a discussion of the hermeneutical issues involved, see Ahlgren, *Teresa of Avila and the Politics of Sanctity,* 77-80, and Weber, *Teresa of Avila and the Rhetoric of Femininity,* 5–16.

of the Encarnación at the age of twenty. There she appears to have been popular both inside and outside the convent. She describes a rather relaxed atmosphere within the convent, including the privilege of visiting her family and entertaining outside visitors in the convent's parlor. Illness and reflection led her to reconsider her religious vocation and to decide to work toward founding a smaller, reformed convent, strictly cloistered and therefore free of outside influences and with increased dedication to mental prayer and contemplation. With help from friends and family she founded the Discalced Carmelite convent of San José in 1562. Her foundations continued; over the course of the next two decades, she would found convents in most of the important cities of sixteenth-century Spain, including Medina del Campo, Toledo, Salamanca, Seville, Segovia, and Burgos. Teresa combined the foundation of these convents with the production of treatises, letters, and other writings which would build a new model for women's religious life.

Indeed, her extensive writing career began at the same time as her reforming activities. Partly in response to questions regarding the nature and orthodoxy of her own prayer experiences, and also as an integral part of her reforming agenda in light of the relative inaccessibility of mystical texts, Teresa penned several spiritual reflections which became *The Book of Her Life*. This widely read book acquired a certain fame during Teresa's life, although it was published only posthumously, in 1588. Still, the book circulated widely among Carmelite circles and was read by members of the royal court. Concern over the book's ideas, particularly Teresa's descriptions of visions and to some degree her conceptualization of the soul's relationship with God, led to Inquisitional inquiries regarding her orthodoxy, the most serious of which involved interviews in the convent she founded in 1575 in Seville. After the interviews, Teresa was ordered into reclusion at the convent of her choice. Retiring to Toledo, Teresa wrote her mystical tour de force, *The Interior Castle*, a chronicling of the seven stages in the soul's mystical journey toward God. One of Teresa's major reasons for writing the *Interior Castle* was her concern that, since the *Life* had been confiscated by the Spanish Inquisition for review, it might never circulate. Ironically, then, the climate of theological suspicion surrounding mystical and visionary experiences actually encouraged the production of more mystical treatises.

The core of Teresa's theological contributions actually centers around the dilemma presented by the perceived need to define and control religious experience. She wanted to demonstrate clearly the accessibility of Christ to all, to highlight the ubiquity of grace available to all sinners,[2] and the ability of all humans to achieve deeper union with God in the temple of their souls. Critical in this process toward union with God were growth in self-knowledge and mental prayer. Within the context of religious life, a supportive community, spiritual direction, and personal commitment to discernment, Teresa had great confidence in the human potential for intimacy with God; this confidence recalled her own personal experience of a strong calling from God, leading her to discover God within herself. The

---

2. As many of her commentators observe, Teresa consistently describes herself as "the most wretched" of sinners. For a discussion of this, see Ahlgren, *Teresa of Avila and the Politics of Sanctity*, 68–72, and Weber, *Teresa of Avila and the Rhetoric of Femininity*, 48–56.

confidence Teresa exhibited in her visions and personal experiences of God was construed as "spiritual arrogance" by some of her contemporaries; others argued that Teresa's visions and holy life exemplified the magnitude of God's grace.[3] Yet Teresa can now be understood as an important defender of the mystical tradition, who presents a distinctive rendering of the mystery of the trinity residing in the individual soul and the possibility of union with this God.[4]

Canonized in 1622, Teresa's mystical doctrine took on increasing importance within the Roman Catholic tradition. Indeed, the spiritual practices and mystical treatises penned by women of Spain and Latin America in the century after Teresa's death reflect her immense influence and lasting appeal. She was proclaimed a doctor of the Roman Catholic Church in 1970.

Bibliography

Ahlgren, Gillian T. W. *Teresa of Avila and the Politics of Sanctity.* Ithaca, N.Y.: Cornell University Press, 1996.

Bilinkoff, Jodi. *The Avila of Saint Teresa: Religious Reform in a Sixteenth-Century City.* Ithaca, N.Y.: Cornell University Press, 1989.

Green, Dierdre. *Gold in the Crucible: Teresa of Avila and the Western Mystical Tradition.* Longmead, England: Element Books, 1989.

Luti, J. Mary. "Teresa of Avila, 'maestra espiritual.'" Ph.D. diss., Boston College, 1987.

Peers, E. Allison. *Handbook to the Life and Times of Saint Teresa and Saint John of the Cross.* Westminster, Md.: Newman Press, 1954.

———. *Mother of Carmel, a Portrait of St. Teresa of Jesus.* London: SCM, 1946.

———. *Studies of the Spanish Mystics.* 3 vols. London: SPCK, 1960.

Teresa of Avila. *The Complete Works of Saint Teresa of Jesus.* Trans. and ed. E. Allison Peers. New York: Sheed & Ward, 1950.

Trueman Dickens, E. W. *The Crucible of Love.* New York: Sheed & Ward, 1963.

Weber, Alison. *Teresa of Avila and the Rhetoric of Femininity.* Princeton, N.J.: Princeton University Press, 1990.

Williams, Rowan. *Teresa of Avila.* Harrisburg, Pa.: Morehouse, 1991.

Thomas Aquinas (1224/25–74)

Thomas Aquinas was born late in 1224 or early 1225 to Landult and Theodora d'Aquino, members of the lower nobility in the Hohenstaufen kingdom of Sicily. He was taken at the age of five to the abbey of Monte Cassino, the motherhouse of Benedictine monasticism, where his parents planned on his becoming abbot. Due to war between the pope and Emperor Frederick II, however, Thomas had to be relocated to Naples for his education. There he became familiar with the thought of Aristotle. To the displeasure of his family, at the age of nineteen he joined the Dominican order at Naples in 1224. Like Francis of Assisi, he had to fight against his family's wishes to join a mendicant order. His family kidnapped him and held him for over a year at Rocaseca before they acceded to his desire to become a Dominican.

---

3. See Ahlgren, *Teresa of Avila and the Politics of Sanctity,* 118–23, 133–40.
4. For an analysis of the reception of this doctrine, see ibid., 126–33.

Life in a mendicant order was attractive to Thomas for several reasons. It was a simple life, modeled upon the simplicity or "poverty" of lifestyle practiced in the apostolic age of the church. It was a form of religious communal living that was located not in the rural countryside, but in the cities, where guilds of scholars and students from the different regions of Europe had come together to form universities. Thomas wanted to cultivate a life of the mind in the context of a simple, spiritually oriented life.

The Dominicans sent Thomas to Paris for his novitiate and theological study under Albert the Great (1245–48). In 1248 Thomas accompanied Albert to Cologne for further study and for cursory lecturing on the Bible as a bachelor of theology. Here his fellow friars reputedly dubbed him the "dumb ox" — a reference to his corpulence and his personal reserve. Thomas developed a close relationship with his teacher Albert, who had been working for many years to produce an encyclopedic summary of Aristotelian thought. Previously Aristotle had been known to medieval Christian scholars only as a logician. Now, however, his original thought in the areas of natural science, metaphysics, and anthropology became known to the Christian West. This discovery of Aristotle represented not only an extension of knowledge, but also a potential threat to traditional Christian belief. Aristotle not only offered a coherent conception of reality, devoid of the Christian God, but also held ideas (e.g., the eternity of the world) that were contrary to the teaching of the Christian church. During his four-year stay in Cologne (1248–52), Thomas was ordained a priest.

In 1252 Thomas was sent back to Paris to prepare for the mastership in theology. From 1252 to 1256, he lectured on the *Sentences* of Peter Lombard, which was a collection of texts from the church fathers, with its topics arranged in systematic order. In 1256/57 Thomas was appointed to the second Dominican chair of theology at the University of Paris. His job required him to lecture, preach, and to engage in academic disputations.

Between the years 1259 and 1272 Aquinas taught throughout Italy, including Naples, Orvieto, Rome, and Viterbo, returning to Paris in 1269. In 1272 Thomas established a Dominican center of studies in Naples. There he followed a daily regimen of early morning confession and Mass, followed by the dictation of his thoughts to his many secretaries until the time for his main meal. After the meal, Thomas went to his cell to pray and rest, returning to dictate until late at night. But during his celebration of Mass on December 6, 1273, the ordinary cycle of Thomas's life changed. Apparently struck by something, he did not resume his work on the third part of the *Summa theologiae*. When asked by his secretary, Reginald of Piperno, why he did not resume work on the *Summa*, Thomas replied, "Reginald, I cannot, because all that I have written seems like straw to me."[1] From that time on, Thomas wrote nothing more. It seems likely that the event of December 6 had a physical as well as a mystical dimension. He spent what would be his last year in prayer.

In 1274 Thomas was directed to go to the Second Council of Lyons, which was to begin early in May. Since the main purpose of the council was the reconciliation

---

1. Weisheipl, *Friar Thomas D'Aquino*, 321.

of Greek Christians with the Latin church, Thomas was asked to bring along a copy of his *Against the Errors of the Greeks,* which he had written at the request of Pope Urban IV in 1263. Thomas set out for Lyons around the beginning of February. He became ill during the journey, however, and asked to be taken to the Cistercian monastery of Fossanuova, where he died on March 7, 1274.

Thomas was canonized in 1323 by Pope John XXII. Despite the fact that several propositions from his writings were condemned by the bishops of Paris and Canterbury in 1277, Thomas's teaching was declared the rule of all teaching and study by Dominicans. In 1567 Pope Pius V gave him the title "Universal Doctor of the Church." In 1879, Pope Leo XIII declared his thought the touchstone of Roman Catholic theology. The Code of Canon Law (1917–18) required Catholic educational institutions to treat philosophy and theology according to his method and principles. The *Catechism of the Catholic Church* (1992) frequently cites Thomas as an authority. Thomas left a decisive stamp on the development of subsequent Catholic theology, not all of it entirely positive. Drawing upon the Aristotelian understanding of biology and previous traditions of the church, Thomas concluded that women were deficient by nature.[2] The scholastic context in which he worked gave his writing an impersonal quality, characterized often by subtle rational distinctions.

Thomas's three most important theological works are his *Commentary on the Sentences,* the *Summa contra Gentiles,* and the *Summa theologiae.* The *Summa contra Gentiles,* written between 1259 and 1264, was intended for use by Dominican missionaries preaching against Muslims, Jews, and heretical Christians in Spain. Because of its intended, apologetic purpose, it tends to make its arguments on the basis of natural reason, rather than by simple appeal to the testimony of the Christian Bible. The *Summa theologiae* was begun in 1265. An encyclopedic book of theological ideas, Thomas left it unfinished. In it Thomas balanced the convictions of faith and the conclusions of reason with recourse to scripture, the church fathers, Augustine, and most particularly Aristotle. Thomas saw nature and grace, reason and revelation, and the natural will and Christian love to be related and complementary. In each pair, the latter term perfects the former, but does not destroy it. Thomas was modest but not skeptical about the human capacity for knowledge and speech about God. We can know that God exists, he wrote, from rational reflection upon the world as an effect of God. We cannot, however, see or comprehend the essence of God in this life. Similarly, we can speak true things about God, but we must remember that appropriate language about God is analogical. In short, Thomas Aquinas formulated an impressive theological system that decisively influenced the western tradition.

Thomas Aquinas lived between the pontificates of two significant popes, Innocent III (1198–1216) and Boniface VIII (1294–1303), in an era of reflection on papal authority. However, Thomas's thought does not provide much ammunition for asserting papal supremacy in the temporal realm. What Thomas writes about the church in his *Exposition on the Apostles' Creed* retains a certain independence from contemporary questions of church and state, recalling instead

---

2. See Hans Küng, *Great Christian Thinkers* (New York: Continuum, 1994), 115–22.

much of Augustine's language about the church. In defining the church Thomas stresses its communal orientation; it is a congregation of believers united over time and space. The community is unified by its oneness in faith, hope, and charity. Doctrinal unity serves as an important form of cement for this community, because Thomas is clear to exclude heretics from it; indeed, Thomas seems to mean "doctrine" by the term "faith." When he examines "hope," he emphasizes that another part of the church's unity stems from its trust in salvation. And later in the same paragraph, he uses the figure of Noah's Ark to represent the church, asserting that there is no salvation outside of it.

The holiness of the church derives from the saving blood of Christ in the Eucharist as well as from the "indwelling of the Trinity." In addition to the more common meaning of universality as throughout the world, Aquinas connects the church in time to past and future members. He asserts that the church exists outside any concrete manifestation of itself, and that it will never cease to be. Finally, the church's apostolicity is affirmed both by the substance of its teachings and by Christ's commission to Peter of the power to bind and loose sin. In his brief exposition Aquinas highlights the salvific function of the church, associating that salvation primarily with doctrine and sacraments, which are to be the major guarantors of the church's unity.

Bibliography

Primary

Thomas Aquinas. *The Aquinas Reader*. Ed. Mary T. Clark. New York: Fordham University Press, 1988.
———. *Introduction to Saint Thomas Aquinas*. Ed. Anton C. Pegis. New York: Modern Library, 1948.
———. *Summa theologiae*. With Latin text and English Blackfriars' translation. New York: McGraw-Hill, 1963–.

Secondary

Chenu, M.-D. *Toward Understanding St. Thomas*. Trans. A. M. Landry and D. Hughes. Chicago: Regnery, 1964.
Davies, Brian. *The Thought of Thomas Aquinas*. New York: Oxford University Press, 1993.
Kretzmann, Norman, and Eleonore Stump, eds. *The Cambridge Companion to Aquinas*. New York: Cambridge University Press, 1993.
Weisheipl, James A. *Friar Thomas D'Aquino: His Life, Thought, and Works*. Garden City, N.Y.: Doubleday, 1974.

Vatican II (1962–65)

The Second Vatican Council was an ecumenical council for the universal church designed to initiate spiritual renewal for the church in light of the challenges of the modern world. Pope John XXIII convoked the council after three years of preparatory commissions designed to study diverse situations, including the state of religious orders, the eastern churches, the role of the laity, the situation of bishops, and the government of dioceses. There were four periods to the council: October 11–December 8, 1962; September 29–December 4, 1963; September 14–November 21, 1964; and September 14–December 8, 1965. Some months after adjourning the first period, on June 3, 1963, John XXIII died. His successor, Paul VI, promised to continue the council and oversaw the remaining sessions.

Over the course of its four years the council enacted four constitutions, nine decrees, and three declarations. The constitutions focused on the church, divine revelation, the liturgy, and the church in the modern world. The decrees addressed the pastoral office of bishops, ecumenism, the eastern churches, the ministry and life of priests, education for the priesthood, renovation of religious life, missionary activity, the role of the laity, and the media. The documents reflect a spirit of analysis and reappraisal of the orientation of Roman Catholicism as well as a genuine concern that the church remain a faithful, visionary, and relevant witness of Christianity in the world.

Lumen Gentium is an ambitious document which seeks to review the variety of ways the Roman Catholic tradition has understood the church, with specific development of scriptural texts on the church as body and spouse of Christ.

In the first section of the document the church is described as "a kind of sacrament or sign of intimate union with God, and of the unity of all humankind."[1] Asserting that the church is an expression of divine reality and therefore essentially mysterious, the document claims, "Already from the beginning of the world the foreshadowing of the Church took place. She was prepared for in a remarkable way throughout the history of the people of Israel and by means of the Old Covenant."[2] Using scriptural metaphors, the document describes how a notion of the church is conveyed through images such as a sheepfold, the field of God to be cultivated, the new Jerusalem, the bride of Christ or "spouse of the spotless Lamb,"[3] the body of Christ, and the mediator of Christ's truth and grace. Yet the document also suggests that these images which point to a mysterious reality are inseparably intertwined with a human and historically present reality.[4] Thus the church is seen to function, as Christ did, within a historical reality and is called to mediate salvation within the confines of the reality: "Just as Christ carried out the work of redemption in poverty and under oppression, so the Church is called to follow the same path in communicating to men [*sic*] the fruits of salvation."[5] Quoting Augustine, the first chapter concludes, "The Church, 'like a pilgrim in a foreign land, presses forward amid the persecutions of the world and the consolations of God,' announcing the cross and death of the Lord until He comes."[6]

---

1. *Lumen Gentium*, in Walter M. Abbott, ed., *The Documents of Vatican II* (New York: Guild Press, 1966), 15.

2. Ibid.

3. Ibid., 19–20.

4. See ibid., 22: "But the society furnished with hierarchical agencies and the Mystical Body of Christ are not to be considered as two realities, nor are the visible assembly and the spiritual community, nor the earthly Church and the Church enriched with heavenly things. Rather they form one interlocked reality which is comprised of a divine and a human element. For this reason, by an excellent analogy, this reality is compared to the mystery of the incarnate Word."

5. Ibid., 23.

6. Ibid., 24. See Augustine, *The City of God*, book 18, chapter 51.

The second chapter of the document explores the nature of the church not solely or even primarily as an organization of hierarchical offices and functions but as the people of God, emphasizing the communal elements of the church. While asserting that the laity and the hierarchial priesthood "differ from one another in essence and not only in degree," *Lumen Gentium* recognizes the priesthood of the faithful as "a participation in the one priesthood of Christ."[7] A latent prioritization of the clergy in matters of the faith appears clearly in several sections of this chapter. The document leaves room for the development of the preaching office of parents and affirms that "the holy People of God shares also in Christ's prophetic office."[8] Further, "The body of the faithful as a whole, anointed as they are by the Holy One, cannot err in matters of belief." However, this unerring quality is ensured by the church's "universal agreement in matters of faith and morals" manifested from bishops down to the last member of the laity in which the people of God receive the Spirit of truth "under the lead of a sacred teaching authority to which it loyally defers."[9] The final section of this chapter affirms a more inclusive understanding of salvation and church by declaring that "those who have not yet received the gospel are related in various ways to the People of God" and, "Those also can attain to everlasting salvation who through no fault of their own do not know the gospel of Christ or His Church, yet sincerely seek God and, moved by grace, strive to do His will as it is known to them through the dictates of conscience."[10]

Additionally, *Lumen Gentium* characterizes "the call of the whole church to holiness" by which "a more human way of life is promoted even in this earthly society."[11] The document leaves for further development what this way of life will mean with respect to justice, although it includes a form of blessing for the poor: "Those who are oppressed by poverty, infirmity, sickness or various other hardships, as well as those who suffer persecution for justice' sake — may they all know that in a special way they are united with the suffering Christ for the salvation of the world."[12]

The church's need to be more engaged in the modern world is taken up in more detail in the document *Gaudium et Spes,* or the Pastoral Constitution on the Church in the Modern World. At its outset the document explains its raison d'être: "For the human person deserves to be preserved; human society deserves to be renewed," and for this to happen the church must offer to humankind its "honest assistance...in fostering that brotherhood of all men which corresponds to this destiny of theirs."[13] Thus *Gaudium et Spes* reinforces the important duty

---

7. Ibid., 27.

8. Ibid., 29.

9. Ibid., 30. Both the notion of inerrancy and the teaching authority of the bishops are reaffirmed later in the document when *Lumen Gentium* declares, "Although the individual bishops do not enjoy the prerogative of infallibility, they can nevertheless proclaim Christ's doctrine infallibly. This is so...provided that while maintaining the bond of unity among themselves and with Peter's successor, and while teaching authentically on a matter of faith or morals, they concur in a single viewpoint as the one which must be held conclusively." Ibid., 48.

10. Ibid., 34, 35.

11. Ibid., 67.

12. Ibid., 79.

13. *Gaudium et Spes,* in ibid., 201.

of the church in "scrutinizing the signs of the times and of interpreting them in the light of the gospel." The context for this activity is the disparity between rich and poor, as the document notes: "Never has the human race enjoyed such an abundance of wealth, resources, and economic power. Yet a huge proportion of the world's citizens is still tormented by hunger and poverty, while countless numbers suffer from total illiteracy."[14] These growing imbalances result in "mutual distrust, enmities, conflicts, and hardships. Of such is man at once the cause and the victim."[15] Yet the inherent dignity of the human person, combined with our "special obligation . . . to make ourselves the neighbor of absolutely every person, and of actively helping him when he comes across our path,"[16] places the church in a unique position to work with the God who "is preparing a new dwelling place and a new earth where justice will abide, and whose blessedness will answer and surpass all the longings for peace which spring up in the human heart."[17]

The two documents, *Lumen Gentium* and *Gaudium et Spes,* were the first major conciliar attempt to define the church both as an institution and as the body of Christ with a clear articulation of the relationship between the church and the world. *Gaudium et Spes* builds upon *Lumen Gentium* in order to make more tangible the mission of the church as it is characterized in the first document. Both documents have provided contemporary theologians with a framework for their continuing analysis of ecclesiology and are heavily cited in later texts. The texts reproduced above describe both the church as a structure, and its sacramental functions, as well as its role in the modern world.

Hans Urs von Balthasar (1905–88)

Hans Urs von Balthasar was born in Lucerne, Switzerland, on August 12, 1905. He was educated in Benedictine and Jesuit schools before attending the University of Zurich, where he pursued doctoral studies in German language and culture. He entered the Society of Jesus on November 18, 1929. After his ordination von Balthasar worked briefly in Munich and then at the University of Basel. In 1950 he left the Jesuits, devoting himself more exclusively to the secular institute called the Community of St. John he had founded with Adrienne von Speyr, a physician and convert to Catholicism.

Von Balthasar was a prolific writer with a remarkable range of expertise. His interest in early Christian writers like Origen, Augustine, and Maximus the Confessor reveals his tendency toward systematic theology with an orientation to mystical theology, and his sensitivity to the presence of God. His theological investigations have an intensely personal quality, expressing his own convictions and designed to inspire contemplation. He is particularly noted for his contri-

---

14. Ibid., 201–2.
15. Ibid., 206.
16. Ibid., 226.
17. Ibid., 237. The document clarifies: "Earthly progress must be carefully distinguished from the growth of Christ's kingdom. Nevertheless, to the extent that the former can contribute to the better ordering of human society, it is of vital concern to the kingdom of God" (ibid.). For conciliar statements on the human person, see pp. 59–63.

butions to the field of spirituality and the history of spirituality. Von Balthasar died on June 26, 1988, two days before he was to receive the insignia of cardinal from John Paul II.

Bibliography

Primary (Select)

von Balthasar, Hans Urs. *Christian Meditation.* Trans. Mary Theresilde Skerry. San Francisco: Ignatius Press, 1989.

————. *Church and World.* Trans. A. V. Littledale with Alexander Dru. New York: Herder and Herder, 1967.

————. *The Glory of the Lord: A Theological Aesthetics.* Trans. Erasmo Leiva-Merikavis. 7 vols. New York: Crossroad, 1982–.

————. *The God Question and Modern Man.* Trans. Hilda Graef. New York: Seabury Press, 1967.

————. *My Work in Retrospect.* San Francisco: Communio Books, 1993.

————. *A Theological Anthropology.* New York: Sheed & Ward, 1967.

Secondary

Gawronski, Raymond. *Word and Silence: Hans Urs von Balthasar and the Spiritual Encounter between East and West.* Grand Rapids, Mich.: Eerdmans, 1995.

Oakes, Edward T. *Pattern of Redemption: The Theology of Hans Urs von Balthasar.* New York: Continuum, 1997.

For Further Reading

General Histories

Ahlstrom, Sydney E. *A Religious History of the American People*. New Haven: Yale University Press, 1972.

Barraclough, Geoffrey, ed. *The Christian World: A Social and Cultural History*. New York: H. N. Abrams, 1981.

Cunliffe-Jones, H., and B. Drewery, eds. *A History of Christian Doctrine*. Philadelphia: Fortress Press, 1980.

González, Justo C. *A History of Christian Thought*. 3 vols. Nashville: Abingdon Press, 1970–75.

Green, Vivian. *A New History of Christianity*. New York: Continuum, 1996.

Jay, Eric G. *The Church: Its Changing Image through Twenty Centuries*. Atlanta: John Knox Press, 1980.

Jedin, Hubert, ed. *History of the Church*. Trans and ed. John Dolan. 10 vols. New York: Crossroad, 1980–83.

Kee, Howard Clark. *Christianity: A Social and Cultural History*. Upper Saddle River, N.J.: Prentice-Hall, 1998.

Latourette, Kenneth Scott. *A History of Christianity*. New York: Harper and Row, 1975.

Marty, Martin E. *A Short History of Christianity*. Philadelphia: Fortress Press, 1980.

McGonigle, Thomas D. *A History of the Christian Tradition: >From Its Jewish Origins to the Reformation*. New York: Paulist Press, 1988.

McManners, John, ed. *The Oxford Illustrated History of Christianity*. New York: Oxford University Press, 1990.

Placher, William C. *A History of Christian Theology: An Introduction*. Philadelphia: Westminster Press, 1983.

Seeberg, Reinhold. *The History of Doctrines*. Grand Rapids: Baker Book House, 1977.

Urban, Linwood. *A Short History of Christian Thought*. Oxford: Oxford University Press, 1995.

Wilken, Robert Louis. *Remembering the Christian Past*. Grand Rapids: Eerdmans, 1995.

Williston, Walker, et al. *A History of the Christian Church*. 4th ed. New York: Charles Scribner's Sons, 1985.

Early Church

Bell, David N. *A Cloud of Witnesses: An Introductory History of the Development of Christian Doctrine*. Kalamazoo, Mich.: Cistercian Publications, 1989.

Chadwick, Henry. *The Early Church*. New York: Penguin Books, 1967.

Ferguson, Everett, ed. *Encyclopedia of Early Christianity*. New York: Garland Publishers, 1990.

Frend, W. H. C. *Martyrdom and Persecution in the Early Church*. Grand Rapids: Baker Book House, 1981.

———. *The Rise of Christianity*. Philadelphia: Fortress Press, 1984.

Kelly, J. N. D. *Early Christian Doctrines*. Rev. ed. New York: Harper and Row, 1978.

McGinn, Bernard. *The Foundations of Mysticism: Origins to the Fifth Century.* Vol. 1 of *The Presence of God: A History of Western Christian Mysticism.* New York: Crossroad, 1994.

McGinn, Bernard, and John Meyendorff, eds. *Christian Spirituality: Origins to the Twelfth Century.* New York: Crossroad, 1985.

Miles, Margaret. *Carnal Knowing: Female Nakedness and Religious Meaning in the Christian West.* New York: Vintage Books, 1989.

Pagels, Elaine. *Adam, Eve, and the Serpent.* New York: Vintage Books, 1989.

Pelikan, Jaroslav. *The Emergence of Catholic Thought.* Chicago: University of Chicago Press, 1971.

Tugwell, Simon. *The Apostolic Fathers.* Harrisburg, Pa.: Morehouse, 1989.

von Campenhausen, Hans. *Ecclesiastical Authority and Spiritual Power in the Church of the First Three Centuries.* Stanford, Calif.: Stanford University Press, 1969.

Wiles, Maurice. *The Making of Christian Doctrine.* Cambridge: Cambridge University Press, 1967.

Medieval/Reformation Church

Brunn, Emlie Zum, and Georgette Epiney-Burgard. *Women Mystics in Medieval Europe.* Trans. Sheila Hughes. New York: Paragon House, 1989.

Bynum, Caroline Walker. *Holy Feast, Holy Fast: The Religious Significance of Food to Medieval Women.* Berkeley: University of California Press, 1986.

Cantor, Norman F. *The Civilization of the Middle Ages.* New York: Harper Collins, 1993.

Colish, Marcia L. *An Intellectual History of the Middle Ages.* New Haven: Yale University Press, 1997.

Delumeau, Jean. *Catholicism between Luther and Voltaire: A New View of the Counter-Reformation.* Philadelphia: Westminster Press, 1977.

Hillerbrand, Hans J., ed. *The Oxford Encyclopedia of the Reformation.* 4 vols. New York: Oxford University Press, 1996.

Lynch, Joseph H. *The Medieval Church: A Brief History.* New York: Longman, 1992.

McGinn, Bernard. *The Growth of Mysticism.* New York: Crossroad, 1994.

Ozment, Steven. *The Age of Reform, 1250–1550: An Intellectual and Religious History of Late Medieval and Reformation Europe.* New Haven: Yale University Press, 1980.

Pelikan, Jaroslav. *The Growth of Medieval Theology.* Chicago: University of Chicago Press, 1978.

———. *Reformation of Church and Dogma (1300–1700).* Chicago: University of Chicago Press, 1984.

Raitt, Jill, ed. *Christian Spirituality: High Middle Ages and Reformation.* New York: Crossroad, 1987.

Tierney, Brian, and Sidney Painter. *Western Europe in the Middle Ages, 300–1475.* New York: McGraw-Hill, 1992.

Modern Church

Aston, Nigel, ed. *Religious Change in Europe, 1650–1914: Essays for John McManners.* New York: Oxford University Press, 1997.

Aubert, Roger. *The Church in a Secularized Society.* New York: Paulist Press, 1978.

Baumer, Franklin L. *Modern European Thought: Continuity and Change in Ideas, 1600–1950.* New York: Macmillan, 1977.

Cragg, Gerald R. *The Church and the Age of Reason.* New York: Penguin Viking, 1974.

Dillenberger, John, and Claude Welch. *Protestant Christianity: Interpreted through Its Development.* 2d ed. New York: Macmillan, 1988.

Engel, Mary Potter, and Walter E. Wyman, Jr. *Revisioning the Past: Prospects in Historical Theology.* Minneapolis: Fortress Press, 1992.

Gerrish, B. A. *Continuing the Reformation: Essays on Modern Religious Thought.* Chicago: University of Chicago Press, 1993.

Graf Reventlow, H. *The Authority of the Bible and the Rise of the Modern World.* Philadelphia: Fortress Press, 1985.

Livingston, James. *Modern Christian Thought.* Upper Saddle River, N.J.: Prentice-Hall, 1997.

McCool, Gerald A. *Catholic Theology in the Nineteenth Century: The Quest for a Unitary Method.* New York: Seabury, 1977.

McGrath, Alister, ed. *The Blackwell Encyclopedia of Modern Christian Thought.* Oxford: Blackwell, 1993.

Miller, Glenn T. *The Modern Church: From the Dawn of the Reformation to the Eve of the Third Millennium.* Nashville: Abingdon Press, 1997.

O'Meara, Thomas F. *Church and Culture: German Catholic Theology, 1860–1914.* Notre Dame, Ind.: University of Notre Dame Press, 1991.

———. *Romantic Idealism and Roman Catholicism: Schelling and the Theologians.* Notre Dame, Ind.: University of Notre Dame Press, 1982.

Pelikan, Jaroslav. *Christian Doctrine and Modern Culture (since 1700).* Chicago: University of Chicago Press, 1989.

Reardon, B. M. G. *Religion in the Age of Romanticism.* Cambridge: Cambridge University Press, 1985.

Schmidt, James, ed. *What Is Enlightenment? Eighteenth-Century Questions and Twentieth-Century Answers.* Berkeley: University of California Press, 1996.

Schoof, Mark A. *A Survey of Catholic Theology, 1800–1970.* New York: Paulist Press, 1970.

Smart, Ninian, et al. *Nineteenth-Century Religious Thought in the West.* 3 vols. Cambridge: Cambridge University Press, 1985.

Thielicke, Helmut. *Modern Faith and Thought.* Grand Rapids: Eerdmans, 1990.

Vidler, Alec. *The Church in an Age of Revolution.* New York: Penguin, 1974.

Welch, Claude. *Protestant Thought in the Nineteenth Century.* 2 vols. New Haven: Yale University Press, 1972, 1985.

Human Person

Cairns, David. *The Image of God in Man.* London: Collins Press, 1973.

Childs, James M. *Christian Anthropology and Ethics.* Philadelphia: Fortress Press, 1978.

Haight, Roger. *The Experience and Language of Grace.* New York: Paulist Press, 1979.

Langford, Peter. *Modern Philosophies of Human Nature: Their Emergence from Christian Thought.* Boston: M. Nijhoff, 1996.

Moltmann, Jürgen. *Man: Christian Anthropology in the Conflicts of the Present.* Trans. John Sturdy. Philadelphia: Fortress Press, 1974.

O'Grady, John F. *Christian Anthropology: A Meaning for Human Life.* New York: Paulist Press, 1975.

Ozment, Steven E. *Homo spiritualis: A Comparative Study of the Anthropology of Johannes Tauler, Jean Gerson and Martin Luther (1509–16) in the Context of their Theological Thought.* Leiden: E. J. Brill, 1969.

Pannenberg, Wolfhart. *Anthropology in Theological Perspective.* Trans. Matthew J. O'Connell. Philadelphia: Westminster Press, 1985.

Part Four

TIMELINE

Chronological Relationships among

Political and Social Events
Intellectual and Cultural Developments
Christian History
Major Christian Writers

Political and Social Events	Intellectual and Cultural Developments	Christian History	Major Christian Writers
37–41 Caligula emperor; unrest in Palestine		c. 30 Crucifixion of Jesus	
41–54 Claudius emperor		48 Council of Jerusalem	
	50–65 Writing career of Seneca the Younger		54–62 Paul's letters
54–68 Nero emperor		60–62 Paul in Rome	
64 Fire in Rome		64 First persecution of Christians	
		c. 67–76 Papacy of Linus	
69–70 Vespasian emperor		70 Fall of Jerusalem	70–85 Synoptic gospels
79–81 Titus emperor	75–79 Flavius Josephus, *History of the Jewish War*	74 Capture of Masada	
		c. 76–88 Papacy of Anacletus	
81–96 Domitian emperor		c. 88–97 Papacy of Clement I	
		95 Domitian persecution	c. 96 *1 Clement*
96–98 Nerva emperor		c. 97–105 Papacy of Evaristus	c. 100 *Didache*
98–117 Trajan emperor		c. 105–15 Papacy of Alexander I	c. 107 Ignatius of Antioch's letters
			c. 108 Polycarp, *Letter to Philippians*
	c. 110 Tacitus, *The Histories*	c. 111 Pliny-Trajan correspondence regarding treatment of Christians	
117–38 Hadrian emperor	c. 120 Tacitus (**b.c. 56**) and Plutarch (**b.c. 46**) die	c. 115–25 Papacy of Sixtus I	c. 120 *Shepherd of Hermas*
122–35 Jewish revolt under Bar Kokhba	c. 125 Pantheon in Rome completed	c. 125–36 Papacy of Telesphorus	
138–61 Antoninus Pius emperor	130–80 Alexandrian gnostic school	c. 136–40 Papacy of Hyginus	
		c. 140–55 Papacy of Pius I	
		144 Marcion expelled from Rome	
161–80 Marcus Aurelius emperor		c. 155–66 Papacy of Anaeletus	c. 155 Justin Martyr, *First Apology*
164–80 Plague in the Roman Empire			c. 160 Justin Martyr, *Second Apology*

Political and Social Events	Intellectual and Cultural Developments	Christian History	Major Christian Writers (b.c. 100)
		c. 165 Polycarp martyred in Smyrna	165 Justin Martyr dies (b.c. 100)
		c. 166–75 Papacy of Soter	
		172 Rise of Montanism	
	c. 170 Pausanias, *Periegesis*	c. 175–89 Papacy of Eleutherius	
		177 Persecution of Christians in Lyons (Blandina martyred)	
180–92 Commodus emperor	180 Catechetical school at Alexandria founded	189–99 Victor I, first Latin-speaking pope	c. 185 Irenaeus, *Against Heresies*
			c. 190 Clement of Alexandria, *Miscellanies*
193–211 Septimius Severus emperor		199–217 Papacy of Zephyrinus	197 Tertullian, *Apology*
	c. 199 Galen, a founder of experimental physiology, dies		c. 200 Irenaeus dies (b.c. 130)
	c. 200 Neo-Platonism; formation of Neo-Hebrew language		c. 200 Tertullian, *On Spectacles*
	203 Origen head of cathechetical school at Alexandria; Plotinus there to 270	c. 203 Martyrdom of Perpetua	c. 207 Tertullian, *Against Marcion*
			213 Tertullian, *Against Praxeas*
211–17 Caracalla emperor			215 Clement of Alexandria dies (b.c. 150)
218–22 Heliogabalus emperor		217–22 Papacy of Callistus I	c. 222 Tertullian dies (b.c. 160)
222–35 Alexander Severus emperor		222–30 Papacy of Urban I	c. 225 Origen, *On First Principles*
	c. 231 Dionysius becomes head of catechetical school at Alexandria	230–35 Papacy of Pontian	c. 233 Origen, *On Prayer*
235–38 Maximinus emperor		235–36 Papacy of Anterus	c. 236 Origen, *Exhortation to Martyrdom*
		236–50 Papacy of Fabian	
244–49 Philip the Arabian emperor			c. 248 Origen, *Against Celsus*
248 Rome attacked by Goths		250 Decian persecution; martyrs revered as saints; Cyprian flees Carthage	
249–51 Decius emperor			

c. 251 Cyprian, *On the Unity of the Catholic Church*	251 Cyprian asserts authority		251–53 Gallus emperor
	251–53 Papacy of Cornelius		
	253–54 Papacy of Lucius I		253–60 Valerian emperor
254 Origen dies (**b.c. 185**)	254–57 Papacy of Stephen I	c. 255 Plotinus, *Enneads*	
	257–58 Papacy of Sixtus II		
	257–60 Valerianic persecutions		
258 Cyprian of Carthage dies (**b.c. 200**)	259–68 Papacy of Dionysius		260–68 Gallienus emperor
	260–63 Debate over Sabellianism		
	261–72 Paul of Samosata, bishop of Antioch; Councils against Paul in **264, 265, and 268**	c. 264 Dionysius dies	
			268–70 Claudius II emperor
	269–74 Papacy of Felix I		270–75 Aurelian emperor
	c. 270 Antony goes to desert		
	275–83 Papacy of Eutychian	c. 276 Manes, founder of Manicheism, dies	
	280–300 Rise of Manichees		
	283–96 Papacy of Caius		284–305 Diocletian emperor
			285 Diocletian divides Roman Empire into East and West
	296–304 Papacy of Marcellinus		
		c. 300 Earliest religious plays	
	303–5 Diocletian persecution	c. 304 Porphyry dies (**b.c. 234**)	307–37 Constantine emperor
	308–9 Papacy of Marcellus I		
	309–10 Papacy of Eusebius		
c. 311 Eusebius, first *Ecclesiastical History*	311 Donatist schism		312 Constantine defeats Maxentius at Milvian Bridge
	311–14 Papacy of Miltiades		313 Edict of Milan guarantees religious toleration
	314 Council of bishops at Arles		

Major Christian Writers	Christian History	Intellectual and Cultural Developments	Political and Social Events
	314–35 Papacy of Sylvester I		316 Constantine condemns Donatists
	323 Arius condemned; Pachomius founds monastery		
c. 324 Eusebius, second *Ecclesiastical History*	325 First Council of Nicea declares Christ *homoousios*, same substance as God		
	328–73 Athanasius, bishop of Alexandria	c. 330 First basilica of St. Peter's in Rome	330–31 Constantinople made capital of Roman Empire
			332 Constantine defeats Goths
c. 335 Athanasius, *Incarnation of the Word*	335 Athanasius condemned and exiled		
	336 Papacy of Mark		
	337–52 Papacy of Julius I		337 Constantine baptized
	337 Athanasius returns to Alexandria		
	339–46 Athanasius's second exile		
340 Eusebius dies (**b.c. 260**)			
346 Pachomius dies (**b.c. 290**)			
	352–66 Papacy of Liberius		
	353 Council of Arles		
356 Athanasius, *Orations Against the Arians*	c. 360 Martin of Tours founds first Gallic monastic community		
357 Athanasius, *Life of Antony*	366–84 Papacy of Damasus I		
367 Hilary of Poitiers dies (**b.c. 315**)			
373 Athanasius dies (**b.c. 300**)			
375 Basil of Caesarea, *On the Spirit*			
377 Ambrose of Milan, *On Virginity*			378 Visigoths defeat Emperor Valens at Adrianople
379 Basil of Caesarea dies (**b.c. 330**)			

Events	Church History	Writings
	381 First Council of Constantinople declares divinity of the Spirit and completes Nicene Creed	**381** Ambrose, *On the Holy Spirit*
		383 Jerome, Vulgate translation of Bible
	384–99 Papacy of Siricius	**384** Jerome, *Letter to Eustochium*
	386 Augustine's conversion to orthodox Christianity	
		c. 390 Gregory of Nyssa, *Life of Moses; On Not Three Gods*
391 Emperor Theodosius prohibits pagan sacrifices	**392–428** Theodore, bishop of Mopsuestia	
	395–430 Augustine, bishop of Hippo	**c. 395** Gregory of Nyssa dies (**b.c. 335**)
		396–97 Augustine, *Confessions*
		397 Ambrose of Milan dies (**b.c. 334**)
	399–401 Papacy of Anastasius I	**399** Evagrius Ponticus dies (**b.c. 345**)
		c. 400 Augustine, *On Christian Doctrine*
	401–17 Papacy of Innocent I	**401–15** Augustine, *Literal Commentary on Genesis*
		404–20 Augustine, *On the Trinity*
		407 John Chrysostom dies (**b.c. 347**)
410 Sack of Rome by Alaric	**411** Pelagian controversy begins	**411–26** Augustine, *City of God*
		413 Augustine, *On the Spirit and the Letter*
	c. 415 John Cassian founds monasteries in Marseilles	
	417 Pope Innocent I condemns Pelagians	
	417–18 Papacy of Zosimus	
	418–22 Papacy of Boniface I	**420** Jerome dies (**b.c. 347**)
		421 Augustine, *Enchiridion*
	422–32 Papacy of Celestine I	**c. 426** John Cassian, *Conferences*

Political and Social Events	Intellectual and Cultural Developments	Christian History	Major Christian Writers
429 Vandals establish kingdom in Northern Africa		**429–31** Nestorius of Constantinople vs. Cyril of Alexandria (christological controversy) **431** Council of Ephesus declares Mary Theotokos **432** Patrick's mission to Ireland **432–40** Papacy of Sixtus III **440–61** Papacy of Leo I, "the Great" **451** Council of Chalcedon condemns monophysitism and defines two natures of Christ	**c. 430** John Cassian, *Institutes* **430** Augustine dies (**b.c. 354**) **c. 435** John Cassian dies (**b.c. 360**)
452 Huns invade Italy **455** Sack of Rome by Vandals		**461–68** Papacy of Hilary **468–83** Papacy of Simplicius	
476 Western Roman Empire collapses	**476** Proclus becomes head of the Platonic Academy at Athens	**483–92** Papacy of Felix II **492–96** Papacy of Gelasius I; two powers theory **496–98** Papacy of Anastasius II	
c. 496 Clodovis, king of the Franks, converts to Christianity	**500** *Codex Bezae*, Greek-Latin text of gospels and Acts of the Apostles; Johannes Stobaios, *Anthology of Greek Literature*	**498–514** Papacy of Symmachus	**after 500** Writing career of Pseudo-Dionysius
507 Franks defeat Visigoths		**513** Council of Tyre **514–23** Papacy of Hormisdas	**c. 515** Pseudo-Dionysius, *Mystical Theology*
	524 Boethius, *The Consolation of Philosophy*	**523–26** Papacy of John I **526–30** Papacy of Felix III	

	529 Benedict founds monastery at Monte Cassino; Council of Orange condemns Pelagianism	
	530–32 Papacy of Boniface II	
527–65 Justinian emperor	**533–35** Papacy of John II	
	535–36 Papacy of Agapitus I	
534 Revised *Code of Justinian* published	**536–37** Papacy of Silverius	
537 Hagia Sophia dedicated under Justinian over an earlier basilica commissioned by Constantine but burned in **532**	**537–55** Papacy of Vigilius	
	553 Second Council of Constantinople affirms Chalcedon	
	556–61 Papacy of Pelagius I	
568 Lombard invasion of Italy	**561–74** Papacy of John III	
	575–79 Papacy of Benedict I	
	579–90 Papacy of Pelagius II	
c. 591 Gregory of Tours, *History of the Franks*	**590–604** Papacy of Gregory I, "the Great"	**c. 591** Gregory the Great, *Moralia on Job*
	597 Gregory's mission to Anglo-Saxons	
c. 600 Pope Gregory I organizes Schola Cantorum and liturgical music	**602** Bishop of London consecrated	**c. 600** Gregory the Great, *Dialogues*
	604–6 Papacy of Sabinian	
	607 Papacy of Boniface III	
	608–15 Papacy of Boniface IV	
614 Jerusalem falls to Persians	**615–18** Papacy of Adeodatus I	
c. 620 Normans invade Ireland	**619–25** Papacy of Boniface V	
632 Death of Muhammad	**625–38** Papacy of Honorius I	

Political and Social Events	Intellectual and Cultural Developments	Christian History	Major Christian Writers
634 Arab armies take Damascus			636 Isidore of Seville dies (b.c. 570)
638 Arab armies capture Jerusalem		640 Papacy of Severinus	
		640–42 Papacy of John IV	
		642–49 Papacy of Theodore I	
		649–53 Papacy of Martin I	
		654–57 Papacy of Eugene I	
		657–72 Papacy of Vitalian	662 Maximus Confessor dies (b.c. 530)
		672–76 Papacy of Adeodatus II	
		676–78 Papacy of Donus	
		678–81 Papacy of Agatho	
		680–81 Third Council of Constantinople rejects monothelitism	
		682–83 Papacy of Leo II	
		684–85 Papacy of Benedict II	
		685–86 Papacy of John V	
		686–87 Papacy of Conon	
		687–701 Papacy of Sergius I	
	c. 700 Lindisfarne gospels copied and illustrated	701–5 Papacy of John VI	
	703–35 Bede helps to establish practice of dating events from the birth of Jesus	705–7 Papacy of John VII	
		708 Papacy of Sisinnius	
710 Entry of Moors into Spain; Spain overtaken by 713		708–15 Papacy of Constantine I	
714–41 Career of Charles Martel		715–31 Papacy of Gregory II	
		731–41 Papacy of Gregory III	c. 732 Bede, *Ecclesiastical History of the English Nation*
732 Martel defeats Muslims at Poitiers			735 Bede dies (b. 673)
		738 Boniface organizes church in Germany	

Events	Papacy	Scholars and Works
752 Pepin proclaimed king of Gaul; Carolingian dynasty established	**741–52** Papacy of Zachary **752** Stephen II, dies before consecration	
754–56 Formation of Papal State	**752–57** Papacy of Stephen II (III)	
	757–67 Papacy of Paul I **768–72** Papacy of Stephen III (IV) **772–95** Papacy of Hadrian I **787** Second Council of Nicea affirms veneration of icons	**778** Ambrose Autpert dies (b. unknown)
790s Alcuin promotes Carolingian revival of learning	**795–816** Papacy of Leo III	
793 Viking raids on England		
c. 800 *Book of Kells*, Irish illuminated text of the gospels		
800 Charlemagne crowned Holy Roman Emperor by Pope Leo III	**816–17** Papacy of Stephen IV (V) **817–24** Papacy of Paschal I **824–27** Papacy of Eugene II **827** Papacy of Valentine **827–44** Papacy of Gregory IV	
829 Basilica of St. Mark in Venice begun		
843 Treaty of Verdun divides Carolingian Empire	**844–47** Papacy of Sergius II **847–55** Papacy of Leo IV	
c. 850 Increasing use of the crossbow		**851** John the Scot, *On Predestination*
853–57 Normans raid France	**855–58** Papacy of Benedict III **858–67** Papacy of Nicholas I	
c. 860 Cyril and Methodius, apostles to the Slavs, invent Cyrillic alphabet	**867–72** Papacy of Hadrian II **869–70** Fourth Council of Constantinople	**c. 862–69** John the Scot, *On the Division of Nature*

Political and Social Events	Intellectual and Cultural Developments	Christian History	Major Christian Writers
c. 875 Vikings settle Iceland		872–82 Papacy of John VIII 882–84 Papacy of Marinus I 884–85 Papacy of Hadrian III 885–91 Papacy of Stephen V (VI) 891–96 Papacy of Formosus 896 Papacy of Boniface VI 896–97 Papacy of Stephen VI (VII) 897 Papacy of Romanus 897 Papacy of Theodore II 898–900 Papacy of John IX 900–3 Papacy of Benedict IV 903 Papacy of Leo V 904–11 Papacy of Sergius III 910 Foundation of Abbey of Cluny; Cluniac reform of Benedictine order initiated 911–13 Papacy of Anastasius III 913–14 Papacy of Lando 914–28 Papacy of John X 928 Papacy of Leo VI 928–31 Papacy of Stephen VII (VIII) 931–35 Papacy of John XI 936–39 Papacy of Leo VII 939–42 Papacy of Stephen VIII (IX) 942–46 Papacy of Marinus II 946–55 Papacy of Agapitus II 955–63 Papacy of John XII 963–65 Papacy of Leo VIII 964 Papacy of Benedict V 965–72 Papacy of John XIII 973–74 Papacy of Benedict VI 974–83 Papacy of Benedict VII	c. 877 John the Scot dies (b.c. 810)
936–62 Otto I, king of Germany and later Holy Roman Emperor (962–73)			
973–83 Otto II, Holy Roman Emperor			

983 Otto III succeeds Otto II, later becoming emperor (996–1002)	c. 1000 manuscript of *Beowulf*; Leif Eriksson believed to reach North America	983–84 Papacy of John XIV
987–1328 Capetian dynasty in France		985–96 Papacy of John XV
990–1029 William, duke of Aquitaine		996–99 Papacy of Gregory V
		998 Beginning of conversion of Russia
		999–1003 Papacy of Sylvester II
		1003 Papacy of John XVII
		1003–9 Papacy of John XVIII
		1009 Norman alliance with papacy
1010 Normans defeat English at Ringmere		1009–12 Papacy of Sergius IV
		1012–24 Papacy of Benedict VIII
1035 Castile becomes a kingdom under Ferdinand I	1037 Avicenna dies (b. 980)	1024–32 Papacy of John XIX
1042–66 Edward the Confessor, king of England		1032–45 Papacy of Benedict IX
		1045–46 Papacy of Gregory VI
		1046–47 Papacy of Clement II
		1047–48 Benedict IX pope again
		1048 Papacy of Damasus II
		1049 Norman alliance collapses
	1050–1125 Romanesque architecture flourishes	1049–54 Papacy of Leo IX
1053 Normans defeat papal army; Pope Leo IX captured		1054 Schism between Western and Eastern Church
		1055–57 Papacy of Victor II
		1057 Peter Damian, monk and reformer, becomes cardinal bishop of Ostia
		1057–58 Papacy of Stephen IX (X)
1059 Lateran Synod issues general prohibition of lay investiture		1059–61 Papacy of Nicholas II, who establishes rules for papal elections by cardinals
	1065 Westminster Abbey consecrated	1061–73 Papacy of Alexander II

Political and Social Events	Intellectual and Cultural Developments	Christian History	Major Christian Writers
1066 William, duke of Normandy, becomes king of England after Norman conquest		1073–85 Papacy of Gregory VII	
1075–85 Conflict between Pope Gregory VII and Henry IV of Germany over lay investiture		1075 Gregory VII's *Dictatus Papae* insists on papal supremacy in temporal and spiritual matters	1078 John of Fécamp dies (**b.c. 990**)
1077 Henry IV does penance at Canossa, is reinstated	c. 1078 Building of Tower of London begins	1076 Gregory excommunicates and deposes Henry IV	1078–79 Anselm, *Proslogion*
1086 William the Conqueror has *Domesday Book* compiled	1088 University of Bologna founded	1084 Foundation of Carthusian order	1088 Berengar of Tours dies (**b.c. 1000**)
1095 First Crusade declared		1086–87 Papacy of Victor III	
1099 Jerusalem recaptured	c. 1100 *Song of Roland*	1088–99 Papacy of Urban II	c. 1099 Anselm, *Why God Became Human*
		1098 Foundation of Cistercian order; Urban II renews treaty with Normans	1102 Anselm, *On the Procession of the Holy Spirit*
		1099–1118 Papacy of Paschal II	1109 Anselm of Canterbury dies (**b. 1033**)
	1120–1200 Early Gothic architecture	1113 Rule of Canons of St. Victor adopted	
		1118–19 Papacy of Gelasius II	
		1119–24 Papacy of Callistus II	
		1121 Foundation of Praemonstratensians	

1122 Concordat of Worms declares investment of bishops the right of ecclesiastical authority	c. 1123 Umar Khayyam dies (**b.c. 1038–42**)	1122 Condemnation of Abelard's works on the Trinity	1123–36 Peter Abelard, *Sic et Non*
		1123 First Lateran Council, first ecumenical council held in the West	c. 1125 Bernard of Clairvaux, *The Degrees of Humility and Pride*
		1124–30 Papacy of Honorius II	1128 Bernard, *On Grace and Free Choice*
			1129 Rupert of Deutz dies (**b. 1077**)
	c. 1132 Abbey of St. Denis built	1130–43 Papacy of Innocent II	c. 1130 Bernard, *On Loving God*
			c. 1135 Bernard, *Sermons on the Song of Songs*
		1139 Second Lateran Council	
1141–44 Geoffrey Plantagenet conquers Normandy	c. 1140 *El Cid* composed; Gratian completes his collection of canon law, *Harmony of Contradictory Laws*	1141 Council of Sens	1141 Hugh of St. Victor dies (**b.c. 1090**)
			c. 1141–51 Hildegard, *Know the Ways*
			c. 1142 Peter Abelard dies (**b.c. 1079**)
1143 Christians take over North Africa	c. 1145 Anna Comnena, historian, dies	1143–44 Papacy of Celestine II	
1145 Second Crusade begins		1144–45 Papacy of Lucius II	
		1145–53 Papacy of Eugene III	
		1153–54 Papacy of Anastasius IV	1153 Bernard of Clairvaux dies (**b. 1090**)
		1154–59 Papacy of Hadrian IV, first English pope	
1155 Frederick Barbarossa crowned emperor	c. 1155 Carmelite order established		1155–58 Peter Lombard, *Sentences*
1158–1214 Alfonso VIII, king of Leon and Castile		1159 Schism between Alexander III and Victor IV	
		1159–81 Papacy of Alexander III	

Political and Social Events	Intellectual and Cultural Developments	Christian History	Major Christian Writers
		1159–64 Victor IV, antipope	**1160** Peter Lombard dies (**b.c. 1095**)
1164 Quarrel between King Henry II of England and Thomas Becket begins	**c. 1160** University of Paris founded **1163** Building of Notre Dame Cathedral (Paris) begins	**1164–68** Paschal III, antipope	**1165** Elisabeth of Schönau dies (**b. 1128**)
1170 Becket murdered	**c. 1170** Chrétien de Troyes, *Lancelot*; Oxford University founded	**1168–78** Callistus III, antipope	**1173** Richard of St. Victor dies (b. unknown) **1173/74** Hildegard, *The Book of Divine Works*
1177 Peace of Venice between Frederick Barbarossa and Pope Alexander III	**1174** Bell tower, "Leaning Tower," of Pisa begun	**1174** Conversion of Peter Valdes; beginning of Waldensian movement	**1179** Hildegard of Bingen dies (**b. 1098**)
		1179 Third Lateran Council **c. 1179–80** Innocent III, antipope **1181–85** Papacy of Lucius III **1184** Council of Verona condemns Cathars, Patarines, and Humiliati	
1185 Norman expedition against Byzantium		**1185–87** Papacy of Urban III **1187** Papacy of Gregory VIII **1187–91** Papacy of Clement III	
1189 Third Crusade begins		**1191–98** Papacy of Celestine III	
	1194 Beginning of reconstruction of Chartres Cathedral **1198** Averroës dies (**b. 1126**)	**1198–1216** Papacy of Innocent III	
1198 Philip Augustus of France quarrels with Pope Innocent III	**c. 1200** *Nibelungenlied* **1200–10** Wolfram von Eschenbach, *Parzifal*	**1200** Innocent interdicts France	

1202 Joachim of Fiore dies (**b.c. 1135**)	1209 Albigensian Crusade	c. **1200–1350** High Gothic architecture	**1202–4** Fourth Crusade
	1210 Innocent III approves Francis of Assisi's first Rule		**1204** Fourth Crusade enters Constantinople; Latin empire established there
c. **1215** *Ancrene Wisse*, English rule for Anchorites	1215 Establishment of Dominican Order; Fourth Lateran Council orders annual confession and communion	1204 Moses Maimonides dies (**b. 1135**)	
	1216–27 Papacy of Honorius III	1209 Cambridge University founded	1215 Magna Carta signed
	1223 Francis' second Rule approved by papacy		1215–50 Reign of Emperor Frederick II
	1227–41 Papacy of Gregory IX		
c. **1240** Hadewijch of Brabant dies (b. unknown)	1241 Papacy of Celestine IV	1230 Walther von der Vogelweide dies (**b. 1172**)	c. **1231** Pope Gregory IX establishes the papal Inquisition
	1243–54 Papacy of Innocent IV		
	1245 First Council of Lyons	1248 Alhambra Palace in Granada begun	
1259 Bonaventure, *The Mind's Road to God*	1254–61 Papacy of Alexander IV		
1259–64 Thomas Aquinas, *Summa contra Gentiles*	1257 Bonaventure becomes general of the Franciscan order	1260 Aristotle's *Politics* translated into Latin	

Political and Social Events	Intellectual and Cultural Developments	Christian History	Major Christian Writers
	1271 Marco Polo travels to the Far East	1261–64 Papacy of Urban IV 1265–68 Papacy of Clement IV 1271–76 Papacy of Gregory X 1274 Second Council of Lyons 1276 Papacy of Innocent V 1276 Papacy of Hadrian V 1276–77 Papacy of John XXI 1277–80 Papacy of Nicholas III 1281–85 Papacy of Martin IV 1285–87 Papacy of Honorius IV 1288–92 Papacy of Nicholas IV	1265–73 Aquinas, *Summa Theologiae* c. 1270 Mechthild of Magdeburg, *Flowing Light of Godhead* 1274 Bonaventure (b. 1221) and Thomas Aquinas (b.c. 1224) die c. 1282 Mechthild of Magdeburg dies (b.c. 1212) c. 1289 Gertrude of Helfta, *Herald of Divine Love* c. 1291 Mechthild of Hackeborn, *Book of Special Grace*
1296–1303 Conflict between Philip IV of France and Boniface VIII 1296 Boniface VIII's *Clericis Laicos* forbids taxation of clergy without papal consent 1302 Boniface asserts papal superiority over kings in *Unam Sanctam*	c. 1292 Roger Bacon, proponent of experimental science, dies (b.c. 1214) 1296 Arnolfo di Cambio designs Florence cathedral	1294 Papacy of Celestine V 1294–1303 Papacy of Boniface VIII 1302 Papal Bull *Unam Sanctam* asserts subjection to pope is necessary for salvation	c. 1297 Angela of Foligno, *The Book* c. 1299 Mechthild of Hackeborn dies (b.c. 1241) 1302 Gertrude of Helfta dies (b.c. 1266)

Historical events	Papacy	Culture	Deaths
1303 Boniface excommunicates Philip; Philip attacks Boniface, who dies in humiliation at Agnani	1303–4 Papacy of Benedict XI		
	1305–14 Papacy of Clement V		1308 Duns Scotus dies (**b.c. 1265**)
	1309 Clement V moves papacy to Avignon, where it remains until **1377**		1309 Angela of Foligno dies (**b.c. 1248**)
	1311–12 Council of Vienne condemns Beguines and spiritualist Franciscans' interpretation of poverty		1310 Marguerite Porete, author of *Mirror for Simple Souls*, executed (b. unknown)
1313–17 Widespread famine and epidemics throughout Europe		c. 1314 Dante, *Divine Comedy*	
	1316–34 Papacy of John XXII		1316 Raymond Lull dies (**b. 1236**)
1324 Marsilius of Padua's *Defender of the Peace* advances conciliar thought and denies papal temporal authority			
	1327 John XXII condemns Marsilius of Padua		c. 1327 Meister Eckhart dies (**b.c. 1260**)
	1334–42 Papacy of Benedict XII	1334 Construction of the papal palace in Avignon begins	
1337 Hundred Years' War between England and France begins		1337 Giotto dies	
	1342–52 Papacy of Clement VI		
1347 Black Death spreads throughout Italy, France, then England. Anti-semitic violence increases			1347 William of Ockham dies (**b.c. 1285**)
		1348–53 Boccaccio, *Decameron*	1349 Richard Rolle dies (**b. 1300**)
	1352–62 Papacy of Innocent VI	c. 1360s Clavichord develops	1361 Johann Tauler dies (**b. 1300**)
	1362–70 Papacy of Urban V		1366 Henry Suso dies (**b. 1295**)
	1370–78 Papacy of Gregory XI		1372 Bridget of Sweden dies (**b. 1301**)
		1374 Petrarch dies (**b. 1304**)	

249

Political and Social Events	Intellectual and Cultural Developments	Christian History	Major Christian Writers
	c. 1375 "Robin Hood" ballads appear		
		1377 Gregory XI returns papacy to Rome from Avignon	
		1378 Beginning of papal schism	c. 1378 Catherine of Siena, *The Dialogue*
		April 9 election of Urban VI (Italian), **1378–89**	
		Sept. 20 election of Clement VII (French), **1378–94**	1378 Julian of Norwich, *Showings* (first version)
		Urban VI remains in Rome; Clement VII returns to Avignon	
1381 Peasants' Revolt in England			1380 Catherine of Siena dies (**b. 1347**)
			1381 Jan van Ruysbroeck dies (**b. 1293**)
			1384 John Wycliffe dies (**b.c. 1338**)
		1389–1404 Boniface IX, Roman pope	1393 Julian of Norwich, *Showings* (second version)
		1394–1417 Benedict XIII, Avignon pope	
	1400 Geoffrey Chaucer dies, leaves *Canterbury Tales* unfinished	1404–6 Innocent VII, Roman pope	
		1406–15 Gregory XII, Roman pope	
	c. 1408 Donatello, *David* (statue)	1409 Council of Pisa attempts to end papal schism, elects a third pope, Alexander V, **1409–10**	
		1410–15 John XXIII, Pisan pope	c. 1410–40 Thomas à Kempis, *The Imitation of Christ*
	c. 1412 Filippo Brunelleschi rediscovers principles of perspective in art	1414–18 Council of Constance condemns Wycliffe and Hus and elects Martin V, **1417–31**	1413 Jan Hus, *On the Church*

People (deaths)	Church	Culture/Learning	Politics & Society
1415 Jan Hus executed (**b.c. 1372**)	**1420** Four Articles of Prague		**1417** End of Great (papal) Schism
c. 1423 Julian of Norwich dies (**b.c. 1342**)		**1425** Louvain University founded	**1429** French recapture Orleans
1429 Jean Gerson dies (**b. 1363**)	**1431–37** Council of Basel		**1431** Joan of Arc burned at stake
	1431–47 Papacy of Eugene IV		**1438** Pragmatic Sanctions of Bourges affirms supremacy of council over pope
	1437–38 Council of Basel transferred to Ferrara; attempted reunification with Eastern Church	**c. 1440** Lorenzo Valla proves *Donation of Constantine* a forgery	**1449** Anti-semitic violence in Toledo
	1439 Council of Ferrara moved to Florence	**1441** Jan van Eyck dies (**b.c. 1390**)	**1453** Hundred Years' War ends; Eastern Roman Empire ends with conquest of Constantinople
	1447–55 Papacy of Nicholas V	**c. 1450** Johannes Gutenberg invents printing press	**1455** Wars of the Roses begin in England
	1455–58 Papacy of Callistus III	**1457** Lorenzo Valla dies	**1469** Marriage of Ferdinand and Isabella
1464 Nicholas of Cusa dies (**b. 1401**)	**1458–64** Papacy of Pius II		**1474** Unification of Castile and Aragon
	1460 Papal bull *Execrabilis* condemns conciliarist theories		
	1464–71 Papacy of Paul II		
1471 Thomas à Kempis dies (**b. 1380**)	**1471–84** Papacy of Sixtus IV		

Political and Social Events	Intellectual and Cultural Developments	Christian History	Major Christian Writers
1478 Spanish Inquisition founded		**1484–92** Papacy of Innocent VIII **1484** Bull *Summis desiderantis affectibus* against witchcraft	
1492 Reconquest of Granada; expulsion of Jews from Spain; arrival of Columbus to Americas	**c. 1485** Sandro Botticelli, *Birth of Venus* **c. 1486** *Malleus maleficarum*	**1492–1503** Papacy of Alexander VI	**1495** Gabriel Biel dies (**b.c. 1420**)
	1494 Humanist Pico della Mirandola dies	**1495–1517** Francisco Jiménez de Cisneros, archbishop of Toledo, promotes humanism **1498** Savonarola (**b. 1452**) burned as heretic	
	1498 Michelangelo, *Pietà*		**1500** Erasmus, *Adages*
	1499 Marsilio Ficino dies	**1500** Papal Jubilee year **1503** Papacy of Pius III **1503–13** Papacy of Julius II	**1503** Erasmus, *Enchiridion*
	1506 New St. Peter's basilica begun in Rome **1508** Foundation of University of Alcalá		
1509–47 Henry VIII, king of England	**1510** Botticelli dies (**b. 1444**)		**1509** Erasmus, *Praise of Folly* **1510** Catherine of Genoa dies (**b. 1447**); her works, *Purgation and Purgatory* and *The Spiritual Dialogue*, are compiled by her disciples **c. 1522**
1511 Pope Julius II founds Holy League of Aragon, England, and Venice to expel French from Italy **1512** Diet of Cologne divides Holy Roman Empire into ten administrative centers		**1512–17** Fifth Lateran Council **1513–21** Papacy of Leo X	

1519 Charles I of Spain elected Holy Roman Emperor Charles V	**1516** Niccolo Machiavelli, *The Prince*	**1517** Luther's *95 Theses* posted	**1515–16** Martin Luther, *Lectures on Romans* **1516** Thomas More, *Utopia*, and Erasmus, *Peraclesis* **1518** Martin Luther, *Heidelberg Disputation*
	1519 Leonardo da Vinci dies (**b. 1452**); Magellan begins trip around the world	**1519** Leipzig Debate between Andreas Carlstadt and Johann Eck	
1521 Diet of Worms declares Luther an outlaw		**1520** Leo X condemns Luther's doctrines and excommunicates him with bull *Exsurge*	**1520** Martin Luther, *Address to the Christian Nobility*, *Babylonian Captivity of the Church*, *Freedom of the Christian*
	1522 Publication of Complutensian Bible at University of Alcalá	**1521** Henry VIII, *Defense of the Seven Sacraments against Luther* **1522–23** Papacy of Hadrian VI	**1523** Ulrich Zwingli, *Short Christian Introduction* **1523–24** Erasmus, *Discourse on Free Will*
1524–25 The Peasants' Revolt in Germany		**1523–34** Papacy of Clement VII	
		1524 Foundation of Theatine order	**1525** Luther, *Bondage of the Will* **1526** Conrad Grebel dies (**b.c. 1498**)
1527 Henry VIII begins legal proceedings to divorce Catherine of Aragon	**1526** William Tyndale publishes translation of Bible		**1527** Hans Denck dies (**b.c. 1500**)
		1528 Foundation of Capuchins	**1528** Zwingli, *Commentary on the True and False Religion*
1529 Ottomans lay siege to Vienna **1530** Diet of Augsburg		**1529** Marburg Colloquy **1530** Augsburg Confession	
		1533 Church of England breaks with Rome	**1531** Ulrich Zwingli dies (**b. 1484**)

Political and Social Events	Intellectual and Cultural Developments	Christian History	Major Christian Writers
1535 Catholic and Lutheran forces overthrow Anabaptist rule in Münster		**1534–49** Papacy of Paul III **1534** Ignatius of Loyola founds Society of Jesus (Jesuits); confirmed by Paul III in **1540** **1535** Ursuline order founded by Angela Merici (**d. 1540**)	**1535** Thomas More dies (**b. 1477**) **1536** Erasmus dies (**b.c. 1467**) **1536** John Calvin, *Institutes of the Christian Religion* (first edition) **1539** Calvin, *Institutes* (second edition) **1539** Menno Simons, *Book of Fundamentals* **1541** Juan de Valdes dies (**b.c. 1490**) **1542** Sebastian Franck dies (**b.c. 1499**)
		1539 Six Articles (England)	
	1543 Nicolaus Copernicus, *On the Revolutions of the Celestial Spheres;* Copernicus dies (**b. 1473**); Andreas Vesalius lays foundation of modern anatomy with *On the Structure of the Human Body*	**1541** Calvin's *Ecclesiastical Ordinances* adopted in Geneva **1542** Establishment of Roman Inquisition (Holy Office) **1545–63** Council of Trent, three major periods: **1545–47, 1551–52, 1562–63**	**1546** Juan Luis Vives (**b.c. 1492**) and Martin Luther (**b. 1483**) die
1547–53 Edward VI, king of England		**1549** *Book of Common Prayer* becomes normative in England; Jesuit Francis Xavier (**d. 1552**) starts mission in Japan	

1551 Martin Bucer dies (**b. 1491**)	1550–55 Papacy of Julius III		1553–58 Mary I, "Bloody Mary," queen of England
1556 Ignatius Loyola dies (**b. 1491**)	1555 Papacy of Marcellus II 1555–59 Papacy of Paul IV		1555 Peace of Augsburg establishes territorial control of religion within Germany 1558–1603 Elizabeth I, queen of England
1559 Calvin, *Institutes* (third edition)	1559 Valdes Index of Prohibited Books		
1560 Philip Melanchthon dies (**b. 1497**)	1559–65 Papacy of Pius IV		
1561 Menno Simons dies (**b.c. 1496**); John Knox, *Book of Discipline*			
	1562 Discalced Carmelite reform begins		1562 Wars of religion begin in France 1563 Thirty-Nine Articles, doctrinal statement of Church of England; given final form in **1571**
1564 John Calvin dies (**b. 1509**) c. 1565 Teresa of Avila, *Life* 1566 Heinrich Bullinger, *Second Helvetic Confession* c. 1568 Teresa, *Way of Perfection* 1572 John Knox dies (**b. 1513**)	1566–72 Papacy of Pius V	1564 Michelangelo dies (**b. 1475**)	
	1572–85 Papacy of Gregory XIII 1575 Oratorians established under Philip Neri		
1577 Teresa, *The Interior Castle* 1579–85 John of the Cross, *The Dark Night* and *The Ascent of Mount Carmel* 1582 Teresa of Avila dies (**b. 1515**)	1585–90 Papacy of Sixtus V		
1588 Luis de Molina, *The Harmony of Free Will with the Gifts of Grace*			1588 English defeat Spanish Armada

Political and Social Events	Intellectual and Cultural Developments	Christian History	Major Christian Writers
			1589 Michael Baius dies (**b. 1513**)
		1590 Papacy of Urban VII	
		1590–91 Papacy of Gregory XIV	**1591** John of the Cross dies (**b. 1542**)
		1591 Papacy of Innocent IX	
		1592–1605 Papacy of Clement VIII	
1598 Edict of Nantes grants religious freedom and civil rights to French Huguenots	**1600** Shakespeare, *Hamlet*		**1600** Luis de Molina dies (**b. 1535**)
	1601 Tycho Brahe dies	**1601** Jesuit Matteo Ricci admitted to Peking	
1603 Scottish and English crowns unite	**1605** Cervantes, *Don Quixote*, Pt. I	**1605** Papacy of Leo XI	**1605** Theordore Beza dies (**b. 1519**)
1605 Gunpowder Plot in England	**1605–6** Shakespeare, *King Lear* and *Macbeth*	**1605–21** Papacy of Paul V	
1607 England establishes first colony in North America at Jamestown	**1608** Telescope invented by Hans Lippershey		**1608** Francis de Sales, *Introduction to the Devout Life*
	1609 Telescope refined and used by Galileo Galilei	**1609** Jesuit reductions established in Paraguay	
		1611 King James Bible published	
			1613 Francisco Suarez, *Defense of the Catholic Faith*
	1614 El Greco dies (**b. 1541**)	**1615** Jesuits have over 13,000 members in 32 provinces	
	1615 Cervantes, *Don Quixote*, Pt. II		
	1616 Cervantes (**b. 1547**) and Shakespeare (**b. 1564**) die		**1617** Francisco Suarez dies (**b. 1548**)
1618 Thirty Years' War begins	**1618–19** Johannes Kepler describes planetary motion	**1618–19** Synod of Dort	

1619 Jakob Böhme, *On the Principles of Christianity*

1621 Robert Bellarmine dies (**b. 1542**)

1622 Francis de Sales dies (**b. 1567**)

1624 Jakob Böhme dies (**b. 1575**)

1620 *Mayflower* lands at Plymouth Rock

1621–23 Papacy of Gregory XV

1622 Congregation for the Propagation of the Faith established

1623–44 Papacy of Urban VIII

1624 Foundation of English deism laid with Lord Herbert of Cherbury's *On Truth*

1626 Facade of St. Peter's in Rome finished

1628 Ignatius of Loyola canonized

1630–42 Puritan migration to New World

1633 Trial of Galileo

1634 Louise de Marillac (**1591–1660**) and Vincent de Paul found the Vincentian Sisters of Charity (formally approved in **1655**)

1625 Hugo Grotius, *The Law of War and Peace*

1625 Jan Brueghel the Elder dies (**b. 1568**)

1626 Francis Bacon dies (**b. 1561**); Santorio Santorio measures human temperature with thermometer for first time

1628 William Harvey discovers circulation of blood; John Bunyan (**d. 1688**) and Jacob van Ruisdael (**d. 1682**) born

1630–80 High Baroque period

1630 Johannes Kepler dies (**b. 1571**)

1631 John Donne dies (**b. 1572**)

1632 John Locke (**d. 1704**), Baruch Spinoza (**d. 1677**), and Jan Vermeer (**d. 1675**) born

---

1619 First enslaved Africans arrive in Virginia

1621 Potatoes planted in Germany for first time

1624–42 Cardinal Richelieu made first minister of France

1626 Dutch establish New Amsterdam (New York after **1664**)

1630 John Winthrop, first governor of Massachusetts Bay Colony, founds Boston

1634 *Ark* and *Dove* land at Maryland colony

Political and Social Events	Intellectual and Cultural Developments	Christian History	Major Christian Writers
		1634 Oberammergau Passion Play performed for first time	
	1636 Harvard College founded	**1636** Roger Williams expelled from Massachusetts; founds Providence	
	1637 René Descartes, *Discourse on Method*; Ben Jonson dies **(b. 1572)**	**1637** Anne Hutchinson expelled from Massachusetts; founds Portsmouth; extermination of Christianity in Japan	**1638** Cornelius Jansen dies **(b. 1585)**
	1638 Pieter Brueghel the Younger dies **(b. 1564)**	**1639** Roger Williams founds first Baptist church in "New World"	
1640 Portugal declares independence from Spain	**1640** Peter Paul Rubens dies **(b. 1577)**		**1640** Jansen's *Augustine* published posthumously
1642 English Civil War begins	**1641** Anthony van Dyck dies **(b. 1599)**	**1642–60** Puritans close theaters in England	
1643 Louis XIV of France begins 72-year reign	**1642** Galileo dies and **(b. 1564)** Isaac Newton **(d. 1727)** born	**1643–47** Westminster Confession	
		1644–55 Papacy of Innocent X	
		1646 Isaac Jogues, S.J., murdered by Iroquois	
1648 Treaty of Westphalia; end of Thirty Years' War		**1649** Maryland Assembly passes Act of Religious Toleration (repealed in **1654**)	
1649–53 English Commonwealth	**1650** Anne Bradstreet publishes first American poem		
	1651 Thomas Hobbes, *Leviathan*		**1652** Gerrard Winstanley, *The Law of Freedom in a Platform*

1653–58 Oliver Cromwell as Lord Protector	1653 Arcangelo Corelli (**d. 1713**) and Johann Pachelbel (**d. 1706**) born 1654 Pascal and Fermat state theory of probability	1655–67 Papacy of Alexander VII 1656 Quakers persecuted in Massachusetts	1656 Pascal, *Provincial Letters*
	1656–65 Bernini works on high altar of St. Peter's in Rome 1659 Henry Purcell (**d. 1695**) and Alessandro Scarlatti (**d. 1725**) born		
1660 Stuart line restored to English crown		1661 Bible translated into Algonquin: first American Bible	1660 Gerrard Winstanley dies (**b.c. 1609**)
	1662 Louis XIV begins to build palace of Versailles; Blaise Pascal dies (**b. 1623**) 1664 Moliere, *Le Tartuffe*	1664 Trappist Order founded in Normandy	
1665 New Jersey founded; the plague kills more than 100,000 in London	1667 Margaret Cavendish becomes member of the Royal Society; no other woman admitted until **1945**	1667–69 Papacy of Clement IX	1666 Bunyan, *Grace Abounding* 1667–74 John Milton, *Paradise Lost*
1668 Spain recognizes Portugal's independence	1669 Rembrandt dies (**b. 1606**) 1670 Spinoza, *Tractatus theologico-politicus*	1670–76 Papacy of Clement X 1671 Rose of Lima (**1586–1617**) is first canonized saint of the New World	
1672 Royal African Company founded; England gains upper hand in slave trade; Czar Peter the Great born (**d. 1725**); France declares war on Dutch 1672–73 Marquette and Joliet expeditions down Mississippi	1673 Moliere dies (**b. 1622**)		

Political and Social Events	Intellectual and Cultural Developments	Christian History	Major Christian Writers
			1674 John Milton dies (b. 1608)
	1675 Jan Vermeer dies (b. 1632); Leibniz invents differential and integral calculus		1675 Philip Spener, *Pia Desideria*
	1677 Baruch Spinoza dies (b. 1632)	1676–89 Papacy of Innocent XI	
1678 La Salle explores Great Lakes	1678 John Bunyan, *The Pilgrim's Progress*, Pt. I		
	1679 Thomas Hobbes dies (b. 1588)		
1681 Royal charter for Pennsylvania			
1682 La Salle claims Louisiana territory for France	1682 Jacob van Ruisdael (b. 1628) and Murillo (b. 1617) die	1682 Four Gallican Articles	
1683 Islamic advance halted as John Sobieski (King John III) of Poland lifts siege of Vienna	1684 John Bunyan, *The Pilgrim's Progress*, Pt. II		
	1685 J. S. Bach (d. 1750), G. F. Handel (d. 1759), and Domenico Scarlatti (d. 1757) born	1685 Louis XIV revokes Edict of Nantes (1598); Huguenots flee France	
	1687 Isaac Newton introduces new cosmology in *Principia Mathematica*		
1688 Glorious or Bloodless Revolution; William and Mary take English throne			1688 John Bunyan dies (b. 1628)
1689 Peter the Great becomes Czar of Russia		1689 Toleration Act in Britain	
	1690 John Locke, *Essay Concerning Human Understanding*	1689–91 Papacy of Alexander VIII	
			1691 George Fox dies (b. 1624)
		1691–1700 Papacy of Innocent XII	
1692 Salem witch trials		1692 Church of England established in Maryland	
			1694 George Fox, *Journal*, published posthumously

1695 John Locke, *The Reasonableness of Christianity*	**1698** Society for Promoting Christian Knowledge established	**1700** Samuel Sewall, *The Selling of Joseph*, first American protest against slavery; John Dryden dies (**b. 1631**)	**1700** Approximate population: France 19 million; England and Scotland 7.5 million; Hapsburg dominions 7.5 million; Spain 6 million
	1700–21 Papacy of Clement XI	**1701** Yale College founded; Jethro Tull's seed drill improves agricultural productivity	**1701–14** War of Spanish Succession
1705 Philip Jacob Spener dies (**b. 1635**)		**1704** John Locke dies (**b. 1632**)	**1703** Delaware separates from Pennsylvania and becomes colony
		1710 G. W. Leibniz, *Theodicy*	**1712** Slave revolts in New York
	1713 Pope Clement XI condemns Jansenism in *Unigenitus*	**1714** Gabriel Fahrenheit (**1686–1736**) constructs mercury thermometer	
		1715 Beginning of Rococo period	
	1716 Teaching of Christianity prohibited in China	**1716** G. W. Leibniz dies (**b. 1646**)	
		1717 Handel, *Water Music*	
		1717–18 Lady Mary Wortley Montagu (**1690–1762**) introduces innoculation in England	
	1719 Jesuits expelled from Russia		
	1721–24 Papacy of Innocent XIII	**1721** J. S. Bach, *Brandenburg Concertos*	
	1722 Moravian community of Herrnhut founded		
	1724–30 Papacy of Benedict XIII		

Political and Social Events	Intellectual and Cultural Developments	Christian History	Major Christian Writers
	1726 Jonathan Swift, *Gulliver's Travels*; Stephen Hales (1671–1761) measures blood pressure		1727 August Hermann Francke dies (b. 1663)
		1730–40 Papacy of Clement XII	1730 Matthew Tindal, *Christianity as Old as Creation*
1732 James Oglethorpe obtains charter to establish Georgia colony		1730–1750s Great Awakening in American colonies	
		1732 Conrad Beissel founds Ephrata Community in Germantown, Pa.	1733 Matthew Tindal dies (b.c. 1657)
	1733–34 Alexander Pope, *Essay on Man*		1736 Joseph Butler, *Analogy of Religion*
	1737 Antonio Stradivari dies (b. 1644)	1738 John Wesley's conversion experience	
	1739–40 David Hume, *A Treatise on Human Nature*	1740–58 Papacy of Benedict XIV	1739 Jonathan Edwards, *Personal Narrative; A History of the Work of Redemption*
1740 Frederick the Great introduces freedom of press and worship in Prussia at beginning of his 46-year reign; Empress Maria Theresa begins her 40-year reign in Austria	1741 Antonio Vivaldi dies (b. 1675)		1741 Jonathan Edwards's sermon "Sinners in the Hands of an Angry God"
	1742 Edmund Halley dies (b. 1656)	1742 Chinese Rite controversy ended by Pope Benedict XIV	
	1748 Hume, *An Enquiry Concerning Human Understanding*		1746 Jonathan Edwards, *A Treatise Concerning Religious Affections* 1748 Alphonsus di Liguori, *Moral Theology*

Religion/Theology	Church/Catholicism	Culture/Science	Politics/History
1752 Joseph Butler dies (**b. 1692**)		**1749** Henry Fielding, *Tom Jones*	
1754 Edwards, *Freedom of the Will*			
1758 Jonathan Edwards dies (**b. 1703**); Swedenborg, *On Heaven and Its Wonders and on Hell*	**1758–69** Papacy of Clement XIII	**1759** Voltaire, *Candide*	
1760 Nikolaus Ludwig von Zinzendorf dies (**b. 1700**)		**1762** Rousseau, *Emile*	**1762** Catherine the Great begins her 34-year reign in Russia
	1763 Johann Nikolaus von Hontheim (pseudonym "Justinus Febronius") publishes *On the Condition of the Church and the Rightful Power of the Bishop of Rome*	**1764** Voltaire, *Philosophical Dictionary*	**1763** France loses North American possessions in Treaty of Paris; rebellion of Pontiac and Ottawa Indians against British
		1765 James Watt improves steam engine; paves way for Industrial Revolution	
		1767 Georg Philipp Telemann dies (**b. 1681**)	
1771 Swedenborg, *True Christian Religion*	**1769–74** Papacy of Clement XIV		**1772** Russia, Prussia, and Austria partition Poland
1772 Emmanuel Swedenborg dies (**b. 1688**)	**1773** Suppression of the Society of Jesus (Jesuits)	**1773** Phillis Wheatley, *Poems on Various Subjects*, first book published by black American	**1773** Boston Tea Party
1774–78 *Wolfenbüttel Fragments* published	**1774** Mother Ann Lee (**1736–84**) leaves England for America, where she founds the American Shakers		
	1775–99 Papacy of Pius VI	**1776** David Hume dies (**b. 1711**); Adam Smith (**1723–90**), *Wealth of Nations*	**1776** Declaration of American Independence

Political and Social Events	Intellectual and Cultural Developments	Christian History	Major Christian Writers
1781 End of American Revolutionary War	**1777** R. B. Sheridan, *The School for Scandal*		**1777** John Wesley, *A Plain Account of Christian Perfection*
1783–1807 Women vote in New Jersey	**1778** Carl von Linné (Linnaeus) (**b. 1707**), Jean-Jacques Rousseau (**b. 1712**), and Voltaire (**b. 1694**) die		
	1781 Kant, *Critique of Pure Reason*		
	1784 Denis Diderot dies (**b. 1713**)	**1784** Wesley's Deed of Declaration; charter of Methodism	
1787 U.S. Constitution signed		**1786** Synod of Pistoia	**1787** Alphonsus di Liguori dies (**b. 1696**)
	1788 Kant, *Critique of Practical Reason*		
1789 Louis XVI calls Estates-General in France; storming of the Bastille; Declaration of the Rights of Man	**1789** William Blake, *Songs of Innocence*	**1789** John Carroll of Baltimore named first American bishop	
		1790 Civil Constitution of the Clergy (France)	
1791 France's new constitution	**1791** Wolfgang A. Mozart dies (**b. 1756**); Benjamin Franklin, *Autobiography*		**1791** John Wesley dies (**b. 1703**)
	1792 Mary Wollstonecraft, *A Vindication of the Rights of Women*		
	1793 Eli Whitney invents cotton gin; Kant, *Religion within the Limits of Reason Alone*		
	1795 James Hutton suggests slow geological evolution in *Theory of the Earth*		
	1796 Edward Jenner finds safe vaccine against smallpox		

1799 Napoleon overthrows the Directory; George Washington dies (**b. 1732**)	1800 Schiller (**1759-1805**), *Maria Stuart*, and Schelling (**1775–1854**), *System of Transcendental Idealism*	1800–23 Papacy of Pius VII	1799 Schleiermacher, *On Religion: Speeches to Its Cultured Despisers*
1801 European population: Italy 17.2 million; Spain 10.5 million; Britain 10.4 million; London 864,000; Paris 547,000; Vienna 231,000	1803 Robert Fulton propels boat by steam power	1801 Concordat between Napoleon and Pope Pius VII	
1803 Louisiana Purchase	1804 Immanuel Kant dies (**b. 1724**); Nathaniel Hawthorne (**d. 1864**) and Ludwig Feuerbach (**d. 1872**) born; Beethoven, *Symphony No. 3*, and Schiller, *Wilhelm Tell*		
1804 Toussaint l'Ouverture leads slave revolt; Haiti gains independence; coronation of Napoleon as emperor	1807 G. W. F. Hegel, *Phenomenology of Spirit*		
1806 Holy Roman Empire dissolved	1808 Goethe, *Faust*, Pt. I and Beethoven, *Symphonies Nos. 5 and 6*		
1807 Great Britain abolishes slave trade	1809 Joseph Haydn dies (**b. 1732**); Charles Darwin (**d. 1882**), Felix Mendelssohn (**d. 1847**), Edgar Allan Poe (**d. 1849**) and Alfred Tennyson (**d. 1892**) born		
	1811 Jane Austen, *Sense and Sensibility*		
1812 Napoleon retreats from Russia in defeat; Jews in Prussia are emancipated	1812 Robert Browning (**d. 1889**) and Charles Dickens (**d. 1870**) are born; Brothers Grimm, *Fairy Tales*	1812 Daughters of Charity of St. Joseph, established in 1809 by Elizabeth Bayley Seton (**1774–1821**), are formally recognized; Sisters of Loretto in Kentucky are founded by Mary Rhodes, Christina Stuart, and Ann Havern	
1812-15 War between U.S. and Britain			

Political and Social Events	Intellectual and Cultural Developments	Christian History	Major Christian Writers
	1813 Jane Austen, *Pride and Prejudice*		
	1814 Johann Fichte dies (**b. 1762**)	1814 Pope Pius VII returns to Rome and restores the Inquisition; also restores the Jesuits	
1815 Congress of Vienna			
	1816 Joseph Niepce, French physicist, makes first photographic paper negative; Rossini, *Barber of Seville*	1816 American Bible Society founded	
1817 San Martín and Simón Bolívar begin liberation of South America		1817 Lutheran and Reformed Churches in Prussia form Evangelical Union; De Lammenais, *Essay on Indifference in Religion* and Joseph de Maistre, *The Pope*; American Colonization Society proposes to buy slaves' freedom and repatriate them in Liberia	
	1818 Mary Wollstonecraft Shelley, *Frankenstein*; Karl Marx born (**d. 1883**)		
1819 Children under age of nine are forbidden to work in England's mills; other children are limited to twelve-hour days		1819 *Theologische Quartalschrift*, oldest continually published journal for Catholic theology, is established	1819 J. S. Drey, *Brief Introduction to the Study of Theology*; Georg Hermes, *Philosophical Introduction to Theology*
1820 Missouri Compromise	1820 Electromagnetism discovered; John Keats, "Ode to a Nightingale" and "Ode on a Grecian Urn"		
1821 Greek War of Independence begins			1821 Joseph de Maistre dies (**b. 1754**) 1821–22 Schleiermacher, *The Christian Faith* (1st ed.)
	1822 Franz Schubert, *Symphony No. 8* (Unfinished)		
1823 Monroe Doctrine		1823–29 Papacy of Leo XII	
	1824 Beethoven, *Ninth Symphony*		1825 Möhler, *Unity in the Church*

1827 John Keble, *The Christian Year*

1830–31 Schleiermacher, *The Christian Faith* (2d ed.)

1832 Möhler, *Symbolism; Or, Exposition of the Doctrinal Differences between Catholics and Protestants*

1833 John Keble's sermon, "National Apostasy"

1826 Pope Leo XII approves the Society of the Sacred Heart, founded by Madeleine Sophie Barat (**1779–1865**)

1829 Oblate Sisters of Providence founded as first African-American congregation in the U.S.; Catholic Emancipation Act allows Catholics in Great Britain to sit in Parliament and hold public office

1829–30 Papacy of Pius VIII

1830 Joseph Smith founds Church of Jesus Christ of Latter-day Saints (Mormons)

1831–46 Papacy of Gregory XVI

1832 Pope Gregory XVI, *Mirari vos*

1833 Beginning of Oxford Movement

1826 James Fenimore Cooper, *The Last of the Mohicans*

1827 Karl von Baer theorizes about the human ovum; Beethoven dies (**b. 1770**)

1828 Francisco Goya dies (**b. 1746**)

1831 G. W. F. Hegel dies (**b. 1770**)

1832 Charles Lyell publishes theory of geological evolution in *Principles of Geology*

1832 Louisa May Alcott (**d. 1888**), Horatio Alger (**d. 1899**), Lewis Carroll (**d. 1898**), and Eduard Manet (**d. 1883**) are born; Johann von Goethe (**b. 1749**), Jeremy Bentham (**b. 1748**), and Sir Walter Scott (**b. 1771**) die

1833 Oberlin College, first in U.S. to admit women and blacks, is founded

---

1828 Isabella van Wagener (**c. 1797–1883**) escapes slavery and takes the name Sojourner Truth

1829 David Walker, *Appeal to the Coloured Citizens of the World*

1830 July Revolution in France; Belgium wins independence from Netherlands

1831 William Lloyd Garrison (**1805–79**) publishes abolitionist periodical *The Liberator*

1832 First Reform Bill (Britain)

1833 Great Britain abolishes slavery; Philadelphia Female Anti-Slavery Society organized by Lucretia Mott (**1793–1880**) as an auxiliary to the exclusively male Anti-Slavery Society

Political and Social Events	Intellectual and Cultural Developments	Christian History	Major Christian Writers
	1834 Victor Hugo, *The Hunchback of Notre Dame*	1834 Leopold von Ranke, *The Roman Popes*	1834 Friedrich Schleiermacher dies (b. 1768) 1835 D. F. Strauss, *The Life of Jesus Critically Examined*; Charles Finney, *Lectures on Revivals of Religion*
1836 Mexicans take the Alamo	1836 Arthur Schopenhauer, *On the Will in Nature*		1836–42 Joseph von Görres, *Christian Mysticism* 1836 Emerson, *Nature*
1837 Queen Victoria of England (1819–1901) begins her 64-year reign; Angelina and Sarah Grimké found the National Female Anti-Slavery Society, one of the few to include women of color from the start	1837 Samuel Morse invents telegraph; Mary Lyon founds Mount Holyoke Female Seminary; Alexander Pushkin dies (b. 1799)	1837 American Presbyterians split into Old and New School; Sarah Grimké, *Letters on the Equality of the Sexes and the Condition of Woman*	
	1838 Dickens, *Oliver Twist* and *Nicholas Nickleby*	1838 Emerson, Harvard Divinity School Address 1839 Pope Gregory XVI condemns slave trade	1838 Johann Adam Möhler dies (b. 1796) 1838–47 Drey, *Apologetics*
1840 World Anti-Slavery Conference (London)	1840 Thomas Hardy (d. 1928), Claude Monet (d. 1928), Pierre A. Renoir (d. 1919), and Auguste Rodin (d. 1917) are born 1841 Feuerbach, *The Essence of Christianity* 1843 J. S. Mill, *System of Logic*; Dickens, "A Christmas Carol"	1841 Catherine McAuley, founder of Sisters of Mercy, dies (b. 1778)	1843 Kierkegaard, *Either/Or* and *Fear and Trembling*
1845 Potato famine in Ireland; U.S. annexes Texas		1844 YMCA founded in England 1845 J. H. Newman becomes a Roman Catholic; U.S. churches split over slavery: e.g., Southern Baptist Convention 1846–47 Brigham Young leads Mormons from Illinois to Utah	1845 Newman, *Essay on the Development of Christian Doctrine*; F. C. Baur, *Paul, the Apostle of Jesus Christ* 1846 Kierkegaard, *Concluding Unscientific Postscript*

1848 Seneca Falls, N.Y., convention for women's rights; revolutions in Paris, Vienna, Berlin, Venice, Milan, and Rome; end of U.S.-Mexican War	1847 Charlotte Bronte, *Jane Eyre*; Emily Bronte, *Wuthering Heights*; William Thackeray, *Vanity Fair*; Thomas A. Edison and Alexander G. Bell are born; Felix Mendelssohn dies (**b. 1809**)	**1846–78** Papacy of Pius IX	**1847** Bushnell, *Christian Nurture*; Baur, *Critical Investigations of the Canonical Gospels*
1849 California gold rush	1848 Karl Marx and Friedrich Engels, *Communist Manifesto*; astronomer Maria Mitchell becomes first woman elected to American Academy of Arts and Sciences	**1848** Count Rossi, papal premier, assassinated; pope flees Rome	
1850 Harriet Tubman (**ca. 1820–1913**) escapes slavery; slaves led to freedom through the Underground Railroad; U.S. population: 23 million and 3.2 million slaves	1850 Nathaniel Hawthorne, *The Scarlet Letter*		
1851 Sojourner Truth addresses Akron women's rights convention	1851 Herman Melville, *Moby Dick*, and Verdi, *Rigoletto*	**1852** First Plenary Council of Baltimore	**1853** Baur, *Church History of the First Three Centuries*; Johann Sebastian Drey dies (**b. 1777**); Philip Schaff, *History of the Apostolic Church*
	1852 Harriet Beecher Stowe, *Uncle Tom's Cabin*, and Emily Dickinson's (**1830–86**) first poem published	**1853** Antoinette Brown Blackwell (**1825–1921**) ordained as first American woman minister (South Butler, N.Y., Congregational Church)	**1854** Kierkegaard, *Attack upon "Christendom"*; Félicité de Lamennais dies (**b. 1782**)
	1854 Florence Nightingale, *Notes on Nursing*	**1854** Pope Pius IX defines Immaculate Conception	**1855** Kierkegaard dies (**b. 1813**)
	1855 Walt Whitman, *Leaves of Grass*		
	1856 Henry Bessemer invents steel converter		
	1857 Gustave Flaubert, *Madame Bovary*		

Political and Social Events	Intellectual and Cultural Developments	Christian History	Major Christian Writers
1859 John Brown hanged for attack at Harpers Ferry, W. Va.	**1859** Darwin, *Origin of Species*; Henri Bergson (**d. 1941**), John Dewey (**d. 1952**), and Edmund Husserl (**d. 1938**) are born; J. S. Mill, "Essay on Liberty"	**1858** American Isaac Hecker founds the Paulist order; Bernadette Soubirous (**1844–79**) experiences visions of Virgin Mary at Lourdes, France	
1860 U.S. Civil War begins		**1860** Ellen G. H. and James White found the Seventh-Day Adventist Church; *Essays and Reviews* (Britain)	**1860** Ferdinand Christian Baur dies (**b. 1792**)
1861 Unification of Italy	**1861/62** Louis Pasteur (**1822–95**) announces "germ theory" of infection		
	1862 Victor Hugo, *Les Misérables*		
1863 Abraham Lincoln declares Emancipation Proclamation	**1863** Mill, *Utilitarianism*	**1863** Munich Congress of Catholic Scholars	**1863** Ernest Renan, *Life of Jesus*
		1864 Pius IX, *Syllabus of Errors*	**1864** Newman, *Apologia pro Vita Sua*
1865 U.S. Civil War ends; German Social Democratic Labor Party, world's first socialist political party, founded; General German Women's Association also founded; Ku Klux Klan founded in Pulaski, Tenn.	**1865** Lewis Carrol, *Alice in Wonderland*	**1865** William and Catherine Booth found the Salvation Army	**1865–67** Baur, *Lectures on the History of Christian Dogma*
	1866 Alfred Nobel (**1833–96**) invents dynamite and Gregor Mendel (**1822–84**) discovers genetics	**1866** Second Plenary Council of Baltimore	**1866** Bushnell, *The Vicarious Sacrifice*; John Keble dies (**b. 1792**)
1867 Second Reform Bill (Britain)			
1869 Elizabeth Cady Stanton and Susan B. Anthony organize the National Woman Suffrage Association; Suez Canal opened		**1869** First Vatican Council begins	

Theology	Church	Culture	History
1870 Newman, *Essay in Aid of a Grammar of Assent*	1870 End of the Papal States	1870 Peter I. Tchaikovsky, "Romeo and Juliet"; Charles Dickens dies (**b. 1812**)	1870–71 Franco-Prussian War
1870–74 Albrecht Ritschl, *The Christian Doctrine of Justification and Reconciliation*	1871 First congress of Old Catholics meets in Munich	1871 Darwin, *The Descent of Man*	1871 Germany united under Emperor Wilhelm I and Chancellor Bismarck
1872 Frederick Denison Maurice dies (**b. 1805**); Charles Hodge, *Systematic Theology*; D. F. Strauss, *The Old Faith and the New*	1872 Jesuits expelled from Germany; Charles Russell founds the Jehovah's Witnesses	1872 Ludwig Feuerbach dies (**b. 1804**)	1874 Frances Willard joins the Women's Christian Temperance Union
1874 Hodge, *What Is Darwinism?*; David Friedrich Strauss dies (**b. 1808**)	1875 Religious orders abolished in Prussia	1874 First exhibit of Impressionist art in Paris	1881 Clara Barton founds American Red Cross
1875 Mary Baker Eddy, *Science and Health*	1878–1903 Papacy of Leo XIII	1876 Alexander Graham Bell invents telephone	1884 Third Reform Bill (Britain)
1876 Horace Bushnell dies (**b. 1802**)	1879 Pope Leo XIII declares Aquinas as the model for Catholic theology; Mary Baker Eddy founds the First Church of Christ Scientist	1880 Feodor Dostoevsky, *The Brothers Karamazov*; Rodin, *The Thinker*	
1878 Charles Hodge dies (**b. 1797**)	1881 Vatican archives opened to scholars	1881 Henrik Ibsen, *Ghosts*; Thomas Carlyle dies (**b. 1795**)	
1882 Edward Pusey dies (**b. 1800**)	1884 Third Plenary Council of Baltimore	1882 Ralph Waldo Emerson (**b. 1803**) and Charles Darwin (**b. 1809**) die	
1885 A. E. Biedermann dies (**b. 1819**)		1883 Karl Marx dies (**b. 1818**)	
		1884 Mark Twain, *Huckleberry Finn*	

Political and Social Events	Intellectual and Cultural Developments	Christian History	Major Christian Writers
	1886 Friedrich Nietzsche, *Beyond Good and Evil*		1886–90 Adolf Harnack, *History of Dogma* 1887 Johannes Evangelist Kuhn dies (**b. 1806**) 1889 Albrecht Ritschl dies (**b. 1822**)
	1889 Robert Browning dies (**b. 1812**)	1889 Catholic University of America opens in Washington, D.C.; Daniel Rudd convenes first Black Catholic Congress in Baltimore	
			1890 John Henry Newman dies (**b. 1801**)
		1891 Pope Leo XIII, *Rerum Novarum*; Catherine Drexel founds Sisters of Blessed Sacrament for Indians and Colored People	
	1892 Toulouse-Lautrec, "At the Moulin Rouge," and Tchaikovsky, "The Nutcracker"		1892 Kähler, *The So-Called Historical Jesus and the Historic, Biblical Christ*; Joseph Ernest Renan dies (**b. 1823**)
1893 Women get the vote in New Zealand 1894 Alfred Dreyfus affair divides France	1894–95 Invention of movie machine and projector 1895 Karl Benz invents first gas-powered car; Guglielmo Marconi invents wireless telegraph; Wilhelm Röntgen discovers the x-ray 1896 First modern Olympic Games (Athens)		1895 Elizabeth Cady Stanton, *The Woman's Bible*
			1897 Charles Hartshorne born
1898 Spanish American War		1899 Dwight L. Moody dies (**b. 1837**); Pope Leo XIII condemns Americanism in *Testem Benevolentiae*	

		1900 Harnack, *The Essence of Christianity*
		1902 Elizabeth Cady Stanton dies (**b. 1815**); Alfred Loisy, *The Gospel and the Church*; William James, *The Varieties of Religious Experience*; Ernst Troeltsch, *The Absoluteness of Christianity and the History of Religion*
		1906/10 Albert Schweitzer, *The Quest for the Historical Jesus*
		1910 William James dies (**b. 1842**)
		1912 Martin Kähler dies (**b. 1835**)
		1914 Johannes Weiss dies (**b. 1863**); Edward Schillebeeckx born

1900 Max Planck announces quantum theory; Sigmund Freud, *The Interpretation of Dreams*; John Ruskin (**b. 1819**), Oscar Wilde (**b. 1856**), and Friedrich Nietzsche (**b. 1844**) die	**1903** National Women's Trade Union League (U.S.) founded	**1903–14** Papacy of Pius X
1903 Wright brothers' first flight		
1904 Giacomo Puccini, "Madame Butterfly"; Anton Chekhov, *The Cherry Orchard*		**1904** Max Weber, *The Protestant Ethic and the Birth of Capitalism*
1905 Albert Einstein formulates Special Theory of Relativity		**1905** Legalized separation of church and state in France
1906 Paul Cézanne dies (**b. 1839**)		
1907 William James, *Pragmatism*; the first Cubist exhibit in Paris		**1907** Pope Piux X condemns "modernism" in *Pascendi dominici gregis*
1910 Igor Stravinsky, *The Firebird*; Mark Twain dies (**b. 1835**)		**1910** First World Missionary Conference (Edinburgh)
1911 Roald Amundsen reaches South Pole; Marie Curie receives Nobel Prize for chemistry		
1912 August Strindberg dies (**b. 1849**)		
1913 D. H. Lawrence, *Sons and Lovers*		
1914 Charles Peirce dies (**b. 1839**)	**1914** Panama Canal opens; World War I begins	**1914–22** Papacy of Benedict XV

Political and Social Events	Intellectual and Cultural Developments	Christian History	Major Christian Writers
1915 First use of chemical warfare	**1915** Einstein postulates General Theory of Relativity		
1916 Margaret Sanger opens first U.S. birth control clinic	**1916** James Joyce, *Portrait of the Artist as a Young Man*		
1917 Bolsheviks seize power in Russia	**1917** Carl Jung, *Psychology of the Unconscious*; Freud, *Introduction to Psychoanalysis*	**1917** Apparitions of Mary at Fatima, Portugal	**1917** Rauschenbusch, *Theology for the Social Gospel*; Otto, *The Idea of the Holy*
1918 World War I ends		**1918** Billy Graham is born	**1918** Romano Guardini, *The Spirit of Liturgy*; Walter Rauschenbusch dies (**b. 1861**)
1918–20 World-wide influenza epidemic kills more than 20 million			**1919** John Macquarrie born; Barth, *The Epistle to the Romans*
1919 League of Nations established	**1919** Bauhaus, founded by Walter Gropius, revolutionizes architecture and industrial arts; T. S. Eliot, "The Wasteland"		
1920 Nineteenth Amendment gives U.S. women the right to vote			**1920** Nathan Söderblom, *Introduction to the History of Religion*
1922 Mussolini seizes power in Italy	**1922** James Joyce, *Ulysses*	**1922–39** Papacy of Pius XI	**1922** Troeltsch, *Historicism and Its Problems*
	1923 Martin Buber, *I and Thou*; Freud, *The Ego and the Id*		**1923** Ernst Troeltsch dies (**b. 1865**)
	1924 Joseph Conrad (**b. 1857**) and Franz Kafka (**b. 1883**) die		
1925–29 Joseph Stalin eliminates rivals in Communist Party	**1925** F. Scott Fitzgerald, *The Great Gatsby*	**1925** John Scopes trial for violating Tennessee law that prohibits teaching of evolution	**1925** Etienne Gilson, *St. Thomas Aquinas*; Gordon Kaufman born
	1926 Ernest Hemingway, *The Sun Also Rises*; John M. Keynes, *The End of Laissez-Faire*		**1926** Jürgen Moltmann born
	1927 Freud, *The Future of an Illusion*; Martin Heidegger, *Being and Time*; first talking picture	**1927** Mexico confiscates church property	

1929 New York stock market crash leads to world depression	1928 Margaret Mead, *Coming of Age in Samoa*; Rudolf Carnap, *The Logical Structure of the World*; Maurice Ravel, "Bolero"; Alexander Fleming discovers penicillin	1929 Lateran Treaty between Mussolini and Pope Pius XI	1928 Ludwig Pastor, *History of the Popes* (begun in 1886); Gustavo Gutiérrez, Hans Küng, Johann Baptist Metz, Schubert Ogden, and Wolfhart Pannenberg are born
	1929 Vienna Circle formed; William Faulkner, *The Sound and the Fury*		1929 Dorothee Soelle born
1931 Jane Addams becomes first woman to receive Nobel Peace Prize		1931 Pope Pius XI, *Quadragesimo anno*	1930 G. K. Chesterton (b. 1874) and Adolf von Harnack (b. 1851) die
	1932 Aldous Huxley, *Brave New World*		1932 Barth, *Church Dogmatics*, Vol. I.1
1933 Adolf Hitler becomes German chancellor	1933 Alfred North Whitehead, *Adventures of Ideas*; Leon Trotsky, *History of the Russian Revolution*; Jung, *Psychology and Religion*	1933 Cardinal von Faulhaber's anti-Nazi treatise "Judaism, Christendom, Germanism"	
		1934–39 Evangeline Booth elected General of the Salvation Army	1934 Eberhard Jüngel and Sallie McFague born; Reinhold Niebuhr, *Moral Man and Immoral Society*
1935 National Council of Negro Women (U.S.) is organized		1934 Barmen Declaration (against Nazism)	
1936 Spanish Civil War begins	1936 A. J. Ayer, *Language, Truth and Logic*		1936 Rosemary Radford Ruether born
	1937 Jean Paul Sartre, *Nausea*; John Steinbeck, *Of Mice and Men*; Picasso, "Guernica"	1937 Papal encyclicals against Nazism and Communism; Oxford Conference (Life and Work); Edinburgh Conference (Faith and Order)	1937 Dietrich Bonhoeffer, *The Cost of Discipleship*; Rudolph Otto dies (b. 1869)
1938 Anti-Jewish violence in Germany (Kristallnacht)	1938 Thornton Wilder, "Our Town"; John Dewey, *Experience and Education*		1938 James Cone born

Political and Social Events	Intellectual and Cultural Developments	Christian History	Major Christian Writers
1939–45 World War II	**1939** Karen Horney, *New Ways in Psychoanalysis* (challenged Freudian understanding of women); Sigmund Freud (**b. 1856**) and William B. Yeats (**b. 1865**) die	**1939** U.S. mission to the Vatican	**1939** David Tracy born; Yves Congar, *Divided Christendom: Principles of a Catholic Ecumenism*
	1940 First electron microscope demonstrated; Richard Wright, *Native Son*; Graham Greene, *The Power and the Glory*	**1939–58** Papacy of Pius XII	**1940** Alfred Loisy dies (**b. 1857**)
1941 Attack on Pearl Harbor; U.S. enters World War II			**1941** Reinhold Niebuhr, *The Nature and Destiny of Man*; Rudolf Bultmann, *New Testament and Mythology*; Elizabeth Johnson born
1941–45 World War II increases demand for women workers; by 1945 women make up more than half the U.S. labor force	**1942** First computer developed in the U.S.; Enrico Fermi (**1901–54**) splits the atom; Albert Camus, *The Stranger*		
1942 Jewish extermination camps are built			
1943 Warsaw Ghetto uprising	**1943** Jean Paul Sartre, *Being and Nothingness*; William Saroyan, *The Human Comedy*	**1943** Pope Pius XII, *Divino Afflante Spiritu*	
	1944 Aaron Copland, "Appalachian Spring"; Tennessee Williams, "The Glass Menagerie"		
1945 Atomic bombs dropped on Hiroshima and Nagasaki; World War II ends; war dead estimated at 35 million plus 10 million in concentration camps	**1945** George Orwell, *Animal Farm*		**1945** Dietrich Bonhoeffer dies (**b. 1906**)
1947 Independence of India declared	**1947** Alfred North Whitehead dies (**b. 1861**)	**1947** Dead Sea scrolls discovered	

1948 State of Israel founded; Gandhi assassinated	**1948** Orwell, *1984*	**1948** World Council of Churches is organized in Amsterdam	**1948** Hartshorne, *The Divine Relativity*; Merton, *The Seven Storey Mountain*
1948–50 Apartheid established in South Africa	**1949** Arthur Miller, "Death of a Salesman"		
1949 U.S.S.R. tests its first atomic bomb		**1950** Pope Pius XII, *Humani Generis*; National Council of the Churches of Christ organized in U.S.: 32 million members; Pope Pius XII proclaims dogma of bodily assumption of Mary	
1950 World population is approx. 2.3 billion; U.N. reports that 480 million out of 800 million children in world are undernourished		**1951** President Truman nominates Gen. Mark Clark as U.S. Ambassador to the Vatican	**1951–63** Paul Tillich, *Systematic Theology*
1952 U. S. explodes first hydrogen bomb	**1952** Samuel Beckett, "Waiting for Godot"; Ralph Ellison, *The Invisible Man*	**1952** Revised Standard Version of Bible published	**1952** Tillich, *The Courage to Be*
	1953 B. F. Skinner, *Science and Human Behavior*; Simone de Beauvoir, *The Second Sex*; Francis Crick and James Watson discover structure of DNA		
1954 *Brown v. Board of Education* outlaws segregation in U.S. schools	**1954** Jonas Salk starts serum innoculation against polio		
1955 Montgomery, Ala., bus boycott begins after arrest of Rosa Parks		**1955** Conference of Latin American Bishops (CELAM) founded	**1955** Pierre Teilhard de Chardin dies (**b. 1881**)
	1956 Albert Sabin develops oral vaccine against polio		**1956** Barth, *The Humanity of God*
	1957 Soviet Union launches Sputnik	**1957** M. L. King forms the Southern Christian Leadership Conference	**1957** Bernard Lonergan, *Insight*
		1958–63 Papacy of John XXIII	
1959 Fidel Castro overthrows Batista in Cuba			**1959** Chardin, *The Phenomenon of Man*

Political and Social Events	Intellectual and Cultural Developments	Christian History	Major Christian Writers
1960 J. F. Kennedy elected U.S. president; U.S. Food and Drug Administration approves "the pill" for contraception	**1960** A.J. Ayer, *Logical Positivism*; laser is developed	**1960** Three women admitted to ministry of Swedish Lutheran Church; Pope John XXIII creates Secretariat for Christian Unity	**1960** Chardin, *The Divine Milieu*
1961 Berlin Wall goes up	**1961** Yuri Gagarin (U.S.S.R.) makes first earth orbit; Ernest Hemingway (**b. 1898**) and Carl Jung (**b. 1875**) die	**1961** Pope John XXIII, *Mater et Magistra*	
1962 Cuban Missile Crisis	**1962** Rachel Carson, *Silent Spring* (concerning effect of pesticides on environment)	**1962–65** Second Vatican Council **1962** Episcopal Church consecrates J. M. Burgess as first black suffragan bishop of Massachusetts	
1963 M. L. King arrested in Birmingham, Ala., demonstration; President Kennedy calls out 3,000 troops; President Kennedy assassinated	**1963** Betty Friedan, *The Feminine Mystique*	**1963** John XXIII, *Pacem in Terris*	
1964 U.S. sends troops to Vietnam; U.S. Civil Rights Act prohibits race and sex discrimination; M. L. King receives Nobel Peace Prize	**1964** *The Autobiography of Malcolm X*	**1963–78** Papacy of Paul VI **1964** Pope Paul VI makes pilgrimage to Holy Land	**1964** Reinhold Niebuhr, *Nature and Destiny of Man*
1965 Malcolm X assassinated in New York; race riots in Watts district of Los Angeles; civil rights violence in Selma, Ala.	**1965** T.S. Eliot dies (**b. 1888**)		**1965** Paul Tillich (**b. 1886**) and Albert Schweitzer (**b. 1875**) die; Moltmann, *Theology of Hope*
1966 National Organization for Women (U.S.) founded		**1966** United Brethren and Methodist Churches vote to merge in **1968** as United Methodist Church; Roman Catholic bishops rule that U.S. Catholics need no longer abstain from eating meat on Fridays (except during Lent)	**1966** Schubert Ogden, *The Reality of God*; Macquarrie, *Principles of Christian Theology*; Hans Urs von Balthasar, *Church and World*

World Events	Culture & Science	Church	Theology
1967 Israel defeats Egypt in Six Day War; President Johnson appoints Thurgood Marshall to Supreme Court; M. L. King leads anti-Vietnam War march in New York; race riots in Cleveland, Newark, Detroit		**1967** Land O'Lakes Statement	**1967** Küng, *The Church*; John Courtney Murray dies (**b. 1904**)
1968 M. L. King and Robert F. Kennedy assassinated; 62 nations sign Nuclear Non-Proliferation Treaty		**1968** Pope Paul VI, *Humanae Vitae* and *Populorum Progressio*; CELAM's Medellín Assembly	**1968** Merton, *Faith and Violence; Conjectures of a Guilty Bystander*; Karl Barth (**b.1886**), Martin Luther King (**b. 1929**) and Thomas Merton (**b. 1915**) die
	1969 Neil Armstrong steps on the moon		**1969** Rahner, *Do You Believe in God?*
			1970 Cone, *A Black Theology of Liberation*
			1971 Küng, *Infallible?: An Inquiry*; Gutiérrez, *A Theology of Liberation*
	1972 Ezra Pound dies (**b. 1885**)		**1972** Lonergan, *Method in Theology*
1973 *Roe v. Wade* decision strikes down antiabortion laws in U.S.; President Allende of Chile, first declared Marxist freely elected as head of state, is ousted by military coup			**1973** Lonergan, *Philosophy of God and Theology*
1973–74 Energy crisis from Arab oil embargo and petroleum shortage		**1974** Four U.S. Episcopal bishops defy church law and ordain eleven women as priests	**1974** Georgia Harkness dies (**b. 1891**)
1974 U.S. President Nixon resigns		**1975** Anglican Church in Canada approves ordination of women; Elizabeth Ann Seton (**1774–1821**) canonized as first American-born saint; previous Episcopal ordination of women is invalidated	**1975** Tracy, *Blessed Rage for Order*

Political and Social Events	Intellectual and Cultural Developments	Christian History	Major Christian Writers
		1976 Episcopal Church approves ordination of women; Archbishop Marcel Lefebvre is suspended by Pope Paul VI for rejecting reforms of Vatican II; convocation of first "Call to Action" Conference	**1976** Rudolf Bultmann dies **(b. 1884)**
1977 U.S. confirms testing of neutron bomb		**1977** Tanzanian black activist Bishop Josiah M. Kibira is elected head of Lutheran World Federation	
1978 Israel and Egypt make peace at Camp David	**1978** First "test tube baby" born to Lesley Brown in England	**1978** CELAM's Puebla Assembly; Pope Paul VI dies; his successor Pope John Paul I dies; Karol Wojtyla becomes Pope John Paul II, first non-Italian pope in 456 years	**1978** Küng, *Does God Exist?*; Rahner, *Foundations of Christian Faith*; Leonardo Boff, *Jesus Christ Liberator*
1979 Muslim revolution in Iran; Sandinistas take control in Nicaragua		**1979** Pope John Paul II is first pope to visit a Communist country (Poland); Vatican declares that Swiss theologian Hans Küng is no longer to be regarded as Catholic theologian	**1979** Schillebeeckx, *Jesus: An Experiment in Christology*
		1979–89 Political activism of Christian conservatives stimulated by Moral Majority	
1980 Solidarity Trade Union movement begun in Poland; 10-year war between Iran and Iraq begins	**1980** Jean Paul Sartre dies **(b. 1905)**	**1980** Oscar Romero, archbishop of San Salvador, is assassinated	**1980** Schillebeeckx, *Christ: The Experience of Jesus as Lord*; Metz, *Faith in History and Society*; Dorothy Day dies **(b. 1898)**
1981 Sandra Day O'Connor becomes first female U.S. Supreme Court justice; Anwar Sadat, president of Egypt, assassinated	**1981** AIDS is identified; U.S. space shuttle makes first flight; IBM launches its personal computer	**1981** South African Presbyterian Church allows interracial marriage in defiance of apartheid laws; Salvation Army withdraws from World Council of Churches in protest of WCC's political support of "guerrilla" movements	**1981** Tracy, *The Analogical Imagination*; Gordon Kaufman, *The Theological Imagination*

1983 Reagan proposes Strategic Defense Initiative; U.S. military invasion of Grenada	1982 Merger of U.S. Presbyterian churches that split in Civil War; World Alliance of Reformed Churches suspends South Africa's two Dutch Reformed churches for heresy of racial segregation	1982 Congar, *Diversity and Communion* 1982–86 Balthasar, *The Glory of the Lord: A Theological Aesthetics*
1983 Astronaut Sally Ride is first American woman to travel in space; Rudolf Nureyev becomes director of Paris Opera Ballet; Alice Walker, *The Color Purple*	1983 U. S. Catholic bishops publish *The Challenge of Peace*	1983 Ruether, *Sexism and God-Talk;* Rahner, *God and Revelation;* Jüngel, *God as the Mystery of the World*
	1984 Vatican publishes "Theology of Liberation"	1984 Macquarrie, *In Search of Deity;* Gutiérrez, *We Drink from Our Own Wells;* Soelle, *The Strength of the Weak;* Karl Rahner (**b. 1904**) and Bernard Lonergan (**b. 1904**) die
	1985 Vatican imposes a year's silence on Leonardo Boff	
1986 Nuclear reactor at Chernobyl (U.S.S.R.) explodes	1986 Desmond Tutu becomes first black archbishop of Cape Town, South Africa; Pope John Paul II becomes first pope in recorded history to visit a synagogue; U.S. Catholic bishops publish *Economic Justice for All*	1986 Elisabeth Schüssler Fiorenza, *In Memory of Her*
1987 Stock market crash; Dow Jones Index falls 23 percent	1987 Jim Bakker, head of "Praise the Lord" television network, resigns after accusations of adultery	1987 L. and C. Boff, *Introducing Liberation Theology;* McFague, *Models of God;* Tracy, *Plurality and Ambiguity*
1988 Toni Morrison's *Beloved* wins Pulitzer Prize; Salman Rushdie's *The Satanic Verses* attacked by some Muslims as blasphemous; Stephen Hawking, *A Brief History of Time*	1988 Eugene A. Marino becomes first black Roman Catholic archbishop in U.S.; Pope John Paul II excommunicates Archbishop Marcel Lefèbvre; Barbara Harris is elected first female Anglican bishop (Massachusetts)	1988 Boff, *Trinity and Society;* Rita Nakashima Brock, *Journeys by Heart;* Hans Urs von Balthasar dies (**b. 1905**)
1988 U.S. B-2 "Stealth" bomber unveiled; Reagan and Gorbachev sign Intermediate-Range Nuclear Forces Treaty	1989 Assassination of six Jesuits and two women at UCA in El Salvador	
1989 Tiananmen democracy protests crushed		

Political and Social Events	Intellectual and Cultural Developments	Christian History	Major Christian Writers
1990 Soviet Union collapses; Germany reunited; Nelson Mandela is freed from South African prison; Sandinistas voted out of office	**1990** Hubble Space Telescope launched	**1990** New Revised Standard Version of Bible, incorporating some inclusive language, is published; *Ex Corde Ecclesiae*	**1990** Jon Sobrino, *Spirituality of Liberation*
1991 Persian Gulf War		**1991** Pope John Paul II, *Centesimus Annus*	**1991** Henri de Lubac dies (**b. 1896**)
1992 Rigoberta Menchú, Mayan activist, receives Nobel Peace Prize; Salvadoran Peace Accords end years of civil war; ethnic cleansing begins in Bosnia		**1992** Vatican issues *Catechism of the Catholic Church*, first "major" catechism since the sixteenth century	**1992** Johnson, *She Who Is*
1993 Israel and PLO agree to process for Palestinian self-rule; new initiatives to end violence in Northern Ireland			**1993** McFague, *Body of God*; Delores Williams, *Sisters in the Wilderness*; Kaufman, *In Face of Mystery*; E. Schüssler Fiorenza, *Discipleship of Equals*
1994 Genocide in Rwanda; Nelson Mandela becomes first black president of South Africa		**1994** Pope John Paul II issues *Ordinatio Sacerdotalis*	**1994** Marjorie Hewitt Suchocki, *The Fall to Violence*; Pedro Casaldáliga, *Political Holiness*; Schillebeeckx, *Church: The Human Story of God*
1995 Yitzhak Rabin, prime minister of Israel, assassinated; Oklahoma City federal building bombed; Dayton Peace Agreement prepares prospect of peace in Bosnia			**1995** Soelle, *Theology for Skeptics*; Yves Congar dies (**b. 1904**)
1996 Guatemalan Peace Treaty ends decades of civil war			
1997 123 nations sign anti-landmine treaty; death of Princess Diana	**1997** Ian Wilmut clones first sheep from adult cell	**1997** Mother Teresa dies (**b. 1910**)	
1998 India and Pakistan test nuclear weapons; peace talks in Northern Ireland		**1998** Juan Gerardi, auxiliary bishop of Guatemala, assassinated; John Paul II, *Ad Tuendam Fidem*, papal letter against theological dissent	